THE ROBERT E. LEE READER

The
ROBERT E. LEE
Reader

Edited by STANLEY F. HORN

KONECKY&KONECKY

Konecky & Konecky
150 Fifth Ave.
New York, NY 10011

Copyright © 1949 Bobbs-Meriill, Company, Inc.

ISBN: 0-914427-83-0

Printed and bound in the USA

To B. W. H.

Introduction

THE purpose of this book is to present a full-length portrait of
Robert E. Lee by means of extracts selected from the writings of
the many who have taken the Confederate commander as their
subject.

There has been no dearth of material. Robert E. Lee has possessed an irresistible appeal for many writers, professional and
amateur. Published works range from that modern biographical
masterpiece, Dr. Freeman's four-volume *R. E. Lee*, back to the
scores of biographies and reminiscences written by those con-
temporaries who knew Lee, who marched under his banners and
who walked with him the paths of peace in the difficult postwar
years. Use has been made also of the many fugitive sketches in
periodicals and newspapers which, though now largely forgotten
or overlooked, shed revealing light on the character of the man.
Lee's official reports and orders, together with his family correspondence, give us an insight into his own innermost thoughts,
both military and personal.

Many of these earlier writings are now obscure, out of print or
not readily available. Some of the books about him have been
concerned chiefly with his military career and are of interest principally to those skilled in the science of war. Some of his biographies have been superficial; some have been sentimental. Out
of this great mass of available material these selections have been
taken and fitted together with a view to giving a readable and
accurate picture of the true Robert E. Lee.

Lee was not merely a great general: he was a great citizen.
Theodore Roosevelt described him as "without any exception the
very greatest of all the great captains that the English-speaking
peoples have brought forth." Many experts in the art of war agree
with this estimate. But his greatness does not rest entirely on his
generalship, and this book is no military history or critique of the
Confederate leader's campaigns and battles. These battles have
been fought over on many a printed page, their strategy and tactics

analyzed and debated by experts. The effort here has been to de-emphasize these battles and refrain from any repetition of their familiar details, except in so far as they may serve as a proper background for the central figures in the foreground. The emphasis is on Lee the man, rather than Lee the soldier. The roar of battle is merely an off-stage noise.

In making the selections for inclusion in this *Reader* there have been no rigid standards as to excellence of writing or fame of writer. It is in no sense an anthology. Rather the selections have been chosen as the fragments that seem best to fit into the mosaic portrait here attempted, a portrait designed to show what manner of man Robert E. Lee really was.

—STANLEY F. HORN

Table of Contents

THE ROBERT E. LEE READER

1

The Lees of Virginia

A PROPER understanding and appreciation of the character and qualities of Robert E. Lee is impossible without some knowledge of the family, social and political background which contributed to the formation of those characteristics.

Lee was a Virginian. This fact dominated his life; it was the controlling consideration in the supreme crisis of his career. Virginia, to be sure, was one of the constituent commonwealths of the United States of America; but to the average Virginian of Lee's day it came natural to think of the state first in point of allegiance. This was particularly true of Robert E. Lee, for the history of his state had been so closely intertwined with the history of his family that the "Lees of Virginia" had long been a familiar identifying phrase. "Virginia is my country. Her will I obey, however lamentable the fate to which it may subject me," Light-Horse Harry Lee had said; and it was instinctive for Robert E. Lee to echo that sentiment of his patriot father.

The Lee family had a proud record of prominence and achievement in old England, long before the original immigrant came to these shores. Launcelot Lee was one of those who fought under William the Conqueror at Hastings. Lionel Lee rode with Richard Coeur de Lion in the Third Crusade, and his armor hangs proudly today in the Tower of London. Sir Henry Lee was knighted by Queen Elizabeth. And in St. George's Chapel of Windsor Castle the Lee banners are still displayed, surmounted by the family arms with their motto: *"Non Incautus Futuri."*

The first Lees who came to Virginia in the earliest Colonial days, with this background of distinction in the old country, naturally assumed places of leadership in the affairs of the Colony, a position which fell like a mantle on succeeding generations of the family. John Adams wrote to Samuel Cooper on February 28, 1779: "The family of Lee . . . has more men of merit in it than any other family." With this heritage Robert E. Lee instinctively and naturally thought of himself primarily as a Virginian, a son of the commonwealth to which his forebears had contributed so much.

Today, however, Lee is regarded by the world not as a Virginian, not as a defeated commander of the Confederate armed forces, but as a great American—a military leader of unsurpassed skill, a gentleman of such nobility of character that he could achieve undying greatness in defeat, without benefit of the decorative halo of victory.

1

How effectively and how thoroughly the great Virginian has been transformed and accepted as a great American is feelingly expressed by one of his Northern admirers, Dr. William E. Brooks.

Lee of Virginia! There have been Lees before him and there will be Lees after, but Robert E. Lee is ever Lee of Virginia. Virginia mothered him, down in the Tidewater where the slow rivers run. To Virginia his heart ever turned in those days when he served in distant places, to Virginia and the white-pillared house on its northern border. It was at Virginia's call that he broke the old army ties and set aside the sober judgment which told him that secession was folly. It was on her fields that he won the fame that ranks him among the greatest of earth's captains. It was in her great Valley that he lived those last busy years when, with a war-weakened body, he strove unrestingly to fit her anew for the tasks of peace. And in her soil he sleeps. Virginia loves him as she does no other. Washington she reverences. Lee she adores.

Yet without in any way raping from Virginia that which she cherishes so greatly, it is time that we should think of him as the common heritage of us all, whether we come from north or south of that line which Mason and Dixon drew, which is only a line but which has been greater than the Chinese wall to our thinking. A past generation thought of him as one who would have destroyed America. It was difficult for that generation to think of him otherwise. They were partners in the event. Those who opposed him shut him out of their hearts because they feared him more than all the rest. Those who with him stood for the Lost Cause made him in their thinking the Hero of that Cause, the superman who emerges from every event, and whom humanity can not do without. So they built a legend about him and, as always is the way with legends, it has stifled the truth. . . .

Yet the truth is greater than the legend, for it is more human. And Lee is intensely human, with some human faults, but also with some great, supremely great, human qualities. . . . And it is these qualities which are our common heritage. In them we may all exult. So those who opposed him, in shutting him out of their affections, have denied themselves and their children something which is rightly theirs. . . . So Virginia must give us the privilege of sharing in him, and we must exercise it.

2

The only writing of Robert E. Lee which he intended for publication is his *Life of General Henry Lee,* inserted as an introduction to his 1869 edition of the latter's *Memoirs of the War in the Southern Department of the United States.* In this biographical sketch of his illustrious father, Robert E. Lee himself gives in restrained prose a brief outline of his family's history in Virginia.

Richard Lee, of Shropshire, during the reign of Charles I came over to the colony of Virginia as secretary and one of the king's privy council. He is described as a man of good stature, comely visage, enterprising genius, a sound head and generous nature. . . . While Prince Charles II was at Breda, Richard Lee went over from Virginia to ascertain if he would protect the colony, should it return to its allegiance to the royal line. Finding no support could be obtained, he retraced his steps and remained quiet until the death of Cromwell, when, with the aid of Sir William Berkeley, Charles II was proclaimed in Virginia King of England, Scotland, France, Ireland and Virginia, two years before his restoration. . . .

This Richard Lee had several children; the two eldest, John and Richard, were educated at Oxford. John took a degree as Doctor of Physic and, returning to his father, died young. . . . Richard spent his time in study, writing his notes in Greek, Latin and Hebrew, and did not improve his paternal estate, which might have produced a princely revenue. He was of the Council of Virginia, filled other offices of honor, and married a Miss Corbyn and left five sons and one daughter at his death, which occurred in Virginia some time after the Restoration. The names of the sons were Richard, Philip, Francis, Thomas and Henry. . . .

Henry, the fifth brother, married Miss Bland; had three sons— John, Richard and Henry—and a daughter, Lettice. John died without issue. Richard lived a bachelor at Lee Hall on the Potomac. Henry married Miss [Lucy] Grymes, had several children, and lived at Leesylvania on the same river. The only sister of these five brothers was united to a Fitzhugh, a family of note in Virginia, and had several children.

The first child [of Henry Lee of Leesylvania and Lucy Grymes] was a daughter, who lived but ten months; the second, Henry Lee, was born on the 29th of January, 1756, at Leesylvania, which is situated on a point of land jutting into the Potomac, three miles above Dumfries, then the county town of Prince William. This village, chiefly built by the enterprise of Scotch merchants, was enriched by a tobacco inspection and enlivened by a theatre. . . .

Henry was preparing himself for the profession of law and about to embark for England to pursue that study under the direction of Bishop Porteus, when the commencement of hostilities with the mother country changed his destiny. Soon after the battle of Lexington he entered the army as captain of cavalry, at the age of nineteen. Besides being present at other important actions in the Northern Department, he was at the battles of Brandywine, Germantown and Springfield, and early became a favorite of Washington.

3

An account of "Light-Horse Harry" Lee's brilliant career in the Revolutionary War is given by his admiring son, Henry Lee, Jr., the elder half brother of Robert E. Lee.

In the difficult and critical operations in Pennsylvania, New Jersey and New York, from 1777 to 1780 inclusive, he was always placed near the enemy, entrusted with the command of the out-posts, with the superintendence of spies, and with that kind of service which required in an eminent degree the possession of coolness, address and enterprise. During the occupation of Phila-delphia by the royal forces, his activity and success in straitening their communications, in cutting off their light parties and inter-cepting their supplies, drew on him the particular attention of the enemy. And, being attacked in consequence, his defence of the Spread Eagle Tavern with only ten men, against Tarleton at the head of two hundred, excited no little admiration. When the dis-tress of the army for provisions reduced Gen. Washington to the necessity of foraging for supplies, as if he had occupied the country of an enemy, a measure which, as may be supposed, excited the most injurious discontent among the inhabitants, Lee being em-ployed on it had the address to execute this painful but necessary duty without exciting the smallest disaffection. He cooperated, so far as cavalry could act, in General Wayne's attack on Stony Point, and procured the intelligence on which it was projected. Indeed, from a part of his correspondence with General Washington which has been preserved, it seems not improbable that Major Lee sug-gested that brilliant enterprise. . . .

In the course of this severe campaign, when desertions from the American army became so frequent as to threaten its dissolution, Major Lee was authorized by General Washington to inflict sum-mary punishment on such deserters as he should take *flagrante delicto*. Being in command of the outposts and always close to the enemy, these offenders often fell into his hands. He commenced accordingly by hanging one of a party; and, to strike a wholesome terror into the main army, sent the lopped and bleeding head to General Washington's camp. This last proceeding was not altogether approved by the Commander in Chief, though, contrary to his apprehensions, it is known to have produced a most salutary effect. . . .

The orders he received and the reports he transmitted during the campaigns of 1779 and 1780 show that General Washington relied on him peculiarly for intelligence respecting the enemy's force and movements. It appears, in short, that at this early period he had so completely engaged the confidence of that great Commander that in an official letter of the 7th of October, 1779, he was directed in future to mark his communications with the word *private,* so that they should not be examined even by the officers of the General's military family.

These services of General Lee, which with various others are not mentioned in his *Memoirs,* gained for him a reputation for talent and patriotism which induced Congress in November, 1780, to promote him to a Lieutenant Colonelcy of dragoons, and to augment his corps by adding to it three companies of infantry, the officers and men composing which he was authorized by General Washington to select from the whole army. With this chosen corps, he was soon detached to join the army of General Greene in the South, where great exertions were required to recover the ground lost by Gates's defeat at Camden. On this occasion, his patriotism exalted by the misfortunes of his country, he expended in the purchase of horses for his dragoons and in equipping his corps a considerable part of the small fortune given him by his father, a contribution for which, though it proved of essential advantage to his country, he never received nor even asked remuneration. . . .

Under the orders of General Greene, his exertions are well known to have been indefatigable and his services various and important. . . . In the course of Greene's operations he was always in the rear when the army retreated, in the van when it advanced, and nearest to the enemy when it was stationary. . . .

After the battle of Eutaw, military operations having been suspended by the excessive heat of the South for a few weeks, Lieutenant Colonel Lee repaired to the headquarters of General Washington on a mission of importance from General Greene, and was present at the siege and surrender of York. . . . When, upon the termination of the last campaign in Carolina, he retired from the army of General Greene on furlough—the only one he obtained during the war—that great officer used the following language in a letter to the president of Congress, February 18, 1782: "Lieutenant Colonel Lee retires for a time for the recovery of his health. I am more indebted to this officer than any other for the advantages gained over the enemy in the operations of the last campaign, and should be wanting in gratitude not to acknowledge the importance of his services, a detail of which is his best panegyric."

4

It is of more than passing interest and significance that Light-Horse Harry Lee, in writing his eyewitness account of the surrender of Cornwallis, should have noted with some asperity his lordship's unwillingness to share the humiliation of defeat. In his letter to Washington, the British commander had suggested "that two officers be appointed by each side to meet at Mr. Moore's house to settle terms of surrender"; and when the actual surrender took place Cornwallis deputed General O'Hara to represent him. Did Robert E. Lee, as he rode to meet General Grant that April morning in 1865, remember his father's pointed comments on the etiquette of capitulation?

Every eye was turned, searching for the British Commander-in-Chief, anxious to look at that man, heretofore so much the object of their dread. All were disappointed. Cornwallis held himself back from the humiliating scene, obeying emotions which his great character ought to have stifled. He had been unfortunate; not from any false step or deficiency on his part but from the infatuated policy of his superior and the united power of his enemy brought to bear upon him alone. There was nothing with which he could reproach himself; there was nothing with which he could reproach his brave and faithful army; why not then appear at its head in the day of its misfortune, as he had always done in the day of triumph? The British general in this instance deviated from his general line of conduct, dimming the splendour of his long and brilliant career.

5

The Revolution at an end, young Colonel Lee found that he had become so enamored of the art of arms that it was difficult to adjust himself to the humdrum routine of civil affairs. Within a few weeks he took unto himself a bride—his third cousin, Matilda Lee, daughter of Philip Ludwell Lee, the eldest son of Thomas. Thomas it was who built Stratford, the famous ancestral home of the Lees, still standing in Westmoreland County on the banks of the Potomac. The original house on this property had been burned, but so high was Thomas' standing that when the news of the disaster reached England, Bishop Meade tells us, "Queen Caroline sent him over a bountiful present out of her own privy purse." With this royal assistance, Thomas Lee built Stratford. From Thomas it descended to his granddaughter Matilda, and here Light-Horse Harry went to live after his marriage to her. A description of the old house by General Robert E. Lee presents a picture of the ancestral house, his birthplace, as he remembered it.

The approach to the house is on the south, along the side of a lawn, several hundred acres in extent, adorned with cedars, oaks and forest poplars. On ascending a hill, not far from the gate, the traveller comes in full view of the mansion; when the road turns to the right and leads straight to a grove of sugar-maples, around which it sweeps to the house. The edifice is built in the form of an H, and of bricks brought from England. The cross furnishes a saloon of 30 feet cube, and in the centre of each wing rises a cluster of chimneys, which form the columns of two pavilions connected by a balustrade. The owner, who before the Revolution was a member of the King's Council, lived in great state, and kept a band of musicians to whose airs his daughters, Matilda and Flora, with their companions danced in the saloon or promenaded on the house-top.

6

Statesmanship was not Light-Horse Harry Lee's forte, but he could not remain inactive in political affairs as his country was going through its formative days, and he was soon elected one of Virginia's representatives in Congress. He also served as a member of the convention in Virginia which ratified the Federal Constitution, was elected governor of the state and served three terms, and later was again elected to Congress. Here he was when Washington died, and here he wrote those resolutions which described Washington in the familiar phrase: "First in war, first in peace and first in the hearts of his countrymen." But in the midst of his political activities "the divine Matilda" died, leaving him with three children, Philip Ludwell, Lucy Grymes and Henry, the first of whom died within a few years. In 1793, while serving as governor, he married Ann Hill Carter, daughter of the distinguished Charles Carter of Shirley, and took her home to Stratford with him. Ann's life at Stratford was not entirely happy. Her husband's financial misfortunes and indiscretions gradually brought them to genteel poverty. In 1806 she went to visit her father at Shirley, but he died soon after her arrival there. Thomas Boyd gives a touching account of those sad months before she gave birth to the baby boy who was named for her Carter brothers, Robert and Edward.

The death of her father was "an afflicting event" and "suspended every inclination," she wrote to her sister-in-law, "but that of enjoying the presence of my only parent," in the quiet rooms of the comfortable old brick house. Remaining there till October, she started back toward Stratford, stopping on the way with the Walkers at Belvoir on the Potomac. When she left, the countryside was bleak and the wind came screaming through the flaps of the open carriage, the only one which remained of the many that had been at Stratford, chilling her as she travelled down the Alexandria road between the bare clay fields toward home. By the time she arrived at Stratford a cold had settled on her chest and she had little to look forward to during the winter but to sit huddled over a charcoal brazier in the gloomy great hall and await the arrival of her fifth child.

Her husband was at home when she arrived, still endeavoring to straighten out his debts and becoming more entangled in the attempt. . . . That he would ever regain anything from the investments into which his too optimistic nature had led him, seemed discouragingly unlikely to Ann Hill Lee. "I know not whether you have a carriage," she wrote to Mrs. Lee of Sully, "but should I get one (which is somewhat doubtful) it can never be appropriated more to my satisfaction than in conveying yourself and dear family to our poor old dwelling." She was miserable, poor, grieving over the death of her father and worried about her sister Mildred, who was very ill.

Sick, depressed, she was in no condition to face the imminent arrival of her fifth child with any cheerfulness. Writing to her sister-in-law at Sully early in January, she expressed her feelings with definite emphasis: "That part of your letter which relates to your expecting another son shortly is so defaced by the seal that I cannot understand it; I applied to your husband for explanation and from his answer I suppose he also has reason for such an explanation—you have my best wishes for your success my dear, and truest assurances that I do not envy your prospects nor wish to share in them."

But on January 19 of that year, 1807, the unwanted child came. It was a boy and they named him Robert Edward. He was born in the high-ceilinged bedroom at the southeast corner of the house where his mother lay on the big four-poster in which the wives of three generations of the Stratford Lees had groaned in childbirth. Richard Henry and Francis Lightfoot, both signers of the Declaration, had been born there. But it was a cold, dismal day; the burning sticks in the shallow fireplace opposite the head of the bed took barely the chill off the room; the window looked out on the brown, wintry garden and Ann Hill's only consolation as she lay breathing weakly from exertion was that she had at last been delivered of her burden.

2

Childhood and Youth

Meanwhile the checkered life of Henry Lee moved on to the crescendo of its tragic climax. As his mounting years exacted their toll, his health failed. The bankruptcy of Robert Morris strained his financial resources. Desperate and unsuccessful land speculations hastened his insolvency. His creditors hounded him relentlessly, and by the spring of 1809 he found himself in the Westmoreland County jail, imprisoned for debt. The disgrace of his imprisonment weighed heavily on him, but his valiant spirit was not broken. Always resourceful, he beguiled his time in prison writing his *Memoirs of the War in the Southern Department of the United States,* a work he had long been planning. His financial difficulties finally composed, he was released from prison and returned to Stratford. Here he continued to work on his book, also exerting himself to disentangle the loose ends of his finances and to salvage something from the wreckage of his fortunes.

But the title to Stratford rested, by inheritance from Matilda, in Henry, Jr., who had now attained his majority, thus becoming the legal owner and master of the old family estate. So, about the beginning of 1810, Light-Horse Harry Lee, his wife and their brood of children—Charles Carter, Sydney Smith, Ann Kinloch and Robert Edward—left the comfortable old mansion in Westmoreland and moved to Alexandria on the Potomac, across the river from Washington, the young and growing capital city.

Robert Lee's youthful years passed pleasantly in Alexandria, despite his mother's constantly failing health and the modest

25

scale of living enforced by the family's reduced circumstances. When he was an old man and was back in Alexandria on a visit, one of his first acts was to walk around to the old house on Cameron Street and see if the snowball bushes he had known as a child were still blooming in the garden. Also, though he was but a small child when he left Stratford, the old family mansion held tender memories for him. In his late years, looking at a picture of the house, he said: "It vividly recalls scenes of my earliest recollections and happiest days. Though unseen for years, every feature of the house is familiar to me." And when, after Appomattox, he found himself and family homeless, his first sentimental thought was to try in some way to purchase Stratford—"there to return and die at home at last."

1

The removal from Stratford to Alexandria constituted a milepost in the lives of Light-Horse Harry Lee and his family. Miss Ethel Armes writes of the impact on the family of the removal to the modest brick town house on a little-city side street.

The library was left intact at Stratford. So were the family portraits, including the Gilbert Stuart portrait of Harry Lee. The greater part of the furniture, which had been there for nearly a hundred years, was also left. Among the few pieces known to have been taken to the new home was Robert's cradle. He had, of course, outgrown it, but in a few weeks it would be needed again. Ann expected her next baby in February. The last of the vehicles was brought out from the huge bare coach house. The Stratford family packed in their belongings and started on their long, rough drive across country. . . .

This move signalized a sharp turning point in the history of the Stratford family; a complete severance with Westmoreland and the past, bringing new horizons for the children and new hope, perhaps, for Ann and Harry Lee. The prelude of Robert's life, and that of his brothers and sister, written at Stratford, was over and done. The first chapter of their new lives was now to begin in a new place—the first chapter of Robert's life, the last of his father's.

After Stratford's broad acres and deep forests, the towering cliffs, the white beach, the mill pond, and the woodland paths and roads, the city of Alexandria must have seemed to the Lee children a cramped and curious place. Many of the houses were in rows; others were set in garden squares separated by box hedges or wrought-iron fences which could be vaulted in a leap. Chimneys were built up their sides instead of being formed into towers as they were at Stratford. Uneven sidewalks of red bricks, flagstones or planks, and long cobblestone streets got lost in the distance and dropped suddenly off into the river. There was no beach, no sea shells, no strange sea weed drifting in with the tides from the Chesapeake. Instead, there were docks and wharves with fleets of sailing ships and boats, far more than ever rode at Stratford Landing.

Yes, Alexandria was a queer place. The Potomac here did not seem to be even related to their river at Stratford. But the city had much the plantation did not have. There was the Friendship Fire Company, with a real engine given by General Washington himself, and a theatre such as Carter had seen in his travels north. There was a Masonic Lodge, a free school, a dancing academy, the Stabler-Leadbeater apothecary shop, and many other shops and stores. Besides all this, horse races took place when the Fairfax Jockey Club met just outside the city. There was a lovely churchyard, like a picture, around their new church—Christ Church. They had rented a house near by at 611 Cameron Street. It was a comfortable two-story brick house with a side yard. Almost the entire first floor might have been placed in the Great Hall at Stratford; but the house was pleasant and cozy, even if it was small. For several years it served as their home.

To Ann and Harry Lee, the move to Alexandria must have had at least some of the recompenses Ann had foreseen. A number of other families in the little Virginia city on the Potomac had also left remote, isolated great houses in the country. The plantation life of a generation before was changing rapidly. The younger sons of the great houses were establishing themselves in the ministry, in law, medicine, in trade, and making their livelihood in towns and cities. . . .

Ann and Harry Lee and their children found themselves in a city of friends. The situation of the Stratford family was, however, strikingly different from that of most of their Alexandria relatives and friends, who were enabled to build beautiful houses and who brought in their furnishings from the country. The belongings of the Stratford family had, for the most part, been left in the Great House. . . . Their limited means did not matter so much in Alexandria as in some other city where they might not have had so many friends.

The poor health of their daughter, Ann Kinloch, remained a source of anxious concern. The child had a serious affliction of the hand and arm which made her peculiarly nervous and delicate. She was under the continual care of physicians in Alexandria and Philadelphia. Eventually, Judge Storrow says, the child's arm had to be amputated. Another daughter was born February 27, 1811. She was named Catherine Mildred for Ann's favorite sister, but she was always called Mildred.

An important factor in the family's rehabilitation, for it was essentially that, was the distinguished character of the new undertaking in which Harry Lee was now engaged: the completion of his *Memoirs*. Many of their friends and neighbors might not read his book; few, doubtless, would buy it. But all would commend the undertaking and respect the author and his family. In this new place, the Stratford children would no longer be the children of a man but recently released from debtors' prison, but the children of Lee the historian. It would again be recalled that the master of Stratford Hall was the famous Light-Horse Harry Lee of the Revolution, "Virginia's Favourite Souldier," and three times her governor. . . .

The convenience of living in Alexandria was a welcome contrast to life in Westmoreland, especially in so stirring a period of the nation's history. On the Potomac, as well as on the Hudson, experiments with steam-propelled boats were continually in progress. Always interested in the economic, industrial and commercial development of his country, Lee must have observed with zest the new methods of transportation by land and water, as they supplemented those with which he was familiar. The changes resulting from Eli Whitney's invention of the cotton gin were absorbing topics. There was much talk of Captains Lewis and Clark of the Northwest Expedition and of Captain Zebulon Pike, all of whom had opened new horizons to the west. Young officers of the United States Army and Navy were taking rank as scientists, explorers, discoverers. Something besides a war machine was being built by them. If the new republic could but have a breathing space—respite from war and talk of war!

2

James Madison was now in the President's chair. War clouds threatened; then the storm of war broke. Harry Lee, although a Federalist, strongly supported the war. His Federalist tendencies, however, led him into an unfortunate affray in Baltimore, where he rushed to the defense of Alexander Hanson, publisher of the *Federal Republican,* which boldly denounced the war. In a riot which ensued Lee was brutally assaulted, his injuries so serious that his life was despaired of. By the summer of 1814 he had recovered sufficiently to undertake a trip to the West Indies in an effort to regain his health. Here he remained until 1818, before he finally was able to arrange passage home on the schooner *Betsy,* bound for Savannah. But he was fated never to reach his Virginia home— or even the *Betsy's* destination. When off Cumberland Island, near Fernandina, he induced the captain of the *Betsy* to set him ashore on the island at "Dungeness," General Nathaniel Greene's old home. Charles C. Jones, Jr., in 1870 set down a record of the closing scenes in Light-Horse Harry Lee's life, a record based on the eyewitness account of General Greene's grandson, Philip M. Nightingale.

Early in February, 1818, about four o'clock in the afternoon, young Nightingale, a lad some fifteen years old, who was amusing himself with boyish sports about the ample grounds, observed a schooner nearing the Dungeness landing. Just before reaching the wharf the schooner came to anchor and a boat was lowered. A feeble old man was assisted into the boat by the captain and mate, who took their seats beside him, and the three were rowed ashore by two sailors. The youth had gone to the landing, where he waited to ascertain the object of the visit and to welcome the guest.

General Lee was lifted from the boat by the sailors who, making a chair with their hands and arms, bore him to the shore. He was pale, emaciated, very weak and evidently suffering much pain. He was plainly, almost scantily attired. The sailors placed upon the wharf an old hair-trunk in a dilapidated condition and a cask of Madeira wine. General Lee brought no other baggage with him.

Beckoning the youth to him, he inquired who he was. Learning that Mrs. Shaw [General Greene's daughter] was at home, and that he was the grandson of General Greene, he threw his arms around him, embracing him with marked emotion. Then, leaning upon him, he walked a short distance from the landing place and sat upon a log. He then bade him go to the house and say to his aunt, Mrs. Shaw, that General Lee was at the wharf and wished the carriage to be sent for him. "Tell her," he added, "I am come purposely to die in the house and in the arms of the daughter of my old friend and compatriot."

Leaving him seated upon the log, young Nightingale hastened to the mansion, communicated the fact of the General's arrival, and delivered his message to his aunt. The carriage was immediately sent, and in it General Lee and his little friend rode leisurely up together, the captain and mate of the vessel walking by the side of the vehicle.

When they arrived at the house, General Lee was so weak that he had to be assisted both in getting out of the carriage and in ascending the steps. Having received a most cordial welcome from Mr. and Mrs. Shaw, he excused himself at once and retired to his room. Such was his feebleness that he kept his room, generally leaving it but once a day, and then only for a little while that he might take a short walk in the garden. . . . Even in these short walks he was able to indulge only for a week or ten days after his arrival. On but a few occasions was he strong enough to dine with the family. His feebleness becoming daily more apparent and oppressive, he was soon entirely unable to leave his room and spent most of his time in a recumbent position.

Shortly after his arrival, all the prominent officers of the Army and Navy stationed in that vicinity called in a body and paid their respects to the distinguished guest. When it became too great an effort for him to leave his room, and he realized the fact that his life was fast ebbing away, he became at times very depressed and irritable. The wound which he had received in Baltimore caused him almost incessant suffering. When the paroxysms of extreme agony were upon him, his exhibitions of commingled rage and anguish were often terrible. . . . A surgical operation was proposed as offering some hope of prolonging his life; but he put an end to the discussion by saying: "My dear sir, were the great Washington alive and here and joining you in advocating it, I would resist."

During his illness he was constantly attended by two surgeons from the fleet [in near-by waters]. The officers of the Army and Navy, usually two at a time, sat up with him every night, ministering most tenderly to his wants. . . . General Lee's sojourn at Dungeness continued nearly two months. His feebleness and emaciation increasing every day, and his paroxysms of agony growing more frequent and longer in their duration, he became utterly exhausted and gradually yielded to the sure and steady approach of the last enemy. . . . He ceased to breathe on the 25th of March, 1818.

As soon as the fact of his demise was known, all the naval vessels in Cumberland Sound showed their colors at half mast. A similar token of respect was manifested at military headquarters on Amelia Island. Arrangements were formed to testify, by the most public funeral honors, the highest regard for the memory of the gallant dead and a just appreciation of the national bereavement. The prominent officers of the Army and Navy came over to Dungeness, with crape upon their side arms, to participate in the obsequies. A company of infantry from the force on Amelia Island and a large detachment of Marines from the fleet formed the military escort. The full Army band was in attendance. The funeral procession moved from the house to the private burial ground near the beach. While it was moving and until the body was committed to the earth, from the *John Adams,* the flag-ship of the fleet, minute guns were fired. The solemn dead march was played by the band. At the grave the customary salutes were fired by the infantry and Marines. There was nothing omitted which, under the circumstances, could contribute to the solemnity of the occasion or aid in compassing the most distinguished funeral honors for this gifted soldier who, by his bright blade, had won such success and honor for the country and, by his intellect and attainments, had given to history some of the most prominent memories of his age and people.

3

Back in Alexandria Harry Lee's widow mourned the passing of her famous husband, but gallantly assumed the task of educating and training her fatherless children. Fortunately her prudent father had definitely entailed his bequest to her so she would be assured of a comfortable life income, protected from the financial ineptitude of her unfortunate husband. Of the family's life in Alexandria, before and after Light-Horse Harry's death, Miss Mason gives us an intimate and interesting glimpse.

The family lived on Cameron Street, near the old Christ Church, then on Orinoco Street, and afterwards in the house known as the Parsonage.

At this period General Henry Lee was absent in the West Indies in pursuit of health; and in one of the admirable letters written to his son Carter, then a student at Cambridge, he says: "Robert, who was always good, will be confirmed in his happy turn of mind by his ever watchful and affectionate mother."

This good mother was a great invalid; one of his sisters was delicate, and many years absent in Philadelphia under the care of physicians. The oldest son, Carter, was at Cambridge; Sydney Smith in the Navy; and the other sister too young to be of much aid in household matters. So Robert was the housekeeper, "carried the keys," attended to the marketing, managed all the outdoor business, and took care of his mother's horses.

At the hour when the other school-boys went to play, he hurried home to order his mother's drive, and would then be seen carrying her in his arms to the carriage and arranging her cushions with the gentleness of an experienced nurse. One of his relatives still lives who was often the companion of these drives. She tells us of the exertions he would make on these occasions to entertain and amuse his mother; assuring her, with the gravity of an old man, that unless she was cheerful the drive would not benefit her. When she complained of cold or drafts, he would pull from his pocket a great jack-knife and newspaper and make her laugh with his efforts to improvise curtains and shut out the intrusive wind which whistled through the crevices of the old family coach.

When he left her to go to West Point his mother was heard to say, "How can I live without Robert? He is both son and daughter to me."

Years after, when he came home from West Point, he found one of the chief actors in his childhood's drama—his mother's old coachman, Nat—ill and threatened with consumption. He immediately took him to the milder climate of Georgia, nursed him with the tenderness of a son, and secured him the best medical advice. But the spring-time saw the faithful old servant laid in the grave by the hands of his kind young master.

General Lee used to say that he was very fond of hunting when a boy, that he sometimes followed the hounds on foot all day. This will account for his well-developed form, and for that wonderful strength which was never known to fail him in all the fatigues and privations of his after-life.

4

A broader, more analytical view of Lee's boyhood life in Alexandria is provided by Dr. Douglas S. Freeman.

This attendance upon his mother continued until Robert left Alexandria. More than anything else, perhaps, his filial attention to her was the prime obligation of his youth, precisely as care for an invalid wife was to be one of the chief duties of his mature years. The man who was to order Pickett's charge at Gettysburg got part of his preparation for war by nursing sick women. The self-command that his mother had inculcated from his babyhood was confirmed at the bedside. Yet his association with his mother did not make the boy effeminate, though it gave him a love for the company of women. He stayed at home uncomplainingly when his mother required his attendance, but when he was free he delighted to swim in the Potomac, to share in the sports of the neighborhood boys, with his cousin and playmate, Cassius Lee, or to follow the chase all day in the rolling country behind Alexandria.

If Robert had a longer holiday he spent it at Chatham, or at Ravensworth with the Fitzhughs, or at Stratford with his brother Henry, who, about the time Robert was ten, married Anne Mc-Carty of Westmoreland County. The dates of his visits to the old home of the Lees are not known, but he must have gone there not infrequently, because in later life he cherished clear memories of a place of which he could have had only the vaguest impressions before the family moved to Alexandria. . . .

As visits and pleasure were interspersed with hard work for Robert, he developed rapidly in physique and in character, and by the time he was thirteen he had learned all that could conveniently be taught him at home and at Eastern View. Accordingly, by 1820, possibly before that year, Robert entered the Alexandria academy. This had been established about 1785, and had been privileged to list Washington as one of its first trustees. Occupying a one-story brick house on the east side of Washington Street, between Duke and Wolfe, the school was made free to all Alexandria boys after January, 1821. Here Robert met at their desks the boys with whom he had played in the fields, and here he came under the tutelage of William B. Leary, an Irishman for whom young Lee acquired enduring respect.

5

Some detailed information about Mr. Leary and also Mr. Hallowell, the two Alexandria schoolmasters who had young Robert Lee as a student, is provided by R. A. Brock.

There always existed a warm friendship between Mr. Leary and his distinguished pupil. After the close of the war he came to Lexington on a special visit to General Lee; and during his Southern tour, the spring before his death, Mr. Leary came a long way to see him, and they had a most pleasant interview. Just after his visit to Lexington, the General wrote his old teacher: "Your visit has recalled to me years long since passed, when I was under your tuition and received daily your instruction. In parting from you I beg to express the gratitude I have felt all my life for the affectionate fidelity which characterized your teaching and conduct toward me. I pray that the evening of your days may be blessed with peace and tranquillity, and that a merciful God may guide and protect you to the end. Should any of my friends, wherever your lot may be cast, desire to know your qualifications as a teacher, I hope you will refer them to me; for of them I can speak knowingly and from experience."

As soon as it was decided that he should go to West Point, he was sent to the school of Mr. Benjamin Hallowell, who was for so many years a famous teacher in Alexandria, in order to perfect himself in mathematics. This gentleman, although espousing the Federal cause during the war, always spoke in enthusiastic terms of his painstaking, successful pupil.

Mr. Hallowell has left this memorandum: "Robert E. Lee entered my school in Alexandria, Va., in the winter of 1824-25, to study mathematics, preparatory to his going to West Point. He was a most exemplary student in every respect. He was never behind time at his studies, never failed in a single recitation, was perfectly observant of the rules and regulations of the institution; was gentlemanly, unobtrusive and respectful in all his deportment to teachers and fellow-students. His specialty was finishing up. He imparted a neatness and finish to everything he undertook. One of the branches of mathematics he studied with me was conic sections, in which some of the diagrams were very complicated. He drew the diagrams on a slate, and although he well knew that the one he was drawing would have to be removed to make room for the next, he drew each one with so much accuracy and finish, lettering and all, as if it were to be engraved and printed."

3

The Training of a Soldier

IN 1825 young Robert Lee had reached the age of eighteen years and had outgrown the educational facilities of Alexandria. It was necessary to make a decision as to his future schooling and his life career, a question which received the thoughtful attention of himself, his mother and his elder brothers—including his half brother Henry. It was perhaps not unnatural that their thoughts should turn to the Army, considering the military fame of the boy's father. Indeed, one of the last letters the father wrote to Robert from the West Indies—and one which the son carefully preserved—discussed eloquently the glories of the military life as demonstrated by the career of Wellington. "Alexander, Hannibal and Caesar among the ancients, Marlborough, Eugene, Turenne and Frederick amongst the moderns, opened their arms to receive him as a brother in glory," wrote Light-Horse Harry Lee to Robert, little dreaming that the quiet lad in Alexandria to whom the letter was addressed would so soon write his own name high up on the list of the great warriors of the world.

His brother Henry used his influence to obtain the desired appointment to the Academy, but one of his cousins wrote in later years that an aunt "took him to Washington and introduced him to General Jackson, who was so much pleased with Robert that he got him his appointment." So Robert Lee placed his youthful feet on the first rung of the military ladder which he was to mount to its very top.

1

Of Robert Lee's four years as a cadet at West Point there is little written record, and that mostly of a negative nature.

36

Making due allowance for the overenthusiasm of an admiring nephew, Fitzhugh Lee's brief account of this period of his uncle's life is about the best available.

The time had now arrived to select a profession, and to the army his inclination pointed—a direction which probably resulted from a son's desire to follow in his father's footsteps, especially when that father had been so distinguished in the profession. He was now a modest, manly youth in his eighteenth year, who resolved to take care of himself and relieve his mother to that extent. His father's career had reflected credit upon his country; could he not hope to do the same? Sydney Smith Lee, his next oldest brother, had already entered the Navy and was supporting himself; so he decided to go in the Army.

The application for an appointment to the United States Military Academy was successful, and in 1825 his name was entered upon the rolls of that celebrated institution. He had now four years of hard study, vigorous drill, and was absorbing strategy and tactics to be useful to him in after-years. His excellent habits and close attention to all duties did not desert him; he received no demerits; was a cadet officer in his class, and during his last year held the post of honor in the aspirations of cadet life—the adjutancy of the corps. . . . It is interesting to notice that his eldest son, George Washington Custis Lee, also entered the Military Academy twenty-one years after his father, was also the cadet adjutant, graduated first in his class, and was assigned to the Engineer Corps.

During his whole course at West Point Robert was a model cadet, his clothes looked nice and new, his cross-belt, collar and summer trousers were as white as the driven snow mounting guard upon the mountain top, and his brass breast and waist plates were mirrors to reflect the image of the inspector. He conscientiously performed his tours of guard duty, whether the non-commissioned officer of the guard was approaching his post or sleeping in his quarters. He never "ran the sentinel post," did not go off limits to the "Benny Havens" of his day or put "dummies" in his bed, to deceive the officer in charge as he made his inspection after taps, and at the parades stood steady in line. It was a pleasure for the inspecting officer to look down the barrel of his gun, it was bright and clean, and its stock was rubbed so as to almost resemble polished mahogany.

Cadet Lee in 1829 became Lieutenant Lee of the Engineer Corps of the United States Army. The cadets who graduate in each class with first honors [Lee was second in his class] are assigned to it and its ranks are kept full of first-class material. Its members are composed of students who obey the regulations, are proficient in their studies and receive few demerits. From this scientific corps distinguished men and great soldiers have issued, and to be an officer in the United States Engineer Corps is a passport anywhere. . . .

Lieutenant Lee entered upon the usual life of a young officer of engineers. His chosen profession had his earnest attention, and every effort was made to acquire information. He knew his studies at West Point were only the foundation upon which to build the life edifice. Without continued application to the principles of engineering and study he could not hope to rise above the ordinary level of the military graduate. So his army career began with the fixed determination to put aside daily pleasures of life where they conflicted with daily hours of duty. . . .

He went much in the society of ladies—always most congenial to him. His conversation was bright, his wit refined and pleasant. Cement, mortar, lime, curves, tangents and straight professional lines disappeared then. He enjoyed a dress parade of this kind, was happy in the drawing-room in the evening, and happy in his work on the parapet next day.

2

The triumphant happiness of young Lieutenant Lee's graduation from the Military Academy in 1829 was clouded by the fact that the life of his mother was rapidly drawing to an end. Immediately following his graduation in July he hastened home and was able to be at her side during her last days, but during the same month she died. He spent the remaining days of his postgraduation leave of absence visiting the Randolph family in Fauquier County and other friends and family connections in Virginia. Among other places visited was "Chatham," the Fitzhughs' ancestral home on the Rappahannock across the river from Fredericksburg—and at Chatham, among other visitors, was also Mary Custis, the daughter of Mr. George Washington Parke Custis, the adopted son of George Washington and the grandson of Mrs. Washington. The Custis family home was at "Arlington" across the Potomac from Washington, and Robert Lee and Mary Custis had known each other from childhood, when their families exchanged visits. But while Robert was visiting at Chatham during his graduation furlough, a sentimental attachment sprang up between him and Mary, and from that time forward neither had an eye for any other.

Years later, in 1863, Lee stood on the hills on the other side of the Rappahannock and looked through his glasses at Chatham on the farther side. Chatham was then the headquarters of the Federal commander, General Burnside, and the Federal guns were bombarding Fredericksburg. Eagerly the Confederate artillerymen trained their guns on the big old house; but gently General Lee stayed their hand. "I could not bear to see Chatham shelled," he told his artillery chief. "It was under those trees that I courted my wife."

But in September [1829] his furlough was over and he was assigned to duty at Fort Pulaski, on Cockspur Island, in the river below Savannah, Georgia. Old Nat, his mother's old coachman, was in desperately bad health; and since his old mistress had just died and he now had no one to care for him, the young lieutenant bundled up the sick old Negro and took him with him to Savannah, where he cared for him until Nat died the next year.

At Savannah Lieutenant Lee entered upon the first duties of his military life. They were not particularly important duties— the minor engineering problems incident to keeping the waters of the sea from the low-lying little island—but Lieutenant Lee gave to this small, insignificant job all that devotion to duty that characterized his whole life; and his reports show his deep concern over the task of keeping up the embankments which the tides and gales insisted on destroying. On February 1st, 1830, he won his first promotion. It was a trivial promotion, merely an appointment from Major Samuel Babcock, in command at Savannah, as "acting assistant commissary of subsistence of the post"; but it must have been very gratifying to the young officer—his first recognition of merit. Here on Cockspur Island Lieutenant Lee remained until December 1st, 1830—his first tour of duty in the Army.

From Savannah he was transferred to Fortress Monroe, across Hampton Roads from Norfolk, and put to work strengthening the fortifications there. The coast defenses had been seriously damaged during the War of 1812; and, now that Andrew Jackson was President, he considered nothing of greater importance than the restoration of these fortifications all along the Atlantic seaboard.

Lieutenant Lee doubtless welcomed the transfer back to Virginia. For one thing, it was convenient to Arlington and Mary Custis; and so effectively did he improve this opportunity to continue his courtship that within six months of his transfer the wedding was announced.

Mary Custis was one of the outstanding belles of Virginia. She had family distinction, wealth and charm. Robert E. Lee was a personable young man of good family, but he had little of this world's goods, and it was hinted that the proud Mr. Custis would have preferred a wealthier husband for his only daughter. But Mary Custis would have no other than Robert Lee; and the objections of her father, if they existed, soon vanished before her great love for the man of her choice. The wedding at Arlington on June 30th, 1831, was according to all accounts a brilliant affair, as befitted the union of a Custis with a Lee. There was the customary round of social festivities following the wedding; but soon Lieutenant Lee was back with his bride at Fortress Monroe, once more engrossed with his blue-prints and drafting-board, acting as assistant to Captain Andrew Talcott who was in charge of the reconstruction of the fortifications.

In 1834 Lieutenant Lee was transferred to Washington, as assistant to Colonel Gratiot, chief engineer of the Army; and in 1835 he was made assistant astronomer of the commission surveying the boundary line between Ohio and Michigan—a very important work, as the accurate surveying of the line was to determine in which state the city of Toledo was located. In 1836 he was back in Washington assigned to duty again as Colonel Gratiot's assistant, and he served in this capacity for two years.

These were two happy years, since it was possible for him and his wife to live with the Custises at Arlington across the river and enjoy with their two infant children the home life thus made possible. Lieutenant Lee (he was now a full-fledged first lieutenant) rode horseback from Arlington to Washington every morning and back home in the afternoon; and he was a familiar figure, cantering through the streets of Washington and Georgetown those two years, on his way to and from the Chief Engineer's office.

Sometimes the roads or the weather prevented the trip on horseback, or an occasional press of work kept him in town. On those occasions he lived with a "mess" in Washington composed of Army officers and several members of President Jackson's cabinet, the Senate and the diplomatic corps. The young Army officers, then as now, enjoyed having a good time during their leisure hours; and sometimes some of the elder and more stately members of the mess were slightly shocked at the frolicsome behaviour of the young men.

One day, as Lee was about to start on horseback for Arlington, he saw one of his Army cronies, Lieutenant Macomb, on the sidewalk and, drawing up alongside him, called out: "Come, get up behind me." Macomb, probably to Lee's surprise, promptly accepted the invitation and, placing his foot in the stirrup, vaulted to the horse's back. Lee, carrying the joke through, galloped off up Pennsylvania Avenue before Macomb could dismount. Turning the corner in front of the Treasury they were spied by the dignified Secretary, Levi Woodbury. His eyes nearly popped out at the sight of two supposedly dignified Army officers riding double up Washington's main thoroughfare; but they bowed gravely to him and galloped on up by the White House, while he turned into the Treasury slowly shaking his head at such didoes.

Even early in life, Lee was exhibiting that trait of character that was afterward to be so valuable to him—that close attention to details and care about having everything just exactly right.

Upon first being stationed in Washington in 1835 he was careful to search out a blacksmith who would shoe his horse carefully in accordance with his own directions; and, having found that man in a smith named Schneider who had a shop on Twentieth and G Streets, he patronized him throughout the rest of his life in Washington. As late as the fall of 1860, when Schneider's blacksmith shop had grown into an iron foundry at the corner of Pennsylvania Avenue and Eighteenth, Lee called on him one day and left with him the drawing of a special kind of coulter he wanted made for use in plowing up some new ground at Arlington. The coulter was later delivered at the farm by a marketman, and Lee did not see Schneider again before the breaking out of the war. But he did not forget the transaction with the Washington blacksmith, and late in 1861, although his mind was crowded with other matters, he found a way to send to Schneider through the lines two gold dollars wrapped in paper in discharge of the old account, accompanied by a note of apology for the delay.

3

Up to this time the Army career of Robert E. Lee was proceeding along conventional lines, with little opportunity for any manifestation of latent talents or brilliance. But in 1837 he was afforded an opportunity for distinction and advancement in his profession through the unpredictable medium of the Mississippi River and its vagaries. At this time the main current of the river became deflected to the Illinois side opposite the city of St. Louis, with the imminent threat that that thriving frontier metropolis would be entirely separated from the river, its only means of transportation. An appeal was made to the Army Engineers for help in staying the threatened change in the river's course, and Lee was placed in charge of the work. General Scott in recommending him said: "Lee is young, but if the work can be done he can do it."

General M. C. Meigs, who served as Lee's assistant on this tour of duty, has provided an interesting account of their experiences in wrestling with the Father of Waters. Meigs describes Lee as "a man then in the vigor of youthful strength, with a noble and commanding presence and an admirable, graceful and athletic figure. He was one with whom nobody ever wished or ventured to take a liberty, though kind and generous to all his subordinates, admired by all women and respected by all men. He was the model of a soldier and the beau ideal of a Christian man."

In the summer of 1837, Lieutenant Robert E. Lee, Corps of Engineers, was ordered by the Engineer Department to proceed to the Mississippi River and, with an appropriation made by Congress for the purpose, to make examination, plans and estimates for the improvement of the navigation of the Mississippi at the harbor of St. Louis, where sandbars threatened to interfere with the use of the water-front of the city, known as the levee, upon which they were encroaching, and where the main channel of the river showed a tendency to change from the Missouri to the Illinois shore. He was also instructed to make surveys and plans for improving the navigation of this river near the point where the Des Moines enters it from the west, and above and about the mouth of Rock River, which enters from the east. At both these points the river flows over ledges of rocks, with a narrow and tortuous channel. During the season of low water all steamboats at these points were obliged to discharge at least a part of their cargo, which was placed upon what were then known as "keel-boats" and towed by horses along the shores to the head of the rapids. The country about these rapids was only then being surveyed and opened for settlement. No railroad had at that time crossed the Alleghanies.

Lieutenant Lee left Washington about June, accompanied by Lieutenant Meigs as his assistant. They went by the way of the Pennsylvania Canal to Pittsburg, where they took a steamer and descended to Louisville, stopping at Cincinnati (both of these were then small cities, compared with what they are to-day). At Louisville they found a small steamboat which had just been completed under the supervision of Captain Shreeves, famous as the inventor and operator of the "snag-boat." His son-in-law, Captain Morehead, was the captain of the surveying boat; and here, with the aid of the boatmen, Lieutenant Lee organized and outfitted a strong surveying-party of river-men. The steamer proceeded to the Des Moines rapids, touching at St. Louis on the way. (St. Louis's principal distinction then was that it was the headquarters of the North-western fur trade. Ashley, Chouteau and Sandford had there their principal offices, and thence despatched expeditions which penetrated the Rocky Mountains and fought battles in Oregon and Washington Territories with the Canadian voyageurs and Scotch servants of the Hudson Bay Company.) Arrived at the lower or Des Moines rapids of the Mississippi, the party attempted to pass the rapids in their steamer, and quickly experienced the difficulties of the navigation by finding themselves fast on the rocks of one of the lower channels. All efforts to float the steamer failed, and the party proceeded to make their survey of these rapids while using the steamer as a base of operations, the surveying-parties leaving the steamer in small boats in the morning and returning at night.

Having completed the survey of the Des Moines rapids, they took passage in a steamer which they found at the head of the rapids, and ascended to Rock Island. There they discovered another steamer wrecked upon a rock in the Rock Island rapids; her hull was stove in and her lower deck was partly under water, but her upper cabin, with its staterooms, was dry and habitable. Holes made for removing the engines yawned in the cabin-floor. Lieutenant Lee made this wreck his base of operations during the survey of the upper rapids. From the stern, after the day's work was over, the young men of the party replenished the larder by fishing for blue catfish, pike and pickerel. About the end of October the work on this part of the river was finished, and they returned to the Des Moines rapids on a passing steamer. At these rapids they found the banks lined with birch-bark canoes and Indian tepees, a tribe of Chippewas having assembled there to receive the fall distribution of presents from the agents. Owing to a rise in the river, they now found themselves able to float their own steamer, in which they returned to St. Louis.

Here the second story of a warehouse on the levee was rented as an office, where the maps giving the results of their surveys of the upper river were prepared. While the reduction of their notes to the form of maps was going on parties were placed in the field on each bank of the river. Signals were established, and the river was thoroughly triangulated and sounded from the mouth of the Missouri to some distance below St. Louis. These surveys were completed and mapped, and the party broke up. The men were discharged, and Lieutenant Lee and Lieutenant Meigs returned to Washington, laying up their steamer for the winter on the Ohio, and passing through Wheeling by way of the Cumberland road. At Frederick, Md., they took cars on the Baltimore and Ohio Railroad, crossing some divides by horse-power. No locomotive had at that time reached Frederick.

Lieutenant Lee made up his report, in which he recommended the improvement of the two rapids by the straightening and widening of the channels and by blasting and moving the rocks which obstructed navigation. He recommended, in regard to the St. Louis problem, the proper course of the dikes to deflect the currents and to close at low water the eastern or Illinois channel by connecting Bloody Island with the eastern shore.

These reports and maps were published by Congress, which for many years continued to make appropriations for the execution of the work designed and recommended by Lieutenant Lee. . . .

The preliminary survey was not the whole of Lieutenant Lee's connection with the improvement of the Mississippi. For some years thereafter he superintended the progress of the work at the points designated. During the prosecution of this work at St. Louis there was much free criticism and adverse prediction indulged in by the people of the threatened city. Heedless of this public clamor, the young Engineer officer pursued the even tenor of his way, and finally convinced his critics by the best of logic, that of success, that there might be some intelligence and ability outside of political assemblies and newspaper offices. . . . Operations at the rapids also were prosecuted in accordance with the plans and under the direction of Lieutenant Lee, and an available channel gradually formed.

4

A more detailed account of the carrying out of the project at St. Louis is given in an article which appeared in a San Antonio paper at the time of Lee's death, quoted by Dr. Jones in his *Reminiscences*.

The almost uniform success of General Robert E. Lee was due probably to the simplicity of the means he invariably adopted to attain even the most gigantic results. As an evidence of this fact, we would call to mind something that our people have never known and the people of St. Louis, those most interested, have likely forgotten. Certain it is that by these latter no official recognition of General (then Brevet-Captain) Lee's services was ever made—not even the poor compliment of a notice in the minutes of the Board of Aldermen.

It will be remembered that many years ago all St. Louis was terrified at the prospect of being isolated by the action of the river current which up to that time had been striking its banks, as it swayed from side to side, almost in front of the city. But, by washing away the banks on the Illinois side, thereby changing the angles of impingement, the stream commenced to gradually wear away the soil below St. Louis, making its way toward the "American bottom," an alluvial tract, and would have finally reached and emptied into a creek some five miles below the city, diverting the river and leaving St. Louis an inland town.

The City Council and the general government made large appropriations, hired the best engineers, built dikes—to find them useless, and were finally obliged to admit that if there was engineering skill sufficient to avert the calamity it could not be found. General Scott was consulted, to know if he could not recommend some one capable of grappling the problem. The general replied: "I know of but one officer, a brevet-captain on my staff. He is young, but if the work can be done he can do it."

Brevet-Captain Robert E. Lee arrived in St. Louis and went to work. Quietly and unostentatiously he prepared his plans, drew his charts, calculated the force and direction of the currents, examined all the discarded plans and determined on his course. All this took considerable time because, as he remarked, "Too much is at stake to trust to any uncertain agencies or leave anything to fortune." So noiselessly were his preparations carried on that the citizens began to murmur at the apparent inactivity of the young officer; the *Republican* and other newspapers attacked him, and at last the city withdrew its appropriation.

Through all this accumulated dissatisfaction, Captain Lee pursued the even tenor of his way, merely remarking when the appropriation was withdrawn by the city: "They have a right to do as they will with their own. The Government has sent me here as an officer of the Army to do a certain work. I shall do it."

The careful preparations were at last completed and everything in readiness: a number of flat-boats—some partially loaded with stones, others fully, according to the depth of water in which they were to sink—moored with strong ropes from each, so that they could be cast loose to the current at one time by one stroke of an axe, and a plug in each so arranged that at a given signal all the plugs could be withdrawn simultaneously. A man stood ready at each line with a hatchet to cut loose; a watch in his hand, with the hour, minute and second indicated when to pull the plug. The signal to "cut loose" was the firing of the captain's pistol, which being given, as with one accord every rope was cut and the boats, exactly as calculated, swung out toward their proper and destined places. Curving at first by the greater force of the current, so accurately had every ounce of pressure been ascertained and provided for that when the moment arrived and every plug was withdrawn the boats went down in a perfect line at right angles to the current as intended. Buoys were fixed, and next day Captain Lee paid an early visit to see if all was safe. All was safe, including the city of St. Louis. Day after day brush, stones, etc., were sunk until the dike thus formed reached the surface of the water. To-day cars cross the same structure, to whose existence a proud city owes its greatness, a silent monument to the genius of one who, though dead, "still lives."

The *Republican* managed to say after the work was complete: "The talented young engineer has succeeded in diverting the current of the river, notwithstanding the fears entertained that such would not be the case."

This is but one notable instance of "Lee's way," which was ever a successful one, whether grappling with a scientific or military problem, whether planning the saving or reduction of a city. Whether in peace or in war, his means were as simple, direct, speedy and efficacious as the results of his efforts were successful, enduring and glorious.

5

A glimpse of the life of the young Army officers on the expedition is provided by a letter written from St. Louis by Lee to his friend, Lieutenant Joseph E. Johnston of the Topographical Engineers, then stationed in Washington. Johnston was then known to his intimate Army friends as "Colonel," and he is so addressed by Lee. The identity of the "Dick" mentioned in the letter is mercifully shrouded in the anonymity of the passing years.

Dear Colonel:

Upon my return here some few days ago from the Rapids I found your letter of the 1st. It did me good to hear of the boys, especially as it was all good. Kan's fishing-project I fear is more natural than feasible, and its merits in so benighted a place as Washington will never be appreciated. I now contemplate you, therefore, as one of the stars in General Scott's staff.

While up the river I fell in with Dick and escorted him from Galena to Burlington, his headquarters. General Brooke happened at Galena while we were there and, besides the pleasure of meeting him again, we had much pleasure in fighting the battles of Old Point over again. But it was done temperately and in a temperance manner, for the general has forsworn strong potations and our refreshment consisted of only soda-water and ice-cream, delicacies that had been untasted by the general for the last *nine* years, and four times a day did we pay our respects to the fountain and freezer.

Dick had been up to Dubuque to let out one of his roads, and, finding some spare days on his hands, "accoutred as he was," he plunged into a pleasure-party for the Falls of St. Anthony that came along in fine spirits, with music playing and colors flying. Would you like to hear of his apparel? A little short-sleeved, short-waisted, short-skirted, brown linen coat, well acquainted with the washboard and intended for a smaller man than our friend; a faded blue calico shirt; domestic cloth pants; a pair of commodious brogans; and a hat torn, broken and discolored. Now, hear him laugh as he presents himself for a dance, arms akimbo, and you have him before you. I believe, though, it was a concerted thing with him, for whom should he meet but his Indian friend "Hole-in-the-Day" and his faithful *Red She,* who showed him his old blanket that she religiously wrapt herself in; but upon examining *his* fingers her good copper rings were not there! He complains bitterly of his present waste of life, looks thin and dispirited, and is acquainted with the cry of every child in Iowa. He is well practised in pork-eating and promiscuous sleeping, and is a friend to Quakers, or rather their pretty daughters. . . .

News recently arrived that the Sioux had fallen upon a party of Chippeways and taken one hundred and thirty scalps. The Hole-in-the-Day, Dick's friend, had gone in advance with the larger party, and they did not come up with him. It is expected that this chief, who is represented as an uncommon man, will take ample revenge, and this may give rise to fresh trouble.

6

Following his successful and satisfactory tour of duty on the Mississippi, Captain Lee was transferred back east and placed in charge of the defenses of New York Harbor, with his headquarters at Fort Hamilton. This made possible a reunion with his steadily growing family—his wife and four children: George Washington Custis, William Henry Fitzhugh, Mildred and Annie.

Here in the officers' quarters at Fort Hamilton he established his home, bringing along Mrs. Lee and the two boys and two girls from Arlington. Mrs. Lee and the children made frequent visits back home to Virginia from time to time, but here at Fort Hamilton the little family spent five happy years together, with all the ups and downs of family life.

Young William Henry Fitzhugh (always called "Rooney" by his father) was a bold and venturesome lad, even in his childhood; and one day when his father was in New York and his mother was out visiting some of the other officers' wives, Rooney strayed off to the big barn where the cavalry horses were kept, although he had been warned against doing so. Boy-like, he lost no time in investigating the fascinating mysteries of the hay-cutter; and before he knew what was happening had cut off the ends of two of his fingers. The surgeon stationed at the fort was in New York City, and there was a great hue and cry raised before surgical attention could be brought to the captain's little son. Captain Lee took this opportunity to point out to his older son, Custis, the tragic results of disobedience and recklessness; but he could not restrain a note of pride as he told of Rooney's patience and courage while waiting for the doctor.

In a letter written to Rooney, then visiting at Arlington, Lee gives a characteristic sample of his kindly relations with his children, relating an anecdote of "a fine boy I heard of in my travels this winter—just 13 years old, the age of Custis," and closing with the admonition: "You and Custis must take great care of your kind mother and dear sisters when your father is dead. To do that, you must learn to be good. Be true, kind and generous, and pray to God to enable you to 'keep his commandments, and walk in the same all the days of your life.' " Then in a lighter tone: "Alec and Frank are well, and the former has begun to ride his pony, Jim, again. Captain Bennet has bought his little boy a donkey, and as I came home I met him riding with two large Newfoundland dogs following, one on each side. The dogs were almost as large as the donkey. My horse, Jerry, did not know what to make of them. I go to New York now, on horseback, every day; one day I ride Jerry and the next Tom, and I think they begin to go better under the saddle than formerly. I hope to come on soon to see that little baby you have got to show me."

Captain Lee was now steadily growing in prestige in Army circles. Whatever his hand found to do he was doing well. In 1844 there came official recognition of his high standing in the form of an appointment to the Board of Visitors at West Point, a great honor for a young officer. Late in 1845 there was bestowed on him the further honor of membership on the Board of Engineers for Atlantic Coast defense. Captain Lee had arrived.

In 1845 Lee was 38 years old. He had been in the Army for 16 years; and, although he had made a good record, it was in the more or less dull and routine work of an Army engineer. There was as yet not the slightest indication that the young man in charge of the New York fortifications was one whose name, within a few years, would be mentioned along with those of Hannibal and Caesar and Napoleon. The country had been at peace since the War of 1812, and there had been no opportunity for American soldiers to try their mettle on the battlefield. But in 1845 there were rumblings of war away to the southward in Mexico. The government was talking about increasing the Army's strength in preparation for possible trouble. It was then that Lee wrote to a friend: "In the event of war with any foreign government, I would desire to be brought into active service in the field; and if that could not be accomplished without leaving the Corps of Engineers I should then desire a transfer to some other branch of the service and would prefer the artillery."

The long-dormant spark of Light-Horse Harry Lee's flaming combativeness was beginning to burn in his quiet son.

4

The Mexican War

===

THE Mexican War grew out of a dispute between the United States and Mexico as to the boundary line between Mexico and Texas, after the Texan Republic had been annexed to the United States of America as one of its constituent states. It was not much of a war as wars go, and the result was never in doubt. It provided, however, a proving ground for the officers of the United States forces; and the names of many of the generals of the Union and Confederate armies are to be found in the annals of the Mexican War in the capacities of lieutenants, captains and majors.

Captain Lee soon had his wish for active service fulfilled. When the war broke out he was assigned to the division commanded by General Wool in General Taylor's army which advanced into Mexico across the Rio Grande. Then, when it was decided that the proper way to invade Mexico was through the Port of Vera Cruz, he was assigned to the staff of General Winfield Scott who was in command of the forces to be engaged. He traveled to Vera Cruz on an army transport, occupying a stateroom with his old friend Joseph E. Johnston; but he wrote home that "poor Joe was sick all the time" and did not enjoy the trip.

The Mexican War was an important milestone in the life of Robert E. Lee. Before it he had been just another good, faithful Army officer. He emerged from the war, at the age of forty-one, with an established reputation as a soldier of great skill and possibilities. General Scott, under whose eye he had served, had marked him down as a man of superior abilities, a reputation which was to influence his whole future life and fame.

1

An incident of Captain Lee's services with General Wool's command during the early days of the campaign is related by General Long "as illustrative of the romance of war and of the daring of its hero."

Shortly before the battle of Buena Vista, General Wool, being ignorant of the position and movements of the enemy, but having been positively assured that Santa Anna had crossed the mountains and was encamped with his whole army at a point only twenty miles distant, determined to send out a scouting-party to ascertain the truth of this report. Captain Lee, who was present, at once volunteered to perform this duty. His offer was accepted, and he was directed to procure a guide and order a company of cavalry to meet him at the outer picket-line as escort. By some means, however, he missed the picket-post and his escort, and ere long found himself several miles beyond the lines with no company but his guide. This was a young Mexican who knew the country, and whom Captain Lee had promised the contents of a pocket-pistol if he should play false.

Dangerous as it was to proceed alone, to return was to abandon the enterprise for that night, and the daring scout galloped on. At a point about five miles from the reported place of encampment of the Mexican army the moonlight displayed numerous tracks of mules and wagons in the road. No artillery-tracks were visible, but these might have been obliterated by the others, and there was abundant reason to conclude that a strong foraging- or reconnoitering-party had passed here. The information thus obtained would have satisfied many officers, yet it was not sufficiently positive for Captain Lee, who determined to go on till he reached the picket-posts of the enemy.

To his surprise, he found no pickets. He concluded that he had missed them as he had those of his own army, and had ridden within the Mexican lines. In confirmation of this opinion, he soon found himself in view of what appeared to be large camp-fires on a hillside at no great distance. His guide, who was by this time in a pitiable state of fright, begged him earnestly to return, saying there was a stream of water just beyond and that he knew that Santa Anna's whole army was encamped on the other side.

But the daring scout was not yet quite satisfied, and, directing the guide to await his return, he galloped boldly forward. Soon he perceived what appeared to be the white tents of a large encampment. Reaching the banks of the stream, he heard beyond it loud talking and the usual noises of a camp.

By this time, however, he was near enough to be able to make better use of the moonlight, and discovered that his white tents were simply a large *flock of sheep,* and that his army was a train of wagons and the drovers of a large herd of cattle, mules, etc. Riding into their camp, he quickly learned from them that Santa Anna had not yet crossed the mountains, and that there were no Mexican forces in that locality.

He galloped back with this important news to the army, where he found his friends in a state of serious apprehension as to his safety, the intended escort having reported his disappearance. "But," said General Lee, "the most delighted man to see me was the old Mexican, the father of my guide, with whom I had been last seen by any of our people, and whom General Wool had arrested and proposed to hang if I was not forthcoming."

Though he had ridden forty miles that night, he was in the saddle again after a three hours' rest. He guided a body of cavalry to and far beyond the point to which he had gone the night before, and succeeded in ascertaining definitely the position, force, etc., of the enemy.

The signal victory of General Taylor at Buena Vista . . . virtually ended the war in the northern Mexican states. Meanwhile . . . General Scott was collecting a large force in the neighborhood of Tampico to operate against Vera Cruz and the city of Mexico. Captain R. E. Lee joined this force by the particular request of General Scott.

2

On his arrival at Vera Cruz, Captain Lee was promptly assigned to the management of the first step in the invasion of

Mexico, the construction of the works to be used by the army of invasion in its siege of the city. Dr. Jones relates an amusing anecdote of the young captain's first experience in actual armed conflicts.

Captain Lee was ordered to throw up such works as were necessary to protect a battery which was to be manned by the sailors of a certain man-of-war, and to use these gallant tars in constructing the work. The time being short, the young engineer pushed on the work very rapidly, and the sons of Neptune began to complain very loudly that "they did not enlist to dig dirt" and they did not "like to be put under a 'land lubber' anyhow."

At last the captain of the frigate—a thorough specimen of a United States naval officer in the palmy days of the service—came to Captain Lee and remonstrated, and then protested, against the "outrage" of putting his men to digging dirt. "The boys don't want any dirt to hide behind," said the brave old tar, with great earnestness and not a few expletives; "they only want to get at the enemy; and after you have finished your banks we will not stay behind them, we will get up on top where we can have a fair fight."

Captain Lee quietly showed his orders and assured the old salt that he meant to carry them out, and pushed on the work amid curses both loud and deep.

Just about the time the work was completed the Mexicans opened upon that point a heavy fire, and these gallant sons of the sea were glad enough to take refuge behind their despised "bank of dirt," feeling very much like the ragged Confederate who said one day, as the bullets flew thick against a pit which he had dug the night before, "I don't begrudge now nary cupful of dirt I put on this bank."

Not long afterwards the gallant naval captain . . . met Captain Lee and, feeling that some apology was due him, said: "Well I reckon you were right. I suppose the dirt *did* save some of my boys from being killed or wounded. But I knew that we would have no use for dirt banks on shipboard, that what we want there is clear decks and an open sea. And the fact is, Captain, I don't like this land fighting anyway. It ain't clean."

3

During the fighting around Vera Cruz Lee had the pleasure of meeting his brother, Sydney Smith Lee, then an officer in the United States Navy, serving on one of the vessels in the supporting naval squadron. In a letter home he told of the encounter with his brother.

The first day this battery opened Smith served one of the guns. I had constructed the battery, and was there to direct its fire. No matter where I turned, my eyes reverted to him, and I stood by his gun when I was not wanted elsewhere. Oh, I felt awfully, and am at a loss what I should have done had he been cut down before me. I thank God that he was saved. He preserved his usual cheerfulness, and I could see his white teeth through all the smoke and din of the fire. I had placed three thirty-two and three sixty-eight pound guns in position. . . . Their fire was terrific, and the shells thrown from our battery were constant and regular discharges, so beautiful in their flight and so destructive in their fall. It was awful! My heart bled for the inhabitants. The soldiers I did not care so much for, but it was terrible to think of the women and children.

4

The first serious engagement of the American forces after leaving Vera Cruz was at Cerro Gordo. General Scott in his report of this battle said: "I am compelled to make special mention of Captain R. E. Lee, Engineer. This officer was again indefatigable during these operations in reconnaisances, as daring as laborious, and of the utmost value. Nor was he less conspicuous in planning batteries and in conducting columns to their stations under the heavy fire of the enemy."

General Twiggs, who commanded the forces actually storming the heights in this battle, said in his report: "Although whatever I may say can add little to the good reputation of Captain Lee of the Engineers Corps, yet I must indulge in the pleasure of speaking of the invaluable services which he ren-

dered me. I consulted him with confidence and adopted his
suggestions with assurance. His gallantry and good conduct
deserve the highest praise."

Colonel Riley in his report spoke of "the intrepid coolness
and gallantry exhibited by Captain Lee of the Engineers when
conducting the advance of my brigade under the heavy flank
fire of the enemy."

In a letter written to his wife from Perote on April 25, 1847,
Captain Lee gave his own account of the Cerro Gordo engagement.

"The advance of the American troops, under Generals Patterson
and Twiggs, were encamped at the Plano del Rio, and three miles
to their front Santa Anna and his army were intrenched in the
pass of Cerro Gordo, which was remarkably strong. The right of
the Mexican line rested on the river at a perpendicular rock, un-
scalable by man or beast, and their left on impassable ravines; the
main road was defended by field works containing thirty-five cannon; in their rear was the mountain of Cerro Gordo, surrounded
by intrenchments in which were cannon and crowned by a tower
overlooking it all—it was around this army that it was intended to
lead our forces.

I reconnoitered the ground in the direction of the ravines on
their left, and passed around the enemy's rear. On the 16th a
party was set to work in cutting out the road, on the 17th I led
General Twiggs's division in the rear of a hill in front of Cerro
Gordo, and in the afternoon, when it became necessary to drive
them from the hill where we intended to construct a battery at
night, the first intimation of our presence or intentions was
known. . . . Soon after sunrise our batteries opened, and I started
with a column to turn their left and to get on the Jalapa road.
Notwithstanding their efforts to prevent us in this, we were perfectly successful, and the working party, following our footsteps,
cut out the road for the artillery. In the meantime our storming
party had reached the crest of Cerro Gordo and, seeing their
whole left turned and the position of our soldiers on the Jalapa
road, they [the Mexicans] broke and fled. Those in the pass laid
down their arms. General Pillow's attack on their right failed.

All their cannon, arms, ammunition and most of their men fell into our hands.

The papers can not tell you what a horrible sight a field of battle is, nor will I, owing to my accompanying General Twiggs's division in the pursuit, and being since constantly in the advance. I believe all our friends are safe. I think I wrote you that my friend Joe Johnston was wounded the day before I arrived at the Plano del Rio while reconnoitering. . . . [He] was doing well and was quite comfortable when I left. . . .

Jalapa is the most beautiful country I have seen in Mexico, and will compare with any I have seen elsewhere. I wish it was in the United States and that I was located with you and the children around me in one of its rich, bright valleys. . . .

This morning I attended the Episcopal service within the fort. It was held on the parade. . . . Many officers and soldiers were grouped around. I endeavored to give thanks to our heavenly Father for all his mercies to me, for his preservation of me through all the dangers I have passed, and all the blessings which he has bestowed upon me, for I know I fall far short of my obligations.

We move out to-morrow toward Pueblo. . . . I accompany the advance. . . . In advance, all is uncertain and the accounts contradictory. We must trust to an overruling Providence, by whom we will be governed for the best, and to our own resources."

5

Henry J. Hunt, afterward a distinguished general officer in the United States Army, was a participant in the Mexican campaign, and thus describes the operations at Contreras, the next point of contact with the Mexicans, where Captain Lee added fresh laurels to his record:

On the 19th of August, 1847, General Scott's headquarters were at San Augustin, a small village four or five miles south of Churubusco. The main road running south from the city of Mexico forks at Churubusco, one branch going to San Augustin, while the other runs in a south-westerly direction, and passes to the east of Contreras and of a somewhat elevated plateau beyond or south of Contreras. The distances from Churubusco to the plateau and from the plateau to San Augustin are each about equal to the distance from San Augustin to Churubusco. This triangular space, included between the two roads and a ridge of hills south of San Augustin as the third side, is called the Pedregal.

This Pedregal is a vast surface of volcanic rocks and scoria broken into every possible form, presenting sharp ridges and deep fissures, exceedingly difficult even in the daytime for the passage of infantry, and utterly impassable for artillery, cavalry or single horsemen. There are occasional intervals, especially near San Augustin, where small fields have been made and tilled; but these little oases grow smaller and more infrequent toward the west, and a mile or two from the plateau cease altogether, so that the country from above Contreras to the range of hills on the south is an almost unbroken field of desolation, such as lava would present if in a state of ebullition. Indeed, it appears like a sea of such lava suddenly congealed, with here and there a clump of hardy bushes and dwarf trees which have managed to force an existence from the apparently sterile rocks. By taking advantage of the small open spaces a difficult, crooked and hardly passable road—not much better than a mule-track—had been opened from San Augustin to the plateau, in front of which it joins the road from the city of Mexico. On this plateau General Valencia had intrenched his fine division, about six thousand strong, with twenty-four guns, which completely commanded the approach from San Augustin. A mile or more north of Contreras and the neighboring hamlet of Anselda, and on the main city road, lay General Santa Anna with a portion of the reserves of the Mexican army.

On the morning of the 19th, General Scott ordered Pillow's and Twiggs's divisions to move from San Augustin toward the plateau, the ground having been previously carefully reconnoitered by Captain R. E. Lee, assisted by Lieutenants Beauregard and Tower of the Engineers. Pillow was directed to improve the road with his force, and, if possible, make it practicable for artillery, while Twiggs was thrown in advance to protect the working-parties.

General Scott in his official report, written that same day, says: "By three o'clock this afternoon the advanced divisions came to a point where the new road could not be continued except under the direct fire of twenty-two pieces of the enemy's artillery . . . placed in a camp strongly intrenched to oppose our operations, surrounded by every advantage of ground. . . . Arriving on the ground an hour later, I found that Pillow's and Twiggs's divisions had advanced to dislodge the enemy, picking their way . . . along his front, and extending themselves toward the road from the city and the enemy's left. . . . The battle, though mainly stationary, continued to rage with great violence until nightfall."

In the mean time portions of Riley's, Persifor Smith's, Shields's and Cadwalader's brigades had made their way across the Pedregal to Contreras, whence they watched the approach of the Mexican troops from the city. . . .

Before sundown all of Riley's—and, I believe, of Cadwalader's, Smith's and Pierce's brigades—were over, and by nine o'clock a council of war, presided over by Persifor Smith and counselled by Captain R. E. Lee, was held at the church.

I have always understood that what was devised and finally determined upon was suggested by Captain Lee; at all events, the council was closed by his saying that he desired to return to General Scott with the decision of General Smith, and that, as it was late, the decision must be given as soon as possible, since General Scott wished him to return in time to give directions for co-operation.

During the council and for hours after, the rain fell in torrents, whilst the darkness was so intense that one could move only by groping. . . .

General Scott . . . says of this same night: "It was already dark, and the cold rain had begun to fall in torrents on our unsheltered troops. Wet, hungry, and without the possibility of sleep, all our gallant corps, I learn, are full of confidence, and only wait for the last hour of darkness to gain the position whence to storm and carry the position of the enemy. Of the seven officers despatched since about sundown from my position, opposite the enemy's centre, and on this side of the field of rocks and lava, to communicate instructions to the hamlet (Contreras), not one has succeeded in getting through those difficulties, increased by darkness. They have all returned.

But the gallant and indefatigable Captain Lee of the Engineers, who has been constantly with the operating forces, is just in from Shields, Smith, Cadwalader, etc., to report as above, and to request that a powerful diversion be made against the centre of the intrenched camp to-morrow morning.

Brigadier-general Twiggs, cut off from the portion of his division beyond the impracticable ground, and Captain Lee, are gone to collect the forces remaining on this side, with which to make that diversion about five o'clock in the morning."

The troops were collected, the diversion made, and the result of the combined movement, made possible only by Captain Lee's services, was the brilliant victory of Contreras early on the following morning.

Subsequently, General Scott, whilst giving testimony before a court of inquiry, had occasion to refer to these operations, and he thus speaks of the service rendered on this occasion by Captain Lee:

"Captain Lee, Engineers, came to me from the hamlet with a message from Brigadier-general Smith about the same time (midnight). He, having passed over the difficult ground by daylight, found it just possible to return to San Augustin in the dark—*the greatest feat of physical and moral courage performed by any individual, in my knowledge, pending the campaign.*"

When we remember that Captain Lee left the council-room at Contreras to pass over miles of such ground as we have described, in a pitch-dark night, without light or company, with the additional danger of wandering either to the right or left and thus falling into the hands of Valencia or Santa Anna, the risk of being met by some of those straggling bands of Mexicans which we had seen in the Pedregal, with no guide but the wind as it drove the cold rain in torrents against his face, or an occasional flash of lightning to give him a momentary glimpse of the country around him, it will be acknowledged that General Scott, considering the object for which this was done, the manner of doing it, and the results, has characterized this deed of devotion by the only terms, exalted as they are, that could appropriately describe it.

6

Among those taking part in the Mexican War was young Lieutenant Raphael Semmes, of the United States Navy, who served ashore on detached duty. Twenty years later he was to share the sorrows of the Confederacy's collapse and surrender with Robert E. Lee, the Commanding General of the Army of Northern Virginia. In Mexico the young naval officer's attention was attracted by the exploits of Captain Lee of the Engineers, and he made mention of them in his account of the fighting in Mexico, published in 1851.

The army of General Scott was full of talent, and the general had the judgment to employ it all in the best manner possible. . . . Among the most prominent of the engineers were Captain Lee and Captain Mason—the former serving at General Scott's headquarters and the latter at those of General Worth. The services of Captain Lee were invaluable to his chief. Endowed with a mind which has no superior in his corps, and possessing great energy of character, he examined, counseled and advised with a judgment, tact and discretion worthy of all praise. His talent for topography was peculiar, and he seemed to receive impressions intuitively which it cost other men much labor to acquire.

On the occasion of which I am speaking, there were two plans presented for the consideration of the general-in-chief by these accomplished engineers. Captain Lee was of opinion that the proper manner of approaching the capital was by the road diverging on the left and leading through San Angel, etc. By this movement we should have but a single obstacle to encounter, the fortified post of Padierna, which he was sanguine of carrying without much loss. Captain Mason, on the other hand, proposed that we should open the main road to Mexico by carrying San Antonio with the bayonet, by a flank movement over the pedregal, or bed of lava. . . . Both of these opinions were favorably received, and both of them partially acted upon. . . .

After a night of rain, the morning of the 19th dawned in a cloudless sky and the sun rose in his usual splendor to light up the lovely valley of Mexico in which the shock of contending armies was so soon to be felt. General Scott, in accordance with the recommendation of Captain Lee, dispatched General Pillow, supported by General Twiggs, to open the road in the direction of Contreras and San Angel. . . . In the meantime, General Persifor F. Smith, commanding the 2nd brigade of Twiggs' division, who had been sent forward under a hot fire to support Magruder's and Collendar's batteries, seeing with the eye of a soldier the nature of the enemy's position and that a front attack was out of the question, determined to try one of the flanks. Being isolated from his division, and having no ready means of communication with it, he undertook the movement of his own responsibility; reconnoitred the ground, with the assistance of Lee and his engineers, and planned and carried out the attack which resulted in the glorious victory of Contreras.

7

Captain Lee not only played an active and important part in the battle of Contreras, guiding the assailing columns through rain and mud and darkness to a position in the rear of the enemy's forces, but also was conspicuous in the later activities of Scott's army. General Long summarizes the closing days of the campaign.

The subsequent movements may be briefly described. The victory of Contreras being complete, General Scott next advanced to Coyoacan, a strongly-fortified place, which Captain Lee was sent to reconnoitre with Captain Kearney's troop, First Dragoons, supported by Major Loring's rifle regiment. Another reconnoissance was sent under Lieutenant Stevens of the Engineers toward the strongly-fortified convent of San Pablo in the hamlet of Churubusco, one mile distant. Captain Lee, having completed his first reconnaisance, was next ordered to conduct Pierce's brigade, by a third road, to a point from which an attack could be made on the enemy's right and rear, thus favoring the movement on the convent and tending to cut off the line of retreat to the capital. Shields was ordered to follow Pierce closely and to take command of the left wing.

The battle, thus ordered, soon raged violently along the whole line. Shields, in particular, was hard pressed and in danger of being overwhelmed by the hosts of the foe. Tidings of this threatened disaster were brought to General Scott by Captain Lee, who was at once ordered to conduct two troops of the Second Dragoons and the Rifles to the support of the left wing. The contest ended in the repulse of the enemy and a brilliant victory for General Scott's army.

This victory was followed by another, on the 8th of September, at the Molino del Rey. The troops were now rapidly approaching the capital city of Mexico, and the Engineer officers, Captain Lee, Lieutenant Beauregard and others, were kept engaged in reconnoissances, which they performed with great daring and success. Then succeeded one of the most daring exploits of the war, that brilliant charge by which were stormed the heights of Chapultepec, a steep hill bristling with walls, mines and batteries, yet up which our infantry columns rushed with a fiery valor and impetuosity which the Mexicans were quite unable to understand. The heights were carried and the enemy put to flight.

In this brilliant affair Captain Lee was wounded and, though eager to advance, was compelled to retire from loss of blood. In his official report General Scott again spoke of him in words of the highest compliment, remarking that he was "as distinguished for felicitous execution as for science and daring," and further stated that "Captain Lee, so constantly distinguished, also bore important orders from me . . . until he fainted from a wound and the loss of two nights' sleep at the batteries."

It is evident, in fact, that General Scott had formed an exalted opinion of the valor and military genius of his young captain of Engineers. He makes, indeed, throughout the reports of his Mexican campaign, frequent mention of three officers of the Engineer corps who were afterward to achieve high distinction in another field—Captain R. E. Lee, First Lieutenant P. G. T. Beauregard, and Second Lieutenant G. B. McClellan. Yet there is every evidence that Captain Lee was his special favorite and there is hardly a despatch in which his name is not honorably mentioned. We may add to the above the statement made by the Hon. Reverdy Johnson that he "had heard General Scott more than once say that his success in Mexico was largely due to the skill, valor and undaunted energy of Robert E. Lee." Years afterward General Scott was heard to declare, "Lee is the greatest military genius in America."

These brilliant services were not left without that recognition which is most dear to the heart of a soldier. Lee was steadily promoted. His gallant conduct at Cerro Gordo brought him the brevet rank of major; his services at Contreras and Churubusco brought him the additional brevet of lieutenant-colonel; and after Chapultepec he was nominated for the brevet rank of colonel—distinctions fully earned by his skill and valor.

The victory last mentioned was immediately followed by the capture of the forts which guarded the roads leading into the city and the occupation of the Mexican capital. This virtually ended the war. There was some guerilla warfare, but no battles of importance, after this achievement, the Mexicans giving up the contest as hopeless.

8

A distinguished soldier's summary of the effect of the Mexican campaign on Lee and his future career is given by General Maurice.

No matter how sure a man may be of his nerves, he is the better soldier when those nerves have been tested under fire and found reliable, and the better leader from the confidence in himself which such experience provides. With this confidence and with much useful experience the Mexican campaign furnished Lee. He had also an ample opportunity for gaining knowledge of the men who were to be his comrades and his foes within a few years. His position in Scott's headquarters brought him into personal touch with most of the officers of the little army and he was able to observe them under the testing conditions of actual service.

McClellan, Gustavus Smith and Beauregard served with him on Scott's staff. Magruder commanded the battery in which Jackson served. Bragg, Sedgwick, A. P. Hill, Porter, Reno, all served in the artillery. Lee's greatest soldier friend, J. E. Johnston, was twice wounded and made himself conspicuous for his dash and courage. Grant served as a lieutenant in the infantry both with Taylor in the early operations of the war and later with Scott's advance on Mexico City. Meade too served on both fronts as an engineer. McDowell was aide-de-camp to Wool, Lee's first general in the campaign. Shields commanded a brigade. Hooker and Pope both served on the staff. Burnside arrived with reinforcements while the march from the sea was in progress. Ewell proved himself to be a dashing dragoon. D. H. Hill and Early both won distinction, and by a prophetic association Longstreet and Pickett were together conspicuous for gallantry in the attack on Chapultepec.

Within fifteen years of the close of the Mexican War these comrades in glory were to be arrayed in opposing ranks. All of them had had with Lee the close association of service against a common foe to add to the intimacy which arises from training in a common school and the links of their small circle. None of them made such use of the knowledge so gained as did Lee.

5

The Years Between

THE Mexican War behind him, Captain Lee resumed his service in the Engineer Corps. His first tour of duty carried him to Florida for an inspection of its coasts and defenses. Then, in April of 1849, he was sent to Baltimore and placed in charge of the building of Fort Carroll on the Patapsco River. During his service at Baltimore he was approached by the Junta of Cuban revolutionists in New York with an offer to take command of the revolutionary forces in Cuba. Lee went to Washington and discussed the matter with Jefferson Davis, then Secretary of War, but refused the flattering offer. In 1852 he was made superintendent of the Military Academy at West Point, and here he served for three years.

In 1855 it was decided by the War Department to organize two new regiments of infantry and two of cavalry to serve on the wild new frontiers created by the extension of the country's boundaries following the Mexican War. E. V. Sumner was named Colonel of the First Cavalry, with Brevet Colonel Joseph E. Johnston as second in command. The Second was commanded by Colonel Albert Sidney Johnston, with Lee serving as his lieutenant-colonel, with the rank of brevet-colonel. The new appointment was a promotion and brought Lee back into the active service which he preferred; but it meant long periods of separation from his family at a time when his boys were growing up and needed a father's care and also when his wife's health was beginning to fail. In addition to the boys—Custis, Rooney and Robert, junior—he now had four girls, Mildred, Annie, Agnes and Mary.

His service on the Texas frontier was a dull routine of un-

67

comfortable camp life and fruitless chases after Comanche Indians or Mexican bandits, but it gave him additional experience
in command, and it afforded him ample time and opportunity
for reflecting and maturing his views concerning the political
questions which were then beginning to shake the country.

1

Robert E. Lee, Jr., has provided a charming reminiscence of
his father's home life during the time the family lived in
Baltimore.

When we lived in Baltimore I was greatly struck one day by
hearing two ladies who were visiting us saying: "Everybody and
everything—his family, his friends, his horse and his dog—loves
Colonel Lee."

The dog referred to was a black-and-tan terrier named "Spec,"
very bright and intelligent and really a member of the family, respected and loved by ourselves and well known to all who knew
us. My father picked up his mother in the Narrows while crossing
from Fort Hamilton to the fortifications opposite on Staten Island.
She had doubtless fallen overboard from some passing vessel and
had drifted out of sight before her absence had been discovered.
He rescued her and took her home, where she was welcomed by
his children and made much of. She was a handsome little thing,
with cropped ears and a short tail. My father named her "Dart."
She was a fine ratter, and with the assistance of a Maltese cat, also
a member of the family, the many rats which infested the house
and stables were driven away or destroyed. She and the cat were
fed out of the same plate, but Dart was not allowed to begin the
meal until the cat had finished.

Spec was born at Fort Hamilton and was the joy of us children,
our pet and companion. My father would not allow his tail and
ears to be cropped. . . . My father was very fond of him, and loved
to talk to him and about him as if he were really one of us. In a
letter to my mother, dated Fort Hamilton, January 18, 1846, when
she and her children were on a visit to Arlington, he thus speaks
of him:

". . . I am very solitary, and my only company is my dog and cats. But Spec has become so jealous now that he will hardly let me look at the cats. He seems to be afraid that I am going off from him, and never lets me stir without him. Lies down in the office from eight to four without moving, and turns himself before the fire as the side from it becomes cold. I catch him sometimes sitting up and looking at me so intently that I am for a moment startled. . . ."

In a letter from Mexico written a year later—December 25, '46, to my mother, he says: " . . . Can't you cure poor Spec? Cheer him up. . . ." In another letter from Mexico to his eldest boy, just after the capture of Vera Cruz, he sends this message to Spec: "Tell him I wish he was here with me. He would have been of great service in telling me when I was coming upon the Mexicans. . . ."

When he returned to Arlington from Mexico, Spec was the first to recognize him, and the extravagance of his demonstrations of delight left no doubt that he knew at once his kind master and loving friend, though he had been absent three years.

2

This was one of the happiest periods of Lee's life, a time when he had greater opportunities for enjoying the companionship of his family—his wife and his growing brood of children. Robert, Junior, tells us of those days:

At forty-five years of age he was active, strong and as handsome as he had ever been. I never remember his being ill. I presume he was indisposed at times, but no impressions of that kind remain. He was always bright and gay with us little folk, romping, playing and joking with us. With the other children he was just as companionable, and I have seen him join my elder brothers and their friends when they would try their powers at a high jump put up in our yard. The two younger children he petted a great deal, and our greatest treat was to get into his bed in the morning and lie close to him, listening while he talked to us in his bright, entertaining way. . . .

Although he was so joyous and familiar with us, he was very

firm on all proper occasions, never indulged us in anything that was not good for us, and exacted the most implicit obedience. I always knew that it was impossible to disobey my father. I felt it in me; I never thought why, but was perfectly sure when he gave an order that it had to be obeyed. My mother I could sometimes circumvent, and at times took liberties with her orders, construing them to suit myself; but exact obedience to every mandate of my father was a part of my life and being at that time.

He was very fond of having his hands tickled and, what was still more curious, it pleased and delighted him to take off his slippers and place his feet in our laps in order to have them tickled. Often, as little things, after romping all day, the enforced sitting would be too much for us and our drowsiness would soon show itself in continued nods. Then, to arouse us, he had a way of stirring us up with his foot—laughing heartily at and with us. He would often tell us the most delightful stories, and then there was no nodding. Sometimes, however, our interest in his wonderful tales became so engrossing that we would forget to do our duty—when he would declare, "No tickling, no story!"

When we were a little older, our elder sister told us one winter the ever-delightful "Lady of the Lake." Of course, she told it in prose and arranged it to suit our mental capacity. Our father was generally in his corner by the fire, most probably with a foot in either the lap of myself or youngest sister—the tickling going on briskly—and would come in at different points of the tale and repeat line after line of the poem—much to our disapproval, but to his great enjoyment.

3

When Lee was appointed superintendent at West Point, the position carried with it the title of "Colonel of Engineers." His son has recorded some interesting incidents of the family life during their residence at the Academy.

My recollections of my father at West Point are fuller and more distinct. He lived in the house which is still occupied by the Superintendent. It was built of stone, large and roomy, with garden, stables and pasture lots. We, the two youngest children, enjoyed it all greatly. Grace Darling and Santa Anna were then with us, and many a fine ride have I had with my father in the afternoons, when, released from his office, he would mount his old mare and, with Santa Anna carrying me by his side, take a five or ten mile trot. Though my pony cantered delightfully, my father would make me keep him in a trot, saying that the hammering I got from that gait was good for me. . . .

My father was the most punctual man I ever knew. He was always ready for family prayers, and at all meal times, and met every engagement, business or social, on the moment. He expected all of us to be the same, and impressed upon us the necessity of forming such habits, for the convenience of all concerned. I never knew him late for the Sunday service at the post chapel. He appeared in uniform some minutes before any one else, and would jokingly rally my mother and sisters for being late or forgetting something at the last moment. When he could wait no longer, he would say, "Well, I am off," and march away to church by himself or with any of us who were ready. Then he took his seat, well up in the middle aisle; and I remember he got always very drowsy during the sermon, and sometimes caught a little nap. . . .

It was against the rules for any cadet to pass beyond certain well-defined limits. Of course, they did sometimes go, and when caught were punished by receiving so many "demerits." My father, riding out one afternoon with me, suddenly came up with three cadets far beyond the limits. When rounding a turn in the mountain road, with a deep, woody ravine on one side, we came upon them. They immediately leaped over a low wall on the ravine side of the road and disappeared from our view. We rode on a minute in silence, when my father said: "Did you know those young men? But no!—if you did, don't say so. I wish boys would do what is right, it would be so much easier for all of us." He knew he would have to report them, but not being sure who they were, I suppose he wished to give them the benefit of the doubt. At any rate, I never heard anything more about it. One of the three asked me the next day if "the Colonel" had recognized them, and I told them what had occurred.

I was now old enough to have a room to myself, and to encourage me to be useful and practical my father made me attend to it, just as the cadets had to do in their quarters in barracks and in camp. He even, for a time, went through the form of inspecting it daily to see if I had performed my duty properly. I remember enjoying it at first, but soon tired of the routine. However, I was kept at it. . . .

He always encouraged me in every healthy outdoor exercise and sport. He taught me to ride, constantly giving me the minutest instructions with the reasons for them. He gave me my first sled, and often came to where we boys were coasting to look on. He also gave me my first pair of skates, and placed me under the care of a reliable person, who should teach me how to use them. . . . It was the same as to swimming, which he was anxious I should learn thoroughly. . . .

I now went to day school, and had always a sympathetic helper in my father. Often he would come into the room where I studied at night and, sitting beside me, show me how to master a hard sentence in my Latin reader or a difficult sum in arithmetic—not by giving me a translation of the sentence nor an answer to the sum, but by showing me step by step the way to the right solution of both. He was very patient, very loving and very good to me. . . .

As Superintendent of the United States Military Academy . . . my father had to entertain a good deal, and I remember well how handsome and grand he looked in uniform, which was the full dress of the army officers then; how genial and bright; how considerate of everybody's comfort of mind and body. He was always a great favorite with the ladies, especially the young ones. His fine presence, his gentle, easy manner and kindly smile put them at once at ease with him.

Among the cadets at this time were my eldest brother, Custis, who in 1854 was graduated at the head of his class, and my father's nephew, Fitzhugh Lee, who was in the third class, besides many relatives and friends. Saturday being a half holiday for the cadets, it was the custom for all social events of which they were a part to take place on that afternoon or evening. Nearly every Saturday a number of these young men were invited to our house to tea, or supper, for it was a good substantial meal. The misery of some of these poor fellows from embarrassment, and possibly from awe of the Superintendent, was pitiable, and evident even to me, a boy of ten. But my father . . . would address himself to the task of making them feel comfortable and at home, and his winning manners and pleasant ways at once succeeded. . . .

While at West Point my father was persuaded to allow R. S. Weir, Professor of Drawing and Painting at the Military Academy, to paint his portrait. As I now remember, there were only one or two sittings, and the artist had to finish the picture from the glimpses he obtained of his subject in the regular intercourse of their daily lives. The portrait shows my father in the undress uniform of a colonel of engineers, and many think it is a good likeness. To me, the expression of strength peculiar to his face is wanting, especially in the lines of the mouth. . . . My father never could bear to have his picture taken, and there are no likenesses of him that really give his sweet expression. It was such a serious business with him that he never could "look pleasant."

4

An intimate view of Lee coping with the duties of his superintendency of the Military Academy is given in one of his letters to Martha Custis Williams ("Markie"). She was a first cousin of Mrs. Lee, and a more distant cousin of Lee himself. Orphaned at an early age, she and her two brothers had been regarded by Lee almost as his own children, and he kept up an affectionate correspondence with her throughout his lifetime.

. . . I have been interrupted by the arrival of General Scott who, with his son-in-law and daughter, Mr. and Mrs. Hoyt, and some friends, called upon the Superintendent. He has had therefore to conduct them into the Library, order a salute in honor of the Commanding General, shew them around the Academies, and conduct them in presence of the Battery, which has just belched forth its thunder. The General has now gone to my quarters, under Major Porter's escort, to repose till dinner, when I shall again have the pleasure of his company and the gentlemen of his suite, with such of our natives as I can collect to do them honour. As my servants have received but short notice for their preparation for dinner, I fear the General will again have an opportunity of taking, if not a hasty, at least a thin plate of soup, and but for an Arlington ham and some of my Shanghai chickens, which I had purposed for my solitary dinner, I should be in doubt whether their hunger could be appeased, as ten additional guests will have to be provided for. But, having given all the required directions, I will wait with patience and *hope* for their execution.

I have just, Markie, accomplished the most unpleasant office I am called on to perform—the discharge of those cadets found deficient at the examination. There were fortunately only nine of them, but all very nice youths, some sons of officers of the Army, one of the Navy, who having neglected their studies, contrary to all advice and efforts to the contrary, must now suffer the penalty, which they acutely feel but which they could not be made to realize. I have just closed their connection with the Academy, signed their last orders, taken leave of them with sincere wishes for their happiness and prosperity, and they have been carried off by the omnibus for the afternoon boat.

5.

A glimpse of General Lee in his capacity as superintendent of the Military Academy, and his contact with a troublesome cadet who later became famous in another line of activity, is given by General Charles Dudley Rhodes.

The new superintendent took a personal, active interest in the every-day life of the cadets, as demonstrated in a marked degree by the Academy records. Whenever a student was in serious trouble, either from violation of some rule or regulation, or through deficiency in studies, it was Lee's custom to write a personal letter to the parents advising them of the matter, and suggesting in a tactful way their influence and cooperation in restoring the cadet concerned to good standing. . . .

In the Academy archives is interesting correspondence regarding the academic troubles of Cadet James A. McNeill Whistler, later the famous artist, honored by many countries. Under date of July 8, 1854, Colonel Lee explains at considerable length in a letter to his immediate superior, General Totten, chief of engineers, that "I can do nothing more in his behalf, nor do I know of anything entitling him to further indulgence." This referred to Whistler's low marks in the subject of chemistry, and his grand total of 136 demerits! But the gentleness of Lee's character is also shown in a letter written to Whistler's mother, informing her that her son was sick in the hospital with an attack of rheumatism. "He does not suffer much pain," writes Lee to the anxious mother, "but his attack does not seem to yield to remedies, and the surgeon has this morning informed me that he fears his lungs are seriously involved." Whistler's discharge from the Academy, ordered by Lee, recalls the great artist's humorous allusion to it, years later. According to Whistler, his instructor in chemistry asked him to define *silicon*. Whistler replied that it was a *gas*. "If," said the artist, "silicon had chanced to be gas, I might now be a major-general in the United States Army."

6

Lee's superintendency was marked by his characteristic efficiency in administration and by some notable improvements in the system of management of the institution. At West Point for three years he had a welcome opportunity to be with his wife and children and enjoy the pleasures of family life. But this chapter in Lee's career came to a close in 1855. Then came his assignment to duty with the newly authorized Second Cavalry, and a new chapter in his life opened. The headquarters of the regiment was first established at Louisville, and here Lieutenant Colonel Lee assumed his new duties on April 20, 1855. Later the regimental headquarters was transferred to Jefferson Barracks in Missouri, and from this location Lee wrote a letter to his wife telling of his experiences in his new command—and giving a hint of that fondness for pets which he shared with his wife and her father.

The chaplain of the post, a Mr. Fish (an Episcopal clergyman and well spoken of) is now absent. . . . We have therefore not had service since I have been here. The church stands out in the trees, grotesque in its form and ancient in its appearance. I have not been in it, but am content to read the Bible and prayers alone, and draw much comfort from their holy precepts and merciful promises. Though feeling unable to follow the one, and truly unworthy of the other, I must still pray to that glorious God without whom there is no help, and with whom there is no danger. That he may guard and protect you all, and more than supply to you my absence, is my daily and constant prayer.

I have been busy all the week superintending and drilling recruits. Not a stitch of clothing has as yet arrived for them, though I made the necessary requisition for it to be sent here more than two months ago in Louisville. Yesterday, at muster, I found one of the late arrivals in a dirty, tattered shirt and pants, with a white hat and shoes, with other garments to match. I asked him why he did not put on clean clothes. He said he had none. I asked him if he could not wash and mend those. He said he had nothing else to put on. I then told him immediately after muster to go down to the river, wash his clothes, and sit on the bank and watch the passing steamboats till they dried and then mend them. This morning at inspection he looked as proud as possible, stood in the position of a soldier with his little fingers on the seams of his pants, his beaver cocked back and his toes sticking through his shoes, but his skin and solitary two garments clean. He grinned very happily at my compliments.

I have got a fine puss, which was left me by Colonel Sumner. He was educated by his daughter, Mrs. Jenkins, but is too fond of getting up on my lap and on my bed; he follows me all about the house and stands at the door in an attitude of defiance at all passing dogs.

7

The work of organizing and outfitting the new regiment at Jefferson Barracks dragged on, month after month. The monotony of this was broken by service on a series of courts-martial, the last of which was at Carlisle Barracks in January 1856, giving him an opportunity to visit his family at Arlington. In his absence Colonel Albert Sidney Johnston com-

pleted the organization of the regiment and marched it over-
land to its assigned post on the Texas frontier. Four companies, under Major Hardee, were stationed at Camp Cooper,
Johnston moving on with the other troopers to Fort Mason.
Lee's court-martial duty ended in February, and late in March
he arrived in Texas to take up his new duties in command of
that portion of the regiment at Camp Cooper, on the Clear
Fork of the Brazos, his first active service in the army in command of troops in the field. General Long tells of his early
service in this capacity.

He reached this post on April 9th, and writes under date of the
12th to the following effect:
"We are on the Comanche Reserve, with the Indian camps
below us on the river belonging to Catumseh's band, whom the
Government is endeavoring to humanize. It will be uphill work,
I fear. Catumseh has been to see me, and we have had a talk, very
tedious on his part and very sententious on mine. I hailed him as
a friend as long as his conduct and that of his tribe deserved it, but
would meet him as an enemy the first moment he failed to keep
his word. The rest of the tribe (about a thousand, it is said) live
north of us, and are hostile. Yesterday I returned his visit, and
remained a short time at his lodge. He informed me that he had
six wives. They are riding in and out of camp all day, their paint
and 'ornaments' rendering them more hideous than nature made
them, and the whole race is extremely uninteresting."
Shortly afterward Colonel Lee with five companies made an
expedition to the headwaters of the Brazos and Wachita rivers,
which occupied him several months. The principal result of this
expedition was the acquisition of geographical information, for
at that time the Comanches were on their annual pilgrimage to
the north of the Arkansas River in search of game for their winter
supply of provisions.
Of his subsequent life in Texas interesting glimpses are obtained from his letters. The Comanches seem to have made plentiful work for the soldiers. Thus, on August 25, 1856, he speaks
of a party of these restless savages who had been on a maurauding
expedition into Mexico, "which is a cloak to cover all their thefts

and murders." They were then seeking to steal north around the cavalry camp, divided into small parties to escape detection. He was about to send out a company of troopers in pursuit, with directions to follow them for twenty days if necessary. He says: "These people give a world of trouble to man and horse and, poor creatures! they are not worth it."

Again . . . he reports several encounters between the troops and the marauding Indians, who were severely punished. "It is a distressing state of things that requires the application of such treatment, but it is the only corrective they understand, the only way in which they can be brought to keep within their own limits."

During this period, however, he himself was absent from his command, having been summoned to Fort Brown, on the Rio Grande, to serve on a court-martial. Here his chief enjoyment seems to have been in the natural surroundings. He writes: "My daily walks are alone, up and down the banks of the river, and my pleasure is derived from my own thoughts and from the sight of the flowers and animals I there meet with. The birds of the Rio Grande form a constant source of interest, and are as numerous as they are beautiful in plumage. I wish I could get for you the roots of some of the luxuriant vines that cover everything, or the seeds of the innumerable flowers."

8

Christmas 1856 was a lonely holiday for Lieutenant Colonel Lee at his frontier post at Fort Brown, Texas. On December 27 he wrote a letter to his wife, hinting of his homesickness and giving an interesting reflection of his views on slavery and national affairs.

The steamer has arrived from New Orleans, bringing full files of papers and general intelligence from "the States." I have enjoyed the former very much, and, in the absence of particular intelligence, have perused with much interest the series of the *Alexandria Gazette* from the 20th of November to the 8th of December inclusive. Besides the usual good reading matter, I was interested in the relation of local affairs, and inferred, from the

quiet and ordinary course of events, that all in the neighborhood
was going on well. I trust it may be so and that you and particularly all at Arlington and our friends elsewhere are well.

The steamer brought the President's message to Congress, and
the reports of the various heads of the Departments, so that we
are now assured that the Government is in operation and the
Union in existence. Not that I had any fears to the contrary, but
it is satisfactory always to have facts to go on; they restrain supposition and conjecture, confirm faith and bring contentment. I
was much pleased with the President's message and the report of
the Secretary of War. The views of the President on the domestic
institutions of the South are truthfully and faithfully expressed.

In this enlightened age there are few, I believe, but will acknowledge that slavery as an institution is a moral and political
evil in any country. It is useless to expatiate on its disadvantages.
I think it, however, a greater evil to the white than to the black
race, and while my feelings are strongly interested in behalf of
the latter, my sympathies are stronger for the former. The blacks
are immeasurably better off here than in Africa, morally, socially
and physically. The painful discipline they are undergoing is
necessary for their instruction as a race and, I hope, will prepare
and lead them to better things. How long their subjection may be
necessary is known and ordered by a wise and merciful Providence.
Their emancipation will sooner result from a mild and melting
influence than the storms and contests of fiery controversy. This
influence, though slow, is sure.

The doctrines and miracles of our Saviour have required nearly
two thousand years to convert but a small part of the human race,
and even among Christian nations what gross errors still exist!
While we see the course of the final abolition of slavery is onward,
and we give it the aid of our prayers and all justifiable means in
our power, we must leave the progress as well as the result in His
hands who sees the end and who chooses to work by slow things,
and with whom a thousand years are but as a single day, although
the abolitionist must know this, and must see that he has neither
the right nor the power of operating except by moral means and
suasion; and if he means well to the slave he must not create angry
feelings in the master. That although he may not approve the

mode by which it pleases Providence to accomplish its purposes, the result will never be the same; that the reasons he gives for interference in what he has no concern hold good for every kind of interference with our neighbors when we disapprove their conduct. Is it not strange that the descendants of those Pilgrim Fathers who crossed the Atlantic to preserve the freedom of their opinion have always proved themselves intolerant of the spiritual liberty of others?

I hope you had a joyous Christmas at Arlington, and that it may be long and often repeated. I thought of you all and longed to be with you. Mine was gratefully but silently passed. I endeavored to find some little presents for the children in the garrison to add to their amusement, and succeeded better than I had anticipated. The stores are very barren of such things here, but by taking the week beforehand in my daily walks, I picked up little by little something for all. Tell Mildred I got a beautiful Dutch doll for little Emma Jones—one of those crying babies that can open and shut their eyes, turn their head, etc. For the two other little girls, Puss Shirley and Mary Sewell, I found handsome French teapots to match cups given to them by Mrs. Waite; then by means of knives and books, I satisfied the boys. After dispensing my presents I went to church; the discourse was on the birth of our Saviour. It was not as simply or touchingly told as it is in the Bible. By previous invitation I dined with Major [George H.] Thomas at 2 P.M. on roast turkey and plum pudding. He and his wife were alone. I had provided a pretty singing bird for the little girl, and passed the afternoon in my room. God bless you all.

9

An engaging picture of Lee in his lighter moments, especially as regards his partiality for pets, is given by Fitzhugh Lee.

Mr. Custis, of Arlington, was very fond of cats, and his large yellow "Tom" was his constant attendant. Some of his household naturally grew fond of these animals, his son-in-law among them. Lieutenant-Colonel Lee would not cut the skirt of his robe, as did Mohammed, to prevent disturbing his cat, which was sitting

on it, nor, like Cardinal Wolsey, give audience with a cat seated
beside him, nor let his cat rest among his papers and books, as did
Richelieu, nor wish a statue with his right hand resting on his
cat, as did Whittington, the famous Lord Mayor of London, but
he liked to see a well-fed puss, such as Gray described in his ode
"On the Death of a Favorite Cat":

> Her conscious tail her joy disclosed,
> The fair round face, the snowy beard,
>   The relish of her paws;
> Her coat that with the tortoise vies,
> Her ears of jet and emerald eyes,
>   She saw and purr'd applause.

From Fort Brown, Texas, February 16, 1857, he tells Mrs. Lee:
"Tell your father Mrs. Colonel Waite has a fine large cat which
she takes with her everywhere. He is her companion by day, and
sleeps on her bed at night. In public conveyances she leads him
in the leash, and carries along a bottle of milk for his use. In her
own carriage he sits on her lap. I have been trying to persuade
her to let me take him up to Camp Cooper, but she says she can't
part from him. He must go to Florida. I have seen some fine
cats in Brownsville in the stores kept by the Frenchmen, but no
yellow ones; the dark brindle is the favorite color on the frontier.
In my walk the other evening I met a Mexican with a wild kitten
in his arms enveloped in his blanket; it was a noble specimen of
the Rio Grande wildcat, spotted all over with large spots like the
leopard. I tried very hard to buy him, but he said he was already
sold. I should prefer one of those at Camp Cooper. I fear though
I should have to keep him chained, for they are very wild and
savage."

And again from Indianola, Texas, March 27, 1857, he writes
to his youngest daughter: ". . . You must be a great personage
now—sixty pounds! I wish I had you here in all your ponderosity.
I want to see you so much. Can you not pack up and come to the
Comanche country? I would get you such a fine cat you would
never look at 'Tom' again. Did I tell you Jim Nooks, Mrs.
Waite's cat, was dead? He died of apoplexy. I foretold his end.
Coffee and cream for breakfast, pound cake for lunch, turtle and

oysters for dinner, buttered toast for tea, and Mexican rats, taken raw, for supper. He grew enormously and ended in a spasm. His beauty could not save him. I saw in San Antonio a cat dressed up for company: He had two holes bored in each ear, and in each were two bows of pink and blue ribbon. His round face, set in pink and blue, looked like a big owl in a full blooming ivy bush. He was snow white, and wore the golden fetters of his inamorata around his neck in the form of a collar. His tail and feet were tipped with black, and his eyes of green were truly catlike.

"But I saw 'cats as is cats' in Sarassa, while the stage was changing mules. I stepped around to see Mr. and Mrs. Monod, a French couple with whom I had passed the night when I landed in Texas, in 1846, to join General Wool's army. Mr. Monod received me with all the shrugs of his nation, and the entrance of madame was foreshadowed by the coming in of her stately cats, with visages grave and tails erect, who preceded, surrounded and followed her. . . . They are of French breed and education, and when the claret and water was poured out for my refreshment they jumped on the table for a sit-to. . . .

"I left the wildcat on the Rio Grande; he was too savage, had grown as large as a small-sized dog, had to be caged, and would strike at anything that came within his reach . . . and would whistle like a tiger when you approached him."

6

Prologue to War

O<small>N</small> July 23, 1857, Colonel Johnston was ordered to report in Washington and to turn over command of the regiment to Lieutenant Colonel Lee. In October of that year, Mrs. Lee's father, George Washington Parke Custis, died. Colonel Lee obtained a leave of absence and returned to Arlington, arriving there on November 11. Mr. Custis was a man of property, and he left a rather complicated will which required careful and tedious administration. Lee was named as executor of the estate and, securing an extension of his leave, he set about the difficult task of untangling the affairs of his father-in-law. The Arlington home place was left to Mrs. Lee for her use and occupancy during her lifetime, then was to go to her son Custis. Martha Washington's old home place, the White House, on the Pamunkey below Richmond, was bequeathed to "Rooney" Lee, and near-by Romancoke was left to young Robert. The Lee girls were left cash bequests; the family silver and Washington relics were all disposed of, as was the other Custis property in Virginia; and it was provided in the will that all the Custis slaves should be set free at the end of five years. The administration of the Custis will proved a tedious and complex task, and Lee, by successive extensions of his leave, stayed on at Arlington until the fall of 1859. Despite the sad cause of his return, and despite his wife's ill health (she was now partially crippled with arthritis), Lee greatly enjoyed the two years he was able to spend with his family—or, at least, with Mrs. Lee and the girls. Custis was with his regiment in California; Rooney had graduated from Harvard and, at the special solicitation of General Scott, had been given a commission in the Army; young Robert was off

83

at a boarding school. Lee devoted his time to rehabilitating the run-down Arlington farm, plowing and sowing the fields, replenishing the livestock and making necessary repairs to the fences and buildings. Despite the pleasure he derived from being at home, his sense of duty weighed heavily on him, and he said: "I feel that I ought to be with my regiment, and this feeling deprives me of half the pleasure I derive from being here." During this time spent at Arlington, however, he was not entirely out of touch with military duties. Once he was called to serve on a court-martial at Newport Barracks, Kentucky; again he served on a court of inquiry at West Point; and in October 1859 he received a sudden call to go to Harper's Ferry to command a detachment of U. S. Marines who had been sent there to suppress a disorder caused by the seizure of the armory by a deluded fanatic named John Brown.

1

Colonel Lee was in Leadbeater's drugstore in Alexandria on the morning of October 17, 1859, when that cloud no larger than a man's hand appeared on the nation's peaceful horizon. There he was found that morning by a messenger bearing a note from the War Department in Washington instructing him to report immediately. The note was brought by a young lieutenant in the First Cavalry, James Ewell Brown Stuart, who was home on leave and, happening to be in the War Department, volunteered to carry the message to Colonel Lee. Stuart accompanied Lee when, in civilian dress, he hurried to the War Department office. Lee learned that some mysterious sort of disturbance had occurred at Harper's Ferry, something in the nature of an armed insurrection. He was told that Army troops and Marines had been ordered there and that he was to go to Harper's Ferry, take command of the forces and quell the disturbance. Lieutenant Stuart, attracted by the prospect of action, asked to be permitted to go along as a volunteer aid. Together they left immediately by railroad for Harper's Ferry. Colonel Lee's official report to Adjutant General Samuel Cooper on October 19 gives his first-hand account of what he did there, told in the starkly simple terms of the professional soldier.

On arriving here on the night of the 17th, I learned that a party of insurgents, about 11 P.M. on the 16th, had seized the watchmen stationed at the armory, arsenal, rifle factory and bridge across the Potomac, and taken possession of those points. They had dispatched six men, under one of their party, to arrest the principal citizens of the neighborhood and incite the negroes to join in the insurrection. The party took Colonel L. W. Washington from his bed about 1½ A.M. on the 17th, and brought him with four of his servants to this place. Mr. J. H. Allstadt and six of his servants were in the same manner seized about 3 A.M. and arms placed in the hands of the negroes. As day advanced and the citizens of Harper's Ferry commenced their usual avocations, they were separately captured, to the number of forty, and confined in one room of the fire-engine house of the armory, which seems early to have been selected as a point of defense. . . .

I made preparations to attack the insurgents at daylight. But for the fear of sacrificing the lives of some of the gentlemen held by them as prisoners in a midnight assault, I should have ordered the attack at once. Their safety was the subject of painful consideration, and to prevent if possible jeopardizing their lives, I determined to summon the insurgents to surrender.

As soon after daylight as the arrangements were made, Lieutenant J.E.B. Stuart, 1st Cavalry, who had accompanied me from Washington as a staff officer, was dispatched under a flag with a written summons, as follows: "Colonel Lee, United States Army, commanding the troops sent by the President of the United States to suppress the insurrection at this place, demands the surrender of the persons in the armory buildings. If they will peaceably surrender themselves and restore the pillaged property, they shall be kept in safety to await the orders of the President. Colonel Lee represents to them, in all frankness, that it is impossible for them to escape; that the armory is surrounded on all sides by troops; and that if he is compelled to take them by force he can not answer for their safety."

Knowing the character of the insurgents, I did not expect the summons would be accepted. I had therefore . . . prepared a storming party of twelve Marines under their commander, Lieutenant Green, and had placed them close to the engine-house and secure from its fire. Three Marines were furnished with sledge-hammers to break in the doors, and the men were instructed how to distinguish our citizens from the insurgents, to attack with the bayonet, and not to injure the blacks detained in custody unless they resisted. Lieutenant Stuart was also directed not to receive from the insurgents any counter propositions. If they accepted the terms offered, they must immediately deliver up their arms and release their prisoners. If they did not, he must, on leaving the engine-house, give me the signal. My object was, with a view of saving our citizens, to have as short an interval as possible between the summons and attack.

The summons, as I had anticipated, was rejected. At the concerted signal the storming party moved quickly to the door and commenced the attack. The fire-engines within the house had been placed by the besieged close to the doors. The doors were fastened by ropes, the spring of which prevented their being broken by the blows of the hammers. The men were therefore ordered to drop the hammers and to use as a battering-ram a heavy ladder, with which they dashed in a part of the door and gave admittance to the storming party. The fire of the insurgents up to this time had been harmless. At the threshold one Marine fell mortally wounded. The rest, led by Lieutenant Green and Major Russell, quickly ended the contest. The insurgents that resisted were bayoneted. Their leader, John Brown, was cut down by the sword of Lieutenant Green, and our citizens were protected by both officers and men. The whole was over in a few minutes. . . .

From the information derived from the papers found upon the persons and among the baggage of the insurgents, and the statement of those now in custody, it appears that the party consisted of nineteen men—fourteen white and five black. That they were headed by John Brown, of some notoriety in Kansas, who in June last located himself in Maryland, at the Kennedy farm, where he has been engaged in preparing to capture the United States works at Harper's Ferry. He avows that his object was the liberation of the slaves of Virginia, and of the whole South; and acknowledges that he has been disappointed in the expectations of aid from the blacks as well as white population, both in the Southern and Northern states. The blacks whom he forced from their homes in this neighborhood, as far as I could learn, gave him no voluntary assistance. . . . The result proves that the plan was the attempt of a fanatic or madman, which could only end in failure; and its temporary success was owing to the panic and confusion he succeeded in creating by magnifying his numbers. . . .

The survivors of the expedition I have delivered into the hands of the marshal of the western district of Virginia and the sheriff of Jefferson County. They were escorted to Charlestown by a detachment of Marines under Lieutenant Green. . . .

I will now, in obedience to your dispatch of this date, direct the detachment of Marines to return to the navy-yard at Washington in the train that passes here at 1¼ A.M. to-night, and will myself take advantage of the same train to report to you in person at the War Department.

2

Colonel Lee's leave expired shortly afterward, and he was back in Texas in February 1860, establishing himself in quarters at San Antonio, which was the headquarters of the Department of Texas, of which he was now in command. His life here was soon enlivened by the necessity for taking action against a Mexican bandit named Cortinas, who had plagued the Rio Grande frontier for several years. Lee himself led an expeditionary force down the lower Rio Grande Valley, and eventually the bandit was driven back into the obscurity of the Mexican interior. From Fort Brown Dr. Jones quotes a letter to Lee's son Custis, which tells something of this campaign, and also mentions a current morsel of Army gossip involving his old friend Joe Johnston.

". . . I have descended the left bank of the river from Eagle Pass, and could find no armed parties on either side of the river.

Everything was quiet. Robberies will be committed by Indians, Mexicans and border men when it can be done with impunity, and always have been done. The last authentic accounts I could get of Cortinas was that with his wife, children and two men he was making his way in Mexican ox-carts into the interior and was 135 miles off. The Mexican authorities, with whom I have been holding a sharp correspondence, *said* they had sent an express to the authorities to arrest him. General Garcia, commanding in Matamoras opposite to me, repeated the assurance. Still I do not expect it to be done and do not like to enter a blind pursuit after a man so far into the interior, with broken-down horses. It is the want of food for them that stops me more than anything else. I can not carry it and do not know that I could find it. The delay in procuring it would defeat my object. . . . Remember me to all friends. My friend, Col. Joe Johnston, is a good soldier and worthy man and deserves all advancement, when it can be done without injustice to others. I think it must be evident to him that it was never the intention of Congress to advance him to the position assigned him by the Secretary. It was not so recognized before, and in proportion to his services he has been advanced beyond any one in the Army, and has thrown more discredit than ever on the system of favoritism and making brevets. . . ."

The allusion to the promotion of Lieutenant Colonel Jos. E. Johnston, whom Secretary John B. Floyd, his cousin, had made in appointing him Quartermaster-General, with the rank of brigadier-general, thus promoting him "over the heads" of Samuel Cooper, Sydney Johnston, R. E. Lee, Sumner, and others who had previously ranked him, was very mild when we remember the extreme sensitiveness of officers about their rank, and that this was a letter from a soldier to his son, also an accomplished soldier, which he never expected to be made public.

But in another private letter Colonel Lee said in alluding to this same matter:

"I rejoice in the good fortune that has come to my old friend Joe Johnston, for while I should not like, of course, that this should be taken as a precedent in the service, yet so far as he is concerned he is every way worthy of the promotion and I am glad that he has received it."

3

In common with most professional soldiers, Lee took no active part and little interest in political affairs. His letters during the latter part of 1860, however, showed how greatly he was disturbed by the widening breach between the North and South. His political philosophy is well expressed in a letter he wrote to his son on January 23, 1861, from Fort Mason:

I received Everett's "Life of Washington" which you sent me, and enjoyed its perusal. How his spirit would be grieved could he see the wreck of his mighty labors! I will not, however, permit myself to believe, until all ground of hope is gone, that the fruit of his noble deeds will be destroyed, and that his precious advice and virtuous example will so soon be forgotten by his countrymen. As far as I can judge by the papers, we are between a state of anarchy and civil war. May God avert both of these evils from us! I fear that mankind will not for years be sufficiently Christianized to bear the absence of restraint and force. I see that four States have declared themselves out of the Union; four more will apparently follow their example. Then, if the Border States are brought into the gulf of revolution, one-half of the country will be arrayed against the other. I must try and be patient and await the end, for I can do nothing to hasten or retard it.

The South, in my opinion, has been aggrieved by the acts of the North, as you say. I feel the aggression and am willing to take every proper step for redress. It is the principle I contend for, not individual or private benefit. As an American citizen, I take great pride in my country, her prosperity and institutions, and would defend any State if her rights were invaded. But I can anticipate no greater calamity for the country than a dissolution of the Union. It would be an accumulation of all the evils we complain of, and I am willing to sacrifice everything but honor for its preservation. I hope, therefore, that all constitutional means will be exhausted before there is a resort to force. Secession is nothing but revolution. The framers of our Constitution never exhausted so much labor, wisdom and forbearance in its formation, and surrounded it with so many guards and securities, if it was intended to be broken by every member of the confederacy at will.* It was intended for "perpetual union," so expressed in the preamble, and for the establishment of a government, not a compact, which can only be dissolved by revolution or the consent of all the people in convention assembled. It is idle to talk of secession. Anarchy would have been established, and not a government, by Washington, Hamilton, Jefferson, Madison and the other patriots of the Revolution. . . . Still, a Union that can only be maintained by swords and bayonets, and in which strife and civil war are to take the place of brotherly love and kindness, has no charm for me. I shall mourn for my country and for the welfare and progress of mankind. If the Union is dissolved, and the Government disrupted, I shall return to my native State and share the miseries of my people; and save in defense will draw my sword on none.

4

In a letter to his cousin "Markie" Williams, at about the same time, Lee gives an expression of his views regarding the approaching clash between the North and South.

My letters from home frequently mention Orton [her younger brother], and in one of the last it was stated that he and Custis were looking forward to captaincies in the Army of the Southern Republic! The subject recalls my grief at the condition of our country. God alone can save us from our folly, selfishness and short sightedness. The last accounts seem to shew that we have barely escaped anarchy to be plunged into civil war. What will be the result I cannot conjecture. I only see what a fearful calamity is upon us and fear that the country will have to pass through for its sins a fiery ordeal. I am unable to realize that our people will destroy a government inaugurated by the blood and wisdom of our patriot fathers, that has given us peace and prosperity at home, power and security abroad, and under which we have ac-

---

* Colonel Lee, of course, here confounds the Constitution of the United States with the "Articles of Confederation." This latter document expresses the purpose of forming "a perpetual union," but when eleven states seceded from the Confederation, formed the Union and adopted a new Constitution, no such phrase was used in the preamble or in any part of that document.

quired a colossal strength unequalled in the history of mankind. I wish to live under no other government, and there is no sacrifice I am not ready to make for the preservation of the Union save that of honour. If a disruption takes place, I shall go back in sorrow to my people and share the misery of my native state, and save in her defence there will be one soldier less in the world than now. I wish for no other flag than the "Star Spangled Banner," and no other air than "Hail Columbia." I still hope that the wisdom and patriotism of the nation will yet save it.

I am so remote from the scene of events and receive such excited and exaggerated accounts of the opinions and acts of our statesmen that I am at a loss what to think. I believe that the South justly complains of the aggressions of the North, and I have believed that the North would cheerfully redress the grievances complained of. I see no cause for disunion, strife and civil war and I pray it may be averted.

5

The crisis of Lee's life was rapidly approaching. On February 4, while at Fort Mason, he received orders relieving him of duty with his regiment and directing him to report to General Scott by April 1.

On his way from Fort Mason to Washington, Lee stopped to eat lunch at a spring on the road to San Antonio, and there he encountered one of the young officers of the Second Cavalry, Lieutenant George B. Cosby, who has left an interesting record of Lee's expression of his sentiments at that time.

He told me that General Scott had ordered him to Washington. Knowing that General Scott had an exalted opinion of General Lee's ability as a soldier, I at once surmised that he was wanted to consult on a campaign against the South, in case of a resort to arms, and told him so. He said he feared that my surmise was true, and that if he found it so he would decline and resign. He further said he had confidence that Virginia would not act on impulse, but would act as she had in the past and would exhaust every means consistent with honor to avert civil war. That if she

failed and determined to secede, he would offer her his services.
That he had ever been taught that his first allegiance was due his
mother state; that he fervently hoped some agreement would be
reached to avert such a terrible war, and there was no personal
sacrifice he would not make to save his beloved country from such
a dreadful calamity; but under no circumstances could he ever
bare his sword against Virginia's sons. As he spoke, his emotion
brought tears to his eyes and he turned away to avoid showing his
emotion, which was greater than he afterwards showed when he
had lost or won some great battle.

He bade me good-by, and I next saw him when I reported to
him in Richmond. He had resigned and Virginia had placed him
at the head of her troops. When I reported, and afterwards saw
him at his rooms, he told me that many in high places seemed to
have no conception of the magnitude of the gigantic struggle before us. The South was totally unprepared for such a war—had no
navy, no powder, manufactories or arms or other essentials. Everything had to be created. But he believed our cause was just
and that all were prepared to make any sacrifice, even to lose their
lives for it. . . . He further said that, above all, we must not under-
rate the Northern people, their courage or ability; we were all
Americans—but he hoped they would not be as united as the
South, for if united they would greatly out-number us and have
facilities to supply everything an army needed.

6

Lee reached home a month ahead of the date set in his orders. An entry in his diary on March 1 says: "Arrived in Alexandria; took a carriage and reached Arlington." On April 1,
in accordance with his orders, he reported to General Scott
and so informed the War Department. The month of March
he spent in watching the relentless development of events
leading to the disruption of the Union. The Confederate
States of America had already been formally organized by the
seceded states, with Jefferson Davis as President, and set up
its seat of government in Montgomery. On March 4 Abraham
Lincoln was inaugurated President of the United States, an

event which fanned the flaming discontent in the South. During March Colonel Sumner of the First Cavalry in Texas was promoted to brigadier general, and Lee on March 28 was promoted to the rank of colonel and given command of Sumner's old regiment, his commission being signed by President Lincoln. There were still hopes that actual warfare could be prevented—and Virginia still remained in the Union. But Lee recognized that his hour of decision was close at hand. On April 12 Fort Sumter was bombarded by the Confederates, and on the fourteenth surrendered. On the fifteenth President Lincoln called for 75,000 volunteers. The war had begun. The hesitating border states, including Virginia, must decide their course. Lee, at home in Arlington, must decide his own personal course. Dr. Freeman tells how he made "the answer he was born to make."

. . . From Washington, on the 17th, there arrived a letter and a message. The letter bore Scott's signature and requested Lee to call at his office on the 18th. The message was conveyed in a note from a Washington cousin, John Lee. It was that Francis P. Blair, Sr., a publicist of Lee's acquaintance . . . desired Lee to meet him the next morning at his house in Washington.

What was afoot now? . . . The answer, in its entirety, Lee did not learn during his lifetime. He never realized how anxious some men high in office and influence had been to save his services to the United States army. In addition to what General Scott had done, Francis P. Blair, Sr., father of Colonel Lee's Missouri friend, Montgomery Blair, had been at work. He had been to President Lincoln, who had authorized him to "ascertain Lee's intentions and feelings." Blair had also discussed the subject with Secretary Cameron and had been directed by him to make a proposition to Lee. It was to explain this that Blair had sent the message to Arlington.

Duly on the morning of April 18 Lee rode over the bridge and up to the younger Blair's house on Pennsylvania Avenue, directly opposite the State, War and Navy Building, where he found the old publicist awaiting him. They sat down behind closed doors. Blair promptly and plainly explained his reason for asking Lee to call. A large army, he said, was soon to be called into the field to enforce the Federal law; the President has authorized him to ask Lee if he would accept command.

Command of an army of 75,000, perhaps 100,000 men; opportunity to apply all he had learned in Mexico; the supreme ambition of a soldier realized; the full support of the government; many of his ablest comrades working with him; rank as a major general— all this may have surged through Lee's mind for an instant, but if so, it was only for an instant. Then his Virginia background and the mental discipline of years asserted themselves. He had said: "If the Union is dissolved and the government disrupted, I shall return to my native state and share the miseries of my people and save in defence will draw my sword on none." There he stood, and in that spirit, after listening to all Blair had to say, he made the fateful reply that is best given in his own simple account of the interview: "I declined the offer he made me to take command of the army that was to be brought into the field, stating as candidly and courteously as I could, that though opposed to secession and deprecating war, I could take no part in an invasion of the Southern States. . . ."

Bidding farewell to Blair, Lee went directly to Scott's office. He sensed Scott's deep interest in his action, and as soon as he arrived he told him what Blair had offered and what he had answered. "Lee," said Scott, deeply moved, "you have made the greatest mistake of your life; but I feared it would be so. . . ." Scott did not stop with this sad observation, but expressed the belief that if Lee were going to resign he ought not to delay. "There are times," Scott is reported to have said, "when every officer in the United States service should fully determine what course he will pursue and frankly declare it. No one should continue in government employ without being actively employed. . . ."

This added a complication that Lee pondered as he left his old commander for the last time. . . . Though willing to resign rather than to fight against the South, he had clung to the hope that he would not have to act unless Virginia seceded. . . . But Scott had now said he should not remain in the army if he was unwilling to perform active duty. . . . Lee, as an officer of the army, might be called upon immediately for duty he could not conscientiously perform. Then he would have to resign under orders. That was a disgrace to any soldier. . . .

But he did not leave his problem behind him as he turned his back on his country's capital. He carried it with him; he wrestled with it. *Was* his position equivocal? Ought he to resign at once, regardless of what Virginia did? He felt that Scott was right, but his own mind was so opposed to secession and his devotion to the Union and to the army proved so strong, now it was put to the test, that he delayed the actual writing of his resignation, hoping against hope. . . .

The next morning, April 19, Lee went into Alexandria on business and there he read the news he had hoped he would never see: Virginia had seceded! . . . The Federal government . . . would certainly take prompt action since the state just across the river from its capital had left the Union. As one of the senior field officers in Washington, he might be summoned at any hour to defend Washington by invading Virginia—which he could not do. Duty was plain. There could be no holding back. The time had come. All the Lees had been Americans, but they had been Virginians first. . . .

So, after midnight on the 19th he sat down and wrote this letter [to Secretary Cameron], not more than fifteen hours after he had received positive information that Virginia had seceded: "I have the honor to tender the resignation of my commission as Colonel of the 1st Regt. of Cavalry. . . ."

To General Scott, that loyal old friend, who had admired him, taught him and advanced him, he penned this letter:

"Since my interview with you on the 18th inst. I have felt that I ought no longer to retain my commission in the Army. I therefore tender my resignation, which I request you will recommend for acceptance. I would have presented it at once, but for the struggle it has cost me to separate myself from a service to which I have devoted all the best years of my life and all the ability I possessed.

"During the whole of that time—more than a quarter of a century—I have experienced nothing but kindness from my superiors and a most cordial friendship from my comrades. To no one, General, have I been as much indebted as to yourself for uniform kindness and consideration, and it has always been my ardent desire to meet your approbation. I shall carry to the grave the most grateful recollections of your consideration, and your name and fame will always be dear to me.

"Save in defence of my native State, I never desire again to draw my sword. . . ."

He came downstairs when he had finished the letters. Mrs. Lee was waiting for him. She had heard him pacing in the room above her and had thought she had heard him fall on his knees in prayer. "Well, Mary," he said calmly, "the question is settled. Here is my letter of resignation and a letter I have written General Scott."

7

First Year of Confederate Service

ON A fine spring morning in April 1861 Robert E. Lee, dressed in the garb of the private citizen he now was, left Arlington—which he was never to see again—and traveled down to Richmond to offer his services to his native state. Virginia had just seceded from the Union, but had not yet joined the young new Confederate States of America. She was, however, raising a force of state troops; and Robert E. Lee was offered, and accepted, the command of these state troops. Soon, however, Virginia joined the Confederacy and Lee was then assigned to the command of the Confederate troops within the state of Virginia—working, of course, under the direction of the President and the Secretary of War. It was an important but thankless task, and Lee longed for assignment to active service in the field; but, true to his sense of duty, he zealously worked at his obscure tasks while others gained the plaudits of early victory.

A delirium of joy swept the South following the rout of the invading Federal army at Manassas in July, and the names of the Southern heroes—Beauregard and Joe Johnston and Stonewall Jackson—were on every lip and in every headline. Lee promptly wrote to his old Mexican War comrade, Beauregard, a warm letter of congratulation: "I can not express the joy I feel at your brilliant victory. The skill, courage and endurance displayed by yourself excite my highest admiration. You and your troops have the gratitude of the whole country, and I offer my heartfelt congratulations at their success." And then, a little wistfully, he wrote to his wife: "I wished to partake in the battle and am mortified at my absence. But the President thought it more important that I should be here. I could not have done as well as has been done, but I could have helped and taken part in a struggle for my home and neighbors."

Meanwhile the Confederate government, wrestling with the age-old problem of military precedence, had created the rank of general, assigning five men to this grade: Samuel Cooper (who was assigned to the post of adjutant general, which position he had held in the United States Army), Albert Sidney Johnston, Robert E. Lee, Joseph E. Johnston and P.G.T. Beauregard. It was specified that they were to rank in the order named, which was the order of their seniority in the old Army. Joseph E. Johnston protested bitterly that he should outrank all the others, thus precipitating a controversy with President Davis which adversely affected Johnston's usefulness throughout the war. Lee took no part in the bickering, satisfied to serve in whatever place and rank assigned to him.

Early in May he wrote to his wife: "Make your plans for a long war. . . . Tell Custis he must consult his own judgment, reason and conscience as to the course he may take. I do not wish him to be guided by my wishes or example. If I have done wrong, let him do better. The present is a momentous question, which every man must settle for himself, and upon principle." Custis, then a lieutenant in the Engineers Corps, did not hesitate long, but resigned his commission and tendered his services to the Confederacy, being given a commission in the engineers. Rooney Lee (who had resigned from the Army two years before, married and gone to farming on his White House plantation) enlisted in the Confederate Army and was made a captain of cavalry. Young Robert, at his parents' bidding, continued (temporarily) his schooling at the university. Lee's brother Smith resigned his commission in the United States Navy, and was made an officer in the Confederate Navy. His nephew, Fitzhugh, also resigned his Army commission, and joined the Confederate cavalry. The Lees of Virginia were in the war.

1

A thoughtful and sound analysis of Lee's personal views in

1861 and his conscientious effort to effect an adjustment of his views to his sense of duty is given by General Maurice.

It was natural that, in the heat and passion aroused by civil war, he should have been held up to obloquy as a traitor to the flag under which he had served, and the country to which he had sworn allegiance. But it is curious that such sentiments should have endured in the minds of some responsible writers long after Robert E. Lee had gone to meet his God.

This is the account which so distinguished an historian as John G. Nicolay gives of Lee's action in April, 1861: "Whether because of family ties (he was a Virginian) or of property interests or of more alluring overtures from the South, Lee on April 20th tendered his resignation to General Scott. On April 22nd, before that resignation had been accepted, he was formally invested by the Virginia Convention with the comand of the Virginia troops, hostile to the United States."

It would, I think, be difficult to compress into a similar number of words a greater misrepresentation of fact.

Even a cursory examination of the evidence should have convinced any one that this is so. I will take Lee's property interests first: His principal estates lay in the valley of the Potomac on the frontier between the contending powers. From his house at Arlington could be seen the capital of the United States. No one will deny that in April, 1861, Lee was an experienced soldier, and that he must have known that his property would inevitably suffer in the event of war. . . . He must equally have been aware that his chances of protecting his property would be greater if he were in command at Washington than they would be if he were at Richmond. . . . Lee was amongst the very few who saw from the first that the war would be long. Within a few days of reaching Richmond, after resigning from the Army of the United States, he was writing to his wife at Arlington: "I think you had better prepare all things for removal from Arlington—that is, plate, pictures, etc., and be prepared at any moment. Where to go is the difficulty. When war commences no place will be exempt, in my opinion; indeed, all the avenues into the State will be the scene of military operations. . . . The war may last ten years. . . ." It is abundantly clear that Lee, more than most men in those critical days, risked by his decision the security of his property and the comfort of those dear to him. Consideration of property did not influence his judgment for a moment.

It is not less preposterous to suppose that he was influenced by more alluring offers from the South. . . . As soon as it became clear that a rupture was imminent, Scott induced Lincoln to make every effort to retain Lee's services for the cause of the Union, and the President sent Mr. Francis Preston Blair to offer to him the command of the active army of the United States. What must such an offer have meant to Lee? It realized what is the honourable ambition of every soldier who enters the service of his country. . . . It was not possible that the South should have made him an offer more alluring than that conveyed to him from President Lincoln, and it is in fact evident that no offer, prior to his decision, was made. When Lee sent in his resignation to Scott, he had made no provision for his future. . . . Lee was actually preparing to enlist as a private in the cavalry when in June, 1861, he received from the Confederate Government the commission to command its forces in the State of Virginia. But, as will be seen, the positions he at first occupied were inferior to that which Lincoln had offered. Ambition had not, any more than considerations of property, influenced Lee's decision.

It is, of course, true that family ties were to Lee a matter of great concern. "I had to meet," he said, "the question whether I should take part against my native State. I have not been able to make up my mind to raise my hand against my relations, my children, my home." Such sentiments, natural as they are, might have induced Lee to resign his commission and to separate himself from the North, but they do not account for the devotion with which he served the South, nor for his repeated and obviously sincere appeals to his troops to fight for, and if need be die for, a just cause. He certainly did not believe slavery to be an institution for which men should fight and die. He had released his own slaves. . . . While Lee thought slavery to be an evil, he believed that more harm than good would result from the attempt to eradicate the evil by force, and there were in 1861 in the North very many who agreed with him in this. It is evident that he would not have resigned his commission in the United States

Army, still less have opposed the Union in arms, if in his mind the retention of slavery had been the chief issue.

Neither did Lee think secession a cause to fight for. . . . He had grave doubts as to whether his State would be right to secede. "Secession is nothing but revolution." . . . Yet Lee held it to be his bounden duty to defend Virginia if she were attacked. That his intention in the first months of 1861 was to do nothing more than resist aggression is, I think, made clear by a letter which he wrote to his sister who lived at Baltimore and was a supporter of the Union. . . . In the anguish of the crisis he had no thought but to go to his State and to suffer with her children. . . . But when Lee got to Richmond and breathed the atmosphere of enthusiasm for a cause which pervaded his State, his attitude of mind changed gradually. He became convinced that Virginia was fighting for the right, and said so again and again to his soldiers. . . .

Lee fought as a man fights who acts on conviction. What, then, was his conviction?

There have been critics of his career who, while expressing every sympathy with him in the terrible situation in which he was placed in April, 1861, have been unable to explain to themselves with any satisfaction his breach of his oath as a regular officer of the Union and his enthusiasm for a cause which, as they say, he must have known to be based on slavery.

As to the first of these criticisms, I would say that Lee did not break his military oath. He resigned his commission and the acceptance of that resignation released him from that obligation. It is true, as Nicolay says, that he went to Richmond before the formal notification that he had ceased to be an officer of the Army of the United States reached him. He assumed that his resignation would be accepted,* and he had reason for that assumption, for in the United States it was recognized that in the event of civil strife the State should permit those in its service who had family ties with the participants in a rebellion to obtain release from service if they so desired. To act otherwise and to force men to fight those near and dear to them would be to make military serv-

---

* On May 2nd he wrote to Mrs. Lee: "I have just received Custis' letter inclosing the acceptance of my resignation. This stated it will take effect on the 25th of April. I resigned on the 20th and wished it to take effect on that day. I cannot consent to its running on further, and he must receive no pay if they tender it beyond that day, but return the whole if need be."

ice an unendurable tyranny. This implicit right to resignation
does not relieve those who act upon it from the pains and penal-
ties attaching to them as rebel citizens, but does absolve them from
the charge of having broken a military oath. The fact that the
authorities at Washingon accepted Lee's resignation and also accepted wholesale resignations of other regular officers who were
of Southern blood shows that this was so.

Those who maintain that Lee must consciously have been fighting for the maintenance of slavery would make of him a casuist.
My reading of his character is different. I have said that his up-
bringing and associations made him take a real and serious interest in political affairs, and I hope to show that in his part in the
conduct of the war he displayed a statesmanlike grasp of situations
which is rarely found in soldiers. But for all that, Lee was not a
politically minded man. His praise of Buchanan's weak and time-
serving message of December, 1860, is sufficient to prove that. He
could not follow political developments to their conclusion with
the logic and perspicacity of Lincoln. He could not foresee the outcome of the struggle between those who advocated limitation and
those who pressed for the extension of slavery. Be it remembered
that in 1861 abolition was the creed of a comparatively small number in the North.

The Lee I see was essentially a simple-minded man, with a keen
sense of duty and a perfect trust in God's providence. His nature
was not such as to make him eager to investigate the complexities
of involved political questions, and his military training was calculated to strengthen his natural distaste for such investigations.
He followed Calhoun in believing the great and leading principle
of the political life of the Union to be that "the general government emanated from the people of the several States forming distinct political communities and acting in their several and sovereign capacity, not from all the people forming one aggregate
political community." He regarded the Union as a great possession, but only so long as it was a free association of free States.

2

Of Robert E. Lee's preparedness for the gigantic task he was approaching, Dr. Freeman gives a masterly analysis, with a due weighing of all the credits and debits.

After his first duty of helping to organize an army—in what capacity he did not yet know—Lee had to anticipate a bloody and a bitter war. What did he know of the grisly art he would have to apply?

In those two unchanging fundamentals of military service, discipline and co-operation, Robert E. Lee had received the precise training of a professional soldier. Obedience to orders was part of his religion. Adverse decisions on his acts he had schooled himself to accept in precisely the same spirit as approval. He could elicit the support of his superiors without flattery, and in the few instances where he had ever had subordinates, he had won their allegiance without threats. He was a diplomat among engineers. Fully qualified to deal with the politician in executive office, he was suspicious of him in the field or in the forum, and none too confident of his sagacity in legislation, though he was as meticulous as his great model, Washington, in subordinating himself, at all times and in all things, to civil authority. His dealings with his brother officers had never been darkened by scheming or marred by jealousy. Of much that West Point taught and of all that it failed to inculcate, his observation had been close and personal. A knowledge of the capacity of some of his prospective opponents had been gained by his service at the academy, in Mexico and in Texas. . . .

Familiarity with the history of war, another fundamental of the training of a leader, was his in limited measure. The American Revolutionary campaigns he had surveyed carefully. His reading of "Light-Horse Harry's" *Memoirs* had been emulous and detailed. Napoleon was the great captain whose battles he had most carefully followed from Jomini, and from such other books as were available. . . . To the Crimean War he had devoted at least casual study. With Hannibal and with Julius Caesar he was not wholly unacquainted.

From these masters of war, and most of all from General Winfield Scott, he had learned the theory of strategy, and had learned it well. He had participated, too, in nearly all the strategical preparation of the most successful series of battles ever fought prior to 1861 by an American army. The strategy he had seen Scott apply had primarily been that of flank attack, based on careful reconnaisance and, where possible, on surprise. Cerro Gordo and Padierna, the two battles which were fought on the basis of Lee's own study of the ground, seem to have meant more in shaping his views of strategy than all his reading. Chapultepec, also, had made a deep impression on him and perhaps suggested the final assault at Gettysburg. The strategical function of the high command he had learned from those same battles in Mexico. That function, as he saw it, was to develop the lines of communication, to direct the reconnaissance, to ascertain the precise position of the enemy, and then to bring all the combatant units into position at the proper time and to the best advantage. In Mexico Scott had never tried to handle his troops in action. He had left that to the divisional commanders; Lee's instinct was to do the same thing.

But if Lee was, in the spring of 1861, a well-schooled theoretical strategist, whose interest lay in that field of war, Scott's methods and his own lack of opportunity had given him a very limited knowledge of tactics. . . . Twenty-six of his thirty-two years in the army had been spent on the staff, and only six in the line. Of these six years something less than three had been passed with troops. At no time had he commanded more than 300 men in the field, and even that number simply for one brief uneventful scout through a desert. Since he had left West Point he had never served with infantry or with artillery, except in the battery at Vera Cruz.

Thanks, however, to the advantages that Scott had afforded him during the campaign from Vera Cruz to Mexico City, he had far more than the staff officer's approach to the duties that awaited him in excited Richmond. In reconnaissance his experience had been sufficient to develop great aptitude. . . . He was an excellent topographer and not without training as an intelligence officer. . . . Fortification, as an engineer, he knew thoroughly. . . .

Such was the positive equipment of Robert E. Lee at the beginning of the War between the States. It was, on the whole, the best equipment with which any soldier entered the struggle, for the capable leaders of Scott's divisions of 1847 were then either dead or too infirm for action, and few of the brigadiers of the Mexican campaigns had displayed special ability. . . .

Admirable as was the training of Lee, it was not complete. He had scant knowledge of militia and little experience with hastily trained volunteers, wide as was his experience with inexpert civilian labor. Only the regular soldier did he know well. Again, from the narrowness of his subordinate command, there was danger that his view would be microscopic. In the third place, all his battle experience had been on the offensive, though the situation and comparative weakness of the South were to compel it to hold to a defensive in the larger sense of the word. Furthermore, having labored so long on detached projects, he was disposed to do work that could have been passed on to others. Most of all was he lacking in any detailed knowledge of the service of supply. . . . Nor had he and most of the other Confederate leaders been reared in a society that gave them a background for this homely but essential part of the work of a successful commanding general. . . .

With Lee's excellent training in some directions set down in one column and his lack of equipment in some particulars placed opposite it, any person who knew him intimately would have said that the man who was now approaching Richmond would show himself a fine strategist, though he might perhaps be a bit theoretical, a popular leader though not a facile tactician—in short, an excellent man to organize an army, to make reconnaissance and to plan battles, but an unknown quantity in handling troops in action. What surprises one who studies the military education of Lee is the entire absence of anything to forecast his great skill in troop movements. . . .

All these were the abstract considerations that might have been argued in the case of any soldier whose background was known. There remained the basic, if less tangible, factor of temperament. He was a gentleman in every impulse: was he too much a gentleman for the dirty business of war? Was there enough of steel in his soul? That respect for civil authority—would it tie his hands in a revolution? Feeling that his duty was performed when he had obeyed his orders and had done his utmost, would he fight for his opinions? Would he escape the "subordinate complex" which is all too familiar in war? If the Southern cause ever depended on him and on him alone, was there in him the stuff of which military dictators are made?

If he thought at all of these things, as his train rolled down to the valley of the Chickahominy, it must have been in the humble conviction that he was not equal to the task that lay ahead, a task of which he was one of the few Southern men to realize the full magnitude. . . . He knew the might and the prestige of the old standard that had been hauled down. . . . He had measured the strength and determination of the North, and he foresaw a bloody test, a long war, a doubtful issue.

3

Lee had hardly assumed his new duties as commander of the armed forces of the state of Virginia, with the rank of General, before he was called on to make a self-sacrificing decision which might have caused a lesser, self-seeking man to hesitate. Governor Letcher had notified President Jefferson Davis of the Confederate States of America that Virginia had seceded and wished to become associated with the new Southern Confederacy. Vice-President Alexander H. Stephens was sent from Montgomery to Richmond to negotiate with the Virginia authorities, his letter of instructions concluding with the positive admonition: "It is indispensable that the control and direction of all offensive military movements should be vested exclusively in the President. Therefore, in your negotiations for the proposed alliance, you will regard it as an essential condition that explicit provision be made conferring this power on the President." An ambitious commander of Virginia's military forces might block the alliance by objecting to the relinquishment of his own authority. Mr. Stephens had strong misgivings, he tells us, as he took up the task assigned him.

With these instructions I went to Richmond and met General Lee. Many persons now think of the Lee of that day in the light of later history. In point of fact he was not the central figure to whom all eyes looked from both sections. His services as military engineer had given him little experience in the command of troops. His brief cavalry service had given him no knowledge of the control of large bodies, and his most important field experience had been at the capture of Harper's Ferry from John Brown. . . .

Outside of the seceded and then Confederated States there was a second combination of States, even more powerful in population and resources than those of the Confederacy, and fully able by *united* action, to dictate to the seceded States. I emphasize the word *united*, for it was only by disuniting these States and securing a suspension of their action that Mr. Lincoln and his most able cabinet succeeded in making a land highway for the passage of invading troops, and at last turning the neutrality of border States into practical co-operation in the supply of money and men for the war. At the head of this second tier of States, every one of them in full sympathy with States-rights doctrines and the *right* of secession, stood Virginia. The military leader of Virginia, and the probable head of the forces of the border States likely to offer armed resistance to the passage of Federal troops over the soil, was Robert Edward Lee. If Virginia did not unite with the Confederacy, but became the leader of this band of neutral and protesting States, there was a combination which might have altered the whole final result.

Upon the day of my arrival in Richmond he had been made Major General of the Virginia army, and this made him the probable head of the forces of the border States.

In the Confederate States he would possibly be subordinate to Albert Sidney Johnston, Joseph E. Johnston, G. T. Beauregard, and I think, on the basis of rank in the old army, to William Henry Walker and G. W. Smith. A Confederate military organization already existed. In addition, the highest Confederate rank was then that of Brigadier-General. General Cooper, as Adjutant-General of the Confederacy, was not to be in the field.

Neither my commission nor any action of the Confederate Congress had made any provision for the rank or position of General Lee. On the day after my arrival this rank of Major General of the Army of Virginia was solemnly conferred upon him by President John Janney, of the convention, in the Hall of Representatives.

Mr. Janney spoke of the sages and heroes of the blood of Lee; of his illustrious father and his great Virginia compatriots; of the unanimous vote of the convention, making him commander-in-chief; and of their faith, that, like Washington, he would be found first in war, first in peace, and first in the hearts of his countrymen. General Lee replied:

"Mr. President and Gentlemen of the Convention: Profoundly impressed with the solemnity of the occasion, for which I must say I was not prepared, I accept the position assigned me by your partiality. I had much preferred your choice had fallen upon an abler man. Trusting in Almighty God, an approving conscience, and the aid of my fellow citizens, I devote myself to the service of my native State, in whose behalf alone will I ever again draw my sword."

As he stood there, fresh and ruddy as a David from the sheep-fold, in the prime of his manly beauty, and the embodiment of a line of heroic and patriotic fathers and worthy mothers; it was thus I first saw Robert E. Lee. I had preconceived ideas of the rough soldier with no time for the graces of life, and by companionship almost compelled to the vices of his profession. I did not know then that he used no stimulants, was free even from the use of tobacco, and that he was absolutely stainless in his private life. I did not know then, as I do now, that he had been a model youth and young man; but I had before me the most manly man and entire gentleman I ever saw.

That this seeming modesty was genuine; that this worth in which his compatriots believed was real; that his character was utterly unselfish, I was to know as the shades of evening fell upon that day, and he sat in my room at the Ballard House, at my request, to listen to my proposal that he resign, without any compensation or promise thereof, the very honor and rank he had that same morning received.

General Lee heard me quietly, understood the situation at once, and saw that he alone stood between the Confederacy and his State. The members of the convention had seen at once that Lee was left out of the proposed compact that was to make Virginia one of the Confederate States, and I knew that one word, or even a look of dissatisfaction from him, would terminate the negotiations with which I was intrusted. North Carolina would act with Virginia, and either the border States would protect our lines, or the battlefield be moved at once down to South Carolina and the borders of Georgia.

General Lee did not hesitate for one moment, and while he saw that it would make matters worse to throw up his commission, he declared that no personal ambition or emolument should be considered or stand in the way.

I had admired him in the morning, but I took his hand that night at parting with feelings of respect and almost reverence, never yet effaced. I met him at times later, and he was always the same Christian gentleman.

Virginia became one of us, and the battlefield, as all men know, and General Lee took subordinate positions which for a time placed him nearly out of sight. The magnitude of his sacrifice of the position of commander-in-chief of the Union army is already appreciated. But the greatness of his self-abnegation in the surrender of the sword of Virginia will not yet be seen unless I show what it at once involved. It is not the man on the battlefield I wish to draw, but a higher thing than a mere sword flourisher—personal character.

Nominally, General Lee lost nothing, but practically, for the time being, he lost everything. The Government moved to Richmond and Mr. Davis directed General Lee, for the time being, to retain his command of the Virginia troops, which was really to make him recruiting and drill inspector.

4

Some idea of the character of the personnel of the armies that gathered in Virginia in early 1861 may be had from a penetrating sketch provided by Robert Stiles, a member of the famous Richmond Howitzers. Stiles had been born in Georgia but had grown up in Connecticut, where his father was a Presbyterian minister. A thoughtful and literate young man, he has left an invaluable record of his experiences and observations during his *Four Years under Marse Robert,* as his book is entitled.

The intellectual atmosphere of the Confederate camps was far above what is generally supposed by the people of this generation, even in the Southern States, and this intellectual aspiration and vigor of the men were exhibited perhaps equally in their religious meetings and services and in their dramatic representations and other exhibitions gotten up to relieve the tedium of camp. But however this may be in general it cannot be denied that the case of the Richmond Howitzers was exceptional in this regard. The corps was organized at the time of the John Brown raid by George W. Randolph, afterwards Secretary of War, and has never been disbanded. In 1861 it was recruited up to three companies and formed into a battalion, but unfortunately the first company was never associated with the other two in the field. The composition of the three companies was very similar; that is, all of them were made up largely of young business men and clerks of the highest grade and best character from the city of Richmond, but included also a number of country boys, for the most part of excellent families, with a very considerable infusion of college-bred men, for it was strikingly true that in 1861 the flower of our educated youth gravitated toward the artillery. The outcome was something quite unparalleled, so far as I know. It is safe to say that not less than one hundred men were commissioned from the corps during the war, and these of every rank from Secretary of War down to a second lieutenant.

Few things have ever impressed me as did the intellectual and moral character of the men who composed the circle I entered the day our guide led my brother and myself to the Howitzer camp. I had lived for years at the North, had graduated recently at Yale, and had but just entered upon the study of law in the city of New York when the war began. Thus torn away by the inexorable demands of conscience and of loyalty to the South from a focal point of intense intellectual life and purpose, one of my keenest regrets was that I was bidding a long good-by to congenial surroundings and companionships. To my surprise and delight, around the camp fires of the First Company, Richmond Howitzers, I found throbbing an intellectual life as high and brilliant and intense as any I had ever known.

The Howitzer Glee Club, trained and led by Frederick Nicholas Crouch, author of "Kathleen Mavourneen," was the very best I ever heard, and rendered music at once scientific and enjoyable. No law school in the land ever had more brilliant or powerful moot court discussions than graced the mock trials of the Howitzer Law Club. I have known the burial of a tame crow to be witnessed not only by the entire command but by scores, perhaps hundreds, of intelligent people from a neighboring town, and to be dignified not only by salvos of artillery but also by an English speech, a Latin oration and a Greek ode, which would have done honor to any literary or memorial occasion at old Yale. . . .

What now of the essential spirit of these young volunteers? Why did they volunteer? For what did they give their lives? We can never appreciate the story of their deeds as soldiers until we answer this question correctly.

Surely it was not for slavery they fought. The great majority of them had never owned a slave and had little or no interest in the institution. My own father, for example, had freed his slaves long years before; that is, all save one, who would not be "emancipated," our dear "Mammy," who clung to us when we moved to the North and never recognized any change in her condition or her relations to us. The great war will never be properly comprehended by the man who looks upon it as a war for the preservation of slavery.

Nor was it, so far as Virginia was concerned, a war in support of the right of secession or the Southern interpretation of the Constitution. Virginia did not favor this interpretation; at least, she did not favor the exercise of the right of secession. Up to President Lincoln's call for troops she refused to secede. She changed her position under the distinct threat of *invasion*—the demand that she help *coerce* her sister states. This was the turning point. . . .

. . . Coming closer down, let us see how the logic of these events wrought itself out among my comrades of the Howitzer Company. We will take as a type in this instance the case of a brilliantly endowed youth of excellent family in Richmond . . . who sealed his fate and his devotion with his life at Gettysburg. He was a student at the University of Virginia in the spring of '61, and perhaps the most extreme and uncompromising "Union man" among all the young men gathered there. Indeed, so exaggerated were his antisecession views and so bold and aggressive was he in advocacy of them, that he became very unpopular and his friends feared serious trouble and even bloody collision. The morning President Lincoln's proclamation appeared he had gone down town on personal business before breakfast, and while there happened to glance at a paper. He returned at once to the University, but not to breakfast; spoke not a word to any human being, packed his trunk with his belongings, left a note for the chairman of the faculty explaining his conduct, boarded the first train for Richmond and joined a military company, before going to his father's house or taking so much as a morsel of food.

What was the overwhelming force which thus in a moment transformed this splendid youth? Was it not the God-implanted instinct which impels a man to *defend his own hearth-stone?* . . .

Here, then, we have the essential, the distinctive spirit of the Southern volunteer. As he hastened to the front in the spring of '61, he felt: "With me is Right, before me is Duty, *behind me is Home.*"

5

In building up a staff for carrying on his official duties in Richmond, there was assigned to General Lee, among others, a young lieutenant named Walter Taylor. Taylor was destined to serve as an aide to Lee during the succeeding years of the war, rising to the position of adjutant general of the Army of Northern Virginia, with the rank of colonel. Fortunately for succeeding historians and students, Colonel Taylor left an entertaining and enlightening record of his four years under the great commander. Of these early days in Richmond, when both he and his general were undertaking new and unfamiliar duties, he says:

I had excellent opportunities at that time to observe General Lee as a worker, and I can say that I have never known a man more thorough and painstaking in all that he undertook. Early at his office, punctual in meeting all engagements, methodical to an extreme in his way of despatching business, giving close attention to details—but not, as is sometimes the concomitant if not the result of this trait, neglectful of the more important matters dependent upon his decision—he seemed to address himself to the accomplishment of every task that devolved upon him in a conscientious and deliberate way, as if he himself was directly accountable to some higher power for the manner in which he performed his duty. I then discovered, too, that characteristic of him that always marked his intercourse and relations with his fellow-men—scrupulous consideration for the feelings and interests of others; the more humble the station of one from whom he received appeal or request, the more he appeared to desire to meet the demand if possible or, if impracticable, to make denial in the most considerate way, as if done with reluctance and regret.

His correspondence, necessarily heavy, was constantly a source of worry and annoyance to him. He did not enjoy writing; indeed, he wrote with labor, and nothing seemed to tax his amiability so much as the necessity for writing a lengthy official communication; but he was not satisfied unless at the close of his office hours every matter requiring prompt attention had been disposed of.

After a day's work at his office he would enjoy above all things a ride on horseback. Accompanied by one or two of his military household, he would visit some point of interest around Richmond, making the ride one of duty as well as pleasure; and no sculptor can ever reproduce in marble or bronze the picture of manly grace and beauty that became in those days so familiar to the people in and around Richmond in the person of General Lee on his favorite horse. After his return from such excursions, in the closing hours of the day, he would take the greatest pleasure in having the little girls of the neighborhood gather around him, when he would talk and joke with them in the most loving and familiar way. . . .

The life then led by General Lee was one of great simplicity and without parade or ostentation; neither then nor later, when in active service with the army, did he care for display of any kind.

6

It was galling to Lee to be forced to remain at a desk in Richmond while the first great battle of the war was being

fought at Manassas by his comrades of the Mexican War, Joe
Johnston and Beauregard. Within a few days, however, President Davis was to satisfy his desire for active service in the
field by assigning him to the difficult task of retrieving the
Confederate situation in the mountains of western Virginia.
Walter Taylor, who accompanied him to the mountains as
his aide, tells us about it.

At this period President Davis became very anxious about the
condition of affairs in the western portion of Virginia. . . . Mr.
Davis wished to send General Lee to that section to restore confidence in the troops and check the Federal advance. There was,
moreover, a lack of harmony between Generals Floyd and Wise,
who were operating separate commands in the Kanawha district,
and it was hoped that the presence of General Lee would tend to
harmonize their differences.

The President held his wish in abeyance until after the battle
of Manassas, and in the latter days of July General Lee left Richmond for his new field of duty. . . . The journey was made as far
as Staunton by rail, and from thence the party proceeded on horseback to Monterey, in Highland County. . . . On arriving at Monterey the delights of a ride on horseback were very seriously impaired by the setting in of a rainy season, and to the same cause
is to be attributed the appalling degree of sickness that then prevailed among the troops, as also the great difficulty experienced in
getting supplies to the front for the army. . . .

After an unsuccessful attempt to surprise the Federal forces at
Cheat Mountain and on Valley River, the Confederates reoccupied
their fortified position at Valley Mountain. Heavy rains continued, the roads were in dreadful condition, and it did not appear
likely that there would be any active movement in that section
for some time. About the 18th or 19th of September General Lee
left Valley Mountain, and proceeded to the Kanawha district.
With only a young subaltern as companion, he made the journey
on horseback. Passing through White Sulphur Springs, the journey was continued to Meadow Bluff, to which point General Floyd
had fallen back with his little army. General Wise was several
miles in advance at Sewell Mountain, confronting Rosecrans' army

with his Legion, having refused to obey General Floyd's order to fall back. . . .

The presence of General Lee reconciled for a time the discordant elements of that army. He promptly advanced General Floyd's command to the position held by General Wise, and so united the army; but to secure discipline and render the force effective it was necessary to have the two commands combined under one commander; and the President, acting upon General Lee's suggestion, sent to General Wise an order relieving him from duty in that department, which, however, contained no reflection upon him. It was only by the tact and good management of General Lee that General Wise was induced to comply with the President's command; and I remember that he told General Lee that he wished him to understand that he left the field and repaired to Richmond in deference to *his* judgment and counsel rather than in compliance with the orders from the Department.

7

The campaign in western Virginia is of particular interest as constituting Lee's first service in the field in the Confederate Army. It was, in fact, his first experience in commanding combat troops, except for the small-scale Indian scouting in Texas; and, so far as could be told from the final failure of the campaign, there was nothing to indicate to the public that he possessed much greater skill than such political generals (and failures) as General Floyd and General Wise. Opposed to the Confederates were two generals who were later to be commanders of Federal armies, McClellan and Rosecrans. A thumbnail sketch of the whole campaign in this theater of action is given by Dr. McCabe.

When General Lee took command of the Virginia forces, he sent Colonel G. A. Porterfield, who had been an officer in the Regular Army of the United States, to Western Virginia, to raise volunteers for the defence of the state. Porterfield proceeded at once to his destination, and, establishing his headquarters at Philippi, a village in Barbour County, issued his proclamation for troops for service in the State army. The people of Western Virginia refused to respond to the call, and at the same time enlisted rapidly in the Federal army.

Porterfield found it impossible to procure recruits, and ascertained that the enemy were collecting troops so rapidly along the Ohio River that unless a Southern army could be sent into Western Virginia, that portion of the state would be speedily overrun by the Federals. He promptly informed General Lee of this and, finding his little command of less than seven hundred men threatened by a Federal column at Grafton, determined to withdraw to Beverley, in Randolph County. Before this resolution could be put into effect, his camp at Philippi was surprised and captured by five thousand Federal soldiers, and his men put to flight, with the loss of several killed and wounded, and a few prisoners.

General Lee, as soon as he received Colonel Porterfield's dispatch, prepared to send troops to Western Virginia. About five thousand infantry, some cavalry, and several batteries of artillery were assembled at Beverley, late in May, and the command bestowed upon Brigadier-General R. S. Garnett, a gallant officer, who had served as General Lee's adjutant-general during the first weeks of the war.

General Garnett after reaching Beverley proceeded to occupy a strong position near that town. With a force of three thousand infantry, six pieces of artillery, and three companies of cavalry, he intrenched himself on the slopes of Laurel Hill, holding the main turnpike from Staunton to Wheeling. This road . . . was his direct line of retreat, being the great highway across the mountains in this region. If cut off from it, his only chance of retreat was by difficult roads over the mountains to the eastward. Five miles below Garnett's position, at Laurel Hill, a road from the west passes through this spur, at a defile known as Rich Mountain, and strikes the main road. To guard this approach against any effort of the enemy to seize his line of retreat, Garnett posted Colonel John Pegram . . . with sixteen hundred infantry and four pieces of artillery at Rich Mountain. . . .

The command of the Department of the Ohio . . . had been entrusted by the Federal Government, early in May, to General George B. McClellan, who had served with distinction in the

Engineer Corps of the Regular Army. As soon as he learned the presence of Porterfield and Garnett in Western Virginia, McClellan determined to cross the Ohio, which properly bounded his department, drive the Southern troops east of the mountains, and occupy the mountain region with his own forces.

It has been seen that the movement against Porterfield was successful. General McClellan now resolved to attack Garnett and, in order to defeat him, directed his march so as to strike the main line of retreat of the Confederate force below the position held by Colonel Pegram, and at the same time to send another column to seize the only other route by which Garnett could retreat, and thus capture the whole force.

Accordingly, on the 11th of July, Brigadier-General Rosecrans, with about three thousand men, was dispatched to attack Pegram's left and rear, while McClellan, with five thousand infantry and some artillery, attacked in front. After a difficult march over the mountain by an unusual road, Rosecrans succeeded in turning Pegram's left, and gaining his rear, and after a short but stubborn fight, Pegram was defeated. Six companies of infantry escaped, but the rest of the Southern force fell into the hands of the enemy.

As soon as General Garnett heard of the result of the fight at Rich Mountain he determined to abandon Laurel Hill and fall back on Huttonsville. Owing to a misconstruction of his orders, the road was left open in the direction of the enemy and blocked some distance from Beverley on his own line of march. This forced him to leave the main turnpike, and retreat by a mountain road into Hardy County. McClellan pursued vigorously, and the Confederates were put to great straits to effect their escape. About five hundred prisoners were taken, and General Garnett himself was killed at one of the fords of Cheat River.

The Confederate loss in the campaign was very slight in killed and wounded, being less than one hundred, but they lost over one thousand prisoners, nearly all their artillery, and the greater part of their baggage.

The disastrous result of the campaign spread a feeling of gloom for a time throughout the South. It was the first defeat the Southern arms had sustained, and the people were totally unused to war. The remnants of Garnett's command retreated to Monterey

in Highland County, where they were soon joined by reënforcements from Richmond; but though temporary successes were frequently gained by the South, McClellan's promptness and boldness gave the Federals a hold upon Western Virginia which they
never relaxed throughout the war.

While Garnett was at Rich Mountain, Brigadier-General Henry
A. Wise was sent to Western Virginia to raise troops in the Kanawha Valley. He established his headquarters at Charleston, and
succeeded in organizing and arming twenty-five hundred infantry,
seven hundred cavalry, and three batteries of artillery, which force
was soon after increased to four thousand men. The Federal army
under McClellan had by this time crossed the Ohio River. A Federal force was at Parkersburg, and the enemy was using every
effort to bring into the Kanawha Valley an army sufficient to drive
Wise out of it. Soon the command of General Cox moved from
the Ohio River to attack him. . . . General Wise at once fell back
to Lewisburg, reaching that place about the 1st of August, after
a retreat which was rendered somewhat difficult by an insufficiency
of transportation.

A few weeks later Brigadier-General John B. Floyd was sent
west of the mountains, with his brigade, which numbered about
eighteen hundred infantry, a battalion of cavalry and a battery of
artillery, to operate in the Valley of the Kanawha. He repaired at
once to the White Sulphur Springs, in Greenbrier County, about
nine miles from General Wise's position. He consulted with General Wise and the two commanders agreed upon an advance towards Gauley River. Unfortunately their columns moved separately, and failed to act in concert at any subsequent period. The
Gauley River was reached, and crossed by Floyd's forces, but Wise
halted on the bank of the stream. Floyd attacked a superior Federal force under Colonel Tyler, at the Cross Lanes in Fayette
County, and defeated it with some loss on the 26th of August. On
the 10th of September he was himself attacked at Carnifex Ferry
on the Gauley by General Rosecrans, who had succeeded McClellan in command of the Federal army in West Virginia. Rosecrans's
force numbered nine thousand men and several batteries of artillery. Floyd had seventeen hundred and fifty men. The Confederates succeeded in maintaining their position against heavy odds

until night, when Floyd recrossed the river. Rosecrans moved forward in pursuit, and forced Floyd and Wise back to Sewell Mountain. Fresh disagreements occurred between the Confederate leaders, and Floyd fell back to Meadow Bluff, eighteen miles west of Lewisburg, and Wise halted on the eastern slope of Sewell Mountain, where he intrenched his position, which he named Camp Defiance. Thus, through the failure of the two Generals to coöperate with each other, the campaign resulted in nothing of value to the Confederates.

Meanwhile, upon the death of General Garnett, General Lee was ordered to Western Virginia to take command of the army in that region. He at once set out from Richmond for Monterey, taking with him reënforcements which, added to the remnants of Garnett's troops, brought the army to about sixteen thousand men. The roads were in a horrible condition, being almost knee deep in mud, and it was with great difficulty that the army could move forward, but advancing steadily westward, General Lee, by the 10th of August, reached the neighborhood of Cheat Mountain, and found it strongly fortified. The position was very formidable, but General Lee determined to endeavor, by strategic movements, to dislodge the enemy from it, when, by pushing forward rapidly with his whole army, he hoped to drive the Federals to the Ohio.

General Reynolds, second in command to Rosecrans, had taken position to cover the approaches to Beverley, with a force of about twelve thousand men. The bulk of this army was strongly intrenched at a point at the junction of Tygart's Valley River and Elk Run, which post was called by the Federals "Elk Water." The rest held the pass at the second summit of Cheat Mountain, on the main road from Staunton to Parkersburg. The mountain had what may be called three distinct summits. The second was the most available for military purposes, and the enemy had strengthened it with a powerful fort or block house in the bend of the road, flanked by intrenchments of earth and logs, protected by dense abattis on every side. On two sides it was impossible to approach this stronghold, for the mountain rose almost perpendicular from the river to the fort.

General Lee felt his way cautiously along the road from Huntersville to Huttonsville, and halted near the Federal position at

Cheat Mountain. Careful reconnoissances developed its immense strength, but Colonel Rust, of the Third Arkansas Regiment, who had made what proved to be a very imperfect reconnoissance of the Federal position, reported that it was perfectly practicable to turn it and carry it by assault. General Lee at once gave orders for a combined attack on the enemy both at Elk Water and Cheat Mountain. The weather was very cold, and the difficulties to be overcome by the troops in occupying the positions assigned them were very great, but, in spite of these obstacles, General Lee succeeded in reaching a point below the enemy at Elk Water, placing other portions of his force on the spurs of the mountain to the east and west of the block house, and moving another part of his army down the river close to the enemy. These dispositions completed, General Lee was ready to attack the Federals at Elk Water, as soon as Colonel Rust's guns should be heard on Cheat Mountain.

Colonel Rust, with fifteen hundred men, was ordered to gain the rear of the fort, where he had reported an assault practicable, and carry the work by storm. After considerable exertion Rust gained the rear of the fort, but saw at a glance that he had been deceived in his former reconnoissance. Indeed the Federal abattis extended so far and was so utterly impenetrable that it was impossible to reach the fort. Seeing this, Colonel Rust decided not to make the assault, and at once withdrew his troops. His failure rendered it useless for General Lee to attack the works at Elk Water, as a victory there would have been useless with the enemy at Cheat Mountain. The Confederate troops were withdrawn and the effort abandoned. . . .

Soon after he had drawn off his troops, General Lee was informed by couriers of the exposed situation of Floyd and Wise, against whom the combined forces of Rosecrans and Cox were advancing. He at once decided to transfer his army to the vicinity of Lewisburg, and endeavor to defeat Rosecrans before the fall rains should render the roads impassable. He reached Floyd's position on the 20th of September and, after conferring with him and inspecting the locality, set out for Camp Defiance where he arrived on the 22d. A close inspection satisfied him that the line held by General Wise on the Sewell Mountain was more advantageous than that of General Floyd at Meadow Bluff, and he at once ordered all his troops forward, and proceeded to strengthen his position. He had left a part of his army to hold the Federal force at Cheat Mountain in check, but, including the commands of Floyd and Wise, he had with him about fifteen thousand men, which was the strength of Rosecrans's army.

Rosecrans, who had been pressing on after Wise and Floyd, now reached the Sewell Mountain and took position on the top and western slope of it; the armies were now in sight of each other, and outpost fights and skirmishes went on constantly. Expecting to be attacked, General Lee made no advance, and the adversaries confronted each other for nearly two weeks. At last, Rosecrans, discovering the true nature of the force opposed to him, on the night of the 6th of October broke up his camp and retreated westward. The retreat was discovered by the Confederates the next morning, but no attempt at pursuit was made. The army was not provided with the means of dragging its artillery through the mud, and its transportation was very deficient.

It must be confessed that General Lee disappointed the expectations of the country in this campaign. He showed less vigor and genius than at any other period of the war.

8

A charming vignette of a private soldier's contact with General Lee during the campaign in western Virginia is given by Sam Watkins, a private in the First Tennessee Regiment.

One evening General Robert E. Lee came to our camp. He was a fine looking gentleman, and wore a moustache. He was dressed in blue cottonade and looked like some good boy's grandpa. I felt like going up to him and saying, "Good evening, Uncle Bob." I am not certain at this late day that I did not do so. I remember going up mighty close and sitting there and listening to his conversation with the officers of our regiment. He had a calm and collected air about him, his voice was kind and tender, and his eye was as gentle as a dove's. His whole make-up of form and person, looks and manner, had a kind of gentle and soothing magnetism about it that drew every one to him and made them love, respect and honor him. I fell in love with the old gentleman and felt like going home with him. I know I have never seen a finer looking man, nor one with more kind and gentle features and manners. His horse was standing nipping the grass, and when I saw that he was getting ready to start, I ran and caught his horse and led him up to him. He took the reins of the bridle in his hand and said, "Thank you, my son," rode off, and my heart went with him. There was none of his staff with him; he had on no sword or pistol or anything to show his rank. The only thing that I remember he had was an opera-glass hung over his shoulder by a strap.

9

General Lee was not unaware of the public's disappointment at the unsuccessful conduct of the nightmarish campaign in western Virginia. In one of his rare displays of sarcasm and bitterness, he wrote to his wife: "I am sorry, as you say, that the movements of our armies can not keep pace with the expectations of the editors of the papers. I know they can regulate matters satisfactory to themselves on paper. I wish they could do so in the field. No one wishes them more success than I do, and I would be happy to see them have full swing. General Floyd has three editors on his staff. I hope something will be done to please them." But the outcome of the campaign did not please the Richmond editors, and they did not hesitate to express their opinion that Lee was an overrated soldier and an incompetent leader. Fitzhugh Lee tells of his uncle's reaction to the censure.

It must be admitted that General Lee retired from West Virginia with diminished military reputation. Great results had been expected from his presence there. Garnett's defeat and death were to be avenged, and the whole of that portion of Virginia speedily wrested from the Federal arms. The public did not understand the difficulties of the situation, or comprehend why he did not defeat Reynolds, or the failure to attack Rosecrans. The news of the expected great victories did not reach Richmond. Men apparently wise shook their heads and said he had been overrated as a soldier; that he relied upon a "showy presence" and a "historic name," and that he was "too tender of blood" and leaned too much to the engineer side of a military question, preferring rather to dig intrenchments than to fight. There were two men, however, who stood by him faithfully in this doubtful period of his career. One of them was the President of the Confederate States, the other the Governor of Virginia. They knew him well, and that the failure of the West Virginia campaign could not be fairly attributed to him.

General Lee remained quiet under the occasional attacks of the public press. He knew that his duty had been discharged conscientiously. He was not aware that he had a "showy presence." On the contrary, he was modest, unassuming and simple. He conducted his campaign in the most unostentatious manner. He had only two aid-de-camps, Colonels Washington and Taylor. The former was killed; the remaining aid-de-camp shared the same tent with him. The mess furniture was of the plainest kind—tin cups, tin plates, tin dishes, which Colonel Taylor says were carried all through the war. In the full zenith of his fame as a great army commander, any one who accepted his hospitality would be obliged to eat from the same old tinware with which he commenced the war in West Virginia.

It is not known that General Lee ever attempted in any way to make explanation or defense of these attacks. In a private letter to Governor Letcher, dated September 17, 1861, he simply states that "he was sanguine of success in attacking the enemy's works on Rich Mountain," that "the troops intended for the surprise had reached their destination, having traversed twenty miles of steep and rugged mountain paths, and the last day through a terrible storm, which had lasted all night, in which they had to stand, drenched to the skin, in a cold rain"; that he "waited for an attack on Cheat Mountain, which was to be the signal, till 10 A.M., but the signal did not come. The chance for surprise was gone. The provisions of the men had been destroyed the preceding day by the storm. They had nothing to eat that morning and could not hold out another day, and were obliged to be withdrawn.

"This, Governor," he writes, "is for your own eye. Please do not speak of it. We must try again. . . ."

General Lee, in obedience to instructions, returned to Richmond, but not amid the shouts of the populace. The bands did not play "See the Conquering Hero Come"; the chaplet of victory was missing from his brow, the scalps of Rosecrans and Reynolds from his belt. The public looked at the cold facts, and were interested in actual results. The difference between war in the mountains and war amid the hills and valleys and green fields was never for a moment considered. . . . There were still passes among the mountains and a few men could hold them against an army, and could only be dislodged by flank and rear attacks over long, steep, circuitous paths. Lee made the attempt when in front of Reynolds. Had his well-laid plans been carried out, possibly he might have defeated the Federal general. In an offensive movement against Rosecrans the elements of success were against him. The naturally strong, elevated position on Sewell Mountain, made still stronger by the methods of an engineer of such great ability as Rosecrans, could not have been easily carried. When it was abandoned, the Federal rear-guard, every few miles, could have found other strong positions where Lee's army could have been detained for days had the condition of his troops and the roads permitted pursuit.

On General Lee's return to Richmond his duties as military adviser at the side of the chief executive officer of the Confederacy were resumed. No response was ever made to public criticisms. His vision swept the future, his vindication would come if opportunity offered.

10

There was one incident of the West Virginia campaign, minor in its nature but important from both a practical and a sentimental standpoint: it was here that Lee first saw the horse which later became his favorite mount and carried him throughout the remaining days of the war and the following days of peace. Thomas L. Broun, the West Virginia farmer who bred him, tells the story of Lee's acquisition of his famous steed, Traveller.

Traveller was raised by Mr. Johnston near the Blue Sulphur Springs, in Greenbrier County, Virginia (now West Virginia); was of the Gray Eagle stock, and as a colt took the first premium under the name of Jeff Davis at the Lewisburg fairs for each of the years 1859 and 1860. He was four years old in the spring of 1861. . . . I purchased him for $175 (gold value) in the fall of 1861 of Capt. J. W. Johnston, son of the Mr. Johnston first above mentioned. When the Wise Legion was encamped about Meadow Bluff and Big Sewell Mountain I rode this horse, which was greatly admired in camp for his rapid, springy walk, his high spirit, bold carriage, and muscular strength. He neither needed whip nor spur, and would walk his five or six miles an hour over the rough mountain roads of Western Virginia with his rider sitting firmly in the saddle and holding him in check with a tight rein, such vim and eagerness did he manifest to go right ahead as he was mounted.

When General Lee took command of the Wise Legion and the Floyd Brigade in the fall of 1861 he first saw this horse and took a great fancy to it. He called it his colt, and said he would need it before the war was over. Whenever the General saw me on this horse he had something pleasant to say about "my colt" as he designated him.

After General Lee was ordered to South Carolina, the Third Regiment of the Wise Legion was subsequently detached from the army in western Virginia and ordered to the South Carolina coast. Upon seeing my brother on this horse near Pocotaligo in South Carolina, General Lee at once recognized the horse and again inquired of him pleasantly about "his" colt. My brother then offered him the horse as a gift, which the General promptly declined, and at the same time remarked: "If you will willingly sell me the horse, I will gladly use it for a week or so to learn its qualities." . . . My brother wrote me of General Lee's desire to have the horse, and asked me what he should do. I replied at once: "If he will not accept it, then sell it to him at what it cost me." He then sold the horse to General Lee for $200 in currency, the sum of $25 having been added by General Lee to the price I gave for the horse in

September 1861 to make up for the depreciation in our currency
from September, 1861, to February, 1862.

In 1868 General Lee wrote to my brother, stating that this
horse had survived the war, was known as Traveller (spelling the
word with a double "l," in good English style), and asking for its
pedigree which was obtained and sent by my brother to General
Lee.

11

The editors and the gossips in Richmond may have been
dissatisfied with Lee's record in western Virginia, but there
was no lessening of the esteem in which he was held by President Jefferson Davis, who later wrote: "He came back carrying
the heavy weight of defeat, and unappreciated by the people
whom he served; for they could not know, as I knew, that if his
plans and orders had been carried out the result would have
been victory rather than retreat. They did not know it, for I
would not have known it if he had not breathed it in my ear,
only at my earnest request and begging that nothing be said
about it. The clamour that then arose followed him when he
went to South Carolina, so that it became necessary to write a
letter to the governor of that state telling him what manner of
man he was. Yet through all this, with a magnanimity rarely
equalled, he stood in silence, without defending himself or
allowing others to defend him; for he was unwilling to offend
any one who was wearing a sword and striking blows for the
Confederacy."

Davis demonstrated his own regard for Lee's talents by immediately assigning him to duty on the South Atlantic Coast,
where he had an opportunity to practice his talents as an engineer by establishing an impregnable system of coast defenses. One of his aides at this time was Major (later general)
A. L. Long, who has written the following sketch of Lee's important service in this sector:

The defences of the coast, embracing numerous vital points,
chiefly occupied General Lee's attention during the period of his

service in this southern department. The character of the work to be done and the method in which he performed it here call for description.

The line of coast extending from the entrance of Chesapeake Bay to the mouth of the Rio Grande presents innumerable bays, inlets, and harbors into which vessels could run either for predatory incursions or with the intention of actual invasion. The Federals, having the command of the sea, it was certain that they would take advantage of this open condition of the coast to employ their naval force as soon as it could be collected, not only to enforce the blockade which had been declared but also for making inroads along our unprotected ocean border. That the system of defence adopted may be understood, it is necessary to describe in detail the topography of the coast.

On the coast of North Carolina are Albemarle and Pamlico Sounds, penetrating far into the interior. Farther south, Cape Fear River connects with the ocean by two channels, the southwest channel being then defended by a small enclosed fort and a water battery. On the coast of South Carolina are Georgetown and Charleston harbors. A succession of islands extends along the coast of South Carolina and Georgia, separated from the main land by a channel which is navigable for vessels of moderate draught from Charleston to Fernandina, Florida. There are fewer assailable points on the Gulf than on the Atlantic. Pensacola, Mobile and the mouths of the Mississippi were defended by works that had hitherto been regarded as sufficiently strong to repulse any naval attack that might be made upon them.

Immediately after the bombardment and capture of Fort Sumter the work of seacoast defence was begun, and carried forward as rapidly as the limited means of the Confederacy would permit. Roanoke Island and other points on Albemarle and Pamlico Sounds were fortified. Batteries were established at the south-east entrance of Cape Fear River, and the works on the south-west entrance of that river were strengthened. Defences were constructed at Georgetown and at all assailable points on the north-east coast of South Carolina. The works of Charleston Harbor were greatly strengthened by earthworks and floating batteries. The defences from Charleston down the coast of South Carolina and Georgia were confined chiefly to the islands and salient points bearing upon the channels leading inland. Defensive works were erected at all important points along the coast.

Many of the defences, being injudiciously located and hastily erected, offered but little resistance to the enemy when attacked. These defects were not surprising when we take into consideration the inexperience of the engineers and the long line of seacoast to be defended. As soon as a sufficient naval force had been collected by the Federals, an expedition under the command of General Butler was sent to the coast of North Carolina and captured several important points. A second expedition, under Admiral Dupont and General T. W. Sherman, was sent to make a descent on the coast of South Carolina. On the 27th of November, Dupont attacked the batteries that were designed to defend Port Royal harbor and, almost without resistance, carried them and gained possession of Port Royal. . . . Later Burnside captured Roanoke Island and established himself in eastern North Carolina without resistance.

The rapid fall of Roanoke Island and Port Royal struck consternation into the hearts of the inhabitants along the entire coast. The capture of Port Royal gave the Federals the entire possession of Beaufort Island, which afforded a safe place of arms for the troops, while the harbor gave a safe anchorage for the fleet. Beaufort Island almost fills a deep indenture in the main shore, from which it is separated for the greater part of its extent by a narrow channel which is navigable throughout. Its northern extremity extends to within a few miles of the Charleston and Savannah Railroad. The main road from Port Royal to Pocotaligo crosses the channel at this point. The evacuation of Hilton Head on the southwestern extremity of Beaufort Island followed the capture of Port Royal. This exposed Savannah, only about twenty-five miles distant, to an attack from that direction. At the same time, the Federals having command of Helena Bay, Charleston was liable to be assailed from North Edisto or Stono Inlet, and the railroad could have been reached without opposition by the road from Port Royal to Pocotaligo.

Such was the state of affairs when General Lee reached Charleston in the early part of November, 1861, to assume the command of the department of South Carolina, Georgia and Florida. His vigorous mind at once comprehended the essential features of the situation, and with his accustomed energy he prepared to overcome the many difficulties that presented themselves. Directing fortifications to be erected on the Stono, the Edisto and the Combahee, he fixed his headquarters at Coosawhatchie, the point most threatened, and directed defences to be erected opposite Hilton Head and on the Broad and Salcatchie to cover Savannah. These were the points requiring immediate attention. He superintended in person the works overlooking the approach to the railroad from Port Royal, and soon infused into his troops a part of his own energy.

The works he had planned rose with magical rapidity. A few days after his arrival at Coosawhatchie, Dupont and Sherman sent their first reconnoissance in that direction, which was met and repulsed by shot from the newly-erected batteries; and now, whether the Federals advanced toward the railroad or turned in the direction of Charleston or Savannah, they were arrested by the Confederate batteries. The people, seeing the Federals repulsed at every point, regained their confidence and with it their energy.

We may at this point introduce a letter addressed to two of his daughters shortly after his journey South, as it gives, in his own words, his opinion of the preceding state of the coast defences, together with some interesting matter relating to his home life:

Savannah, 22 Nov., 1861

"My Darling Daughters: I wish I could see you, be with you and never again part from you. God only can give me that happiness. I pray for it night and day. But my prayers, I know, are not worthy to be heard. . . . I am much pleased at your description of Stratford and your visit there. It is endeared to me by many recollections and it has always been the desire of my life to be able to purchase it. Now that we have no other home, and the one we so loved has been for ever desecrated, that desire is stronger with me than ever. The horse chestnut you mention in the garden was planted by my mother. I am sorry the vault is so dilapidated. You do not mention the spring, one of the objects of my earliest recollections. How my heart goes back to those happy days! . . . This is my second visit to Savannah. I have been down the coast as far as Amelia Island to examine the defences. They are poor indeed, and I have laid off work to employ our people a month. I hope our enemy will be polite enough to wait for us. It is difficult to get our people to realize their position. . . ."

The most important points being now secured against immediate attack, the general proceeded to organize a system of sea-coast defence different from that which had been previously adopted. He withdrew the troops and material from those works which had been established on the islands and salient points, which he could not defend, to a strong interior line, where the effect of the Federal naval force would be neutralized. After a careful reconnoissance of the coast he designated such points as he considered it necessary to fortify. The most important positions on this extensive line were Georgetown, Charleston, Pocotaligo, Coosawhatchie and Savannah. Coosawhatchie, being central, could communicate with either Charleston or Savannah in two or three hours by railroad, so in case of an attack they could support each other. The positions between Coosawhatchie and Savannah and those between Charleston and Coosawhatchie could be reinforced from the positions contiguous to them. There was thus a defensive relation throughout the entire line. . . .

The house at Coosawhatchie selected by General Lee for head-quarters was of just sufficient capacity for himself and military family. . . . The general was as unpretentious in the interior arrangement of his quarters as were his exterior surroundings. His simple camp-equipage and that of his staff comprised the entire furniture of the house. The table-service consisted of a neat set of tin-ware, plates, dishes and cups made to fit into each other for convenience in packing. The bill of fare corresponded in frugality to the plainness of the furniture. The general occupied the head of the table, and always seasoned the meal with his good humor and pleasant jests, often at the expense of some member of the staff who seemed to miss the luxuries of the table more than himself.

The extensive line of operations that demanded his attention caused Lee to be almost constantly on the move, first at one place, and then at another, where important work was in progress. It was remarkable how his quiet, confident manner stimulated the men to exertion whenever he came among them. . . .

About the middle of March [1862] Lee was directed to proceed to Richmond. By that time he had established a strong interior line of defence extending from Winyaw Bay to the mouth of St. Mary's River. This line, being bravely and skilfully defended, proved to be an impenetrable barrier to the combined efforts of the land and naval forces of the enemy constantly employed on the coast, until it was carried by Sherman in his unopposed march through Georgia and South Carolina.

In order that the importance of this series of defensive works may be understood, it is necessary to know what it accomplished. It protected the most valuable agricultural section of the Confederacy, ensured the safety of Charleston and Savannah, and covered the principal line of communication between the Mississippi and the Potomac. Besides these important results, it produced a desirable effect by diffusing among the inhabitants a sense of security they had not felt for many months.

12

Paul Hamilton Hayne, in the language of the poet that he was, gives us a glimpse of Lee at this stage of his career.

A scene witnessed by us at Fort Sumter, on an afternoon in 1861, comes vividly back to memory. Leaning upon a great Columbiad which occupied an upper tier of the fortress, we were engaged in watching the sunset when voices and footsteps toward the right attracted our notice.

Glancing round we saw approaching us the then commander of the fort, accompanied by several of his captains and lieutenants; and, in the middle of the group, topping the tallest by half a head, was perhaps the most striking figure we had ever encountered— the figure of a man seemingly about fifty-six or fifty-eight years of age, erect as a poplar, yet lithe and graceful, with broad shoulders well thrown back, a fine, justly-proportioned head posed in unconscious dignity, clear, deep, thoughtful eyes and the quiet, dauntless step of one every inch the gentleman and soldier.

Had some old English cathedral crypt or monumental stone in Westminster Abbey been smitten by a magician's wand and made to yield up its knightly tenant restored to his manly vigor, with a chivalric soul beaming from every feature, some grand old Crusader or "red-cross" warrior who, believing in a sacred creed and espousing a glorious principle, looked upon mere life as nothing in the comparison, we thought that thus would he have appeared, unchanged in aught but costume and surroundings! And this superb soldier, the glamour of the antique days about him, was no other than Robert E. Lee, just commissioned by the President, after his unfortunate campaign in western Virginia, to travel southward and examine the condition of our coast fortifications and seaboard defenses.

8

Adviser to the President

EARLY in 1862 the affairs of the Confederacy
were at a low ebb. The people, drugged by the easy victory at
Manassas, had relaxed their efforts and were suffering the fatal
consequences of overconfidence. In the west the Federals had
captured Fort Henry and Fort Donelson; Nashville, the stronghold and armory of that region, had been evacuated by the
Confederates. In Virginia the Federal forces, now under the
command of General George B. McClellan, were being drilled
and supplied and organized into a powerful fighting force. Before the threat of their power, General Johnston was preparing
to withdraw his army to the line of the Rappahannock, and
gave evidence that he might retreat further. The Federals had
also landed forces on the Peninsula below Richmond, and
were beginning a gradual advance from that direction, with
only a skeleton Confederate force under General Magruder
to oppose them.

In the face of these developments, the people of the Confederate States—and especially of Virginia—began to grumble and
to voice questions as to the capacity of their leadership. There
were open suggestions that President Davis should relinquish
his personal direction of the movements of the armies and turn
that task over to an active military leader. There was much
discussion and debating of this proposal in Congress, the final
outcome being the issuance of an order by the President proclaiming that "General Robert E. Lee is assigned to duty at the
seat of government, and under the direction of the President
is charged with the conduct of military operations of the armies of the Confederacy."

That qualifying phrase "under the direction of the Presi-

dent" robbed the position of any real authority, and rendered
the assignment unwelcome to Lee. Obedient to superior authority, however, he promptly repaired to Richmond and assumed his new duties. Thus he was available when fickle opportunity knocked at his door a few weeks later.

1

Some idea of the confusion in Richmond at this time, and
the constant harassment and interruption under which Lee
and other officials had to try to perform their duties, may be
had from the observations of an intelligent English gentleman
who had enlisted as a private in the Confederate army and
spent a short furlough in Richmond after the battle of Manassas.

The Government offices were quiet and business-like, but no
other part of the capital was so. The hotels were crowded to excess, as they always are; and great numbers of officers in expensive
uniforms strutted about on "sick leave," many of whom had never
been in the army at all and after running up bills with all classes
of tradesmen would suddenly depart for parts unknown. The
marvel was that people could be so deceived, for it is no exagger-
ation to say that every third man was dignified with shoulder-
straps, and collectively they far out-numbered all the officers at
Manassas! In theatres, bar-rooms and shops, on horseback and on
foot, all wore the insignia of office. Not one was to be found of
less rank than captain, and as for colonels—their name was legion!
I was measured by a youth for a pair of boots, and bought some
dry-goods of another, one morning: in the evening I saw both of
them playing at billiards at the Spottswood, dressed out in bran-
new uniforms with insignia belonging to the rank of major! This
was sufficient explanation, and it did not at all surprise me afterwards to hear that nearly all the thousand and one gambling hells
were kept by "captains," "majors" and "colonels." General Winder, the provost marshal, subsequently made it a punishable offence for any to assume uniforms except soldiers. The change was
sudden and ludicrous in effect.

The floating population of Richmond was made up of the strangest elements. Some came to see friends, others with wonderful inventions or suggestions for Government. Not a few were impressed with the idea that the Cabinet needed their advice and counsel; but the majority of these strangers came with the modest determination to offer their services at large salaries, pretending that if they were not accepted for this or that office some state or other would feel humbled, perhaps secede from the Confederacy, and I know not what.

It was laughable indeed to hear the self-sacrificing Solons holding forth in bar-rooms or in private. Their ideas of all things military were decidedly rich and would have astonished poor Johnston or Beauregard, who were put down as mere schoolboys beside them. General Washington Dobbs, who had been engaged all his life in the leather business somewhere in Georgia, had come up to proffer his valuable services as brigadier; but, being unsuccessful, his patriotism and indignation electrified the whole private family where he boarded. Colonel Madison Warren, some poor relation of the English blacking-maker, had lived in some out-of-the-way swamp in the Carolinas; he came to Richmond to have a private talk with the President, to let him know what he thought about General McClellan and old Scott. Not getting an audience, he offered himself for the vacancy of quartermaster-general; and, not being accepted, was sure that Jefferson Davis was a despot and that the Southern Confederacy was fast going to the devil.

Smith had a self-loading, self-priming field-piece that would fire a hundred times a minute and never miss. Each gun would weigh only twenty tons and cost $10,000. He had asked a commission to make a thousand of them only, was willing to give Government the patent right gratis, and they would not listen to him! How could the South succeed when neglecting such men as Smith? Jones was another type of a numerous class of patriots. Tracts were necessary food for the soldiers. He (Jones) only wanted the Government to start a large Bible and tract house, give him the control of it, and he would guarantee to print as many as were needed and sell them as cheaply as anybody else—considering the high price of everything. Jones, like a thousand others, did not succeed with any of the departments; and, after being jammed and pushed about in the various lobbies and staircases for a whole month, arrived at the conclusion that the Confederate Government was not sound on the Bible question and, therefore, ought not to be trusted in this enlightened and gospel-preaching age!

2

Into this maelstrom of confusion Robert E. Lee was precipitated in those early days of 1862, to manage the military affairs of the Confederacy—"under the direction of the President." How he assumed his new burden of responsibility, how he quietly set about the work of building up and co-ordinating the Confederate military resources is outlined by Dr. Freeman.

During the terrible months Lee had been in western Virginia, mountains had broken the winds of contention and distance had kept from him the worst alarms. In South Carolina and in Georgia, engrossed in the details of a difficult defense, he had heard little of the confidential news that came only to the President and to the War Department. Now that he was back at the storm-centre of the Southern struggle, consulted by Davis and having free access to the files, he soon learned the dark inwardness of a situation that had changed much for the worse since he had left the Confederate capital in November.

Disaster was in the air. The defeats at Fort Henry and Fort Donelson had led the Confederates under Albert Sidney Johnston to evacuate most of Kentucky and part of western Tennessee. The newspapers that Lee read on his arrival in Richmond contained the gloomy intelligence that Fort Columbus, the advanced Confederate position on the Mississippi, thirty miles south of the confluence of the Ohio, had been abandoned by his old West Point friend, Leonidas Polk. There was danger that all the Southern posts on the river, from Columbus as far down as Memphis or beyond, would fall to the victorious and overwhelming Federal forces. Nowhere, since a small Federal column had been destroyed at Ball's Bluff on the Potomac, October 22, 1861, had there been a substantial Confederate success on land to relieve the gathering gloom. Southern commissioners in Europe had not been received at a single court. . . .

The worst was not known, even to Congress. The Confederacy's supply of powder was nearly exhausted. The arsenals were almost bare of weapons. Expected shipments of arms from across the Atlantic were being delayed by a blockade that was already demonstrating the silent, decisive influence of sea-power, which the Confederates were powerless to combat. The army might soon be without the means to fight. Hope of relieving the blockade was raised for a day when the frigate *Merrimac,* cut down to the water's edge and covered with railroad iron, awkwardly steamed forth from Norfolk on March 8 as the Confederate ram *Virginia* and destroyed the *Congress* and the *Cumberland,* but she was challenged the next day by an ironclad as curious as herself, the *Monitor.*

The faith of the public had fallen with the misfortunes of their cause. Gone was the old boastfulness that had humiliated Lee. Silent were the platform-patriots who had predicted the complete defeat of the United States within ninety days after the first gun had been fired. The prophets had been confounded, the weak were despairing, the courageous were anxious. . . .

A week and more Lee spent in study of the general situation, without definite assignment to duty. On March 13 there were important developments. Davis then received his first official information that Johnston had evacuated the Manassas line on March 8-9, had retreated twenty-five miles southward along the Orange and Alexandria Railroad, and had halted his army on either side of the north fork of the Rappahannock River. The same day, unknown to the Confederates, a Union council of war at McClellan's headquarters decided on the line of advance for the vast Army of the Potomac that was now equipped to the last tent-peg. And on that identical, ill-omened 13th, Lee received an impossible assignment to duty.

Behind it lay conflict between the President and Congress. . . . Mr. Davis's disposition to direct military operations in person had provoked much criticism. . . . He asked in effect that . . . legislation creating the post of commanding general be enacted, so that the appointee could act, in a sense, as military or technical head

of the War Department. Congress acquiesced but . . . the measure
. . . provided for a commanding general . . . and authorized the
officer so named to take personal command of any army in the
field at any time. . . . The President saw in the move an invasion
of his constitutional rights as commander-in-chief of the army and
navy. . . . He vetoed the measure and simultaneously assigned
General Lee "to duty at the seat of government," charged "under
the direction of the President"—that phrase asserted his authority—
"with the conduct of military operations in the armies of the Confederacy." . . .

The Charleston Mercury said that he was being reduced "from
a commanding general to an orderly sergeant." Lee himself said:
"It will give me great pleasure to do anything I can to relieve
[the President] and serve the country, but I cannot see either advantage or pleasure in my duties. But I will not complain, but
do the best I can." . . .

The duties of the post were to prove vexing and varied and
were never to be finished. He could not know when the President
would call him to a long, futile conference, or what new problem from an unfamiliar field a hard-beset commander would present by telegraph with a plea for instant answer. . . . Broadly
speaking, Davis entrusted to him the minor, vexatious matters of
detail and the counselling of commanders in charge of the smaller
armies. On the larger strategic issues the President usually consulted him and was often guided by his advice, but in no single
instance was Lee given a free hand to initiate and direct to full
completion any plan of magnitude. . . . Public confidence in his
qualities as a commander was not what it had been in 1861. In his
whole career there was not a period of more thankless service, but
there were few, if any, during which he contributed more to sustain the Confederate cause.

3

In his capacity as military adviser to President Davis, Lee
held a position somewhat similar to the Chief of a General
Staff in other more permanently organized governments and
military establishments. In this capacity he was entrusted with

the responsibility for advising the government as to the over-all strategy to be followed and also supervising the organization of the Confederacy's armed forces. His contribution to the Confederate cause in this latter capacity was not attended with any great publicity and was overshadowed by his later brilliant career as a field commander, but it has not been overlooked by such a keen student of military affairs as Major General Sir Frederick Maurice, the distinguished British soldier and military writer.

Little has been said of Lee's work as an organizer, yet it had a great influence on the course of the war. I have already said he was one of the very few who from the first saw that the war would be long. The fact that the enlistment of the first volunteers in the North was for ninety days is sufficient evidence of the authoritative view held on that side. Lee endeavoured to persuade Davis to make enlistment compulsory and for the duration of the war, and though the Confederate Government was not at first prepared for so drastic a measure, he did succeed in getting it to accept the enlistment of volunteers without limit as to numbers, for the duration of the war, after a first enactment limiting service to twelve months had been adopted. In April, 1862, he persuaded the authorities of Richmond to get a Conscription Act passed, nearly a year before such a measure was adopted at Washington.

In three other respects his plans of preparation seem to have been from the first superior to those adopted in the North. His own experiences had convinced him of the importance of having an efficient staff, and he took special pains to make this provision from his exiguous resources; he was equally convinced of the importance of having what in modern armies is called an "order of battle" scientifically arranged; as a cavalry officer he attached a high value to that arm, for which the landowners and farmers of the South furnished splendid material. Until a late stage in the war the staff work of the Southern armies, if very far from perfect when judged by present standards, was better than that of the Northern forces; the organization of the Southern troops in brigades and divisions and the establishment of a hierarchy of command were more adapted to the requirements of war than was the system first devised at Washington, that is to say, the Confederate order of battle was superior to the Federal until Hooker reorganized the army of the Potomac in January, 1863; the Southern cavalry was, until the middle of 1863, superior not only in its personnel, as was in the circumstances natural, but in its organization and methods. So for the first half of the period of the war, Lee's capacity as a military organizer conferred definite advantages on the South.

But Lee's most pressing concern at the beginning of the war was with the defence of Richmond. Not only was it necessary for the South to act defensively until at least the nucleus of an army was prepared, but the cause of State Rights to which the Confederacy was pledged, imposed extreme caution in invading the territory of Maryland without the explicit consent of that State, which it was hoped to induce to join the Southern cause. There were three avenues of approach to Richmond: by the Orange and Alexandria Railroad to Manassas Junction and thence across the Rappahannock; by Harper's Ferry and up the Valley of the Shenandoah; and by sea through Fortress Monroe and the Yorktown Peninsula. Lee, as he had told his wife, expected that "all the avenues into the State" would be the scene of military operations, and he prepared to meet attack in each of the three. He early predicted that Manassas would be the scene of one of the first battles, and there he assembled the chief Southern force. Jackson first, and then J. E. Johnston, were sent to Harper's Ferry, and defensive lines covering Richmond were prepared on the Yorktown Peninsula. It is evident that the South owed much to these timely dispositions. Not a little of the Confederate success at the first battle of Manassas was due to the familiarity of the troops with the ground on which they fought, while a rich return was to be gained for the familiarity with the Valley which Jackson early acquired.

Such were Lee's preoccupations during the first months of war, throughout which he worked in close accord with President Davis. The Confederate President had, for a statesman, an unusual degree of military experience. He was a West Pointer, and had been at the Military Academy at the same time as Lee. He had served both in the United States infantry and dragoons, and then resigned his commission. When the Mexican War broke out, he volunteered for service and became colonel of a Mississippi regiment, while he was Secretary of War in Mr. Pierce's administration. He had then had excellent opportunities for getting to know the small band of regular officers of the United States Army and he showed himself to be not only a good judge of men, but to have the firmness of character not to be moved from his judgment either by popular clamour or by temporary failures on the part of those in whose qualities he had convinced himself he had good reason to believe. It happened that the first performances of both Lee and Jackson in the field were unsuccessful, and the Press of Richmond was free with criticisms, particularly of the former, but Davis never wavered in his support of Lee either then or at any other time, while Lee was consistently loyal to the President, and there is no word of criticism of the statesman to be found throughout the soldier's correspondence. The Constitution of the Confederacy followed that of the Union in making the President Commander-in-Chief of its forces, and Lee had no desire to oust him from that position. In July, 1861, Lee wrote to his wife: "I have never heard of the assignment to which you allude—of Commander-in-Chief of the Southern Army—nor have I any expectation or wish for it. President Davis holds that position."

4

Lee's innate talent for military affairs, coupled with his familiarity with the military and economic resources of the Federal government, prevented his entertaining the popular delusion of a short war and a quick victory for the Confederate States. He looked for a long war, and formulated his basic strategy on this theory, as General Maurice explains.

We find that Lee in his strategy employed three methods, each admirably adapted to the means available and to the political situation at the time. In the first period his policy was, as I have said, purely defensive. He was seeking time to prepare the means for bolder courses, for no one knew better than he that defence by itself is but a sorry weapon. In the second period he was seeking every opportunity to attack, not merely on the battlefields of Virginia, but in the territory of his enemy. He never forgot that he had seen from the heights of Arlington the domes of Washington. He believed that the surest way to cause the North to abandon the attempt to impose union by force of arms would be to seize the seat of the Federal Government, or at least to isolate it from the rest of the Union. So while defending Richmond he had always an eye upon Washington.

Military critics are agreed that Napoleon's mastery of the art of war was never more completely displayed than in his first great campaign in Italy. Lee's campaigns of 1862 are also supreme in conception, and have not been surpassed, as examples of strategy, by any other achievement of their kind or by any other commander in history. Both men had, when they were called to positions of responsibility, a complete grasp of the fundamental principles of war. There are in war few comparisons more striking than that between the inaction of the Southern forces after the first battle of Manassas and Lee's energy, promptness, decision and boldness in action after the second battle at the same place. True, as I have shown, Davis must take his share of blame for the loss of opportunity in 1861, but in 1862 the President was the same, it was the soldier who was different. One is forced to the conclusion that his absence from Davis's side at this time was fraught with consequences. The evidence is clear that the hastily formed levies of the Confederacy at Manassas were almost as disorganized by victory as were the Federal troops by defeat, and Davis had made out for himself a good answer to the charge that he was responsible for stopping an immediate pursuit. But when order had been restored and the unreadiness of the Union was revealed, it is hard to believe that Lee, if he had been given the chance, would not have galvanized the leaders of the Confederacy into action before the winter set in. The troops flushed with victory needed no spur.

The third period of the war, reckoned from the point of view of a consideration of Lee's strategical methods, dates from the failure at Gettysburg. After that battle Lee saw that the growing power of the North and the increasing determination of its people made it impossible to force them to abandon the struggle by an offensive campaign in the border States, even if that campaign were successful. Henceforth the policy for the South was to endeavour to convince the North that the subjugation of the Confederacy was either a task beyond their means or one which would bring them more loss than gain. Lee's procedure was then, not as in the second period to seek to force a decision by boldness and enterprise, but to avoid decision and to cause delay. The Campaign of the Wilderness, of Spottsylvania, and the North Anna is a classical example in military history of how these objects should be sought. In method it was fifty years ahead of the times, and I believe that if the Allies in August, 1914, had applied Lee's tactical methods to the situation which then confronted them the course of the World War would have been changed.

5

The immediate and imminent problem confronting the Confederate military authorities in the spring of 1862 was the defense of the Confederate capital itself. "On to Richmond" was the war cry in the North, and it was no secret that with the coming of favorable weather a powerful thrust would be made against that city. Throughout the winter months the armies of Joe Johnston and McClellan (who had succeeded McDowell after First Manassas) faced each other in the neighborhood of Centreville in a long-drawn-out exhibition of masterly inactivity. But in March the Federal forces began to stir, and there were signs that the contemplated avenue of attack was by way of the Peninsula. President Jefferson Davis tells of the plans made to defend against this movement.

As soon as we ascertained that the enemy was concentrating his forces at Fortress Monroe, to advance upon our capital by that line of approach, all our disposable force was ordered to the Peninsula, between the James and York Rivers, to the support of General John B. Magruder, who, with a force of seven to eight thousand men, had, by availing himself of the Warwick River . . . constructed an intrenched line across the Peninsula, and with equal skill and intrepidity had thus far successfully checked every attempt to break it, though the enemy was vastly superior in numbers to the troops under General Magruder's command. . . .

As a second line of defense, a system of detached works had been constructed by General Magruder near to Williamsburg, where the width of the Peninsula available for the passage of troops was only three or four miles. The advantage thus secured to his forces, if they should be compelled to retreat, will be readily appreciated. . . .

Such was the condition of the Virginia Peninsula between the York and James Rivers when General McClellan embarked the mass of the army he commanded in northern Virginia and proceeded to Fortress Monroe; and when the greater part of our army, under the command of General J. E. Johnston, was directed to move for the purpose of counteracting this new plan of the enemy. . . .

As soon as it was definitely ascertained that General McClellan, with his main army, was on the Peninsula, General J. E. Johnston was assigned to the command of the Department of the Peninsula and Norfolk, and directed to proceed thither to examine the condition of affairs there. . . .

6

Joe Johnston was given his new assignment in the course of a conference with President Davis and Lee in Richmond to which he had been summoned. In his *Diary* J. B. Jones (the "Rebel war clerk") makes a touching reference to the scene as Johnston left the conference for his new command: "The President took an affectionate leave of him; and General Lee held his hand a long time, and admonished him to take care of his life." General Johnston here takes up the narrative of events.

I went to the Peninsula as soon as possible, reaching General Magruder's headquarters early in the morning; and passed the day in examining his works and in obtaining all the pertinent information General Magruder could give. That officer had estimated the importance of at least delaying the invaders until an army capable of coping with them could be formed; and he opposed them with about a tenth of their number on a line of which Yorktown, intrenched, made the left flank. This boldness imposed upon the Federal general, and made him halt to besiege instead of assailing the Confederate position. This resolute and judicious course on the part of General Magruder was of incalculable value. It saved Richmond, and gave the Confederate government time to swell that officer's handful of an army.

Before nightfall I was convinced that we could do no more on the Peninsula than delay General McClellan's progress toward Richmond. I thought it of great importance that a different plan of operations should be adopted without delay; and, leaving General Magruder's headquarters at nightfall, I hastened back to Richmond to suggest such a one, and arrived next morning early enough to see the President in his office as soon as he entered it. After describing to him Magruder's position and the character of his defensive arrangements, I endeavored to show that, although they were the most judicious that that officer could have adopted when he devised them, they would not enable us to defeat McClellan. Instead of only delaying the Federal army in its approach, I proposed that it should be encountered in front of Richmond by one quite as numerous, formed by uniting there all the available forces of the Confederacy. . . . The great army thus formed, surprising that of the United States by an attack when it was expecting to besiege Richmond, would be almost certain to win; and the enemy, defeated a hundred miles from Fort Monroe, their place of refuge, could scarcely escape destruction.

The President, who had heard me with apparent interest, replied that the question was so important that he would hear it fully discussed before making his decision, and desired me to meet General Randolph (Secretary of War) and General Lee in his office at an appointed time for the purpose. At my suggestion he authorized me to invite Major Generals Smith and Longstreet to the conference. I was confident of the support of the former, for we had discussed the general question and agreed that the Confederate government ought to meet McClellan's invasion with all its available forces.

The conference began more than an hour before noon by my

describing General Magruder's defensive arrangements. Major General Smith was then asked to give his opinion, and suggested the course we had agreed upon. . . . General Randolph, who had been a naval officer, objected to the plan proposed because it included at least the temporary abandonment of Norfolk, which would involve the probable loss of the materials for many vessels-of-war contained in the navy yard there. General Lee opposed it because he thought that the withdrawal from South Carolina and Georgia of any considerable number of troops would expose the important seaports of Charleston and Savannah to the danger of capture. He thought too that the Peninsula had excellent fields of battle for a small army contending with a great one, and that we should for that reason make the contest with McClellan's army there. General Longstreet took little part, which I attributed to his deafness. . . .

At six o'clock the conference was adjourned by the President, to meet in his house at seven. The discussion was continued there, although languidly, until 1 A.M., when it ceased; and the President, who previously had expressed no opinion on the question, announced his decision in favor of General Lee's opinion, and directed that Smith's and Longstreet's divisions should join the Army of the Peninsula and ordered me to go there and take command. . . . The belief that events on the Peninsula would soon compel the Confederate Government to adopt my method of opposing the Federal army reconciled me somewhat to the necessity of obeying the President's order.

7

So Joe Johnston rode off to his new command, nursing the expectation—almost the hope, it seems—of being able later to say "I told you so!" to Davis and Lee. President Davis has left his own record of the conference and of subsequent events on the Peninsula.

Though General Johnston did not agree with this decision, he did not ask to be relieved, and I did not wish to separate him from the troops with whom he was so intimately acquainted, and whose confidence I believed he deservedly possessed. . . .

About the middle of April a further reënforcement of two divisions from the Army of Northern Virginia was added to our forces on the Peninsula, which amounted, when General Johnston assumed command, to something over fifty thousand.

The work of strengthening the defenses was still continued. On the 16th of April an assault was made on our line, to the right of Yorktown, which was repulsed with heavy loss to the enemy, and such serious discomfiture that henceforward his plan seemed to be to rely upon bombardment, for which numerous batteries were prepared. . . .

By the following telegram sent by me [on May 1] to General Johnston . . . the contents of that which I had received from him . . . will be readily inferred:

"Accepting your conclusion that you must soon retire, arrangements are commenced for the abandonment of the navy-yard and removal of public property both from Norfolk and Peninsula. Your announcement today that you would withdraw to-morrow night takes us by surprise, and must involve enormous losses, including unfinished gunboats. Will the safety of your army allow more time?"

My next step was to request the Secretary of War, General Randolph, and the Secretary of the Navy, Mr. Mallory, to proceed to Yorktown and Norfolk to see whether the evacuation could not be postponed, and to make all practicable arrangements to remove the machinery, material, ordnance and supplies for future use. . . . General Randolph, in his testimony before a joint special committee of the Confederate Congress, said:

"A few hours after we arrived in Norfolk, an officer from General Johnston's army made his appearance, with an order to General Huger to evacuate Norfolk immediately. . . . As that would have involved heavy losses in stores, munitions and arms, I took the responsibility of giving General Huger a written order to delay the evacuation until he could remove such stores, munitions and arms as could be carried off. . . . Mr. Mallory . . . gave similar instructions to the commandant of the navy-yard. . . . The evacuation was delayed for about a week. . . ."

8

Despite the delay, the Confederate losses in equipment and materiel incident to the evacuation of Norfolk were enormous. Among other things, the surrender of the navy yard made necessary the destruction of the famous ironclad *Virginia*. All of the heavy guns had to be left behind in the fortifications around Norfolk; also, "a very large number of picks and spades, many of them entirely new," which were to be sorely needed in the construction of the defenses of Richmond, were abandoned.

At Williamsburg Johnston fought a rear-guard action with McClellan's pursuing forces, the engagement taking on the proportions of a minor battle. Johnston tells of his movements following the fighting at Williamsburg.

The day after the action . . . the army was concentrated near Barhamsville. The army remained five days in this position, in line facing to the east, Longstreet's right covering the Long Bridges and Magruder's left the York River Railroad; it was easily and regularly supplied by the railroad and could no longer be turned by water.

Intelligence of the destruction of the ironclad *Virginia* was received on the 14th. I had predicted that its gallant commander, Commodore Tatnall, would never permit the vessel to fall into the hands of the enemy. The possession of James River by the naval forces of the United States consequent upon this event, and their attack upon the Confederate battery at Drewry's Bluff, suggested the necessity of being ready to meet an advance upon Richmond up the river, as well as from the direction of West Point. The Confederate forces were in consequence ordered to cross the Chickahominy on the 15th. On the 17th the army encamped about three miles from Richmond in front of the line of redoubts constructed in 1861. Hill's division, in the centre, formed across the Williamsburg road; Longstreet's on the right, covering the river road; Magruder's on the left, crossing the Nine Mile road; and Smith's in reserve, behind Hill's left and Magruder's right.

After reaching the Chickahominy, General McClellan's troops

advanced very slowly. Sumner's, Franklin's and Porter's corps were on and above the railroad, and Heintzelman's and Keyes's below it and on the Williamsburg road. The last two, after crossing the stream at Bottom's Bridge on the 22nd, were stationary apparently for several days, constructing a line of entrenchments two miles in advance of the bridge. They then advanced, step by step, forming four lines in advancing. I hoped that their advance would give us an opportunity to make a successful attack upon these two corps by increasing the interval between them and the larger portion of their army remaining beyond the Chickahominy.

9

As Johnston maneuvered his troops, steadily moving backward, there was great apprehension in Richmond, both on the part of the military authorities and the civilian population. An inside view of the official attitude toward Johnston's strategy as the Federal army drew closer and closer to Richmond is provided by a member of the Confederate Cabinet, John H. Reagan, of Texas.

Slowly our troops fell back and the Federals advanced, until it became a concern of the Government where the gage of battle would be accepted. When General Johnston reached the vicinity of the Chickahominy, on the high ground bordering the river swamp, he formed his line to give battle, and sent a dispatch to President Davis advising him of the fact. The Cabinet was in session when the dispatch was received; and the members suggested to the President the manifest danger of General Johnston's offering battle to a superior force with his rear on such a stream as that of the Chickahominy, where the swamp was wide with no road or bridges sufficient to enable him to retreat if he should be defeated. A further question was raised as to whether the President should not call General Johnston's attention to this. Mr. Davis declined to do so, saying that when we entrusted a command to a general we must expect him, with all the facts before him, to know what is best to be done; that it would not be safe to undertake to control military operations by advice from the capital.

This I know to have been his policy throughout the war, adverse critics to the contrary notwithstanding.

The next morning, instead of receiving the report of a battle, the President received a dispatch from General Johnston saying that he was retiring across the Chickahominy and would contest the crossing of that stream with McClellan. There was in the Cabinet an expression of relief when his dispatch was read. The Chickahominy was crossed some twenty-five miles from Richmond.

The day after this crossing was made, I rode down to our lines and camped that night with Hood's brigade and the next day marched with it to where we went into camp, a little below Rockets, a suburb of Richmond. About the hour of noon, as I was returning to my residence, in passing the Executive Office I saw the President coming out. He hailed me and requested that when I had got my dinner I should come and go with him down to the Chickahominy to see General Johnston. As I rode off I said to him that he would not have to go to the Chickahominy to see the General. From what occurred afterward it was apparent that he had not caught my words.

After dinner we rode out through Rockets, and on reaching the high ground the President asked me what those tents were, indicating an encampment a half mile or so from us. I told him they were the tents of Hood's brigade.

"No!" he exclaimed; "Hood's brigade is down on the Chickahominy."

I replied that I had camped with it the night before and had come there with it. Riding on a little further I remarked, "If you want to see General Johnston, he is in the brick house off to our right."

Again he objected, not seeming to be able to realize the situation: "No, General Johnston is down on the Chickahominy." To which I answered that I had seen him and his staff go to that house that day. The look of surprise which swept over his face showed a trace of pain.

Mr. Davis and one of his staff officers (I believe it was Colonel Ives) turned off to the General's headquarters, and I rode on to Hood's camp. The President never told me what occurred between him and General Johnston, but his staff officer did. He said the President inquired of the General why he was in the suburbs of Richmond and had not contested the crossing of the Chickahominy with General McClellan. General Johnston's answer was that the army was out of provisions, that the ground near the Chickahominy was low and marshy and the water bad; and that he had brought the army near Richmond where the ground was dry, the water good, and to be that much nearer needed supplies. The President inquired if Richmond was to be given up without a battle; and, not getting a satisfactory reply as to whether it would or not, said to General Johnston that if he was not going to give battle he would appoint some one to the command who would. This will throw light on what subsequently occurred between them.

The President's anxiety was known to the Cabinet. He invited General Robert E. Lee, who was then acting in the capacity of military adviser or consulting-general to the President, to meet with the Cabinet, and when we were convened Mr. Davis announced his solicitude and requested General Lee's opinion as to the next best line of defense, if Richmond should be abandoned. General Lee, after discussing the question as a military engineer, stated that the next best line of defense would be at Staten River. "But," he added, "Richmond must not be given up—it shall not be given up." As he spoke the tears ran down his cheeks. I have seen him on many occasions and at times when the very fate of the Confederacy hung in the balance; but I never saw him show equally deep emotion.

10

Johnston finally had his army where he wanted it—on the outskirts of Richmond where, in his opinion, he could best give battle to his adversary. McClellan had been advancing slowly and in considerable uncertainty. When he took his army to the Peninsula it was with the distinct understanding that McDowell's army, left behind to guard Washington, would be sent to join McClellan's right flank before Richmond. Stonewall Jackson's activities in the Valley, however, made the Washington authorities reluctant to send McDowell so far away from the capital. McClellan at length realized that he would have to wage his attack on Richmond without Mc-Dowell's help, and proceeded accordingly. General E. M. Law, who took part in the fighting around Richmond, tells of the first clashes in the series of engagements there in the summer of 1862.

It was not until the 24th of May that McClellan's army was in position along the east bank of the Chickahominy and the struggle for Richmond itself began.

The Federal army, holding the line of the Chickahominy from Mechanicsville to Bottom's Bridge, at once commenced the construction of military bridges between those points, and before the end of May McClellan's left wing was advanced by throwing the two corps of Heintzelman and Keyes across the river. The latter took position and entrenched on a line running in front of Seven Pines on the Williamsburg Road, with its right extending across the York River Railroad in front of Fair Oaks station. Heintzelman was placed in supporting distance in the rear near Savage's Station.

McClellan's outposts were now within five miles of Richmond—almost near enough to realize President Lincoln's suggestion, when he inquired by telegraph on May 26th, "Can you get near enough to throw shells into the city?" This amiable desire was not destined to be gratified, for during the afternoon and night of the 30th of May a heavy rain-storm occurred, flooding the low grounds of the Chickahominy and threatening the destruction of the military bridges constructed by the Federal army.

The two wings were to a certain extent isolated, and General Johnston took advantage of this condition of affairs to attack Keyes' corps near Seven Pines on the 31st of May. This corps was assailed by D. H. Hill's division and thoroughly routed. Heintzelman came to its support, but by this time the divisions of Longstreet and G. W. Smith had united in the attack with D. H. Hill, and this corps fared little better than that of Keyes. By the most strenuous exertions, Sumner's Federal corps was thrown across the almost ruined bridges during the afternoon and night of the 31st, and this timely reinforcement, together with the intervention of night, saved the left wing of McClellan's army from destruction.

The tardy movements of some of the Confederate commanders on the extreme right delayed the attack several hours beyond the time when it should have been made, and this delay was fatal to the complete success of General Johnston's plans. While G. W. Smith's division, to which I was attached, was warmly engaged near the junction of the Nine Mile Road and the York River Railroad, General Johnston rode up and gave me an order as to the movements of my command. Night was rapidly approaching and he seemed anxious to urge forward the attack with all possible speed so as to clear the field of the enemy before night. He was moving with the troops and personally directing the advance when he received a severe wound in the shoulder and was compelled to relinquish the command. The Confederates had been checked on their left wing by the arrival of Sumner's corps, and the fighting ceased just after dark. It was renewed on our right wing on the morning of the 1st of June, without advantage to either side, and by 2 o'clock P.M. the battle was over, without having accomplished the purpose for which it was fought.

General G. W. Smith, an officer of acknowledged ability, succeeded General Johnston in command of the Confederate army on the night of the 31st of May. But during the afternoon of the next day, June 1st, he in turn relinquished the command to General Lee, under orders from President Davis. Our right wing was at once withdrawn from its advanced position, and Smith's division on the left followed the next day.

As I was standing near the Nine Mile Road a day or two after the battle, General Lee passed along the road, accompanied by two staff officers. I had never seen him before, and he was pointed out by some one near me. I observed the new commander of the Army of Northern Virginia very closely and with a great deal of interest. General Johnston was universally beloved and possessed the unbounded confidence of the army, and the commander who succeeded him must be every inch a man and a soldier to fill his place in their confidence and affection. General Lee had up to this time accomplished nothing to warrant the belief in his future greatness as a commander. He had made an unsuccessful campaign in western Virginia the year before, and since that time had been on duty first at Charleston and then in Richmond. There was naturally a great deal of speculation among the soldiers as to how he would "pan out." The general tone, however, was one of confidence, which was invariably strengthened by a sight of the man himself.

Calm, dignified and commanding in his bearing, a countenance strikingly benevolent and self-possessed; a clear, honest eye that could look friend or enemy in the face; clean-shaven, except for a closely-trimmed mustache which gave a touch of firmness to the well-shaped mouth; simply and neatly dressed in the uniform of his rank, felt hat and top boots reaching to the knee; sitting his horse as if his home was in the saddle—such was Robert E. Lee as he appeared when he assumed command of the Army of Northern Virginia in the early days of June, 1862, never to relinquish it for a day until its colors were furled forever at Appomattox.

11

A close-up view of some of the action at Seven Pines is provided by Secretary Reagan. Reagan, an enthusiastic Texan, had promised the men of Hood's Texas Brigade that if they got into a battle near Richmond he would try to be with them. Accordingly, on the morning of the day of the battle, May 31st, he rode from Richmond to the battle front with President Davis.

We found General Lee with General Magruder at the headquarters of the latter. I left them and rode on with General Hatton until we overtook his brigade and, leaving the General, passed on to where General G. W. Smith was putting the Confederate brigades into battle as they came up. . . . In going to the front, I met General Randolph, the Secretary of War, who on learning my purpose to join the Texas men advised, "You had better go back with me; Yankee bullets have no respect for Postmaster-Generals."

On reaching General Smith I inquired of him where I would find Hood's brigade. He said he could not tell me, but that if I would take the right-hand road of the three that branched off there and kept a lookout to the right I might possibly find it in half a mile or so. I rode on to the field at Fair Oaks House, and saw some men across the railroad at the far side of the field. It was cloudy, and that, together with the smoke of the field, kept me from knowing who they were until I got near them. When I reached them they raised a shout, and that seemed to have invited the opening of the enemy's artillery on them. The firing was quite rapid. About one half of the brigade was there, but on account of the boggy condition of the ground the field officers and the remainder of the brigade had not been able to reach that place and there were no officers present above the rank of captain. They requested me to lead them in a charge. In the absence of all information and authority as to what should be done, I thought it best not to risk such a step.

The men lay down and were being furiously shelled when I saw some persons ride up to Fair Oaks House, nearly midway between where we were and the Federal batteries. Through the smoke I thought it to be General Johnston and his staff, and galloped to where they were. General Johnston was in the house. I did not dismount and did not see him, but the Hon. Muscoe Garnett . . . and Major J. D. Banks, two members of his staff, were in the yard and I somewhat emphatically expressed my surprise that the commander of an army in a great battle should put himself in a position where he could not live long, saying that his example would encourage no one, as the officers and men could not know where he was. This statement was taken to him, and I was advised by the officer who took it that his only answer was that this was no time to look for safe places. . . .

I passed across the field into the woods beyond it, and there found President Davis and Generals Lee and Magruder under a fire of small arms. I protested against the President's unnecessary exposure and said to them that I had just left General Johnston where he was in great danger, exposed as he was to the enemy's fire. A few minutes later a courier came from our left and announced that General Hampton had been wounded; and at nearly the same time another announced that General Johnston had been killed; and after a short interval he was brought past us on a stretcher, apparently in a lifeless condition.

President Davis at once gave General Lee verbal direction to take command of the army and to issue the necessary orders. The archives of the War Department show that he was appointed to the command three days later, but he assumed control of the field during the battle, as indicated.

12

The battle of Manassas had given the people of Richmond their first intimation of the actualities of war; but the fighting at Seven Pines had brought the conflict to their doorstep. As the artillery boomed and the musketry crackled in the very suburbs of the city, and as the pathetic tide of wounded began to trickle into the city from the bloody field of Seven Pines, Richmond came to know war at ghastly first hand. An English soldier in the Confederate ranks gives his impression of the local scene.

Although the number of our wounded was not considerable, the Government endeavoured to provide comfortably for them; and for this purpose stores and warehouses in various parts of the city were fitted up and surgeons, public and private, detailed to superintend them. There were several "committees for the wounded" in operation among the better class of citizens, and everything that private means could do was devoted to the needy. From sunrise until sunset the bedsides of our poor fellows were never deserted by kind friends, and I have known frequent instances where ladies attended, night after night, for weeks, fanning, washing and feeding them, reading or writing for them, etc., so that the poor boys were oftentimes even bored by their many attentions and unceasing care. Scores were taken from military hospitals into private families and tended for months, free of charge, and treated more affectionately than they might have been even at home. First-class surgeons gave their advice and attention gratuitously, and I know several medical men of standing who neglected lucrative practice to assist our men. Some took them home and cared for them there; others instituted private hospitals for their proper treatment; and I remember instances where individuals have been comfortably provided with homes and proper scientific treatment for many months, not being allowed to depart until fully recovered from wounds or ailments. Frequently, during the battle of Seven Pines, I saw hundreds of citizens drive their vehicles near the battle-grounds and convey away the wounded; to see a muddy, ragged, bandaged soldier lolling in a fine silk-trimmed carriage was no uncommon sight.

In fact, so great was the anxiety of citizens to carry off the wounded, that one of their omnibuses, approaching too near the enemy's lines on Sunday morning, was captured by an ambuscading party and carried off in great triumph as a rebel trophy. The omnibus was but one of many furnished by hotels for this humane purpose, and several were capsized in the mud and rendered useless for all future service.

The poor wounded soldiers seemed perfectly contented with their treatment and lay in bed smoking cigars or drinking brandy toddy, as happy as lords. In fact, many of them rather liked the change and would not exchange their honourable scars for any amount, cigars, brandy, fine food and raiment were such a contrast to rags, constant duty, hard fare and incessant marching.

Some soldiers who came out of camp to visit these invalids would look round with almost a jealous eye upon the many comforts provided for them. Ragged, sunburnt and ill-fed as they were, many could but jocularly smile and good-humoredly wish some friendly bullet had thrown *them* into such comfortable quarters. When the wounded in turn visited their comrades in camp, their appearance was so much improved, they looked so bright and cheerful and had so many stories to tell about pleasures and pastimes, that our doctors caught many feigning sickness in order to be sent to hospitals in town.

The theatres were a great source of temptation, and as convalescents were permitted to attend them with properly signed passes, these places were nightly crowded with military audiences, scores having arms in slings or bandaged heads. Such pieces, such music, such yelling and laughter were never heard before. The poor Germans in the orchestra were tired to death with repeats of "Dixie," "My Maryland" and the "Marseillaise"—tunes which the audience accompanied with vocal efforts of their own or embellished with a running accompaniment of stamps and howling.

"Blood and thunder" productions were greatly in vogue, and those pieces wherein most of the characters were killed rose decidedly in the ascendant. "A tip-top fight" was what the boys delighted in, and an unlucky hero would never fall without an accompanying yell of "Bring on your ambulance!" Had these men had free access to liquor, its effect would have been disastrous; but this was successfully prohibited, thanks to the vigilance of the provost-marshal, General Winder.

The greatest amount of affection seemed to be lavished upon privates; officers for the most part were treated coldly by the masses and allowed to shift for themselves as best they could, for it was considered far more honourable to carry a musket than to loiter around Richmond in expensive gold-corded caps and coats.

Volumes might be written upon the great kindness shown to our troops by the ladies of Virginia. Although the women of Winchester, Leesburg, Charlottesville and other places did much for the common cause, their noble-hearted and open-handed sisters of Richmond far surpassed them all. Nothing that human nature could do was left undone; and although much of this kindness and care was thrown away upon rude, uncouth objects, their humanity, patience and unceasing solicitude are beyond all praise. . . .

The field hospitals presented an awful sight. I entered one, but never desire to see another. It was an old dilapidated house, with scarcely anything standing except the brick chimney. The sufferers lay inside and outside on straw, but such was the flow of blood that all their garments, bedding, straw and everything around was of a bright red colour. In one corner I saw a large pile of arms and legs; many already dead were lying on the grass with blankets thrown over them, while not far distant in the woods a party was engaged in digging long trenches for sepulture. These things were passing under the eyes of all, and those just brought in from the field were spectators of operations going on, hearing moans and groans constantly. Sickening as such sights were, our men bore up under it wonderfully well, and did not wince at all when called upon to take their place upon the unhinged door which served as an operating table.

Yet how could all this be otherwise? Such is the reality of war, and those who paint it in glowing colours, with all the pomp and circumstance of triumph, should never fail to add a few words of truth against encouraging the sacrifice of life for the sake of ambition and unsubstantiated causes. Had it not been for the great love evinced for us by the good people of Richmond, hundreds of wounded would never have answered roll-call again; and but for their paternal care, coupled with the extraordinary exertions of Government, the increasing warm weather would have added greatly to our bills of mortality.

13

While occupied with the pressing problem of defending Richmond against the approaching forces, General Lee had the war brought home to him in a closely personal manner. His youngest son and namesake, Robert, was a student at the University of Virginia when the war began in 1861 and, like his elder brothers, was eager to join the Confederate Army. He was then dissuaded by his father, with the assurance that the war would last long enough for him to take part in it after he had completed his schooling. But a year of inactivity was all that the young enthusiast could stand, and he tells of his enlistment—in the ranks—in the famous Rockbridge Artillery.

But in the spring of '62 he allowed me to volunteer, and I having selected the company I wished to join, the Rockbridge Artillery, he gave his approval, and wrote me to come to Richmond, where he would give me my outfit. He was just as sweet and loving to me then as in the old days. I had seen so little of him during the last six years that I stood somewhat in awe of him. I soon found, however, that I had no cause for such a feeling. He took great pains in getting what was necessary for me.

He writes to my mother [March 15, 1862]:

". . . On returning to my quarters last night after 11 P.M. Custis informed me Robert had arrived and had made up his mind to go into the army. He stayed at the Spottswood, and this morning I went with him to get his overcoat, blankets, etc. There is great difficulty in procuring what is good. They all have to be made, and he has gone to the office of the adjutant-general of Virginia to engage in the service. God grant it may be for his good as He has permitted it. I must be resigned. I told him of the exemption granted by the Secretary of War to the professors and students of the university, but he expressed no desire to take advantage of it. It would be useless for him to go, if he did not improve himself, nor would I wish him to go merely for exemption. As I have done all in the matter that seems proper and right, I must now leave the rest in the hands of our merciful God. I hope our son will do his duty and make a good soldier."

The baggage of a private in a Confederate battery was not extensive. How little was needed my father, even at that time, did not know, for though he was very careful in providing me with the least amount he thought necessary, I soon found by experience that he had given me a great deal too much. It was characteristic of his consideration for others and the unselfishness of his nature, that at this time, when weighed down, harassed and burdened by the cares incident to bringing the untrained forces of the Confederacy into the field, and preparing them for a struggle the seriousness of which he knew better than any one, he should give his time and attention to the minute details of fitting out his youngest son as a private soldier.

I think it worthy of note that the son of the commanding general enlisting as a private in his army was not thought to be anything remarkable or unusual. Neither my mother, my family, my friends nor myself expected any other course, and I do not suppose it ever occurred to my father to think of giving me an office, which he could easily have done. I know it never occurred to me, nor did I ever hear, at that time or afterwards, from anyone, that I might have been entitled to better rank than that of a private because of my father's prominence in Virginia and in the Confederacy.

9

Active Command—Richmond Relieved

MUCH as Lee may have thirsted for active service in the field, he would have been the last to desire to achieve such advancement through the misfortune of another—least of all through the wounding of his old friend Joe Johnston, whom he had affectionately admonished so recently to take care of himself. But, no matter how it came to him, the command of the army was now in his hands. He was no longer a desk general. He must take charge personally of the movements of the Confederate troops now clinging precariously to the outskirts of Richmond and trying to hold at arm's length the enveloping forces of McClellan. The engagement at Seven Pines had been little better than a drawn battle. The Federals had been checked, but there was no reason to expect them to do anything other than tighten their pressure on the city's defenses. It was now Lee's duty to evolve some plan for loosening that pressure—and not merely to make plans, but put them into effect, shoulder personally the responsibility for success or failure. Already he had weakened McClellan and disrupted his plans by suggesting the movements of Stonewall Jackson which held McDowell in defense of Washington. But McClellan's Army of the Potomac still greatly outnumbered Richmond's defending forces. The test of Robert E. Lee's skill as a strategist and tactician was at hand, with the fate of the Confederate capital depending on the outcome.

1

It would be hard to imagine more unpropitious circumstances than those in which Lee took command of the forces defending Richmond from the encircling movement of McClellan's large and well-equipped army. Colonel Marshall impressively sums up these discouraging conditions.

The Southern people were greatly depressed, and their reverses had inspired painful doubts of their ability to cope with their powerful adversary. One after another, the hopes of succour upon which they had relied had been disappointed, and the conviction that they could depend upon them vanished at a moment when they seemed to have reached the crisis of their fate. All eyes were turned to the impending struggle for the possession of Richmond. The army engaged in its defence was inferior in numbers to that of the enemy and imperfectly supplied with arms and equipment. It had been retreating almost continuously since it left Centreville and had now reached a point beyond which it could not retire without the loss of the Confederate capital and the sacrifice of those vital interests which depended upon its possession. It had just undergone a change of officers, and its ranks were filled with raw and inexperienced recruits. Weak in everything but the spirit, intelligence and patriotism of the men who composed it, it was made weaker by the infirmities of its own organisation. At a time when it most needed all that confidence in its commander could impart, a leader who possessed and deserved that confidence had been stricken down.

It was at this extreme moment, when the exultant North was eagerly and confidently expecting the reward of its great efforts, and the despondent South regarded its cause as almost lost, that a man as yet comparatively unknown caught the standard as it fell from the stricken hand that had carried it so bravely, and bore it resolutely to the front. But it was not only the unpromising condition of affairs or the imminence of the public danger that rendered the position of General Lee difficult and embarrassing. He did not shrink from the grave responsibilities and arduous labours which he knew must be encountered to relieve his country from its danger, but to enable him to perform the task with hope of success he greatly needed the confidence of the people and of the army. It cannot be denied that when he first took command at Richmond he had yet to acquire both.

General Lee had submitted to the unjust judgment of his countrymen without repining. Aware of his ability to direct the greatest affairs, longing to share in the exciting events taking place
around him, he never asked for service of his own choice, but was
content to perform with all his energies such duties as were assigned to him. His only desire was that the work should be done,
he cared not by whom; and in this spirit he endured without a
murmur enforced obscurity and unmerited condemnation, and
felt an unselfish pride in the exploits of his more fortunate
brethren in arms. He pursued the path of duty with equal and
unfaltering steps through the unseen labours of the office and
through commands sterile of opportunities for distinction.

Now that path led him to the foremost place in the eyes of his
country. His patient waiting at last had its reward; the bloody
drama had reached a stage worthy of his intervention; and in the
midst of universal despondency, oppressed by the consciousness
that he did not possess the confidence of the people or of the army,
he entered modestly and humbly, but with unshaken resolution,
upon the performance of his arduous task.

2

As Colonel Marshall suggests, at the time Lee took over the
command of the army from the wounded Johnston, there was
by no means universal satisfaction with the change in commanders. Critics did not hesitate to compare the supposed
abilities of Lee and Johnston, to the disparagement of Lee.
General Maurice gives the judgment of a modern military
critic of recognized competence.

J. E. Johnston, who may be taken as the type of the good ordinary general, saw no alternative to assembling the largest possible number of Confederate troops around Richmond, and there
hazarding all upon the issue of a battle with McClellan. On May
10th he had written to Lee: "If the President will direct the concentration of all the troops of North Carolina and Eastern Virgina,
we may be able to hold Middle Virginia at least. If we permit
ourselves to be driven beyond Richmond, we lose the means of

maintaining this army. A concentration of all our available forces may enable us to fight successfully. Let us try."

Johnston was so completely convinced that this was the only possible course that he unwittingly interfered with Lee's plans. The limits of Johnston's command do not seem to have been precisely defined, and he assumed that he controlled certain detachments which he had left behind when his army moved to Richmond and reënforcements which were on the way to him. Lee not only proposed to unite Ewell and Jackson for the attack upon Banks, but to strengthen Jackson by two brigades which were coming up from North Carolina. Johnston sent orders to Ewell to move eastwards nearer to Richmond and ordered the reënforcements to himself. Jackson at once telegraphed to Lee for instructions, the President supported Lee and the confusion was put right. Johnston had, indeed, first approved of the movement against Banks, but in the middle of May the situation around Richmond appeared to him to be too desperate to allow of so hazardous an enterprise. He was a fine soldier, his men were devoted to him; it was on his representation that Davis agreed to leave Jackson in the Valley for the purpose of keeping the Federal forces in and west of it away from Richmond, at the time when the news of McClellan's move to the Peninsula first became known; as a commander on the battlefield he was possibly Lee's equal, but he lacked that wider vision, that power to look calmly beyond the dangers and perils of his immediate front to the situation in the whole theatre of war, that power, in short, which takes Lee out of the ranks of the good ordinary and places him in the select band of the supreme generals.

The attitude and conduct of the two men in those critical days of May, 1862, seem to me to place beyond question Lee's superiority as a commander over Johnston. I am therefore surprised to find that Ropes, for whom, as an historian, I have the very greatest respect, after admitting that Lee possessed a combination of qualities, physical, mental and moral, which marked him out among the leaders in the Civil War, says of him: "In intellect it may be doubted whether he was superior to the able soldier whom he succeeded; indeed, Joseph E. Johnston possessed as good a military mind as any leader on either side." When McClellan was hammering at the gates of Richmond, Lee saw that the way to save the town was to make McDowell defend Washington; Johnston looked only to the prospect of a battle with McClellan. There we have a measure of the intellect of the two men.

3

The long-range strategy and plans formulated by Lee upon succeeding to the command of the Confederate Army before Richmond are effectively summarized and elucidated by Colonel Marshall, who was at his chief's side in a confidential capacity during those epochal days and was in position to know better than perhaps anybody else what thoughts were coursing through the commander's mind.

To arrive at a correct understanding of the events which marked the history of the three years during which General Lee held command, it is necessary to consider them in relation to the policy of defence which he devised. The battles and strategic movements which attracted so much attention were not separate and distinct events, entirely independent one of the other, but formed parts of one plan of warfare, adopted by General Lee at the time he took command of the army and steadily pursued until his means were exhausted.

It is neither just to him nor consonant with the truth to measure his success by the issue of each engagement, or to judge of his skill by the consequence of each movement. The war in Virginia, with all its chances and changes, was in fact all one campaign. The battles on the Chickahominy and at Manassas, the invasion of Maryland, and the invasion of Pennsylvania, all had a common object. They were results of a plan of defence based upon a survey of all the circumstances, a plan deemed by General Lee to be the best adapted to meet the necessities of this country and to secure final success. The necessities of the country required that General Lee's measures should be adapted to its capacity to sustain a war of such magnitude, and that they should neutralize the enemy's great superiority. The population of the South available for military service was less than one-fifth of that of the United

States. . . . The North could readily raise new armies, while the means of the South were so limited that a few bloody victories might leave it powerless to continue the struggle. . . . For this reason the plan of compelling the enemy to grant peace by a campaign of conquest was impracticable. . . .

On the other hand, it was equally imprudent to remain entirely on the defensive, and await the attack of the enemy. Such a policy would reduce the contest to a mere trial of strength and resources, and the issue of such a trial could be easily foreseen. . . . Nor did the policy of retreating before the enemy and drawing him further into the interior of the country promise greater advantages. . . .

In these circumstances there was but one course left for General Lee to pursue, if he would save Richmond from the peril which he knew would attend its investment by the large army of the enemy. He must give occupation to that army, and such occupation as would compel the largest concentration of its forces. By this means he might even induce the enemy to withdraw troops from other parts of the Confederacy, and thus obtain additional reinforcements for himself. . . .

The great advantages which the enemy would have in besieging Richmond were so apparent that it was a saying of General Lee that Richmond was never so safe as when its defenders were absent. His meaning was that the safety of Richmond depended upon our ability to employ the enemy at a distance and prevent his near approach to the city. Such was the policy adopted by him, a policy which procured the comparative security of Richmond, from the time the Army of Northern Virginia moved northward in 1862 to the time when, worn out with more than two years' exhausting war, it was forced to retire within the entrenchments of its capital. . . .

As it was the manifest policy of the Federal Government to conclude the war speedily, and to feed the growing impatience of the people with successes which would give assurance of such a result, so on the other hand it became the policy of General Lee to disappoint these hopes and encourage the belief that the war would be of indefinite length. The means to accomplish this end were to frustrate the enemy's designs; to break up campaigns undertaken with vast expense and with confident assurance of success;

to impress upon the minds of the Northern people the conviction that they must prepare for a protracted struggle, great sacrifices of life and treasure, with the possibility that all might at last be of no avail; and to accomplish this at the smallest cost to the Confederacy. . . .

It will be seen how the blows struck by General Lee's army upon the northern border of Virginia, and beyond the Potomac, relieved the pressure of the enemy upon the whole Atlantic Coast, paralyzed his efforts in western Virginia, and even diverted troops from the remote regions of the lower Mississippi. But the people could not foresee all the advantages of the successful prosecution of this system of defence, and regarded with dissatisfaction a policy which seemed to expose them to certain and immediate danger. These circumstances added largely to the difficulties and embarrassments of General Lee, but they did not deter him from pursuing steadily and in spite of all opposition the plan by which alone he believed the war might be prosecuted to a successful issue.

4

Lee had fully realized, as Colonel Marshall points out, that the way to save Richmond was to force McDowell to defend Washington instead of joining McClellan, and Lee had effectively pinned McDowell down by the expedient of creating a threat to Washington by demonstrations by Stonewall Jackson in the Shenandoah Valley. Jackson's "Valley Campaign," an essential precedent to Lee's brilliant relief of the siege of Richmond, is one of the outstanding masterpieces of military history, and the details of the campaign are available in many historical works and military textbooks. Fitzhugh Lee gives a brief but comprehensive summary of Stonewall's whirlwind action against the various forces opposing him, a campaign brilliant in itself and a vital factor in the strategy of Lee's defense of Richmond.

After his [Jackson's] return from Romney he was at Winchester, then Woodstock, some forty miles below, then following

Shields from Strasburg, and on March 23rd attacked him at Kerns-
town and was repulsed. Banks, who was on his way from the Valley to Manassas, was ordered back to destroy this bold soldier; and
Blenker, with ten thousand men on his way to Fremont, was instructed to report to him as he followed Jackson up the Valley,
where later the latter took up position at Swift Run Gap in the
Blue Ridge Mountains, the Shenandoah River being in his front,
his flanks protected by the mountain sides, while Ewell was not
far away across the mountains in his rear at Gordonsville.

"Stonewall" did not like to be cooped up in the mountains,
and wrote General Lee at Richmond, asking him to re-enforce him
with five thousand men. . . . On April 29th Lee replied that his
request could not be complied with, but suggested his union with
General Edward Johnson, who had some thirty-five hundred men
near Staunton. Lee was anxious to gain success in the Valley, because it would retard the offensive campaign against Richmond,
and informed Jackson that if he was strong enough to hold Banks
in check, Ewell might, by uniting with Anderson's force between
Fredericksburg and Richmond, attack and possibly destroy Mc-
Dowell, then at Fredericksburg. Banks had some twenty thousand men then at Harrisonburg watching General Edward Johnson, and six thousand men, under Milroy and Schenck, had moved
west of the mountains, and were in front of Johnson, while Fremont was marching with ten thousand men to join them.

Evading Banks at Harrisonburg, Jackson moved to Staunton,
joined his force with Johnson's and defeated Milroy and Schenck;
Ewell marched then from Gordonsville to the Valley and Banks
fell back to Strasburg. Jackson, having disposed of the two Federal commanders, returned with great swiftness, united with
Ewell, defeated the Federal forces at Front Royal, and then pushed
on with great rapidity to attack Banks who, hearing of his approach, fell back to Winchester where he was defeated and followed to the Potomac River.

The defeat of the Federal troops in the Valley and Jackson's
presence on the Potomac produced consternation at the Federal
capital. General McDowell, who had commenced his march from
Fredericksburg to join McClellan, was turned back toward Washington, being directed to send twenty thousand men of his com-

mand at once to the Shenandoah Valley to reinforce Fremont, who had moved down the Valley to get in Jackson's rear and capture him. McClellan wanted McDowell badly and McDowell desired to go to his support, and both generals practically intimated to the Washington authorities that they were scared, that they did not think Washington was in danger of capture by Jackson and that moving a part of McDowell's troops to the Shenandoah Valley would not succeed in destroying Jackson's forces.

Jackson in the mean time, having disposed of Banks, determined to prevent the union of Shields (who had arrived from McDowell's army) with Fremont, and by a series of brilliant manœuvers fought the battles of Cross Keys and Port Republic, holding one commander at arm's length while he hammered the other. By this admirable campaign, in which his great military genius was displayed, McClellan was deprived of the co-operation of McDowell's army, while Jackson contributed largely to the success of the battles around Richmond.

His splendid work in the Valley is summed up by one of his biographers: "In three months he had marched six hundred miles, fought four pitched battles, seven minor engagements, daily skirmishes, defeated four armies, captured seven pieces of artillery, ten thousand stand of arms, four thousand prisoners and a very great amount of stores." His movements produced a panic at the Federal capital.

5

To make immediate plans for the active defense of Richmond, Lee needed exact knowledge of the location of McClellan's army. He was particularly interested in the Federal right wing, north of the Chickahominy, which he suspected was "in the air" and therefore vulnerable to attack. To confirm this suspicion he sent out a scouting party of cavalry under General James Ewell Brown Stuart—the same Stuart who, as a young lieutenant of the First Cavalry, had accompanied him to Harper's Ferry in 1859; the same "Jeb" Stuart who was to make his name synonymous with brilliance in the movements of the cavalry of the Army of Northern Virginia. One of those who rode with Stuart, John Esten Cooke, has left a word picture of the flashing cavalryman.

General James E. B. Stuart, who now made his first prominent appearance upon the theatre of the war, was a Virginian by birth, and not yet thirty years of age. Resigning his commission of lieutenant in the United States Cavalry at the beginning of the war, he had joined Johnston in the Valley and impressed that officer with a high opinion of his abilities as a cavalry officer. . . . In person he was of medium height; his frame was broad and powerful; he wore a heavy brown beard flowing upon his breast, a huge mustache of the same color, the ends curling upward; and the blue eyes, flashing beneath a "piled-up" forehead, had at times the dazzling brilliancy attributed to the eyes of the eagle. Fond of movement, adventure, bright colors, and all the pomp and pageantry of war, Stuart had entered on the struggle with ardor, and enjoyed it as the huntsman enjoys the chase. Young, ardent, ambitious, as brave as steel, ready with jest or laughter, with his banjo-player following him, going into the hottest battles humming a song, this young Virginian was, in truth, an original character, and impressed powerfully all who approached him.

One who knew him well wrote: "Every thing striking, brilliant and picturesque seemed to centre in him. The war seemed to be to Stuart a splendid and exciting game, in which his blood coursed joyously, and his immensely strong physical organization found an arena for the display of all its faculties. The affluent life of the man craved those perils and hardships which flush the pulses and make the heart beat fast. He swung himself into the saddle at the sound of the bugle as the hunter springs on horseback; and at such moments his cheeks glowed and his huge mustache curled with enjoyment. The romance and poetry of the hard trade of arms seemed first to be inaugurated when this joyous cavalier, with his floating plume and splendid laughter, appeared upon the great arena of the war in Virginia."

Precise people shook their heads, and called him frivolous, undervaluing his great ability. Those best capable of judging him were of a different opinion. Johnston wrote to him from the west: "How can I eat or sleep in peace without *you* upon the outpost?"

Jackson said, when he fell at Chancellorsville: "Go back to General Stuart, and tell him to act upon his own judgment, and do what he thinks best. I have implicit confidence in him." Lee said, when he was killed at Yellow Tavern: "I can scarcely think of him without weeping." And the brave General Sedgwick, of the United States Army, said: "Stuart is the best cavalry officer ever *foaled* in North America!"

6

What started out to be a mere scouting trip by Stuart and his troopers developed into an exploit of such spectacular proportions as to gain everlasting fame in military annals. Penetrating so far to the enemy's rear that it seemed unlikely he could return the way he came, Stuart adopted the bold procedure of riding entirely around the opposing army and coming back into Richmond from the opposite side. "Stuart's ride around McClellan" has become almost legendary in the stories of the war. A vivid first-hand account of it is available from Heros von Borcke, the astonishing Prussian soldier, who from sheer love of adventure had made his way to the Confederate States and thrown in his lot with Stuart.

It was two o'clock in the morning [June 12], and we were all fast asleep, when General Stuart's clear voice awoke us with the words, "Gentlemen, in ten minutes every man must be in his saddle!"

In half the time all the members of the Staff were dressed and the horses had been fed; and the ten minutes were scarcely up when we galloped off to overtake the main body, which we reached by about five o'clock. Our command was composed of parts of the different regiments of the brigade, and consisted of about 2500 cavalry, with two pieces of horse-artillery.

None of us knew where we were going; General Stuart only communicated the object of the expedition to the colonels commanding; nevertheless every one followed our honoured leader with perfect confidence. We marched the whole day long without halting, and towards evening bivouacked near the little town of

Taylorsville in Hanover County, where we were already within the enemy's lines. At daybreak we again mounted our horses, and our vanguard was soon reported to have met with a party of the enemy's dragoons, who on their approach had hurried off in hasty flight. Without waiting to pursue them, we continued our march, greeted everywhere with enthusiasm by the inhabitants, especially the ladies, who for a long time had seen none other than Federal troops. . . .

A few miles from Hanover Court-house we surprised a picket of the enemy's cavalry, every man of which fell into our hands from the suddenness of our attack. Whilst we were occupied with sending the prisoners to the rear, our advance-guard came back at a run, hotly pursued by a large body of the enemy's dragoons. Our leading squadron spurred immediately forward to meet the attack, and . . . I joined them as with loud war-cries they hurled themselves against the blue masses of the enemy. The Yankees were not able to withstand the impetuous onset of the Virginia horsemen, and after a melee of a very few minutes, there commenced a most exciting chase, which was continued for nearly three miles. . . . Half an hour later our advance-guard again came in collision with the enemy, who had rallied and, with strong reinforcements, were awaiting us. . . . The enemy's lines were broken and in full flight, leaving many of their dead and wounded, and a large number of prisoners . . . in our hands. . . . The enemy made one more attempt to rally, but their lines were broken by our furious attack; they fled in confusion, and we chased them in wild pursuit across an open field, through their camp, and far into the woods.

When we had returned to their camp, the work of destruction began. Every one tried to rescue for himself as much as possible of the articles of luxury with which the Yankees had overloaded themselves, but few succeeded in the end; for, in accordance with the well-laid plan of our leader, flames flashed up, now in one place, now in another, and in a few minutes the whole camp was enveloped in one blaze, hundreds of tents burning together presenting a beautiful spectacle. . . .

We now found ourselves in the heart of the enemy's position, and their encampments lay around us on all sides. At one point of our journey, the house occupied by the Federal Commander-in-Chief, General McClellan, as his headquarters . . . was plainly visible at the distance of about two and a half miles. Our situation would have been one of extraordinary peril, had not the boldness and rapidity of our movements disabled and paralysed our adversaries.

On either side of the road we constantly seized upon unsuspecting Federal soldiers, who had no idea of the close proximity of the dreaded Stuart until collared by his horsemen. A considerable number of waggons laden with goods and provisions fell into our hands, among them one containing the personal stores of General McClellan, with his cigars, wines and other dainties. But we could not be burdened with booty, so the entire train was committed to the flames, the champagne popped bootlessly, and the cabanas wasted their fragrance on the air. Three transport ships which lay in the river Pamunkey near at hand, laden with wheat, corn and provisions from all quarters, were seized by us, together with the guard and agents stationed there, and ere long the flames mounting towards heaven proclaimed how complete was our work of destruction. . . .

Towards evening we reached the railroad which was so useful to the enemy in giving them communication with the north; and just as the demolition of the road-bed was about to begin, the train was seen coming up. Without delay General Stuart posted a portion of his men on either side of the embankment, with orders to fire if the train refused to stop at the station. The train moved slowly nearer and nearer, puffing off the steam, and we could soon perceive that it was laden with soldiers. . . . As the command to stop was disregarded, but on the contrary the movement of the train was accelerated, firing began along our whole line. The engine-driver was shot down by Captain Farley, to whom I had lent my blunderbuss; but before the deadly bullet reached him he had put the train in somewhat quicker motion, so that we could not make ourselves masters of it.

A battle of the strangest description now arose. Some of the soldiers in the train returned our fire, others sprang out to save themselves by flight, or lay down flat at the bottom of the carriages. The train, though its motion had been quickened, was not going at so rapid a pace that we could not keep up with it by galloping hard. . . . We heard later that few of the occupants of the train had escaped unhurt; the greater part were either killed or severely wounded. . . . After having done as much injury as we could to the railroad, we proceeded on our march, whilst the last beams of the sun lighted up the scene of destruction.

It had been a hard ride and a hard day's work, and my parched tongue was cleaving to the roof of my mouth, when one of our men galloped up to me and held out a bottle of champagne, saying, "Captain, you did pretty hot work to-day. I got this bottle of champagne for you out of McClellan's waggon. It will do you good." Never in my life have I enjoyed a bottle of wine so much. Late in the evening a baggage-train and two sutler's waggons fell into our hands, and we took possession of a large quantity of luxuries, such as pickles, oysters, preserved fruits, oranges, lemons and cigars.

About ten o'clock we had an hour's rest to feed our horses, and then rode on all the night through towards the Chickahominy River, which we reached at five o'clock in the morning. From the reports we had received we expected to find little difficulty in fording the stream, but who can describe our astonishment at finding it so swollen by the rain . . . that the water was more than fifteen feet deep! At the same time our rear-guard announced that a whole division of the enemy was on our track. Every one felt the weight of the danger that threatened us, every one looked with anxiety towards our leader, who, with the greatest possible calmness and coolness, gave his orders and made his arrangements. Two regiments and two pieces of horse-artillery were ordered, in case of an attack, to cover our retreat; whilst all the other available men were dismounted, some of them being employed to build bridges, the others to swim the river with the horses. . . . Towards noon all were in safety on the other bank, General Stuart being the last man to cross the bridge, which we then destroyed. . . . We had still to march the remainder of the day and all the night before we could rest in security. . . . We were in the saddle almost uninterruptedly for two days and two nights, fighting for a considerable part of the time. . . . On the morning of the 15th we arrived safely within our lines, and bivouacked about six miles from Richmond.

7

A summary of Lee's plans for the relief of Richmond, the plans which were to develop into the famous Seven Days' battles, is given by Edmund Lee Childe.

Thanks to the intelligence which Stuart brought back, General Lee saw that the Federal right could be easily turned for, so to speak, it was unguarded. He resolved to profit by this circumstance. His first care, on assuming the command, had been to construct along his lines works of defence sufficiently strong for a part of his army to hold them against all the Federal army, leaving the rest of the Confederate troops free to take the offensive. The time was favourable. Jackson, the conqueror of Shields and Fremont, was in a situation to join his soldiers with the Confederate army under Richmond. He was, therefore, recalled, with the recommendation to operate this movement as secretly as possible so that the enemy might not know he had left the Valley.

To this end recourse was had to a strategem. On the 11th of June Whiting's division of Lee's army were loaded in several trains at the terminus of the Danville railroad at Richmond. They were made to cross the river at a point near Belle Isle, where there were at that moment a considerable number of Federal prisoners about to be released and sent down the James River. The trains loitered a long time, and the prisoners were able to convince themselves that all these Confederate soldiers were sent by Lee to reinforce Jackson, who was only waiting for them to march on Washington. McClellan, in effect, believed this report of the liberated prisoners. The trains did set out in the direction indicated, but returned the same night. Jackson, on his part, by a clever combination of marches and counter-marches made believe that he was descending the Valley towards the upper Potomac, and then disappeared suddenly. Even his soldiers were ignorant whither he was leading them. They had received orders not to ask the names of the villages they passed through, and to reply to all questions: "I don't know." So well, that Jackson, having surprised a soldier stealing cherries, and asking him his name and regiment, could get him to say nothing else but: "I don't know."

On the 15th of June Jackson's division arrived at Ashland, fif-

teen miles north of Richmond. Here he left his tired soldiers and
rapidly betook himself to the city. Crossing the streets at night,
he arrived without being recognised at the house which served
for Lee's headquarters near Fair Oaks Station. There took place
the first interview since the commencement of the war between
these two remarkable men.

Lee's plan was to take the Federal right wing in front and rear,
throw it back on the centre, and thus force McClellan to issue from
his intrenchments and deliver battle in order to maintain his
communications with the Pamunkey. Consequently Jackson was
to direct his march on Pole Green Church, nearly in the direction
of Stuart's reconnoitring expedition. This latter, with a large part
of the cavalry, was stationed at Jackson's extreme left, to surround
the Federals more surely. General Branch was to defile by Meadow
Bridge on Mechanicsville, while General A. P. Hill would bear
directly on Mechanicsville, supported by the concentrated fire of
all the Confederate batteries raised along the Chickahominy. The
position of Mechanicsville once carried, General D. H. Hill would
support Jackson's operation, who was charged to attack on the rear .
and squeeze everything that came his way as in a vise, all the time
pressing on the Confederate centre. Longstreet was to support
General A. P. Hill, and the two corps united had for their mission
to occupy the enemy's lines at New Bridge. Generals Huger and
Magruder were meanwhile to defend the works before Richmond,
making demonstrations against the centre, and to advance if the
enemy retreated, pursuing him vigorously. On the roads abutting
on the capital were posted sentries and detachments of cavalry to
watch the movements of the enemy. Reserves of infantry were
ready to support them in case of an unforeseen attack. The soldiers
were ordered to carry provisions for three days. As the Confederates occupied the inner (that is, the shorter) line, it was easy for
them, if needed, to concentrate themselves rapidly, either for attack or defence.

McClellan, on his side, since the battle of Seven Pines had been
content to fortify his position, seeking to divine the schemes of
his adversary. He had quietly given up the offensive part to Lee,
and during the rest of this campaign the Federal forces offered the
strange spectacle of an army invading a country and, although

very superior in number and resources, awaiting the attack instead of pressing forward and engaging himself in conflict. McClellan had also committed the remarkable blunder of so disposing his army that the Chickahominy flowed between its two wings, thus cutting its centre at right angles. The wings could only communicate with each other by means of bridges and roads, always very bad because of the marshy nature of the ground bordering the river. Sudden overflows might at any moment carry away the bridges, in which case the two halves of his army could not possibly succour each other. Having established his base of operations on the Pamunkey, which was unnecessary, he was compelled to keep his right wing between that river and Richmond to protect his communications. Had he chosen the James, all need of remaining north of the Chickahominy would have disappeared and this dangerous position, the holding of both banks of a stream which could play him a bad turn, would have no further shade of excuse or reason for its continuance.

For the rest, McClellan felt the peril of his position so much that he was thinking of changing his base of operations when a deserter from Jackson's division arrived on the 24th of June and informed him that that general was preparing to march on his right flank.

8

D. H. Hill, one of the participants in the conference of Lee's generals in Richmond in preparation for the ensuing battle, has left a record of that dramatic event which is revealing of the men engaged. Particularly significant is the evidence, here first exhibited, of Lee's practice of leaving to his subordinates the details of putting his battle plans into effect.

While encamped, about noon on Monday, the 23d of June, 1862, on the Williamsburg road, about a mile from the battle-field of Seven Pines, in command of a division of the Confederate army, I received an order from General Lee to report immediately at his quarters on the Mechanicsville road. On approaching the

house which the general occupied, I saw an officer leaning over
the yard-paling, dusty, travel-worn and apparently very tired. He
raised himself up as I dismounted, and I recognized General Jackson, who till that moment I had supposed was confronting Banks
and Frémont far down the Valley of Virginia. He said he had
ridden fifty-two miles since 1 o'clock that morning, having taken
relays of horses on the road.

We went together into General Lee's office. General Jackson
declined refreshments, courteously tendered by General Lee, but
drank a glass of milk. Soon after, Generals Longstreet and A. P.
Hill came in, and General Lee, closing the door, told us that he
had determined to attack the Federal right wing and had selected
our four commands to execute the movement. He told us that he
had sent Whiting's division to reënforce Jackson, and that at his
instance the Richmond papers had reported that large reënforcements had been sent to Jackson "with a view to clearing out the
Valley of Virginia and exposing Washington." He believed that
General McClellan received the Richmond papers regularly, and
he (Lee) knew of the nervous apprehension concerning Washington. He then said that he would retire to another room to attend to
some office work, and would leave us to arrange the details among
ourselves. The main point in his mind seemed to be that the crossings of the Chickahominy should be uncovered by Jackson's advance down the left bank, so that the other three divisions might
not suffer in making a forced passage.

During the absence of General Lee, Longstreet said to Jackson:
"As you have the longest march to make, and are likely to meet
opposition, you had better fix the time for the attack to begin."
Jackson replied: "Daylight of the 26th." Longstreet then said:
"You will encounter Federal cavalry and roads blocked by felled
timber, if nothing more formidable; ought you not to give yourself more time?" When General Lee returned, he ordered A. P.
Hill to cross at Meadow Bridge, Longstreet at the Mechanicsville
Bridge, and me to follow Longstreet. The conference broke up
about nightfall. . . .

That night my division marched across to the neighborhood of
Mechanicsville Bridge. To conceal the movement our camp-fires
were freshly lighted up by a detachment after the troops had left,

and a company was sent some miles down the Charles City road to send up rockets, as though signaling an advance in that direction.

9

After all Lee's planning, the time eventually arrived when those plans must be put into execution, when the planned battle must be waged. Freeman dramatically pictures Lee's reflections on the fateful evening of the twenty-fifth before the beginning of hostilities.

Toward evening . . . the rain had ceased, and as the anxious people of Richmond looked out from the housetops, they saw a rainbow covering the camps of their defenders. It was an omen, the superstitious affirmed. Yet there were many who had no faith in the omen or in the commander of the army. Critics were still to be found on every corner; those who had doubted Lee's qualities of command continued to murmur so dubiously that his admirers had to defend him. At that very hour, perhaps, the editor of *The Richmond Enquirer* was writing for his next day's paper an appeal for confidence in Lee. "Impatient critics," he said, "are still busy with comments upon a policy, the facts leading to which they do not know, and upon which, if they did, they could form no reliable opinion."

Back through the fading rainbow, unmindful of critics, Lee returned to his headquarters. For part of the way he went over the road he and Davis had followed that last night in May, not quite four weeks before, when the President had told him he wished him to assume command of the army. Then the fields and the highways had been full of the wounded, victims of a bungled battle that only the optimist could style a victory. Now, under the summer stars, in the meadows, the men were lighting their camp-fires, and the teamsters were feeding their horses in the knowledge that the cooking of three days' rations meant a new battle. What could Lee have thought as he rode silently by, and heard the echo of the soldiers' banter, the music of their boyish laughter?

At the Dabbs House the servants were packing the camp equipage and the office was ready to be abandoned, for, with the dawn, headquarters would be in the field, and none could say where sunset would find them on the morrow. Lee ate his supper, received the last reports, wrote a letter to President Davis, telling him of the affair on the Williamsburg road, questioned the staff once more about the movements of the troops that night, and then sought a few hours' sleep.

The eve of the great struggle for the possession of Richmond; the eve of the first battle Lee had ever directed under the Southern flag! Was everything prepared? Had he forgotten any essential? Would he have the advantage of surprise, or was the enemy at that hour preparing for him? The column that was to make the turning movement was strong enough; the force he would hurl against the enemy's right certainly outnumbered the Federal brigades north of the Chickahominy; the artillery was prudently apportioned; the attacking divisions were well-led; the general staff had done its work carefully; the wagon-train would not be long. If Magruder and Huger put up a bold front [south of the Chickahominy], they would be able to hold off the enemy until Lee's advance had passed New Bridge. Then, if the Federals attempted to drive into Richmond, he would recross the river and be on their heels, just as he had promised the President he would be. But . . . was he expecting too much of inexperienced staff officers? The only maps that the engineers had prepared were little more than sketches; would they suffice; were they accurate? Were the roads so narrow and so numerous, in a tangled country, that they would confuse the commanders? Above all . . . was the plan understood? Was it subject to two interpretations in any particular? Was it over-complicated? It provided for the convergence on the heights of the Chickahominy of columns that were to approach by three routes, Jackson's turning column after a long march from the north, A. P. Hill across Meadow Bridge, Longstreet and D. H. Hill by way of Mechanicsville pike. Would they meet at the same time and on the appointed line, or . . .?

It was getting late; the birds were beginning to stir; that low, continuous sound was the creaking of the complaining wagons on the road; that muffled pulsing, as regular as the beat of an untroubled heart, was the tramp of D. H. Hill's men on the way to their rendezvous. The day of battle had come!

10

Lee was not alone in his anxiety. As the days passed by in that June of 1862, with the Federal army ringing Richmond in its very suburbs, the tension and apprehension in the Confederate capital steadily mounted. The people knew that the new commander of the Army of Northern Virginia was strengthening the defenses of the city and building up the personnel and supplies of the army. It was taken for granted that a battle for the possession of Richmond was not far off—but there was no indication as to when that battle might be fought. J. B. Jones, the war clerk diarist, was by reason of his position more closely in touch with affairs than the ordinary noncombatant. His diary reflects the thrill he experienced on the morning of June 26, when there passed through his hands a message from General Lee which gave a hint that this was the day.

To-day a letter, hastily written by General Lee to the Secretary of War, stated that his headquarters would be at ———, or *beyond* that point, where couriers could find him if there should be anything of importance the Secretary might desire to communicate during the day. *This is the day of battle!* Jackson is in the rear of McClellan's right wing! I sent this note to the Secretary at once. I *suppose* Mr. Randolph had been previously advised of General Lee's intention to fight to-day, but I do not *know* it. I know some of the brigadier-generals in the army do not know it, although they have all been ordered to their commands. This is no uncommon order; but it is characteristic of Lee's secretiveness to keep *all* of his officers in profound ignorance of his intentions, except those he means to be engaged. The *enemy* cannot possibly have any intimation of his purpose. . . .

After dinner I repaired, with [my son] Custis and a few friends, to my old stand on the hill north of the Jews' Cemetery, and sat down in the shade to listen. Many persons were there, as usual—for every day some firing could be heard—who said, in response to my inquiries, that distant guns had been heard in the direction of the Pamunkey River.

"That is Jackson!" I exclaimed, as the sounds were distinctly discerned by myself, "and he is in their rear, behind their right wing!"

All were incredulous, and some doubted whether he was within a hundred miles of us. But the sounds grew more distinct and more frequent, and I knew he was advancing. But how long could he advance in that direction without being overwhelmed? Everywhere else along the line such a deathlike silence reigned that even the dropping fire of the pickets, usually so incessant, could be heard.

This suspense continued only a few minutes. Two guns were heard northeast of us, and in such proximity as to startle some of the anxious listeners. These were followed by three or four more, and then the fire continued with increasing rapidity. This was General A. P. Hill's division in *front* of the enemy's right wing, and Lee's plan of battle was developed. Hill was so near us as to be almost in sight. The drums and fifes of his regiments, as they marched up to the point of attack, could be easily heard; how distinctly then sounded his cannon in our ears! And the enemy's guns, pointed in the direction of the city, were as plainly discerned. I think McClellan is taken by surprise. . . .

Another hour, and the reports of the cannon come with the rapidity of seconds, or 3600 per hour! And now, for the first time, we hear the rattle of small arms. And lo! two guns farther to the right—from Longstreet's division, I suppose. And they were followed by others. This is Lee's grand plan of battle—Jackson first, then Hill, then Longstreet—time and distance computed with mathematical precision! The enemy's balloons are not up now. They *know* what is going on, without further investigations up in the air. The business is upon earth, where many a Yankee will breathe his last this night. McClellan must be thunderstruck at this unexpected opening of a decisive battle.

11

Mr. Jones, as he sat on his hill with the other Richmond citizens on the morning of June 26th, listening to the cannonading and musketry from the direction of Mechanicsville, evidently knew something of Lee's plan of battle. He thought he was speaking from the safe vantage point of prior knowledge when he said "That is Jackson!" to his unbelieving listeners— but it was not Jackson! It had indeed been planned for Jackson to advance at 3 A.M. on the twenty-sixth and fall on McClellan's exposed right wing while Hill hammered it from the front; Jackson himself had set that as the time he would be there and all the battle plans had been fixed on that basis. But the morning of the twenty-sixth found Jackson and his men just leaving Ashland on their march for Cold Harbor, and this delay almost upset Lee's well-laid plans at the very outset. Everybody else was ready; Hill had concentrated near the Meadow Bridge and had sent General Branch to the point where the Brook Road crosses the swamp. Then they waited anxiously for Jackson, who did not make contact with McClellan's outposts until late in the afternoon, nearly sunset. Dr. McCabe tells us of the developments.

. . . General Jackson was to notify General Branch of his advance. Branch was to cross immediately upon receiving this message and, as soon as he had uncovered the Meadow Bridge, A. P. Hill was to pass over. General Branch did not receive General Jackson's message until ten o'clock on the morning of the 26th, owing to the delay in the latter's advance from Ashland. He immediately passed the swamp with his brigade and moved in the direction of Meadow Bridge. He met with more opposition than he had expected, and his advance was very slow.

General A. P. Hill had expected to commence his movement early in the morning, but these unavoidable delays detained him also. He waited impatiently until three o'clock in the afternoon of the 26th of June, but no tidings came from Jackson or Branch. He knew they were engaged with the enemy, but as yet the latter had failed to open the way for him. Every moment was precious now that the movement had begun, and further delay might hazard the success of the whole plan. In view of this, he determined to advance at once.

Field's brigade . . . was promptly moved upon the bridge, which it captured at once. . . . The whole division was enabled to cross the swamp in safety. Following the road for a few hundred yards, the command wheeled abruptly to the right and, moving through the fields, marched direct upon Mechanicsville. The enemy greeted the advance with a heavy fire of artillery, but General Field . . . swept forward steadily and, after a sharp conflict, drove the Federals from Mechanicsville.

Up to this time the Confederates had encountered only the advanced forces of the enemy. The real position selected by the Federals was one of great strength. It was about a mile back of Mechanicsville and was located immediately on the left bank of Beaver Dam Creek. . . . The Federal position, naturally strong, had been selected with great care, and was defended by several lines of infantry and artillery (the former posted in rifle pits) extending from the base of the hill to the top. The line was held by the corps of Major-General Fitz John Porter, General McClellan's ablest lieutenant.

As Hill's troops pressed on, they came under the fire of the Federal guns on Beaver Dam Creek. . . . A brief inspection of their position satisfied General Hill that it was too strong to be carried by a direct assault, and as he momentarily expected to hear the sound of Jackson's guns on the left, he refrained from making a direct attack. . . . Pender's brigade was thrown forward, to the right of Field's, in an attempt to force a passage of the creek at Ellison's Mill. He made a gallant attack, charging several times with great vigor, only to be driven back by the withering fire of the Federals. A part of D. H. Hill's command having now arrived, another effort was made to turn the Federal left, with the same result.

The battle ended at nine o'clock, the enemy having been driven from Mechanicsville to their works on Beaver Dam Creek, which they held successfully against all efforts to dislodge them. The Confederates passed the night on the ground they had won. Their loss was heavy—between three and four thousand. The Federal loss was much smaller.

By six o'clock in the afternoon, the movement of General A. P. Hill having uncovered the Mechanicsville Bridge, the divisions of Generals D. H. Hill and Longstreet were put in motion. At nine o'clock the greater portion of these troops were over the stream.

D. H. Hill was ordered to move by the Upper Cold Harbor Road and coöperate with Jackson, while Longstreet was advanced to the support of A. P. Hill. . . .

General McClellan was informed of the approach of Jackson, and seeing his danger he at once ordered General Porter to fall back from Beaver Dam Creek toward the New Bridge . . . and shortly before daylight the troops began to retire, burning such things as they could not carry off. . . .

At night General Jackson bivouacked at Hundley's Corner. During the day he had borne steadily away from the Chickahominy, and had gained ground towards the Pamunkey, thus securing a position from which he could descend the next day on the Federal rear at Cold Harbor. . . .

12

President Davis had known Robert E. Lee for a good many years. He knew him to be an affable gentleman in his personal relations, he knew of his knowledge and skill in military affairs, but he had never seen him actually in command of troops on a battlefield. He was soon to find that Lee, the commander, was an entirely different person from Lee, the socially correct gentleman, or Lee, the desk-bound military adviser. Mrs. Constance Cary Harrison, one of the wartime belles of Richmond, tells of an incident at the opening of the Seven Days which must have been an eye opener to President Davis.

When General Lee had crossed the Chickahominy, President Davis, with several staff-officers, overtook the column, and, with the Secretary of War and a few other non-combatants, forded the river just as the battle of Mechanicsville began. General Lee, surrounded by members of his own staff and other officers, was found a few hundred yards north of the bridge, in the middle of the broad road, mounted and busily engaged in directing the attack then about to be made by a brigade sweeping in line over the fields to the east of the road and toward Ellerson's Mill, where in a few minutes a hot engagement commenced. Shot, from the enemy's guns out of sight, went whizzing overhead in quick succession, striking every moment nearer the group of horsemen in the road as the gunners improved their range.

General Lee observed the President's approach, and was evidently annoyed at what he considered a foolhardy expedition of needless exposure of the head of the Government, whose duties were elsewhere. He turned his back for a moment, until Colonel Chilton had been dispatched at a gallop with the last direction to the commander of the attacking brigade; then, facing the cavalcade and looking like the god of war indignant, he exchanged with the President a salute, with the most frigid reserve of anything like welcome or cordiality. In an instant, and without allowance of opportunity for a word from the President, the general, looking not at him but at the assemblage at large, asked in a tone of irritation: "Who are all this army of people, and what are they doing here?"

No one moved or spoke, but all eyes were upon the President; everybody perfectly understood that this was only an order for him to retire to a place of safety, and the roar of the guns, the rattling fire of musketry and the bustle of a battle in progress, with troops continually arriving across the bridge to go into action, went on. The President twisted in his saddle, quite taken aback by such a greeting—the general regarding him now with glances of growing severity. After a painful pause the President said, deprecatingly: "It is not my army, General." "It certainly is not *my* army, Mr. President," was the prompt reply, "and this is no place for it"—in an accent of command.

Such a rebuff was a stunner to Mr. Davis, who, however, soon regained his serenity and answered: "Well, General, if I withdraw, perhaps they will follow," and, raising his hat in another cold salute, he turned his horse's head to ride slowly toward the bridge—seeing, as he turned, a man killed immediately before him by a shot from a gun which at that moment got the range of the road. The President's own staff-officers followed him, as did various others; but he presently drew rein in a stream, where the high bank and the bushes concealed him from General Lee's repelling observation, and there remained while the battle raged. The Secretary of War had also made a show of withdrawing, but improved the opportunity afforded by rather a deep ditch on the roadside to attempt to conceal himself and his horse there for a time from General Lee, who at that moment was more to be dreaded than the enemy's guns.

13

On the morning of the twenty-seventh Jackson moved forward, swinging to the east and completely flanking the Federal position on Beaver Dam, which Porter abandoned early in the morning without further resistance. McClellan's communication with his base at White House was thus imperiled, and he was forced into a quick decision to transfer his base to the James River. To protect his retreat to the James, Porter was withdrawn to a position along Powhite Creek, on which Gaines' Mill is located, on a high ridge in a bend of the Chickahominy near Cold Harbor—a strong position, well protected by artillery. If Lee was perturbed by the mishandling of his plans in his first important engagement, he gave no outward sign of it. He had fixed his headquarters at a house on the Hogan plantation; and there, to quote an observer, "calm and collected, he was seated beneath a verandah in the rear of the house. A crowd of officers were on the walks and greensward. They conversed in whispers while their chief, aside and alone, seemed buried in his own thoughts, his fine countenance impressed with a serious air, but without a shade of inquietude or irresolution." Meanwhile the Confederate forces were moving into position for the assault on McClellan's right wing which would destroy it or force it to flee in retreat across the river. E. M. Law, whose brigade played a prominent part in the ensuing battle of Cold Harbor, tells of the engagement.

A. P. Hill's division, which had the Confederate advance nearest the Chickahominy, pushing on from Ellerson's Mill, appeared in Porter's front at about two o'clock P.M., and at once commenced the attack. This was a grave mistake, for Longstreet's division, which was to support Hill, was not up, and Jackson's flanking column, having a much longer distance to march, was not in position on our left. The Federal line stood firm against the repeated assaults of A. P. Hill's troops. . . .

In the meantime Jackson's column, reinforced by D. H. Hill's division, was moving steadily to the left, in the direction of Cold Harbor. All along the line of march were evidences of the hasty retreat of the Federals. Dense clouds of smoke rising from their abandoned camps indicated to us, before we reached them, that such stores as they could not carry off in their retreat were being destroyed. This was a sore disappointment to the hungry Confederates, whose mouths watered at the sight of the good things they rarely enjoyed, but now reduced by the flames to a condition much too over-done to satisfy their whetted appetites. I heard many hearty and rather profane expressions of disgust at the conduct of our Yankee friends who showed such a want of hospitality in receiving us on this visit to their quarters. . . .

Our movements were strangely slow; we seemed to be feeling our way instead of moving promptly upon well-known points and with a well-defined purpose. Even after Porter's line of battle had been developed in our front there was much uncertainty and delay in getting the various Confederate commands in proper position for a general and decisive attack. The wooded and marshy character of the ground on which the Confederates had to move to reach the enemy contributed in some measure to produce this result. But the real trouble was that the Confederate officers, even those in high command, knew little or nothing of the topography of the country in which they were operating. An accurate map in the hands of each division commander would have saved many valuable lives at Gaines' Mill as well as at Ellerson's, and time enough would have been gained to have brought the whole Confederate force upon the field at the former place several hours before it actually reached there. . . . The Federals, on the other hand, knew the country thoroughly; they had occupied it for several weeks and during that time their engineer officers had inspected it carefully and had made accurate maps. In short, they knew every road, stream and bridle-path in it. . . .

While A. P. Hill was engaging the center of Porter's line, D. H. Hill's division was pushing around to the extreme Federal right, and Jackson had brought up Ewell's and a portion of his own division into the interval between the two Hills. It was after 4 o'clock P.M., when the left wing of the Confederate army moved to the attack. . . .

The firing was heavy and continuous as we approached the field, and when Ewell's and D. H. Hill's divisions joined in the attack, the roar of musketry became deafening, the heaviest I have ever heard on any field. . . . The final advance of the Confederate left under D. H. Hill was made just before dark, and resulted in the complete rout of the Regulars under Sykes, whose troops retreated in confusion to the swamps of the Chickahominy. . . .

That portion of the Federal line in front of A. P. Hill and Longstreet was of the most formidable character. . . . By 5 o'clock the battle was in full progress all along the line. Longstreet's and A. P. Hill's men were attacking in the most determined manner, but were met with a courage as obstinate as their own. After each bloody repulse the Confederates only waited long enough to reform their shattered lines or to bring up their supports, when they would again return to the assault. Besides the terrific fire in their front, a battery of heavy guns on the south side of the Chickahominy were in full play upon their right flank. There was no opportunity for manoeuvering or flank attacks. The enemy was directly in front and he could only be reached in that direction. If he could not be driven out before night it would be equivalent to a Confederate disaster, and would involve the failure of General Lee's whole plan for the relief of Richmond. It was a critical moment for the Confederates.

While matters were in this condition Whiting's division arrived in rear of that portion of the line held by the remnants of A. P. Hill's division. . . . As we moved forward to the firing we could see the straggling Confederate line lying behind a gentle ridge that ran across the field parallel to the Federal position. . . . Passing over the scattering line of Confederates on the ridge, we broke into a trot down the slope toward the Federal works. Men fell like leaves in the autumn wind; the Federal artillery tore gaps in the ranks at every step; the ground in rear of the advancing column was strewn thickly with the dead and wounded. Not a gun was fired by us in reply; there was no confusion and not a step faltered as the two gray lines swept silently and swiftly on; the pace became more rapid every moment; when within thirty yards of the ravine, and the men could see the desperate nature of the work in hand, a wild yell answered the roar of Federal musketry and they rushed for the works. The Confederates were within ten paces of them when the Federals in the front line broke cover and, leaving their log breastworks, swarmed up the hill in their rear, carrying away their second line with them in their rout. . . . Anderson's brigade, till then in reserve, passed through on the right and led the way for Longstreet's division; while on the left the roll of musketry receded toward the Chickahominy, and the cheering of the victorious Confederates announced that Jackson, Ewell and D. H. Hill were sweeping that part of the field.

The battle was won. The Federal infantry was in full flight toward the swamps of the Chickahominy and the bridges in their rear. The first great battle of the "Seven Days" fight for Richmond was over, and the tired Confederates slept victorious upon one of the best contested fields of the war.

14

The overwhelming nature of the Confederate victory is reflected in the vivid eyewitness account which the correspondent of the *New York Tribune* sent from the battlefield.

At six o'clock the enemy commenced a determined attack on our extreme right, evidently with a design of flanking us. It was an awful firing that resounded from that smoke-clouded valley—not heavier than some in the earlier part of the engagement, but more steady and determined. It was only by over-bearing exhausted men with fresh ones that the enemy succeeded in turning that flank—as at length he did succeed, only too well; and he accomplished it in three-quarters of an hour. At the expiration of that time our officers judiciously ordered their men to fall back; the order was not obeyed so judiciously, for they ran back—*broken, disordered, routed.* Simultaneously the wounded and skulkers about the buildings used as hospitals caught a panic, whether from a few riderless horses plunging madly across the field or from instantaneously scenting the rout, does not appear. A motley mob started pell-mell for the bridges. They were overtaken by many just from the woods, and it seemed as if Bull Run were to be repeated.

Meanwhile the panic extended. Scores of gallant officers endeavored to rally and re-form the stragglers, but in vain; while many officers forgot the pride of their shoulder-straps and the honor of their manhood and herded with the sneaks and cowards. . . .

That scene was one not to be forgotten. Scores of riderless, terrified horses dashing in every direction; thick flying bullets singing by, admonishing of danger; every minute a man struck down; wagons and ambulances and cannon blockading the way; wounded men limping and groaning and bleeding amid the throng; officers and civilians denouncing and reasoning and entreating, and being insensiby borne along with the mass; the sublime cannonading, the clouds of battle-smoke and the sun just disappearing, large and blood-red—I can not picture it, but I see it and always shall.

15

The arrival of Jackson and his men on the battlefield at Cold Harbor completed Lee's pincers movement on McClellan's right flank, and insured the success of this, the first of a number of such military coups by Lee and Jackson. The meeting of the two commanders on the field, following the rout of the Federals, was a dramatic incident which has been recorded by one of the observers and participants in the battle, John Esten Cooke.

Jackson . . . rode forward to Cold Harbor where General Lee awaited him, and the two soldiers shook hands in the midst of tumultuous cheering from the troops, who had received intelligence that Jackson's corps had joined them. The contrast between the two men was extremely striking . . . Lee, the grave commander-in-chief, with his erect and graceful seat in the saddle, his imposing dignity of demeanor, and his calm and measured tones, as deliberate as though he were in a drawing-room. Jackson was a very dif-

ferent personage. He was clad in a dingy old coat, wore a discolored cadet-cap, tilted almost upon his nose, and rode a raw-
boned horse with short stirrups which raised his knees in the most
ungraceful manner. Neither in his face nor figure was there the
least indication of the great faculties of the man, and a more awk-
ward-looking personage it would be hard to imagine. In his hand
he held a lemon, which he sucked from time to time, and his demeanor was abstracted and absent.

As Jackson approached, Lee rode toward him and greeted him
with a cordial pressure of the hand.

"Ah, general," said Lee, "I am very glad to see you. I had hoped
to be with you before!"

Jackson made a twitching movement of his head, and replied
in a few words, rather jerked from his lips than deliberately uttered.

Lee had paused, and now listened attentively to the long roll
of musketry from the woods where Hill and Longstreet were engaged; then to the still more incessant and angry roar from the
direction of Jackson's own troops, who had closed in upon the
Federal forces.

"That fire is very heavy," said Lee. "Do you think your men
can stand it?"

Jackson listened for a moment, with his head bent toward one
shoulder, as was customary with him, for he was deaf, he said, in
one ear, "and could not hear out of the other," and replied briefly:

"They can stand almost anything! They can stand that!"

He then, after receiving General Lee's instructions, immediately
saluted and returned to his corps.

16

The battle of Cold Harbor, despite the bungling of the
preceding day, was a brilliant Confederate victory. McClellan's army was routed, and there was every reason to expect
that it would be destroyed before it could reach its new base
on the James. But the next few days supplied a classic example of how the best-laid plans of a commanding general can be
frustrated by the ineptitude of his subordinates. General Long

summarizes briefly the disappointing outcome of the bungled encounters with McClellan's retreating forces at Savage's Station, Frazier's Farm and Malvern Hill.

The next morning Lee directed Stuart with his cavalry, supported by Ewell's division of infantry, to seize the York River Railroad. McClellan was thus cut off from his base of supplies, and reduced to the necessity of retreating by one of two routes— the one by the Peninsula, the other by the James River under the cover of the gunboats. He chose the latter as the shortest and easiest.

General Lee remained on the 28th on the north side of the Chickahominy in observation of McClellan's movements. Instructions were sent at the same time to Magruder to keep a vigilant watch on the Federals and without delay report any movement that might be discovered. These instructions were not as faithfully executed as they should have been, for the retreat of the Federals had commenced on the morning of the 28th, and was not discovered until the morning of the 29th, when the Federal lines were found by two engineer officers . . . to be abandoned, although the Confederate picket lines were in many places less than half a mile from the Federal lines.

The safe retreat of McClellan to the James is mainly due to the advantage thus gained. When General Lee on the morning of the 29th found that the Federal army was in retreat he ordered an immediate pursuit. All of the troops on the north of the Chickahominy, with the exception of the divisions of Ewell and Jackson, and Stuart's cavalry, which were to remain in observation lest the Federals might change their line of retreat, were ordered to recross that stream with the view of overtaking the retreating columns.

General Lee on recrossing the Chickahominy found Magruder, Huger and Holmes preparing to pursue the retreating Federal army. At twelve o'clock the pursuit was commenced, and about three Magruder came upon Sumner's corps, which was in position near Savage's Station. General Heintzelman having retired, Sumner's and Franklin's corps had to receive Magruder's attack unsupported. Sumner held his position with great obstinacy until night ended the conflict. This determined stand enabled the Federal army to make a safe passage of the White Oak Swamp.

In the afternoon of the 29th Jackson was directed to cross the Chickahominy and relieve Magruder in the pursuit. Lee directed the other divisions of his army to march by several roads leading in the direction of McClellan's line of retreat, with the view of striking his column in the flank while Jackson pressed him in the rear. About three o'clock on the 30th, Lee, with the divisions of Longstreet and A. P. Hill, struck the Federal column at Frazier's Farm, and a fierce combat ensued which was closely contested until night. Contrary to his expectations, he was not supported in this attack by Generals Jackson and Huger, consequently McClellan again escaped and continued his retreat during the night to Malvern Hill.

The delay on the part of General Jackson was very unusual. The explanation of his delay on this occasion was that, being greatly exhausted by long marches and battles for more than a week, he sought a short repose. His staff, out of mistaken regard for their general, permitted him to sleep far beyond the time he had allowed himself. When he awoke he was greatly chagrined at the loss of time that had occurred, the damage of which he was unable to repair.

Though General Lee accomplished all that was at first proposed, yet had the parts assigned to some of his subordinates been performed with the exactness that was naturally expected, the results of his operations would have been far greater than those shown in the sequel.

On the morning of the 1st of July it was discovered that McClellan had occupied in force the strong position of Malvern Hill, while his powerful artillery swept every approach and the shot of the gunboats fell beyond the Confederate lines. After a careful reconnoissance of McClellan's position, Lee determined to attack his left. His first line, composed of the divisions of Magruder, D. H. Hill and Jackson, was advanced under cover of the wood near the base of the hill. Magruder was ordered to attack the Federal left, while Hill and Jackson threatened their center and right. The attack was delayed until near sundown, when Magruder made a most gallant assault. By dint of hard fighting his troops gained the crest of the hill and forced back the Federal left, but were in turn driven back. The firing continued along the line until ten o'clock. The Confederates lay upon their arms where the battle closed, ready to resume the fight as soon as the daylight should appear.

Under the cover of the night, McClellan secretly retired, his retreat being facilitated by a heavy fall of rain, which deadened the sound of his withdrawal. The Confederates the next morning, groping through the dense fog, came upon the abandoned lines. This was the first information they had of the retreat. McClellan had now gained the protection of the Federal gunboats; therefore Lee did not immediately pursue, but ordered a day's rest, which the troops greatly needed. McClellan continued his retreat to Harrison's Landing on the James River, where he took up a position. Lee advanced the next day to that neighborhood and after a careful reconnoissance of the Federal lines deemed it inadvisable to attack; and, as there was no probability of the Army of the Potomac speedily resuming operations, he returned to his former camp near Richmond to rest, recruit and reorganize his army.

17

Stonewall Jackson's unwonted lack of vigor at White Oak Swamp, and the consequent failure of the Confederate attack at Frazier's Farm, have been the subject of much discussion among military critics and historians. At the time it must have been a painful disappointment to Lee, but there was no sign of any such disappointment in his next meeting with Jackson, after Stonewall had finally crossed the swamp and resumed an active part in the pursuit of McClellan. The Richmond Howitzers were engaged in the fighting, and here Robert Stiles had an opportunity to witness the meeting between Lee and Jackson after Frazier's Farm, and their discussion of plans for pressing the pursuit of the retreating enemy.

All of us had been longing for a sight of Jackson. It is impossible to exaggerate or even to convey an adequate idea of the excitement and furor concerning him about this time, both in the army and among the people.

On Sunday evening, not far from Savage Station, I had been struck directly over the heart by a spent ball, which glanced from a buckle but blackened my breast and nauseated me somewhat. Next morning, still feeling badly and the battery remaining stationary for a time, I had retired a little from the line and was half reclining at the foot of a huge pine that stood on the edge of the Williamsburg road. Hearing the jingle of cavalry accoutrements toward the Chickahominy, I looked up and saw a half-dozen mounted men, and riding considerably in advance a solitary horseman whom I instantly recognized as the great wizard of the marvelous Valley Campaign which had so thrilled the army and the country.

Jackson and the little sorrel stopped in the middle of the road, probably not fifty feet off, while his staff halted perhaps a hundred and fifty yards in his rear. He sat stark and stiff in the saddle. Horse and rider appeared worn down to the lowest point of flesh consistent with effective service. His hair, skin, eyes and clothes were all one neutral dust tint, and his badges of rank so dulled and tarnished as to be scarcely perceptible. The "mangy little cadet cap" was pulled so low in front that the visor cut the glint of his eyeballs.

A ghastly scene was spread across the road hard by. The Seventeenth and Twenty-first Mississippi, of our brigade, had been ordered into the woods about dusk the evening before and told not to fire into the first line they met; but the poor fellows ran into a Federal brigade and were shocked and staggered by a deadly volley. Splendid soldiers that they were, they obeyed orders, held their own fire, laid down and took the enemy's. Almost every man struck was killed, and every man killed shot through the brain. Their comrades had gone into the woods as soon as it was light, brought out the bodies and laid them in rows, with hands crossed upon the breast, but eyes wide-staring. A sickly summer rain had fallen in the night and the faces of the dead were bleached with more than death's pallor. Every eyeball was strained upward toward the spot where the bullet had crashed through the skull, and every forehead stained with ooze and trickle of blood. Men were passing through the silent lines, bending low, seeking in the distorted faces to identify friends.

Jackson glanced a moment toward this scene. Not a muscle quivered as he resumed his steady gaze down the road toward Richmond. He was the ideal of concentration—imperturbable, resistless. I remember feeling that if he were not a very good man he would be a very bad one. . . .

A moment later and his gaze was rewarded. A magnificent staff approached from the direction of Richmond, and riding at its head, superbly mounted, a born king among men. At that time General Lee was one of the handsomest of men, especially on horseback, and that morning every detail of his dress and equipment of himself and horse was absolute perfection. When he recognized Jackson he rode forward with a courier, his staff halting. As he gracefully dismounted, handing his bridle rein to his attendant, and advanced, drawing his gauntlet from his right hand, Jackson flung himself off his horse and advanced to meet Lee, little sorrel trotting back to the staff where a courier secured him.

The two generals greeted each other warmly, but wasted no time upon the greeting. They stood facing each other, some thirty feet from where I lay, Lee's left side and back toward me, Jackson's right and front. Jackson began talking in a jerky, impetuous way, meanwhile drawing a diagram on the ground with the toe of his right boot. He traced two sides of a triangle with promptness and decision; then, starting at the end of the second line, began to draw a third projected toward the first. This third line he traced slowly and with hesitation, alternately looking up at Lee's face and down at his diagram, meanwhile talking earnestly; and when at last the third line crossed the first and the triangle was complete, he raised his foot and stamped it down with emphasis, saying "We've got him": then signalled for his horse and when he came, vaulted into the saddle and was off. Lee watched him a moment, the courier brought his horse, he mounted, and he and his staff rode away.

The third line was never drawn—so we never "got" McClellan.

18

The Seven Days' battles marked the introduction of some innovations in warfare which later came to be important factors in the practice of the military science. The Federal forces, aided by a visiting German scientist, Count Zeppelin, were experimenting with the use of balloons for aerial reconnoitering of the Confederate position, an experiment which the Confederates tried vainly to imitate. Lee, on the other hand, when first brought to Richmond to look after its defenses, had conceived the idea of mobile, armored artillery, and the Federals were given a taste of this new and novel weapon as they retreated across the Peninsula. An Englishman with Lee's army tells about it.

While our troops were cautiously advancing through the deserted camps, a strange phenomenon came into sight on the line of railroad from Richmond. Mr. Pearce (Government ship-builder) had constructed an iron-clad, one-gun battery on the framework of a freight truck, the front and sides being cased with thick iron plates, having timber inside eighteen inches thick, the sides and front slanting towards the top which was open. A 32-pound rifle had its mouth through an embrasure in front, a well-protected locomotive shoving it forward, the driver being protected by a surrounding wall of cotton bales. Its motion was slow, for the battery weighed some sixty tons and several shaky wooden bridges had to be crossed. Having arrived at a point where the Nine Mile Road crosses the railroad, General Griffith of the Mississippi Brigade was speaking to the engineer when the enemy fired a shell at it, a fragment of which struck Griffith, and he shortly afterwards expired beneath a tree. The "Railroad Merrimac" instantly advanced and was soon engaged in dispersing the flying enemy, its large shells exploding right and left in the woods with loud detonations.

Large columns of white sulphurous smoke now rose up into the sky, their beautiful spiral forms and broad-capped tops looking like mammoth pillars of ivory rising from the dark and distant line of timber. The enemy were destroying ammunition; but to prevent further waste of such valuables the "Merrimac" ran along towards Savage Station and routed several batteries drawn up to oppose its progress.

The destruction caused by this single gun was very great; for, having arrived within full view of the enemy's retreat, their long lines of waggons and glitter of bayonets presented conspicuous marks for the gunners, who fired constantly on every side inflicting much loss.

19

Colonel Taylor remarks, with a candor and gallantry all too rare in military writing:

In considering the causes that contributed to prevent a more complete victory to the army under General Lee, after all that has been said, we cannot emphasize too strongly the fact that more was not accomplished because of the character and personality of the men behind the guns on the Federal side. The army under General McClellan was made up largely of the flower of the manhood of the Northern and Eastern states, and his lieutenants were men and soldiers of a very high type. The system of bounties and substitutes that subsequently prevailed in the recruiting of the ranks of the Federals had not then begun to operate, and under the generally acknowledged and remarkable administrative powers of General McClellan his army had been raised to the highest degree of efficiency. Nothing less than an army of the finest material, most excellently officered, could have so well resisted the terrible blows delivered by the Confederates under General Lee.

General Lee in his report says: "Under ordinary circumstances the Federal army should have been destroyed. Its escape was due to the causes already stated. Prominent among these is the want of correct and timely information. This fact, attributable chiefly to the character of the country, enabled General McClellan skilfully to conceal his retreat and to add much to the obstructions with which nature had beset the way of our pursuring columns; but regret that more was not accomplished gives way to gratitude to the Sovereign Ruler of the universe for the results achieved. The siege of Richmond was raised and the object of a campaign which had been prosecuted after months of preparation at an enormous expenditure of men and money, completely frustrated. More than ten thousand prisoners, including officers of rank, fifty-two pieces of artillery, and upward of thirty-five thousand stands of small arms were captured. The stores and supplies of every description which fell into our hands were great in amount and volume, but small in comparison with those destroyed by the enemy."

20

Lee's gratification at relieving Richmond from the strangle hold of McClellan's army was diluted by his regret that the greatest possible results had not been attained. "The Federal army should have been destroyed," he said in his official report, and subsequent students of the campaign have been inclined to agree with him. Dr. Freeman, after perhaps the most thorough study of the Seven Days made by any critic, explains the failure.

The Federal army was not destroyed, as Lee had hoped it would be, for four reasons: (1) The Confederate commander lacked adequate information for operating in a difficult country because his maps were worthless, his staff work inexperienced, and his cavalry absent at the crisis of the campaign; (2) the Confederate artillery was poorly employed; (3) Lee trusted too much to his subordinates, some of whom failed him almost completely; and (4) Lee displayed no tactical genius in combating a fine, well-led Federal army. When these four factors are given their just valuation, the wonder is not that an honest commander had to admit that he had failed to realize his full expectation. Rather is the wonder that so much of success was attained. . . .

So appears the campaign after seventy years. At the time, it provoked conflicting opinions. Hostile critics of President Davis and of General Lee, balancing successes against failures, professed disappointment with Lee's generalship and with the results obtained. Said *The Charleston Mercury*, "Much as we praise the strategy, projected as we hear, by General Johnston, some time since, by which McClellan has been beaten on the Chickahominy, the blundering manner in which he has been allowed to get away, the desultory manner in which he has been pursued by divisions instead of our whole force, enabling him to repulse our attacks, to carry off his artillery, and, finally, to make a fresh stand with an army reinforced, are facts, we fear, not very flattering to the practical generalship of General Lee." Some of General Johnston's friends jealously grumbled that their hero would have made a better showing than Lee if he had been supported by the administration in concentrating as large an army as Lee had. Robert Toombs wrote Vice-President Stephens that Lee was "far below the occasion." And so for other critics less distinguished.

But the public saw the successes, not the shortcomings. Especially in Richmond, press and people did not judge the Seven Days as a series of close battles but in their proper light, as a campaign of strategy that began with the first move to transfer Jackson from the Valley and ended when McClellan was caged and impotent at Harrison's Landing, with his plan of operations hopelessly shattered. They remembered the panic of May; they did not forget how they had seen the glow of bombardment and had heard above the anxious beating of their own hearts the defiant challenge of the enemy's guns. And in the contrast between June 1 and July 4 they read a mighty achievement. "The people at large," one observer testified, "greeted Lee as the author of a great deliverance worked out for them." Some were most eulogistic: "The operations of General Lee . . . ," *The Richmond Dispatch* affirmed, "were certainly those of a master. No captain that ever lived could have planned or executed a better plan. . . . Its success places its author among the highest military names." A correspondent of *The Richmond Enquirer* insisted, "Never has such a result been achieved in so short a time with so small cost to the victors. I do not believe the records of modern warfare can produce a parallel when the battle is considered in this aspect." Lee, said *The Richmond Whig*, "has amazed and confounded his detractors by the brilliancy of his genius, the fertility of his resources, his energy and daring. He has established his reputation forever, and has entitled himself to the lasting gratitude of his country." Thoughtful men saw in the outcome a vindication of the President's policy, and the hope of a long period of successes in arms.

More important, far, than popular acclaim was the confidence and admiration aroused among the soldiers in the ranks. Within a month the "King of Spades" became the father of his men, trusted and idolized. He gave them the *causerie de bivouac* that Napoleon considered essential to the morale of a victorious army. Stories of his simplicity, of his devotion, and of his humility began to go the rounds. The troops already felt that he was superior to the best general the enemy had, and that their lives and their cause were safe in his hands. After this first campaign, their faith in him was unbounded.

21

Dr. Freeman's mature and scholarly judgment as to the effect of the Seven Days' battles on Lee and his army and the relationship between them is paralleled in the comments of Robert Stiles, who served in the Confederate ranks during those history-making days.

Whatever effect the Seven Days' battles may have had upon other reputations, Federal or Confederate . . . there is one name and fame which those seven days gave to history and to glory, as to which the entire world stands agreed, and all the after chances and changes of the war but expanded the world's verdict.

When we contemplate Lee's great plan and the qualities of leadership which those operations revealed in him, we know not which most to admire—the brilliance, the comprehensiveness or the almost reckless audacity of the scheme and of the man. It is a singular fact, and one which seems to demand explanation, that the prominent impression which Lee invariably seems to make is that of roundness, balance, perfection; and yet unquestionably his leading characteristic as a general is aggressive audacity. Take for example his leaving but 28,000 of 80,000 men between McClellan and Richmond, and with the other 52,000 crossing a generally impassable stream and attacking McClellan's 105,000 in entrenched positions. Mayhap old Jubal Early, who knew Lee and knew war as well as any other man on either side, has the right of it and suggests the true explanation when he says, speaking of this very operation: "Timid minds might regard this as rashness, but it was the very perfection of a profound and daring strategy."

And when we attempt to measure the effect of these Seven Days' battles—when we note that within less than one month from the day he took command of an army with which he had had no previous personal connection, Lee had completely secured its confidence and correctly estimated its capabilities, had conceived and perfected his great plan and every detail essential to its successful execution, had begun to put it into operation and actually delivered his first great blow; when we note further that within a week after that blow was struck Richmond was entirely relieved and within a few weeks more Washington was in serious peril and the United States Government had called for three hundred thousand more men; when, we say, all this is considered, we may as well ask when did the weight of one great Captain's sword, only this and nothing more, cause the scales of war to dip with such a determined, downward sag?

One of the most important features of these seven days of battle was that it was the first prolonged wrestle of the Army of Northern Virginia, the struggle that really gave birth to that army; that gave it experience of its own powers, cohesion, character, confidence in itself and in its great commander—and proper estimate of its great opponent, the Army of the Potomac and its commander. Then, too, these days of continuous battle tested the individual men, and especially the officers of the army, winnowing the chaff from the wheat and getting rid of some high in command who did not catch the essential spirit of the army or assimilate well with it, or bid fair to add anything of value to it; at the same time this week of continuous battle brought to the front men who had in them stuff out of which heroes are made and who were destined to make names and niches for themselves in the pantheon of this immortal army.

22

Richmond's relief from the immediate threat of invasion was a tonic to the people and an inspiration to the soldiers, but some of the carping critics found it embarrassing to be forced to admit that they might be wrong in the estimate of Lee's ability they had so vociferously proclaimed at the time of his ill-fated campaign in western Virginia. One of the most vitriolic of Lee's detractors at that time was Mr. E. A. Pollard, editor of the *Richmond Examiner,* and it is amusing to read the squirming comment he made following the Seven Days.

A great deal was claimed for "generalship" in the battles around Richmond; and results achieved by the hardy valor of our troops were busily ascribed by hollow-hearted flatterers to the genius of the strategist. . . .

The vulgar and unintelligent mind worships success. The extraordinary and happy train of victories in Virginia seems to have had no other significance or interest to a number of groveling minds in the South than as a contribution to the personal fame of General Lee, who, by no fault of his own, was followed by toadies, flatterers and newspaper sneaks in epaulets, who made him ridiculous by their servile obeisances and excess of praise.

The author does not worship success. He trusts, however, that he has intelligence enough to perceive merit, without being prompted by the vulgar cry; he is sure that he has honesty and independence enough to acknowledge it where he believes it to exist. The estimation of General Lee made in some preceding pages was with reference to his unfortunate campaign in western Virginia. It was founded on the events of that campaign, in which there is no doubt General Lee blundered and showed an absurd misconception of mountain warfare; and so far as these events furnished evidence for the historian, the author believes that he was right, unprejudiced and just in ascribing the failure of that campaign to the misdirection of the commanding general.

If, however, it can be shown, as now seems to be likely from incomplete events, that on wider, clearer and more imposing fields General Lee has shown qualities which the campaign in the mountains of Virginia had not illustrated, the friends of this commander may be assured that the author will be honest and cordial in acknowledging the fact.

23

A feature of the Peninsula campaign, of particularly keen interest and concern to General Lee, was McClellan's advancing forces' envelopment of the old Custis estate, "White House" on the Pamunkey, where Mrs. Lee and her daughter Mary had gone from Arlington. Major W. Roy Mason, of General Field's staff, tells of the part he played in bringing the Lee ladies back within the Confederate lines, just as the Seven Days' action was getting under way.

One day in June, 1862, General Lee rode over to General Charles W. Field's headquarters at Meadow Bridge and asked for me. I should say here that on leaving home to enter the army I carried a family letter of introduction to General Lee; and on account of that, and also my relationship to Colonel Charles Marshall, an aide on his staff, my visits at army headquarters were exceptionally pleasant.

When General Lee approached me on this occasion, he said: "Captain, can General Field spare you a little while?" I replied, "Certainly, General; what can I do for you?" "I have some property," he answered, "in the hands of the enemy, and General Mc-Clellan has informed me that he would deliver it to me at any time I asked for it."

Then, putting aside his jesting manner, he told me that his wife and Miss Mary Lee, his daughter, had been caught within the Federal lines at the White House, the residence of General W. H. F. Lee, his son, and he desired me to take a courier and proceed with a flag of truce to Meadow Bridge and carry a sealed dispatch to General McClellan. At the Federal headquarters I would meet the ladies and escort them to Mrs. Gooch's farm, inside our lines.

I passed beyond the pickets to the second bridge, where I waved my flag of truce, and was asked by the Union officer of the guard to enter. When I reached the picket, the officer said he had been ordered not to permit any flag of truce to pass through his lines until he had communicated with the headquarters of General McClellan. I waited on the bridge, and when the courier returned he had orders to bring me before the general. The officer insisted on blindfolding me, and positively forbade my courier accompanying me. I was then led through the camps, where I could hear the voices of thousands, laughing, talking or hallooing. After riding an hour, a distance as I supposed of three or four miles, I reached headquarters and was relieved of my bandage. The general came out and gave me a hearty welcome; and when he heard that I had been blindfolded he was so indignant that he placed the officer, my guide, under arrest. I had never seen him so excited.

He asked me into the house, produced his liquors, and gave me a dinner of the best, after which we discussed the situation at length. He asked me no questions which it would compromise our cause to answer, but we calmly reviewed the position of things from our separate points of view, and he inquired anxiously after all his old friends. (General McClellan and my brother-in-law, General Dabney H. Maury, C.S.A., formerly captain, U.S.A., had been classmates and devoted friends, and the general had visited my father's house and my own at Fredericksburg.)

About 3 o'clock in the afternoon, looking down the road, we saw a carriage approaching. The curtains were cut off, and it was drawn by a mule and a dilapidated old horse, driven by a negro of about ten or twelve years, and followed by a cavalry escort. General McClellan, jumping up hastily, said: "There are Mrs. Lee and Miss Mary now." As the carriage stopped before the door, General McClellan, greeting the ladies with marked cordiality, at once introduced me, and remarked to Mrs. Lee that the general (her husband) had chosen me as her escort through the lines, and that, by a strange coincidence, he (McClellan) had found in me a personal friend. He offered to accompany us in person to the river, but this was declined by Mrs. Lee as entirely unnecessary.

When we reached Mrs. Gooch's farm and our own pickets, cheer after cheer went down the long line of soldiers. Near the house we were met by General Lee and a large number of officers assembled to honor the wife and daughter of their chief.

Before leaving for Richmond, Mrs. Lee handed me from a basket, under the carriage-seat, two fine tomatoes, the finest I had ever seen, remarking that she supposed such things were scarce in the Confederacy. The seeds of these tomatoes I preserved, and some years after the war General Lee ate some tomatoes at my table and praised them; whereupon we told him, to his astonishment, that those were the Lee tomatoes, and that they had been distributed all over the state under that name, from the seed of those given me by his wife.

24

When Lee took up his residence in Richmond in 1861 he established himself at a house on Franklin Street, later occupied by Mrs. Lee and their daughters, a house which is now one of Richmond's historic shrines. A glimpse of life in this house is given by one of the family friends who was a frequent visitor.

When General Lee came to Richmond in '61, the house at 707 East Franklin Street was offered him by Mr. John Stewart, a wealthy and worthy citizen of Henrico County. It was nicknamed "The Mess" and, before Mrs. Lee and her daughters arrived, was occupied by the General (when he was in town), General Custis Lee, Major Coxe, Captain Ferdinand C. Hutter, Robert Shirley Carter, Chapman Leigh and others—a merry party of young officers who made the house ring with jest and song, and who scoffed at danger and defeat.

The wrench from Arlington was not without tears. When Robert E. Lee cast his lot with Virginia, his wife's words to him were: "Whichever way you go will be in the path of duty. You will think it right, and I shall be satisfied." Arlington was the living record of Mrs. Lee and her ancestors; the museum of the most complete collection of Washington relics on the earth; the scene of Robert Lee's courtship and marriage; the birthplace of his children. But the grandeur of Arlington was over; the pall of war hung over the land. A band of homeless women looked not for luxurious living, but for a shelter till the struggle was past. Behind was a stately mansion hallowed with historic association, tinged with the exquisite color of early love-making and the riper joy of wedlock, echoing with the prattle of little children, blessed with the companionship of grown-up sons and daughters. It was hard to leave it; but hosts of friends offered outstretched sympathy, and greater issues than sentiment and comfort were at stake. . . .

To break with Arlington was to sever the associations of three generations; and a knotty question also arose—where should they go? After deliberation the "White House," Martha Custis's old home (now the property of W. H. F. Lee) seemed their proper destination. . . . When they first left Arlington they went to "Cedar

Grove," the plantation of a kinsman on the Potomac, where they
remained for some time. . . . Afterward they went to "Chantilly,"
one of the stately homes of Fairfax, on their way to the "White
House." Mrs. Lee was then cheerful and confident of the success
of the cause for which she had already made great sacrifice. It was
not long before the White House, in its exposed condition upon
the Pamunkey and well in the lines of the United States army,
was considered unsafe, and the little party started for Richmond.
They were made prisoners of war at Hanover Court House and
detained there for one week. Before Mrs. Lee left the White House
she tacked upon the front door a card bearing the request that
Union soldiers would not desecrate the home of George Washington's wife.

Mrs. Lee's experience as a prisoner was very dismal. She heard
the wildest rumors of the fall of Richmond, of the overwhelming
army which would then pursue the retreating Southerners, of the
peril and hardships to which her dear ones were exposed. . . . She
became frantic from the reports which were brought to her, and
sent to General McClellan and asked him to send her to Richmond. In consequence, her carriage was ordered, the colored
driver was dismissed and a Union soldier mounted the boot and
drove the ladies to the Confederate lines under a flag of truce.
Then a Confederate soldier took his place and drove them in to
Richmond, to 707 East Franklin Street. The moment she entered
the door she became one of "The Mess." She was prepared to
share a soldier's life; she was not afraid of hardship; she was ready
for danger. . . .

When Mrs. Lee became one of "The Mess" she was a handsome woman with red-brown eyes and abundant grayish hair.
Her chief characteristic—amidst the grandeur of Arlington, at the
gay watering places, or in Richmond during the crucial period of
her life—was a simple sincerity of heart and manner. She did not
care for dress or show, and was in this respect a sharp contrast to
her husband, who was always attired in the most fastidious and
elegant manner. . . .

"No. 707" became a common meeting place. People came to
talk of victory or sorrow; they could stay here if they had nowhere
else to go; they gathered here to work; the disheartened came for

comfort from the tender, loving wife of the commander-in-chief, whose nature was sympathetic, who was intelligent, agreeable and brave. Mourning mothers came to her in their agony; wives of heroes brought her their joy over recent success; friends came without ceremony and partook of what they could get. . . .

Soon after Mrs. Lee came to Richmond a merciless rheumatism bound her to her chair. In the back room, opening on a veranda shadowed by ailanthus trees, her days were spent. But her spirit quailed not before physical infirmity; her quick mind planned, in emergency, various industries for the soldiers' comfort, as well as homely devices for the welfare of "The Mess." She gathered together the young girls and infused into them a working interest. They began to knit and sew, to scrape lint and to make bandages. . . . Life at Richmond then was a shifting panorama; sick people were coming in and well ones going out. It was a restless turmoil— one day of hope, a night of anguish, a morning of joy or sorrow. In these varying scenes Mrs. Lee's chamber was a Mecca. Seated in her wheeled chair, she listened and strengthened, and smiled even when her own heart ached. . . .

25

Another personal incident of the Seven Days' campaign which must have given great personal pleasure to the over-burdened commander of the Confederate forces was his first meeting with his young son Robert, after the boy had joined the Rockbridge Artillery in March and gone off to fight under Stonewall Jackson. It was the day after the battle of Cold Harbor.

The tremendous work Stonewall's men had performed, including the rapid march from the Valley of Virginia, the short rations, the bad water and the great heat, had begun to tell upon us, and I was pretty well worn out. . . . My battery had not moved from its bivouac ground of the previous night, but was parked in an open field all ready, waiting orders. Most of the men were lying down, many sleeping, myself among the latter number. To get some shade and to be out of the way, I had crawled under a caisson, and was busy making up many lost hours of rest. Suddenly I was rudely awakened by a comrade prodding me with a sponge-staff as I had failed to be aroused by his call, and was told to get up and come out, that some one wished to see me.

Half awake, I staggered out and found myself face to face with General Lee and his staff. Their fresh uniforms, bright equipments and well-groomed horses contrasted so forcibly with the war-worn appearance of our command that I was completely dazed. It took me a moment or two to realize what it all meant, but when I saw my father's loving eyes and smile it became clear to me that he had ridden by to see if I was safe and to ask how I was getting along. I remember well how curiously those who were with him gazed at me, and I am sure that it must have struck them as very odd that such a dirty, ragged, unkempt youth could have been the son of this grand-looking victorious commander. . . .

After McClellan's change of base to Harrison's Landing on James River, the army lay inactive around Richmond. I had a short furlough on account of sickness, and saw my father; also my mother and sisters, who were then living in Richmond. He was the same loving father to us all, as kind and thoughtful of my mother, who was an invalid, and of us, his children, as if our comfort and happiness were all he had to care for. His great victory did not elate him, so far as one could see.

10

The Best Defense

=========

L EE's master stroke against McClellan in the furious Seven Days' campaign had indeed raised the siege of Richmond and afforded immediate relief to that beleagured city. But the well-equipped, well-trained and disciplined army under McClellan, in its camp at Harrison's Landing on the James, was rapidly recovering from the demoralizing effects of defeat. Although defeated, McClellan still had there in a strong position in close proximity to Richmond an effective fighting force of some 90,000 men, and their presence constituted an ever-present threat to the security of Richmond and to Lee's numerically inferior army defending it. For one thing, there was the danger that he might transfer his army across the James—as Grant did three years later—and assail Richmond through its southern back door at Petersburg, but, fortunately for the Confederates, McClellan's suggestion of this was disapproved.

In any event, Lee realized that it would be a surrender of all he had gained to sit quietly by and wait for McClellan to resume the offensive. An offensive movement on the part of the Confederates was clearly indicated as the most desirable strategy, and Lee's thoughts naturally turned to his favorite ruse of relieving Richmond by threatening Washington. To add to the complexity of his problem, however, a new factor had been introduced into the equation. General John Pope, who had gained a spurious reputation for ability in the western theater of the war, had been brought to Washington and given command of a new army created by joining the forces of McDowell, Banks and Frémont. The resulting force of 43,000 men was but little less than Lee's total effective force.

Pope had assumed command with an incredibly bombastic announcement, dated from "Headquarters in the Saddle," in which he introduced himself to his troops in braggart words which, in view of subsequent developments, he must have regretted to his dying day:

"I have come to you from the west, where we have always seen the backs of our enemies; from an army whose business it has been to seek the adversary and beat him when found; whose policy has been attack, not defense. I presume I have been called here to pursue the same system, and to lead you against the enemy. It is my purpose to do so, and that speedily.

"Meantime, I desire you to dismiss from your minds certain phrases which I am sorry to find much in vogue amongst you. I constantly hear of taking strong positions and holding them; of lines of retreat and bases of supplies. Let us dismiss such ideas. The strongest position a soldier should desire to occupy is one from which he can most easily advance against the enemy. Let us study the probable lines of retreat of our opponents, and leave our own to take care of themselves. Let us look before and not behind. Success and glory are in the advance. Disaster and shame lurk in the rear. . . ."

Lee was wise enough to estimate Pope's braggadocio at its true value; but, nevertheless, the very existence of an army of 43,000 men between Washington and Richmond, added to the threat of McClellan's 90,000 at Richmond's doorstep on the James, placed Lee and the Army of Northern Virginia in a distinctly uncomfortable position, a position from which it would have to be extricated by bold and resourceful action. And Lee provided just such action.

1

Lee was not affected, beyond the point of amusement, by Pope's address to his troops from his "Headquarters in the Saddle," but Pope adopted further tactics which moved Lee to one of his rare outbursts of indignation and protest against the tactics of the enemy. Pope on July 23 issued a general order in which he directed his subordinates to "arrest all disloyal male citizens within their lines or within their reach in rear of their commands," and that those who refused to take the oath of allegiance "shall be conducted South, beyond the extreme pickets of this army, and notified that if found again, anywhere within our lines, or at any point in the rear, they will be considered as spies and subjected to the extreme rigor of military law." He also decreed that private homes would be "razed to the ground" if any of his troops were fired on by "bushwhackers," and that any person detected in such an act "shall be shot without waiting civil process." To effectuate this, five private citizens were seized by General Steinwehr and held as hostages. Pope also instituted a policy of subsisting the army off the enemy's country, a policy which soon promoted excesses on the part of the soldiers, especially in view of the pointed hint in Pope's orders that "No guard will be placed over private houses or private property of any description. . . . Soldiers were called into the field to do battle against the enemy, and it is not expected that their force and energy shall be wasted in protecting private property of those most hostile to the Government." Comment on the effect of Pope's new ideas, from a Northern viewpoint, was included in a July 31 dispatch to the *New York World* from its correspondent with Pope's army.

Unless these innovations are guarded by far more stringent safeguards against irregular and unauthorized plundering, we shall let loose upon the country at the close of the war a torrent of unbridled and unscrupulous robbers. Rapid strides toward villainy have been made during the past few weeks. Men who at home would have shuddered at the suggestion of touching another's property, now appropriate remorselessly whatever comes to their reach. Thieving, they imagine, has now become an authorized practice. . . .

I know a case where a family were just seating themselves to supper. Soldiers came that way and, going in, swallowed everything. That was not all, but whatever indoors and out of doors the soldiers wanted was readily appropriated, and the proprietor of the place told me sorrowfully that they had ruined him—he never could now get out of debt. I hardly regretted his misfortune so much on his account as for the influence of this thieving upon the soldiers. . . . Unless a check is given to this promiscuous and unauthorized plundering, the discipline and value of the army will be destroyed; and when the enlistments have expired, we shall let loose a den of thieves upon the country.

One favorite form in which this exhibits itself is in the passing of Philadelphia [counterfeit] Confederate notes. Whenever we advance into a new section, the floodgates are immediately opened, and the *fac-simile* Confederate notes are poured out upon the land. They pass readily, and seem to be taken gladly for whatever is held for sale. . . . Horses and other valuable property are often purchased with this bogus currency. . . .

And so these practices are going on until, I believe, if it is not checked we shall unfit the men to be soldiers now or citizens hereafter. Such has been the influence of these new orders—this new way of dealing with the Confederates.

2

The Confederate reaction to Pope's new policy was prompt and vigorous. A general order issued by Adjutant General Samuel Cooper at Richmond denounced Pope's policy, stating that he had "now determined to violate all the rules and usages of war, and to convert the hostilities hitherto waged against armed forces into a campaign of robbery and murder against unarmed citizens and peaceful tillers of the soil." It set forth that the Confederate government was "thus driven to the necessity of adopting such just measures of retribution and retaliation as shall seem adequate to repress and punish these barbarities," specifically providing that General Pope, General Steinwehr and their subordinate commissioned officers were "expressly and specifically declared to be not entitled to be considered as soldiers." This order was forwarded by Lee to General Halleck at Washington with an accompanying letter in which Lee expressed himself with unusual warmth and vigor.

. . . The military authorities of the United States have commenced a practice changing the whole character of the war, from such as becomes civilized nations into a campaign of indiscriminate robbery and murder.

The general order issued by the Secretary of War of the United States . . . directs the military commanders of the United States to take the private property of our people for the convenience and use of their armies, without compensation.

The general order issued by Major General Pope on the 23rd day of July . . . directs the murder of our peaceful inhabitants as spies, if found quietly tilling the farms in his rear, even outside of his lines, and one of his Brigadier Generals, Steinwehr, has seized upon innocent and peaceful inhabitants to be held as hostages, to the end that they may be murdered in cold blood if any of his soldiers are killed by some unknown persons whom he designates as "bushwhackers."

We find ourselves driven by our enemies by steady progress towards a practice which we abhor and which we are vainly struggling to avoid. Under these circumstances this Government has issued the accompanying general order which I am directed by the President to transmit to you, recognizing Major General Pope and his commissioned officers to be in the position which they have chosen for themselves—that of robbers and murderers and not that of public enemies entitled, if captured, to be treated as prisoners of war.

The President also instructs me to inform you that we renounce our right of retaliation on the innocent, and will continue to treat the private enlisted soldiers of General Pope's army as prisoners of war; but if, after notice to your Government that we confine repressive measures to the punishment of commissioned officers, who are willing participants in these crimes, the savage practice threatened in the order alluded to be persisted in, we shall be reluctantly forced to the last resort of accepting the war on the terms chosen by our enemies, until the voice of an outraged humanity shall compel a respect for the recognized usages of war.

3

These unpleasant diplomatic amenities disposed of, Lee settled down to the more congenial task of studying the military problem confronting him. Colonel Taylor, who was at

Lee's side during these trying times, tells of the steps taken by the Confederate commander to prove the soundness of the old axiom that "the best defense is a good offense"; of how he daringly divided his army in the face of superior enemy forces, and how he successfully carried out this dangerous maneuver.

The army under General Pope was then occupying the line of the Rappahannock River, and seriously threatened the line of railroad from Richmond to Gordonsville. The purpose of General Pope, as related by him before the Committee on the Conduct of the War, was to have marched upon Gordonsville and Charlottesville, destroying the railroad, and then to move upon Richmond from the west.

It was imperative, then, for General Lee to check the advance of General Pope's army. The Confederate commander, with the small force at his command, was surely beset with difficulties at this time. One adversary with ninety thousand men was but a day's march from the Confederate capital, safely intrenched, and ready to take advantage of any invitation to attack, or any false step of his opponent. Another adversary with forty-three thousand men, unopposed, threatened to move upon his unprotected communications, and advance upon the capital from the west. To oppose the two, he had an army of about sixty-five thousand men available for operations in the field.

After allowing his army to enjoy a rest of about ten days, General Lee detached General Jackson, with the troops of his command, embracing his old division of four brigades and Ewell's division of three brigades, with orders to proceed toward Gordonsville, which point he reached on July 10th, and to move against General Pope. General A. P. Hill was soon ordered to follow with his division, and to join General Jackson. While these movements were being made, General Lee covered the city of Richmond with his remaining divisions.

On the 9th of August General Jackson attacked and defeated a part of the army of General Pope at Cedar Run. . . . Rickett's division of McDowell's corps reached the scene of action late in the day and served to check the Confederate advance. During the night General Pope was further reinforced by the arrival of Sigel's corps, so that on the morning of the 10th General Jackson was confronted by the greater part of Pope's army, and the other part was but a short distance away and hurrying to his support. . . . Under the existing conditions General Jackson could not resume the offensive. He had accomplished all that he dared to undertake with the force under his command: he had attacked a portion of the army under General Pope, routed it before it could be reinforced, greatly alarmed the authorities at Washington, and given to them a final argument, if one was needed, in favor of the withdrawal of the army under General McClellan from its position on James River to the support of the army in front of Washington. General Jackson therefore decided to retire on the night of the 11th toward Gordonsville.

Already the strategy of General Lee had accomplished the desired results. On the 4th of August General McClellan received orders to withdraw his army from the Peninsula. . . . The defeat of Banks' corps at Cedar Run greatly excited the fears of the Federals for the safety of Washington, and additional and urgent orders were sent to General McClellan to hasten the abandonment of the position at Harrison's Landing and the removal of his army to the front of Washington, to avert the threatened attack upon that city. . . .

General Lee had now become pretty well convinced, from the reports that reached him, of the proposed withdrawal of McClellan's army from its position on James River. . . . It therefore appeared that active operations on the James River were no longer contemplated by the Federals, and that the most effectual way to relieve Richmond from any danger of attack from that quarter would be to reinforce General Jackson and advance upon General Pope. . . .

Accordingly, on the 13th of August General Longstreet was ordered to proceed to Gordonsville. . . . General Stuart was directed to move with the main body of his cavalry to that point, and General R. H. Anderson was directed to . . . follow General Longstreet. These forces having assembled in the neighborhood of Gordonsville, General Lee determined to advance against the enemy at once.

4

Colonel Taylor speaks of the reports that reached General Lee regarding the transfer of McClellan's army from the James to the Washington front. How this report reached him is graphically told at first hand by that stormy petrel, John S. Mosby, the partisan ranger, who brought the news to General Lee in person. Mosby had been captured in a brush with the enemy a few weeks previously, then included in a batch of prisoners exchanged in early July and was sent along with them on an army transport to the exchange point on the James River near Richmond. But Mosby was already an experienced and skillful scout, trained to keep his eyes open and study the meaning of the things he saw.

When we arrived at Hampton Roads, I saw a large number of transports with troops lying near. As a prisoner I kept up my habits as a scout and soon learned that they were Burnside's troops who had just come from North Carolina. If they were reinforcements for McClellan, it would indicate that he would advance again on Richmond from his new base on the James. On the other hand, if they sailed up the Chesapeake, it would show that they were going to join Pope, and that McClellan would be withdrawn from the Peninsula. This was the problem that I had to solve. It was a pivotal point in the campaign. . . .

On the fourth day several steamers with prisoners from their places of confinement in the North anchored near us, and I was told that we were to start that evening up the James River, to the point where the commissioners would meet for the exchange. During the day I saw the transports with Burnside's troops weighing anchor and passing out by the fort. I had become pretty well acquainted with the captain of the steamer that brought us down from Washington, and found out that he was a Confederate in sympathy; so when he was going ashore for his orders, I asked him to find out where the transports were going. When he returned he whispered to me that Aquia Creek, on the Potomac, was the point. That settled it—McClellan's army would not advance, but would follow the transports northward.

I was feverish with excitement and anxiety to carry the news to General Lee, but nobody suspected what I had discovered, nor did I hear any comment on the movement of Burnside's troops. I was so restless that I sat nearly all night on the deck of the steamer, watching for the day star.

Early in the morning we arrived at the landing, and I was the first to jump ashore. As I was in a hurry and afraid of being detained by some formality in exchanging, I whispered to the Confederate Commissioner that I had important information for General Lee, and asked him to let me go. He made no objection.

It was a hot day in August, and I set out alone to walk twelve miles to headquarters. Some one in Washington had given me a patent-leather haversack and a five-dollar greenback. The latter I had invested in lemons at Fortress Monroe, for the blockade kept them out of Virginia. After trudging several miles I was so exhausted and footsore that I had to lie down by the roadside; but I held on to my lemons. A horseman—one of Hampton's legion—came along, and I told him how anxious I was to get to General Lee. He proved a benefactor indeed, for he put me on his horse, walked to his camp with me, got another horse and rode to General Lee's headquarters with me. . . .

I found myself in, what was then to me, the awful presence of the Commander-in-Chief. We had never met before, but I was soon relieved of embarrassment; General Lee's kind, benevolent manner put me at ease. I found him looking over a map on the table. As quickly as I could, I told him that Burnside's troops had been sent to Pope. . . . After I had finished my story, he asked me a few questions. I remember very well that he inquired on what line I thought the next movement against Richmond would be made, and that I considered it a high compliment that he should ask my opinion on such an important matter. He then called one of his staff into the room and told him to have a courier ready to go to General Jackson. . . . As soon as Jackson got the news about Burnside, he hastened to strike Pope at Cedar Mountain before reinforcements could reach him. . . .

When I rose to leave General Lee at this my first meeting with him, I opened my haversack and put a dozen lemons on the table.

He said I had better give them to some of the sick and wounded in the hospitals; but I left them and bade him good-by.

5

Having determined to assume the offensive, Lee moved his whole army below Orange Court House to a position south of Clark's Mountain, where he could make use of the fords of the Rapidan on Pope's flanks. General Long tells of Lee's movements after he reached this position, and of the difficulties that beset him in putting his plans into operation.

On the 18th, Lee and his staff ascended Clark's Mountain and reconnoitred the Federal position. In plain view before them lay Pope's army, stretched out in fancied security, and to all appearance in utter ignorance of the vicinity of a powerful foe. It was evident from that elevated position that the two armies were about equally distant from Culpeper Court-house, and that the Confederate force was in a position to gain the Federal rear. The absence of the cavalry, however, prevented an immediate advance, and Lee retained his position till the next day, satisfied that the enemy was still in ignorance of his danger. On the afternoon of the 19th the signal-station on the top of the mountain notified the Confederate commander that a change had occurred in the situation of affairs. The enemy had evidently taken the alarm. There was a bustle in the camp that indicated a move, as if Pope had suddenly learned the peril of his position and was preparing for a hasty flight toward the Rappahannock.

As it afterward appeared, Pope had learned of Lee's vicinity through the capture of Lieutenant Fitzhugh of Stuart's staff, on whom he had found a letter revealing the fact of the movement of the Confederate army. On gaining this important and somewhat startling information, he had immediately given orders to break camp and retreat in all haste to the line of the Rappahannock.

During this interval General Stuart himself had run a serious risk of capture. The main body of the cavalry, under Fitz Lee, failing to make their appearance at the point where Stuart awaited them, he had become impatient and advanced with some members of his staff to meet them. On the night of the 17th he occupied a house at Vediersville, intending to continue his search for the cavalry the next morning. At an early hour of that morning a squadron of Federal cavalry which was out reconnoitering suddenly made its appearance in front of the house which sheltered the Confederate general. The surprise was complete but, fortunately, the Federals did not dream of the valuable prize within their reach. Ere they were able to grasp the situation Stuart had become aroused and apprised of his imminent peril. He instantly sprang up and, without hat or haversack, rushed for the rear door of the house. There he sprang on his horse without heed of saddle or accoutrements and rode hastily into the woods, followed by those members of his staff who had accompanied him. The Federals learned only too late of the valuable prize which had slipped through their fingers, and had to content themselves with the hat and haversack of the dashing leader of the Confederate cavalry.

The retreating Federal army was followed by Lee in rapid pursuit, but it had crossed the Rappahannock by the time he reached the vicinity of that stream. Pope on crossing the river took up a position on the left bank, his left covering Rappahannock Station, his right extending in the direction of Warrenton Springs. Lee confronted him on the right bank of the river. The two armies remained thus opposed two or three days, during which nothing occurred except some unimportant skirmishing between the cavalry and the outposts.

When it became known in Washington that Pope had been compelled to retreat and recross the Rappahannock, the Federal authorities made every effort to rapidly reinforce him by troops drawn from the Army of the Potomac and from Burnside's force, which had been withdrawn from North Carolina. General Lee, in order to retard the forwarding of troops and supplies to the Federal army, ordered Stuart to turn Pope's right, gain his rear, inflict as much damage as he could upon the Orange and Alexandria Railroad, and gain information of the enemy's movements.

Stuart, in compliance with his instructions, crossed the Rappahannock late in the afternoon of the 21st, a few miles above Warrenton Springs, with a brigade of cavalry and, screening his movements by the mountain-spurs and intervening forests, he proceeded

toward the village of Warrenton, passing that place after nightfall, and advanced direct upon Catlett's Station on the railroad. Arriving in the midst of a violent storm, he surprised and captured
the Federal encampment at that place, which he found to contain
General Pope's headquarters. He secured Pope's letter-book and
papers, with many other valuable articles. . . . He returned, bringing with him his valuable booty, without the loss of a man. By the
capture of Pope's papers, Lee gained an accurate knowledge of the
situation of the Federal army.

6

The papers captured by Stuart showed Lee that troops were
moving from every direction to reinforce Pope. In such circumstances it was necessary for Lee to take some definite action—to advance or to retire. John Esten Cooke tells how
brilliantly the Confederate commander reacted to this crisis.

It was thus necessary to act with decision, and General Lee resolved upon a movement apparently of the most reckless character.
This was to separate his army into two parts and, while one remained confronting the enemy on the Rappahannock, send the
other by a long circuit to fall on the Federal rear near Manassas.
This plan of action was opposed to the first rule of the military
art, that a general should never divide his force in the face of an
enemy. That Lee ventured to do so on this occasion can only be
explained on one hypothesis, that he did not highly esteem the
military ability of his opponent. . . . The wooded character of the
theatre of war generally rendered such movements practicable, and
all that was requisite was a certain amount of daring in the commander who was called upon to decide upon them. This daring
Lee repeatedly exhibited, and the uniform success of the movements indicates his sound generalship.

To command the force which was now to go on the perilous
errand of striking General Pope's rear, General Lee selected Jackson, who had exhibited such promptness and decision in the campaigns of the Valley of Virginia. Rapidity of movement was neces-

sary above all things, and if any one could be relied upon for that, it was the now famous Stonewall Jackson. . . . Crossing the Rappahannock at an almost forgotten ford, high up and out of view of the Federal right, Jackson pushed forward day and night toward Manassas, reached Thoroughfare Gap in the Bull Run Mountains west of that place, passed through and completely destroyed the great mass of supplies in the Federal depot at Manassas. The whole movement had been made with such rapidity . . . that Manassas was a mass of smoking ruins almost before General Pope was aware of the real danger. Intelligence soon reached him, however, of the magnitude of the blow aimed by Lee and, hastily breaking up his camps on the Rappahannock, he hurried to attack the force assailing his communications. The first part of General Lee's plan had thus fully succeeded. General Pope . . . had disappeared suddenly, to go and attack the enemy in his rear. General Lee promptly moved in his turn, with the great corps under Longstreet, and pushed toward Manassas, over nearly the same road followed by Jackson.

The contest of generalship had now fully begun, and the brain of General Lee was matched against the brain of General Pope. It is no part of the design of this writer to exalt unduly the reputation of Lee and detract from the credit due his adversaries. . . . Of General Pope, however, it must be said that he suffered himself to be outgeneraled in every particular; and the pithy comment of General Lee, that he "did not appear to be aware of his situation" sums up the whole subject. . . .

Jackson reached and destroyed Manassas on the night of August 26th. . . . Then, having achieved his aim, Jackson fell back toward Sudley . . . and retired before the great force hastening to rescue them. He had with him about twenty thousand men, and General Pope's force was probably triple that number. Thus, the point was to hold General Pope at arm's-length until the arrival of Lee; and, to accomplish this great end, Jackson fell back beyond Groveton. There he formed line of battle, and waited.

. . . Under these circumstances, the true policy of General Pope was to obstruct Thoroughfare Gap, the only road by which Lee could approach promptly, and then crush Jackson. On the night of the 27th, General McDowell was accordingly sent thither with forty thousand men; but General Pope ordered him, on the next morning, to Manassas where he hoped to "bag the whole crowd," he said—that is to say, the force under Jackson. This was the fatal mistake made by General Pope. Thoroughfare Gap was comparatively undefended. While General Pope was marching to attack Jackson, who had disappeared, it was the next thing to a certainty that General Lee would attack *him*.

All parties were thus moving to and fro; but the Confederates enjoyed the very great advantage over General Pope of knowing precisely how affairs stood, and of having determined upon their own plan of operations. Jackson, with his back to the mountain, was waiting for Lee. Lee was approaching rapidly, to unite the two halves of his army. General Pope, meanwhile, was marching and countermarching, apparently ignorant of the whereabouts of Jackson, and undecided what course to pursue.

General Lee, in personal command of Longstreet's corps, reached the western end of Thoroughfare Gap about sunset, on the 28th, and the sound of artillery from the direction of Groveton indicated that Jackson and General Pope had come in collision. . . . It was certainly calculated to excite his nerves if they were capable of being excited. . . . Lee accordingly pressed forward, reached the Gap, and the advance force suddenly halted; the Gap was defended. The Federal force posted here . . . was small and totally inadequate for the purpose; but this was as yet unknown to General Lee. His anxiety under these circumstances must have been great. Jackson might be crushed before his arrival. He rode up to the summit of the commanding hill which rises just west of the Gap, and dismounting directed his field-glass toward the shaggy defile in front. . . . After reconnoitring for some moments without moving, he closed his glass slowly, as though he were buried in reflection and deliberating at his leisure, and, walking back slowly to his horse, mounted and rode down the hill.

The attack was not delayed. . . . The assault was successful. The small force of the enemy at the eastern opening of the Gap retired, and, by nine o'clock at night, General Longstreet's corps was passing through. All the next morning (August 29th) Longstreet's troops were coming into position on the right of Jackson, under the personal supervision of Lee. By noon the line of battle was formed. Lee's army was once more united. General Pope had not been able to crush less than one-half that army, for twenty-four hours nearly in his clutches, and it did not seem probable that he would meet with greater success, now that the whole was concentrated and held in the firm hand of Lee.

7

A participant's personal impressions of some of the interesting features of Jackson's march have been left by Major W. Roy Mason.

On the 23rd of August, as our brigade . . . was passing through an oak forest several miles from our starting-point in the morning, General Field and his staff riding leisurely at its head, we were hailed by General Fitzhugh Lee who, with his staff, had alighted on one side of the road. He requested us to dismount, as he had something to show us. He then slipped behind a big oak tree, and, in a moment or two, emerged dressed in the long blue cloak of a Federal general that reached nearly down to his feet, and wearing a Federal general's hat with its big plume. This masquerade was accompanied by a burst of jolly laughter from him that might have been heard for a hundred yards.

We inquired as to what this meant, and he told us that the night before he had made a raid upon Pope's headquarters, near Catlett's Station, with orders to capture him. He had surrounded his tent, but upon going in had found only the supper-table spread there, and near it a quartermaster and one or two minor staff-officers whom he took greatly by surprise. Pope's cloak and hat were in the tent, and he was told that the general had taken them off on account of the heat, and had walked down through the woods to visit the headquarters of some other general—where, they did not know. Being pressed for time, and anxious to retreat from a position that might soon become a dilemma, General Fitz Lee requested the quartermaster to open the military chest of his chief, which was found to contain . . . $350,000 in greenbacks, after which, mounting the Federal officers behind three of his men, he prepared to go. He did not forget to take the supper from the table, however, or the uniform coat and hat from the chair. . . .

We reached Manassas Plains on the morning of the 27th. . . . That evening we took possession of the enormous commissary and quartermaster stores of the enemy.

The buildings that sheltered them were sheds reaching . . . for many hundred yards and containing everything necessary to the equipment of an army, but, having only ambulances with us, we could carry nothing but medical supplies, which we found in abundance. The first order that General Jackson issued was to knock out the heads of hundreds of barrels of whisky, wine, brandy, etc., intended for the [Pope's] army. I shall never forget the scene when this was done. Streams of spirits ran like water through the sands of Manassas, and the soldiers on hands and knees drank it greedily from the ground as it ran.

General C. W. Field and staff took possession of the Federal headquarters. When we reached them, we found spread upon the table, untouched, a breakfast of cold chicken, lamb and biscuit, and coffee that by this time had also grown cold. It had not been spread for us, but—"*Telle est la fortune de la guerre.*" There was also a barrel of cut sugar, a sack of Java coffee and similar luxuries. There I found . . . a bed with feather pillows and bolster, upon which I at once threw myself, begging to be allowed to rest, if but for ten minutes.

In a short time General A. P. Hill sent us an order to burn all the quartermaster and commissary stores with all the buildings, and requested me to superintend the execution of the order. It was with the greatest pain that I complied with this order, as there were so many things that we of the South absolutely required; but we had no wagons to transfer them. It must be remembered that we were within twenty miles of Washington, with Pope's enormous army between us and Longstreet's corps. . . .

Before I executed my order in burning the commissary and quartermaster stores, however, I took the bolster-case from the headquarters tent, and filled it with cut sugar and tied it at one end, and filled the pillow-case with Java coffee, and succeeded in strapping both behind my horse, for which small act of providence I was amply praised by General Field.

8

A close-up and vivid picture of the man-killing hardships incident to the movement of a great army is found in the pages of the journal kept by John Dooley, an enlisted man in Long-street's corps, where is set down his reaction to the march to join Jackson at Manassas.

Day after day and night after night did we tramp along the rough and dusty roads, 'neath the most broiling sun with which the month of August ever afflicted a soldier, through rivers and their rocky valleys, over mountains and through rocky glen—on, on, scarcely stopping to gather the green corn from the fields to serve us for rations. Oh, how often when the mid-day sun poured down his fiercest beams, how often when my weary legs, feeling like lumps of bruised flesh, mechanically as it were moved one after the other (at the dead of night), how often was I tempted to lay down my musket and acknowledge myself conquered by the num-berless hardships and terrible fatigue of the campaign. But I felt it my duty to endure everything, and above all my pride sustained me; and from the bottom of my heart I was wont on occasions of such temptation to ask of God to give me renewed strength to en-able me to complete that arduous campaign.

During these marches the men were oftentimes unrecognizable on account of the thick coverings of dust which settled upon the hair, eye-brows and beard, filling likewise the mouth, nose, eyes and ears; and the poor victims are much like hard-toiling millers, although much more so.

Sometimes the road leads through the woods, and then how de-lightfully cool we feel, how lustily we cheer and sing our chorus with redoubled enthusiasm; for one of the chief helps in our com-pany towards keeping up gaiety and a cheerful heart is to march in time to some popular air which we all sing in chorus and repeat over and over again. I really think, nay I am sure, that half the fatigue of a march may be avoided or unfelt if the men have music to cheer their drooping spirits and enliven their lagging steps.

Miles upon miles of desolate track may be seen every day through fertile fields which should be teeming with rich harvests of luxuriant grain, but now they are trodden under foot by ruthless foes whose retreating steps are scarcely more destructive than the march of their avenging pursuers. Here the fences thrown down and the rails half burnt; the smoking homestead and the houseless, breadless orphan appeal to heaven for retribution upon a wanton cowardly foe whose brutal orders have been but too faithfully executed by a depraved and savage soldiery. . . .

Our marches were constant and nearly always prolonged into the night. One day I was sent some distance back to see if his regiment's wagons were very far behind and, if possible, to bring them up with the regiment. I found the road in our rear blocked completely by wagons of every description—commissaries', quartermasters', ordnance, etc., etc. The train extended to the rear at least ten or fifteen miles and his regiment's wagons were some three or four miles from our position; and I was informed that all the wagons of the whole corps had their proper place in line and could not, even though there was room on the road, leave the position assigned them. Our men were taking up their line of march and I was told to remain behind and bring up his regiment's wagons.

Here I had a fine view of nearly the whole of Longstreet's Corps. I stood upon a slight eminence and watched each brigade as it left in column last night's bivouac and marched towards a mill race which flowed nearly at the bottom of our slope. It was a glorious sight to see this little army, in so many divisions, approaching and crossing this stream at several points. The sun burst out from the heavy mist which had enveloped it and, glancing along the guns and accoutrements of the soldiers, filled meadow, hill and stream and heart with blithesome gaiety. How they shout and sing and laugh and joke while brigade after brigade pass by and ford the stream. Few care how wet they get; necessity urges, and what must be done they'll do quickly.

All the morning they were passing this stream, and to my inexperienced eye there appeared at least a hundred thousand men. But I learned afterwards that we had not at most more than thirty thousand in this corps.

The wagons are passing at another portion of the stream, and I stand waiting for ours to make their appearance, but in vain. Nearly every second wagon comes to a halt in the middle of the stream, which is deep, and the wagons are heavy and the horses, unlike the well-fed beasts of the Yankees, are weak and they must drink; and so there is much ado about getting out of the stream and clambering up the ground on the other side, which is anything but a level plain.

There I waited until late in the evening for our regimental train to come up, but it didn't come. I wish some of the wiseacres at home, who sit in cozy offices and write censorial articles about the inefficiency of Generals in failing to follow up their victories and in annihilating this and t'other army, could have stood where I did on that memorable day and watched the slow process of this immense train of wagons which was almost steadily passing here all day and at nightfall scarce one-half had crossed the little stream. They might then understand what it is to move a large army over rough, muddy and rocky roads, having but one road for troops, baggage, ordnance, ammunition, quartermaster's stores and commissaries. . . . To anyone who watched the progress of our army and the immense wagon trains, etc., absolutely necessary for its maintenance, it must have been evident that (en masse) celerity of movement was not and could not be (with either defeat or victory) our forte.

I grew weary watching wagon after wagon as it passed this little stream and still no sign of our own; I decided that our teams would come along just as quickly were I there or not; so I abandoned my post, following the road the army had taken, and trusting to come up with our men during the night. . . .

Before I leave this vicinity let me tell you that two men were hung at Stephensburg by a drum-head court martial, Gen. Longstreet commanding. The first of these men was a deserter, a West Virginian, and had been a captain in our army last year. Yesterday he was found in Stephensburg, recognized by his old companions, tried, condemned and executed. The other was a Yankee spy of remarkable daring. Gen. Lee, it appears, had dispatched a courier (a private of Hampton's Legion, many of whom wore a dingy-brown uniform) to General Longstreet to take various positions at the different fords in the Rappahannock which the enemy might occupy or prevent our crossing. The Yankee spy intercepted the courier in a lonely spot, killed him, took his dispatch, and dressed

himself in the dead man's brown suit of clothes. Hastening on to
General Longstreet he, instead of presenting his orders, announced
verbally that the General should march in an almost totally different direction from that commanded. Longstreet was perplexed,
the courier is detained. An officer of the General's Staff (formerly
of Hampton's Legion) does not recognize the courier; the body of
the murdered courier is found; and the spy is tried, condemned
and executed.

9

When Lee at length led Longstreet's men into position on
the right of Jackson's embattled corps, the stage was set for the
second battle of Manassas. The battle, fought on almost exactly the same ground as the first battle of the same name in
the summer of 1861, was one of the outstanding masterpieces
of Lee's military genius. General Maurice gives us a concise
but comprehensive sketch of it.

The perilous manoeuvre had been accomplished, and an opportunity highly favourable to the Confederates had been created.
While Pope was bringing his corps up piecemeal to attack Jackson,
Longstreet stood stretching well beyond the Federal left, ready to
strike a deadly blow. On this day Jackson had to play the part of
Wellington at Waterloo, and stand the pounding until Longstreet,
in the role of Blücher, gave the *coup-de-grace*. But the *coup* was
not given. Three times did Lee urge Longstreet forward, three
times did Longstreet find reason, which seemed to him good, for
not attacking. Longstreet was an obstinate man. It may be that
the experience of Malvern Hill weighed heavily on him, but it is
clear that he was obsessed by one idea. He believed the recipe for
victory to be to manoeuvre an army into a position such that the
enemy would be compelled to attack at a disadvantage, and there
await the blow. That belief of Longstreet's and consequent unwillingness to attack was later to be disastrous to the Confederate
cause, and it is at least probable that it saved Pope's army from
annihilation on August 29th. Longstreet had in front of him
Porter with very inferior numbers, and was so placed that he could

have speedily enveloped Porter's flank. Curiously enough, while Lee was pressing Longstreet to attack, Pope, who appears to have been unaware that Longstreet's whole force was in the field, was doing the same thing to Porter, who prudently refrained from so desperate a measure until he had more certain information of the force opposite him. After the battle Porter was dismissed for failing to do the very thing that Longstreet hoped he would do.

A share of the responsibility for Longstreet's inaction must be Lee's. One of the few defects of his generalship was a curious reluctance in battle to back his own judgment against that of his chief subordinates and to enforce his will upon them. It is a hard thing for a commander to draw the line correctly between undue interference and excess of liberty. Lee once described the principles which guided his conduct in battle. "My interference in battle would do more harm than good. I have then to rely on my brigade and division commanders. I think and work with all my power to bring the troops to the right place at the right time; then I have done my duty. As soon as I order them forward into battle, I leave my duty in the hands of God." This, as a system of command, is sound to a point. It is entirely applicable to the commander-in-chief of such huge armies as fought in the Great War, but in forces of the size which Lee commanded some more direct intervention when battle is joined is sometimes necessary. Lee was disposed to err on the battlefield in not asserting his authority enough. He suffered, as the French say, from the defects of his qualities, for it is probable that, if his character had allowed him to be more assertive, he would not have inspired in those he led the devotion which made them endure as men have rarely endured.

Having failed to get Longstreet to move on the 29th, Lee changed his plans for the 30th. He was aware that Pope would have taken advantage of the respite allowed him to bring all his troops within reach in due order to the battlefield. The reënforcements he had ordered from Richmond, numbering more than 20,-000 men, were fast approaching. They had, in fact, crossed the Rappahannock. He therefore decided to await Pope's attacks, to place Longstreet in position to assault the Federal left, and to watch for an opportunity to strike back.

Pope, who never throughout the battle grasped the situation, was deceived by some readjustments which Lee made in his line of battle into thinking that the Confederates were retreating. About noon he ordered an attack upon Jackson. Jackson stood firm and the Federals suffered severely from enfilading fire from Longstreet's guns. Pope then made the crowning mistake of taking troops from his left opposite Longstreet to support the attack on Jackson. The opportunity for the counter-attack had come, and Lee ordered a general advance. Longstreet, who was now fighting a battle after his own heart, had seen the chance and was already on the move. The Federal left was driven in. Their reserves behind Pope's center and right were ordered to the left to meet the new danger, and Jackson's attack, crashing forward against troops who had already suffered a repulse, completed the Confederate victory.

The effect of Jackson's destruction of the stores at Manassas and of the marches to and from which had preceded Pope's attacks had increased the strain of battle almost to breaking point. "The complete prostration of his troops from hunger and fatigue" of which Pope speaks was the natural reaction from gallant efforts made in adverse conditions. The prostration was increased by a retreat at night. Jackson's men were, however, too exhausted, Longstreet's too far off, for a prompt and vigorous pursuit of Pope into the position at Centreville to which he retreated. But on September 1st Pope threw up the sponge and wrote to Halleck that the army "should draw back to the entrenchments in front of Washington." Halleck perforce agreed; the retreat was continued, and on September 2d, McClellan was placed in command of all the troops within the defences of the capital.

10

An incident of Second Manassas as unexpected as it was pleasant to General Lee was his chance meeting with his son Robert during the heat of the battle. Robert tells of this encounter with his father, the first time they had met since the Seven Days' fighting around Richmond.

When I again saw my father, he rode at the head of Longstreet's men on the field of Manassas, and we of Jackson's corps, hard pressed [by Pope] for two days, welcomed him and the divisions which followed him with great cheers.

Two rifle-guns from our battery had been detached and sent to join Longstreet's advance artillery, under General Stephen D. Lee, moving into action on our right. I was "Number 1" at one of these guns. We advanced rapidly, from hill to hill, firing as fast as we could, trying to keep ahead of our gallant comrades, just arrived. As we were ordered to cease firing from our last position we took, and the breathless cannoneers were leaning on their guns, General Lee and staff galloped up, and from this point of vantage scanned the movements of the enemy and of our forces.

The General reined in "Traveller" close by my gun, not fifteen feet from me. I looked at them all some few moments and then went up and spoke to Captain Mason of his staff, who had not the slightest idea who I was. When he found me out he was greatly amused, and introduced me to several others whom I already knew. My appearance was even less prepossessing than when I had met my father at Cold Harbor, for I had been marching night and day for four days, with no opportunity to wash myself or my clothes; my face and hands were blackened with powder-sweat, and the few garments I had on were ragged and stained with the red soil of that section. When the General, after a moment or two, dropped his field glass to his side, and turned round to his staff, Captain Mason said: "General, here is some one who wants to speak to you." The General, seeing a much-begrimed artillery-man, sponge-staff in hand, said: "Well, my man, what can I do for you?" I replied, "Why, General, don't you know me?" and he, of course, at once recognized me, and was very much amused at my appearance and most glad to see that I was safe and well.

11

Lee was remarkably fortunate in passing through the entire four years of the war without a wound, although never shielding himself from the fire of the enemy. At Second Manassas, however, he did suffer an injury which was not only painful and troublesome, but which must have reduced his effectiveness during the important campaigning just ahead.

At this time a serious mishap befell General Lee, that made life a trial to him for several weeks, and came near depriving the army of his presence. It happened on the day after Pope's army had retreated, when General Lee halted for conference with General Longstreet. The party had dismounted near a high railroad embankment and culvert. General Lee, surrounded by a number of general and staff officers, held his horse with the bridle loosely depending from his arm. Suddenly a large number of prisoners, with a guard, swarmed over the embankment and scurried in the direction of General Lee and party. My recollection is that they moved in great haste because the fire from the enemy made it unsafe on the embankment. This sudden apparition frightened General Lee's horse, and he quickly threw up his head and jumped backward. General Lee was thrown violently to the ground, and both wrists were seriously sprained and the small bones of one hand broken. He had no use of either hand, and for some days each arm had to be carried in a sling. He could not ride his horse, and for some time thereafter moved in an ambulance. This was a sore trial to the general's patience. The ambulance could not go into many places where a horse would have carried him, and so his movements were greatly hindered: all this in addition to the physical suffering he was experiencing.

11

Maryland, My Maryland

THE invading Federal army having been driven out of Virginia and into the fortifications of Washington, Lee was confronted with the necessity for making a quick decision as to what to do next. No doubt he recalled the fruitlessness of the previous Confederate victory at Manassas and was resolved that on this occasion his victorious army would not be permitted to sacrifice its gains by inactivity.

As a matter of practical fact, it was virtually impossible for him to remain where he was. The immediate vicinity had been fought over and foraged by two armies for a week and was destitute of provisions. His line of communications with Richmond was 150 miles long, and was now interrupted by reason of the fact that Pope in his retreat had burned the bridges over the Rappahannock and the Rapidan. Lee's only alternative was to retreat or to advance. There was no advantage in going back closer to Richmond, except to shorten his line of supply; and such a movement would have the disadvantage of surrendering the gains of the campaign just completed, making it easy for the Federals to invade Virginia again. It was not feasible to advance directly against Washington, well fortified and on the farther side of a deep river.

Lee, in these circumstances, decided to move up the river a few miles above Washington and there cross over into Maryland. This course seemed to possess numerous advantages. In the first place, it would immediately get the troops into a region where they could live off the country. Then, too, such a movement was calculated to draw the Federal Army out of Washington in pursuit of him and thereby remove the threat of immediate invasion. It was also thought that the presence of the victorious Confederate Army in Maryland might cause the hesitant Marylanders to rally to the Southern cause—not to mention such an army's demoralizing influence on the Northern people.

So, on the fourth of September, hardly giving the tired soldiers time to catch their breath after all their marching and fighting of the preceding few days, the Army of Northern Virginia started to cross the Potomac at the fords near Leesburg, and by the seventh the whole army was north of the river—the first movement of a Confederate army into Northern territory.

1

The crossing of the Potomac River by the Army of Northern Virginia marked the opening of a new chapter in the war, the carrying of the fighting beyond the frontiers of the Confederacy. From the beginning the policy of the South had been, as expressed in Jefferson Davis's words: "All we want is to be let alone." But now the Confederate armed forces were carrying the war into the enemy's country—not exactly the enemy's country, it was hoped, for there was a belief that Maryland might still be induced to join the Confederacy if given an opportunity, protected by Confederate arms. The crossing of the river, aside from its effect on anybody else, exerted a strongly beneficial psychological effect on the soldiers in Lee's army. They were in high spirits as they made the crossing, as related by John Esten Cooke.

Maryland was now undefended; and the smoke of battle had scarcely lifted from the plains of Manassas when the victorious columns of Lee were in motion toward the upper Potomac. . . .

"On to Maryland!" was the watchword, and the veterans of Jackson moved forward at the signal, joyous, elated, confident of victory, and burning with ardor at the thought that the fair fields of Virginia, the homes of their loved ones, would be relieved of the horrors of war. No time was lost by General Lee in commencing his movement. It was necessary to gain a foothold in Maryland before the disorganized forces of the Federal Government were

again put in fighting condition, and the campaign began with
energy and rapidity. . . .

On the 5th the passage of the Potomac was effected without resistance. The scene is said to have been inspiring. "When our
army reached the middle of the river, which they were wading,"
says an army correspondent, "General Jackson pulled off his hat,
and the splendid band of music struck up the inspiring air of
'Maryland, my Maryland,' which was responded to and sung 'with
the spirit and with the understanding' by all who could sing; and
the name of all who could then and there sing was legion." . . .

Jackson had thus obtained an undisturbed foothold upon the
soil of Maryland, and his troops indulged in rosy dreams of the
exciting scenes and novel triumphs of a march through the rich
and unexplored territory of that enemy who had so long laid
waste the fields of Virginia. . . . But even the novel and attractive
scenes before them had not been sufficient to enable a large portion of the troops to overcome the exhaustion of the immense
march from the Rappahannock, together with the want of rest and
food. A large portion of the command . . . had broken down in
the rapid advance; all along the road from Manassas to Leesburg
thousands of stragglers, with weary frames and bleeding feet, were
toiling slowly on in the wake of the army; and the southern bank
of the Potomac swarmed with thousands of men who had sunk
down to obtain the rest which nature demanded and without
which they could advance no further. Before this great force
could rejoin the different corps, General Lee resumed his march;
the enemy pressed forward on his rear, the way was barred, and
the Army of Northern Virginia continued its march and fought
its enemies with less than two-thirds of its numbers. . . .

The reception of the Confederate forces in Maryland was not
encouraging. That ancient commonwealth . . . was now called
upon to decide, by its acts, whether the Southern proclivities
claimed for it were only theoretical, or such as to spur its people
on to overt acts against the Federal Government. The response
seemed to indicate an almost complete indifference, if not open
hostility, to the Confederates. . . . They had entered a portion of
the State entirely dissimilar to the lower counties, where the Southern sentiment was powerful. Here the Union feeling was in the

ascendant, as in Western Virginia, and little encouragement met the Southern arms. . . . There were, however, many exceptions to this want of cordiality in the demeanor of the people. One Marylander fed in a single day six hundred Southern soldiers; officers and men were urged to stop and use the houses and all they contained; many ladies sewed day and night on garments for the ragged troops; and from the houses of a few daring gentlemen waved white handkerchiefs and the Confederate flag. . . .

General Lee had given the strictest orders in relation to depredations by the troops; and the same writer adds, "Though thousands of soldiers are now roaming through the town [Frederick], there has not been a solitary instance of misdemeanor." A Marylander, Colonel Johnson, commanded the strong provost guard; no Union man was molested; "pay as you go" was the policy of the Southern leaders; and all kinds of property used by the troops, even the fence rails which they burned, were carefully paid for.

2

The depredations of General Pope's army in Virginia had been so unrestrained, there were fears north of the Potomac that General Lee's invasion of the North might be featured by retaliatory measures. To quiet any such apprehension, and to give an outline of his true purpose in leaving Virginia, Lee issued a proclamation:

Headquarters Army of Northern Virginia
Near Fredericksburg, September 8, 1862

To the People of Maryland:

It is right that you should know the purpose that has brought the army under my command within the limits of your state, so far as that purpose concerns yourselves.

The people of the Confederate States have long watched with the deepest sympathy the wrongs and outrages that have been inflicted upon the citizens of a Commonwealth allied to the states of the South by the strongest social, political and commercial ties.

They have seen, with profound indignation, their sister state deprived of every right, and reduced to the condition of a conquered province. Under the pretense of supporting the Constitution, but in violation of its most valuable provisions, your citizens have been arrested and imprisoned upon no charge and contrary to all forms of law. The faithful and manly protest against this outrage made by the venerable and illustrious Marylanders—to whom in better days no citizen appealed for right in vain—was treated with scorn and contempt. The government of your chief city has been usurped by armed strangers; your Legislature has been dissolved by the unlawful arrest of its members; freedom of the press and of speech have been suppressed; words have been declared offences by an arbitary desire of the Federal Executive, and citizens ordered to be tried by military commission for what they may dare to speak.

Believing that the people of Maryland possessed a spirit too lofty to submit to such a government, the people of the South have long wished to aid you in throwing off this foreign yoke, to enable you again to enjoy the inalienable rights of freemen, and restore independence and sovereignty to your state.

In obedience to this wish, our army has come among you and is prepared to assist you with the power of its arms in regaining the rights of which you have been despoiled. This, citizens of Maryland, is our mission, so far as you are concerned. No constraint upon your free will is intended—no intimidation will be allowed. Within the limits of this army, at least, Marylanders shall once more enjoy their ancient freedom of thought and speech. We know no enemies among you, and will protect all of every opinion. It is for you to decide your destiny, freely and without restraint. This army will respect your choice, whatever it may be; and, while the Southern people will rejoice to welcome you to your natural position among them, they will only welcome you when you come of your own free will.

R. E. LEE, General commanding.

3

One of Lee's generals, Major General John G. Walker, who had been left with his division to guard Richmond when the Army of Northern Virginia started its campaign against Pope in August, did not overtake the main body of the army until after it had crossed the Potomac on its invasion of Maryland and was camped near Frederick. Here he reported to Lee, and he has written a firsthand account of Lee's plans for the approaching campaign as revealed to him that day.

I went at once to General Lee, who was alone. After listening to my report, he said that as I had a division which would often, perhaps, be ordered on detached service, an intelligent performance of my duty might require a knowledge of the ulterior purposes and objects of the campaign.

"Here," said he, tracing with his finger on a large map, "is the line of our communications, from Rapidan Station to Manassas, thence to Frederick. It is too near the Potomac, and is liable to be cut any day by the enemy's cavalry. I have therefore given orders to move the line back into the Valley of Virginia, by way of Staunton, Harrisonburg and Winchester, entering Maryland at Shepherdstown.

"I wish you to return to the mouth of the Monocacy and effectually destroy the acqueduct of the Chesapeake and Ohio canal. By the time that is accomplished you will receive orders to coöperate in the capture of Harper's Ferry, and you will not return here, but, after the capture of Harper's Ferry, will rejoin us at Hagerstown, where the army will be concentrated. My information is that there are between 10,000 and 12,000 men at Harper's Ferry, and 3,000 at Martinsburg. The latter may escape toward Cumberland, but I think the chances are that they will take refuge at Harper's Ferry and be captured. Besides the men and material of war which we shall capture at Harper's Ferry, the position is necessary to us, not to garrison and hold, but because in the hands of the enemy it would be a break in our new line of communications with Richmond.

"A few days' rest at Hagerstown will be of great service to our men. Hundreds of them are barefooted, and nearly all of them are ragged. I hope to get shoes and clothing for the most needy. But the best of it all will be that the short delay will enable us to get up our stragglers—not stragglers from a shirking disposition, but simply from inability to keep up with their commands. I believe there are not less than from eight to ten thousand of them between here and Rapidan Station. Besides these we shall be able to get a large number of recruits who have been accumulating at Richmond for some weeks. I have now requested that they be sent forward to join us. They ought to reach us at Hagerstown. We shall then have a very good army, and," he smilingly added, "one that I think will be able to give a good account of itself."

"In ten days from now," he continued, "if the military situation is then what I confidently expect it to be after the capture of Harper's Ferry, I shall concentrate the army at Hagerstown, effectually destroy the Baltimore and Ohio road, and march to this point," placing his finger at Harrisburg, Pennsylvania. "That is the objective point of the campaign. You remember, no doubt, the long bridge of the Pennsylvania Railroad over the Susquehanna, a few miles west of Harrisburg. Well, I wish effectually to destroy that bridge, which will disable the Pennsylvania Railroad for a long time. With the Baltimore and Ohio in our possession and the Pennsylvania Railroad broken up, there will remain to the enemy but one route of communication with the West, and that very circuitous, by way of the Lakes. After that I can turn my attention to Philadelphia, Baltimore or Washington, as may seem best for our interests."

I was very much astonished at this announcement, and I suppose he observed it, for he turned to me and said:

"You doubtless regard it hazardous to leave McClellan practically on my line of communication, and to march into the heart of the enemy's country?" I admitted that such a thought had occurred to me.

"Are you acquainted with General McClellan?" he inquired. I replied that we had served together in the Mexican war, under General Scott, but that I had seen but little of him since that time.

"He is an able general, but a very cautious one. His enemies among his own people think him too much so. His army is in a very demoralized and chaotic condition, and will not be prepared for offensive operations—or he will not think it so—for three or four weeks. Before that time I hope to be on the Susquehanna."

Our conversation was interrupted at this point by the arrival of Stonewall Jackson, and after a few minutes Lee and Jackson turned to the subject of the capture of Harper's Ferry. I remember Jackson seemed to be in high spirits, and even indulged in a little mild pleasantry about his long neglect of his friends in "the Valley," General Lee replying that Jackson had "some friends" in that region who would not, he feared, be delighted to see him.

The arrival of a party of ladies from Frederick and vicinity, to pay their respects to Lee and Jackson, put an end to the conversation, and soon after I took my departure.

4

During the early days of the Maryland campaign there occurred one of those dramatic episodes which, stranger than fiction, played such a large part in the history of the war—the discovery by General McClellan (who had succeeded Pope) of Lee's entire plan of campaign, as set out in his Secret Order No. 191. The Indiana bluecoat, John M. Bloss, who found the fateful document, has left an account of the incident.

On September 13, Company F, 27th Indiana, was placed on the skirmish line in front of our brigade. We moved forward rapidly and soon reached the suburbs of Frederick. It was a warm morning and we threw ourselves upon the grass to rest. While lying there I noticed a large envelope. It was not sealed, and when I picked it up two cigars and a paper fell out.

The cigars were divided and, while the needed match was being secured, I began to read the enclosed document. As I read, each line became more interesting. It was Lee's order to his army, giving his plans for the next four days from that time and, if true, was exceedingly important. I carried it back to Captain Kopp of our company, and together we took it to Colonel Colgrove. He was at that time talking to General Kimball. They read it, I imagine, with the same surprise I had felt, and immediately started with it to General McClellan.

The order made known not only Lee's position, but his intent. . . . It showed that Lee proposed to divide his army on the 10th and that at this time, the 13th, it was really separated into five divisions and that three divisions were far away. . . . McClellan's army was practically concentrated and could strike McLaws or Hill or both. . . .

The time when I found the dispatch could not have been later than 10 o'clock on the 13th. I saw General Kimball start with it to McClellan's headquarters; he had a good horse, understood the importance of the dispatch, and has since told me that he carried it directly to General McClellan.

In about three-quarters of an hour after it was found, we noticed orderlies and staff officers flying in all directions, and soon the whole army was rapidly moving forward, the enemy attacked and driven over the Catoctin Mountains and across the Middletown Valley, and those who knew of the lost dispatch attributed this movement to it.

5

In after years there were some, including General Longstreet, who were inclined to cast doubt on the importance of the famous Lost Dispatch and its influence on General McClellan's movements. Any such doubts seem to be effectively disposed of by William Allan, that faithful chronicler of the Army of Northern Virginia.

The part played by this lost dispatch is a perfectly simple and plain one, and nothing but special pleading can obscure its importance. There are few soldiers on either side who do not recognize its decisive influence. General Lee . . . looked on it as a controlling factor in all the subsequent operations, and there was no doubt in his mind as to its supreme importance.

Besides transferring the theatre of war from Confederate territory and securing supplies for his army, General Lee expected that his invasion of Maryland would force the Federal army to leave Washington to oppose his progress. To inflict further damage upon that army was, of course, his prime object. Nor were his expectations ill-founded, for as soon as he entered Maryland the Federal army set out from the lines of Washington to meet him. This army, though largely superior in numbers to Lee, was much hampered in its movements by many causes. The half of it had just suffered a terrible defeat, and the work of reorganizing must be carried on while the army was moving. The change of commanders had taken place under discouraging circumstances; and General McClellan, though restored to power, did not possess the confidence of the Washington administration. An excessive sensitiveness as to the safety of Washington was the idea uppermost in the mind of Halleck, the Federal commander-in-chief, and caused him to clog McClellan still farther by incessant cautions, lest his bold adversary should make a flank attack upon the capital when once the Federal army was out of reach of it. Add to this that McClellan was one of the slowest and most cautious of commanders.

Some of these things, of course, General Lee did not know, but he knew well the bad condition of the Federal army; indeed, probably under-rated the rapidity with which it was recuperating. He knew the sensitiveness of the Federal government in regard to Washington; he knew the military character of the man opposed to him. Lee did not intend to fight McClellan east of South Mountain, nor to dispute the passage of that barrier with him. On the contrary, he desired to draw him into the country west of that range and then, when the Federal army was out of reach of Washington, he proposed to give battle on his own terms.

While awaiting the slow advance of the Federal army the feebleness of Halleck, or his antagonism to McClellan, gave Lee an unexpected chance to strike a blow. Some ten thousand men had been retained at Harper's Ferry, and invited capture. To Lee's bold but accurate judgment it was evident that a part of his army might be employed for some days in the capture of this garrison and its large material of war, and that his force could then be reunited in the Hagerstown Valley before McClellan would be ready to fight. . . .

No one can sit down and read the history of the Federal movements at that time without being convinced that, but for the captured dispatch, McClellan's progress would have been even slower than Lee anticipated. He was creeping along at a rate that would have given Lee all the time he wanted, and the farther McClellan got from Washington the more urgent became Halleck's cautions. The movements to the south of the Potomac of Walker and Jackson to complete the investment of Harper's Ferry confirmed Halleck in his fears. On September 12th President Lincoln telegraphed McClellan, "Jackson is crossing at Willamsport. Probably the whole rebel army will be drawn from Maryland." September 13th Halleck telegraphed, "Until you know more certainly the enemy's force south of the Potomac you are wrong in thus uncovering the capital." Again, on the 14th, Halleck said, "I fear you are exposing your left and rear." Even as late as the 16th Halleck expressed the conviction that Lee's plan was to re-cross the Potomac, turn McClellan's left, and cut him off from Washington. Halleck's fears thus made the case more favorable than Lee could have anticipated. But, apart from this, there was no ground then, as there is none now, for deeming Lee's expectations unreasonable. . . .

Lee's infantry left Frederick on the 10th; McClellan entered it on the 12th. Not a very keen pursuit, one would say. On the 13th McClellan obtained the lost dispatch, and at once everything changed. The groundlessness of Halleck's fears was evident; the movement of Confederate troops to the south of the Potomac was designed against Harper's Ferry—not, as Halleck thought, against Washington. Lee's whole plan of campaign was revealed to his antagonist; not simply his present position, but the movements for some days to come of every division of his army became known to McClellan. . . . McClellan, it is plain, did not under-rate the importance of the dispatch. He gave vent to demonstrations of joy at his good fortune in finding the lost order, and at once set to work to relieve Harper's Ferry and seize the opportunity presented by the division of Lee's army.

6

William Miller Owen, an observant young lieutenant in the Washington Artillery, which was in the van of the Confederate advance, has recorded the movements and events leading up to Lee's bloody battle with McClellan at Sharpsburg on the Antietam.

On the 13th it was reported that a cavalry skirmish had occurred at Frederick, and that McClellan with a large army, was following in our wake. We found excellent lager beer and cigars in Hagerstown, and the "secessionists" entertained us hospitably.

On the 14th the enemy, under McClellan, reached Turner's Gap near Boonesboro, and attacked D. H. Hill's division of 3,000 men. Longstreet's corps marched at daylight from Hagerstown to his relief. McClellan had caught us in a bad fix, for Jackson and A. P. Hill are still away at Harper's Ferry. Our column (Longstreet's) moves as fast as it can, and the firing at Boonesboro is distinctly heard. As we reached the outskirts of Boonesboro, at 3 o'clock, we met an ambulance, conveying the body of General Garland, who had been killed during the afternoon. Upon reaching the gap, two divisions . . . of Longstreet's corps were sent up the mountain to aid D. H. Hill; but it soon became manifest that our forces were not sufficient to resist McClellan's entire army, and, in view of this, Gen. Lee, at dark, ordered the troops to withdraw. Gen. Fitz Lee, of the cavalry, estimates McClellan's force at 100,000 men.

At 11 P.M. Longstreet and D. H. Hill, having been withdrawn, are marched in the direction of the Potomac to Sharpsburg, so that they may connect with Jackson and Hill when they shall come from Harper's Ferry.

The road is blocked with wagons and our movements are necessarily slow. General Lee and staff pass by and urge every one to move along as fast as possible. Reports are received that the enemy's cavalry occupies Sharpsburg.

We reached the vicinity of that town early in the morning of the 15th, crossed the Antietam by a stone bridge, and formed line of battle along the range of hills between the town and the stream, with our backs to the Potomac.

On the opposite shore of the Antietam the banks are quite steep and afford good position for artillery. Longstreet's corps forms the right of the main road, and D. H. Hill on the left. All the batteries present are placed in position along the ridge. Longstreet says, "Put them all in, every gun you have, long range and short range."

On the ridge near the First company were the batteries of Bachman and Riley, and here Gen. Lee established headquarters.

A courier arrives in hot haste, with news that Jackson has captured Harper's Ferry with its garrison of 12,000 men, 70 pieces of artillery and 13,000 small arms.

"This is indeed good news," said General Lee; "let it be announced to the troops"; and staff officers rode at full gallop down the line and the announcement was answered by great cheering.

Our lines were scarcely formed when the enemy appeared upon the opposite bank of the Antietam, and our artillery opened upon him a few guns, just to let him know that we were going no further and were at bay. Couriers were sent to Jackson and Hill to come to us as soon as possible. Our numbers in their absence are fearfully small, hardly 15,000 men, being those of Longstreet, D. H. Hill and Stuart's cavalry; and McClellan has 100,000; but they must be but hastily raised militia regiments, and don't count for much. Where do all these men come from? Pope had but 50,000 after the battle at Groveton last month.

All this day our thin line faced the whole of McClellan's army, and it closed with a little artillery practice on each side. . . .

For some unknown reason General Lee expressed his belief that there would not be much fighting on the morrow. He did not then know, as we learned afterwards, that McClellan held the key to all his movements, by having in possession a most important order, lost by General D. H. Hill at Frederick, and expected, from the information obtained, to crush Lee's army. McClellan was reported as saying, "If I don't crush Lee now, you may call me whatever you please."

At daylight, on the morning of the 16th, the enemy is in plain view on the high ground upon the opposite bank of the Antietam. His batteries are in position. They open fire, and become annoying. We reply . . . but the distance is too great to make a duel effective, and the firing is stopped by order of Gen. Lee. . . .

Riding through the town to find Gen. Longstreet, I met Gen. Lee on foot, leading his horse by the bridle. . . . The shells of the enemy were falling in close proximity to him, but he seemed perfectly unconscious of danger.

7

The sanguinary battle which ensued around the village of

Sharpsburg along Antietam Creek is described succinctly by
Robert S. Henry.

All day of the fifteenth [of September] Lee, with but half his
little army, stood to await attack, while off to the south the Union
garrison at Harper's Ferry, cooped up and ringed by artillery fire
plunging from the heights above them, was surrendering to Jackson. McClellan, however, did not attack that day—although he
could have put in line at any time after noon sixty thousand effec-
tives, more than three to one against Lee. Nor did he attack on
the sixteenth, except for pushing Hooker's corps across the creek
north of Lee's left and marching them toward Lee's flank until,
about dark, Meade's division made contact with the Confederates,
too late to do more.

Lee's decision to stand and fight a vastly superior army at Sharpsburg, with the Potomac at his back, is the most questionable of his
career. It was bold to the point of rashness—but Lee and the Confederacy were in a situation where boldness, and ever more boldness, was their only hope of success. The consequences of defeat
at Sharpsburg would have been appalling, but the possibilities of
victory, political and diplomatic, made it worth while to take the
risk. And, besides, Lee and the Army of Northern Virginia had
met this army coming against them before, and they could count,
with reason, upon its being handled cautiously. In the existing
situation, and with the combined military, political and diplomatic
problem which faced Lee, it is likely that he did the wise thing
by his decision at Sharpsburg to take risks with McClellan.

On September fifteenth, Harper's Ferry surrendered. Jackson
left A. P. Hill to complete the surrender, handle the prisoners,
eleven thousand of them, and gather up the spoils, while he
marched at once to rejoin his chief at Sharpsburg. On the way there
he heard of McClellan's advance to the line of the Antietam. "I
thought I knew McClellan," said Jackson to Walker, riding alongside, "but this movement of his puzzles me." Jackson did know
his man—they had been together at West Point—but he did not
know, then, of the lost order.

Of the tactical details of Sharpsburg, fought on September seventeenth, the bloodiest single day's fighting of the whole war, it is

not necessary to speak. McClellan, having on the field more than two men to every one that Lee had or could bring up, was yet unable to drive the Confederates from their battle position. Divisions and corps crossed the Antietam and advanced through the corn-fields or pasture lands on its slopes; through the woods on either side of the little white brick Dunkard Church on Lee's left; and, finally, across that sunken road along the Confederate center which was that day baptized as the Bloody Lane—but it was as divisions and corps they advanced, and not as an army. Wherever they pressed too strongly, Lee pushed in his scant reserve to stiffen the bending line, hesitating not at all to bring men from the right to support the failing left, or from the last of his reserves to sustain either flank, as the need arose. McClellan, with heavy reserves available, cautiously kept them as reserves instead of using them at the critical time and place.

Finally, in the afternoon of this most terrible day, McClellan sent forward his left wing, on the southern end of the line, to cross the Antietam by the old stone bridge, since known as Burnside's Bridge, and by the lower fords. At the bridge stood Toombs—Brigadier-General Robert Toombs he was now, and no longer a secessionist orator or the Secretary of State of the Confederacy. Almost had he been kept out of this battle. In the days before Cedar Mountain, while the troops were yet in Virginia, General Toombs had gone away one afternoon to call on one of his old Congressional friends living near by. While he was away, orders came from Longstreet, corps commander, for his brigade to move out and picket one of the fords of the Rapidan. Toombs, returning from his visit, found his troops moving, and moving on an order which had not come through him. Conceiving this to be in derogation of his military dignity, he peremptorily ordered them back to their camps, and left the ford unguarded. It was through this ford, it is said, that Pope's raiding cavalry got off with Stuart's dispatch book, giving away the first of Lee's plans. At any rate, Longstreet relieved Toombs of his command, and placed him in technical arrest. At the urgent entreaty of Toombs he was restored to command in time to take part in the battle, and right worthily he and his brigade stood and fought and held the line of the lower Antietam for an hour or more. And then when, after all, the weight of Burnside's corps pushed the Confederates back and up the hill and into the outskirts of the village, there came up through the corn-field to the south the division of Ambrose Hill, the "Light Division," which that day through September heat had marched from Harper's Ferry at top speed to take its part in the battle.

The division deployed as it came up and charged Burnside's corps in flank—a most demoralizing charge, with their red-shirted commander in front, joyous in the nick of battle. In peace this Hill, with his deep-set eyes and his beard of patriarchal proportions, was the mildest of men. In battle, he was born to fight—and, about Petersburg, to die. Is it any wonder that Jackson, in his dying delirium, and Lee, in his last breath, each called on Hill?

The battle was over, at fearful cost. Lee, with less than forty thousand men, lost about eight thousand that day; McClellan, who started the day with seventy thousand, lost more than twelve thousand.

During the night and early the next morning reenforcements numbering more than his losses joined McClellan. For Lee there were no reenforcements—but all through the day after the battle, with his shattered troops, he remained in position, inviting attack, and even considered a turning movement against McClellan's right flank. That night, however, urged by Longstreet and Jackson, he withdrew from his battle positions and forded the Potomac to the Virginia side, without any real molestation from the Union Army —then or for many weeks afterward.

8

During the closing, critical hours of the battle of Sharpsburg, General Lee had another battlefield encounter with his cannoneer son Robert, who has recorded the touching incident.

As one of the Army of Northern Virginia, I occasionally saw the commander-in-chief on the march or passed the headquarters close enough to recognise him and members of his staff, but a private soldier in Jackson's corps did not have much time, during that campaign, for visiting, and until the battle of Sharpsburg I had no opportunity of speaking to him.

On that occasion our battery had been severely handled, losing many men and horses. Having three guns disabled, we were ordered to withdraw, and while moving back we passed General Lee and several of his staff, grouped on a little knoll near the road. Having no definite orders where to go, our captain, seeing the commanding general, halted us and rode over to get some instructions. Some others and myself went along to see and hear.

General Lee was dismounted, with some of his staff around him, a courier holding his horse. Captain Poague, commanding our battery, the Rockbridge Artillery, saluted, reported our condition and asked for instructions. The General, listening patiently, looked at us—his eyes passing over me without any sign of recognition—and then ordered Captain Poague to take the most serviceable horses and men, man the uninjured gun, send the disabled part of his command back to refit, and report to the front for duty. As Poague turned to go, I went up to speak to my father. When he found out who I was, he congratulated me on being well and unhurt. I then said:

"General, are you going to send us in again?"

"Yes, my son," he replied with a smile. "You all must do what you can to help drive these people back."

9

Both sides were stunned by the fury of the Sharpsburg fighting. Major Jed Hotchkiss tells of conditions on the Confederate side, and quotes Colonel Stephen D. Lee as to the conference of Lee and his generals following the battle.

Sharpsburg was a stand-up, hand-to-hand fight, as brave and furious as any the world ever saw, and the Confederate soldiers had in it proved themselves more than a match, in a fair and open conflict, for their Federal foes. The losses on both sides indicate the nature of the struggle. The living of both armies, as the sounds of battle died away, sunk to profound slumber, such as only follows a day of battle, in the very lines where they had fought and amid the horrors of the carnage of the bloody battlefield.

At nightfall Lee held the line of the Hagerstown turnpike and of the road leading south from Sharpsburg, and the line on his left which Jackson had chosen before the battle as the one he would hold; and his unconquerable veterans were ready to renew the combat at his word of command. The Federals had really gained and held no advantages of position.

Colonel Stephen D. Lee, the Confederate chief of artillery, stated to the writer that an hour after dark on the 17th General Lee summoned his division commanders to meet him at his head-quarters in the wood in the rear of Sharpsburg, and as each came up he quietly asked him: "How is it on your part of the line?" Longstreet replied: "As bad as can be"; Hill, "My division is cut to pieces"; Hood declared with great emotion that he had "no division left." Colonel Lee asserted that all of these officers advised that the army should cross the Potomac before daylight; but that General Lee, after a profound pause, said: "Gentlemen, we will not cross the Potomac to-night. You will go to your respective commands, strengthen your lines, send two officers from each brigade toward the ford to collect your stragglers and bring them up. Many others have come up. I have had the proper steps taken to collect all the men who are in the rear. If McClellan wants to fight in the morning, I will give him battle again."

Some 5,000 Confederate stragglers joined their comrades during the night of the 17th, and the morning of the 18th dawned upon the lines of contending forces, drawn up face to face at close range and ready for a renewal of the mighty struggle; but both stood on the defensive, and not a gun was fired during the livelong day. Lee was not only willing but eager to renew the battle, in which he was earnestly seconded by Jackson, who suggested that if fifty heavy guns were sent to the Nicodemus Ridge beyond his left they could silence the Federal guns on the Poffenberger Ridge and open the way for falling on the Federal right. Colonel S. D. Lee accompanied Jackson, at General Lee's suggestion, to reconnoiter the chances for success in such an attempt. The chief of artillery pronounced the undertaking not only impracticable but extremely hazardous and, to the great disappointment of both Lee and Jackson, the movement was abandoned.

Learning during the afternoon of the 18th that large reinforcements were advancing to McClellan from both the North and East, Lee determined to cross into Virginia; and that night, in good order, and leaving nothing behind him but his dead and wounded who could not be moved, he crossed his army through the Potomac. At the same time Stuart crossed his cavalry through the river at a ford on Lee's left, went up it to Williamsport and recrossed and threatened McClellan's right and rear, thus engaging his attention while Lee took his long trains and his army back into Virginia.

10

General Walker, whose men were the last of the Confederates to cross the Potomac on the retreat from Sharpsburg, gives us a striking picture of General Lee on that trying occasion.

As night closed down [on the 17th], the firing along the whole line ceased; one of the bloodiest and most hotly contested battles of the war had been fought. The men of my division—worn out by a week's incessant marching and fighting by day and night— dropped down where they were, and could with difficulty be roused, even to take their cooked rations, brought up from our camp in the rear. . . .

During the whole of the 18th the two armies rested in the positions which they had occupied at the close of the battle. There was a tacit truce, and Federal and Confederate burying-parties passed freely between the lines.

We had fought an indecisive battle, and although we were, perhaps, in as good a condition to renew the struggle as the enemy were, General Lee recognized the fact that his ulterior plans had been thwarted by this premature engagement, and after a consultation with his corps commanders he determined to withdraw from Maryland. At dark on the night of the 18th the rearward movement began; and a little after sunrise of the next morning the entire Confederate army had safely recrossed the Potomac at Shepherdstown.

Detained in superintending the removal of a number of the wounded of my division, I was among the last to cross the Potomac. As I rode into the river I passed General Lee, sitting on his horse in the stream, watching the crossing of the wagons and artillery. Returning my greeting, he inquired as to what was still behind. There was nothing but the wagons containing my wounded, and a battery of artillery, all of which were near at hand, and I told him so. "Thank God!" I heard him say as I rode on.

11

The Maryland invasion, culminating in the battle of Sharpsburg, or Antietam, has been the subject of much discussion and controversy by military experts and other writers. What seems to be a fairly well-balanced estimate of the campaign is given by one writer who took part in it, John Esten Cooke.

General Lee and his adversary had displayed conspicuous merit in the campaign thus terminated, and we shall pause for a moment to glance back upon this great passage at arms.

. . . General McClellan . . . had assembled an army, after the defeat at Manassas, with a promptness for which only his own great personal popularity can adequately account, had advanced to check Lee, and had fully succeeded in doing so; and had thus not only protected the fertile territory of Pennsylvania from invasion, but had struck a death-blow for the time to any designs General Lee might have had to advance on the Federal capital. If the situation of affairs at that moment be attentively considered, the extreme importance of these results will not fail to appear. It may perhaps be said with justice that General McClellan had saved the Federal cause from decisive defeat. There was no army to protect Washington but the body of troops under his command; these were largely raw levies, which defeat would have broken to pieces, and thus the way would have been open for Lee's march upon Washington or toward Philadelphia—a movement whose probable result would have been a treaty of peace and the independence of the Southern Confederacy. All these hopes were reversed by McClellan's rapid march and prompt attack. In the hours of a single autumn day, on the banks of the Antietam, the triumphant advance of the Confederates was checked and defeated. And, if the further fact be considered that the adversary thus checkmated was Lee, the military ability of General McClellan must be conceded. . . .

The merit of Lee was equally conspicuous, and his partial failure in the campaign was due to circumstances over which he had no control. His plan, as was always the case with him, was deeplaid, and every contingency had been provided for. He was disappointed in his aim by three causes which he could not foresee. One was the great diminution of his force, owing to the rapidity of his march, and the incessant fighting; another, the failure in obtaining recruits in Maryland; and a third, the discovery by General McClellan of the "lost dispatch," as it is called, which revealed Lee's whole plan to his adversary. In consequence of the "finding" of the order of march, McClellan advanced with such rapidity that the laggards of the Southern army on the hills north of Leesburg had no opportunity of joining the main body. The gaps in the ranks of the army thus made were not filled up by Maryland recruits; Lee fell back, and his adversary followed, no longer fearful of advancing too quickly; Jackson had no time after reducing Harper's Ferry to rejoin Lee at Hagerstown; thus concentration of his troops and a battle somewhere near Sharpsburg were rendered a necessity with General Lee. . . .

From what is here written, it will be seen that Lee was not justly chargeable with the result of the Maryland campaign. He had provided for every thing as far as lay in his power. Had he not been disappointed in events to be fairly anticipated, it seemed his force would have received large accessions, his rear would have closed up, and the advance into Pennsylvania would have taken place. Instead of this, he was forced to retire and fight a pitched battle at Sharpsburg; and this action certainly exhibited on Lee's part military ability of the highest order. The force opposed to him had been at least double that of his own army, and the Federal troops had fought with a gallantry unsurpassed in any other engagement of the war. That their assault on Lee failed was due to the fighting qualities of his troops and his own generalship. His army had been manoeuvered with a rapidity and precision which must have excited even the admiration of the distinguished soldier opposed to him. He had promptly concentrated his forces opposite every threatened point in turn, and if he had not been able to carry out the axiom of Napoleon, that a commander should always be superior to the enemy at the point of contact, he had at least done all that was possible to effect that end, and had so far succeeded as to have repulsed if not routed his adversary. This is the main feature to be noticed in Lee's handling of his troops at Sharpsburg. An unwary or inactive commander would have there suffered decisive defeat, for the Confederate left wing numbered, throughout the early part of the battle, scarcely more than four thousand men, while the column directed against it amounted first to eighteen thousand, and in all to forty thousand. To meet the impact of this heavy mass, not only desperate fighting, but rapid and skillful manoeuvering was necessary. . . .

Military critics, examining this great battle with fair and candid eyes, will not fail, we think, to discern the truth. That the Southern army, of less than forty thousand men, repulsed more than eighty thousand in the battle of Sharpsburg was due to the hard fighting of the smaller force, and the skill with which its commander manoeuvered it.

12

Lee himself was not unmindful of the qualities displayed by his army in the Maryland campaign, and he was quick to give voice to his admiration in a congratulatory order issued to the troops as soon as they had gone into camp on the Virginia side of the river.

In reviewing the achievements of the army during the present campaign, the commanding general can not withhold the expression of his admiration of the indomitable courage it has displayed in battle and its cheerful endurance of privation and hardship on the march. Since your great victories around Richmond you have defeated the enemy at Cedar Mountain, expelled him from the Rappahannock and, after a conflict of three days, utterly repulsed him on the plains of Manassas and forced him to take shelter within the fortifications around his capital. Without halting for repose you crossed the Potomac, stormed the heights of Harper's Ferry, made prisoners of more than eleven thousand men, and captured upward of seventy-five pieces of artillery, all their small arms, and other munitions of war. While one corps of the army was thus engaged, the other insured its success by arresting at Boonesborough the combined armies of the enemy, advancing under their favorite general to the relief of their beleaguered comrades.

On the field of Sharpsburg, with less than one-third his numbers, you resisted from daylight until dark the whole army of the enemy and repulsed every attack along his entire front of more than four miles in extent. The whole of the following day you stood prepared to resume the conflict on the same ground, and retired next morning without molestation across the Potomac. Two attempts subsequently made by the enemy to follow you across the river have resulted in his complete discomfiture and being driven back with loss. Achievements such as these demanded much valor and patriotism. History records few examples of greater fortitude and endurance than this army has exhibited, and I am commissioned by the President to thank you in the name of the Confederate States for the undying fame you have won for their arms.

Much as has been done, much more remains to be accomplished. The enemy again threatens with invasion, and to your tried valor and patriotism the country looks with confidence for deliverance and safety. Your past exploits give assurance that this confidence is not misplaced.

13

Lee's retreat from Sharpsburg was accomplished in an orderly and leisurely manner. McClellan seemed to have had enough fighting for the present, and did not pursue his retreating enemy. The Army of Northern Virginia went into camp near Winchester and spent several weeks there licking its wounds and doing all it could to recuperate. Later, after McClellan had crossed to the south side of the Potomac and advanced to Warrenton, Lee, with Longstreet's corps, took a position near Culpeper, Jackson remaining in the Valley near Winchester. Those weeks of rest and relaxation were of great value to Lee's army physically; and there also seemed to develop at this time a closer bond of mutual understanding and affection between the commander and his men. John Esten Cooke has commented on it.

General Lee and his army passed the brilliant days of autumn in the beautiful valley of the Shenandoah . . . and the benign influence of their surroundings was soon seen on the faces of the troops.

A Northern writer who saw them at Sharpsburg describes them as "ragged, hungry and in all ways miserable"; but their forlorn condition, as to clothing and supplies of every description, made no perceptible difference in their demeanor now. In their camps along the picturesque little stream called the Opequan . . . the troops laughed, jested, sang rude camp-ballads and exhibited a joyous indifference to their privations and hardships, which said much for their courage and endurance. Those who carefully considered the appearance and demeanor of the men at that time saw that much could be effected with such tough material, and had another opportunity to witness, under circumstances calculated to test it, the careless indifference to the past as well as the future peculiar alike to soldiers and children. These men, who had passed through a campaign of hard marches and nearly incessant battles, seemed to have forgotten all their troubles and sufferings. The immense strain upon their energies had left them apparently as fresh and efficient as when the campaign begun. There was no want of rebound; rather an excessive elasticity and readiness to undertake new movements. They had plainly acquired confidence in themselves, rightly regarding the event of the battle of Sharpsburg, where they were so largely outnumbered, as highly honorable to them, and they had acquired still greater confidence in the officers who commanded them. . . .

The great events of the war continually modified the relations between him [General Lee] and his men; as they came to know

him better and better he steadily rose in their admiration and regard. At this time—the autumn of 1862—it may be said that the
troops had already begun to love their leader and had bestowed
upon him as an army commander their implicit confidence. . . .
The men universally felt that their commander was equal to any
and every emergency. . . . Lee had already impressed the army with
a profound admiration for his soldiership. From this to the sentiment of personal affection the transition was easy; and the kindness, consideration and simplicity of the man made all love him.
Throughout the campaign Lee had not been heard to utter one
harsh word; a patient forbearance and kindness had been constantly exhibited in all his dealings with officers and men; he was
always in front, indifferent plainly to personal danger, and the men
looked now with admiring eyes and a feeling of ever-increasing affection on the erect, soldierly figure in the plain uniform, with
scarce any indication of rank, and the calm face, with its expression of grave dignity and composure, which remained unchanged
equally on the march and in battle.

It may be said that when he assumed command of the army before Richmond the troops had taken him on trust; now they had
come to love him, and when he appeared the camps buzzed, the
men ran to the road, called out to each other: "There goes Mas'
Robert!" or "Old Uncle Robert!" and cheers followed him as he
rode by.

14

Among the visitors to the Army of Northern Virginia while
it was in camp near Winchester was Colonel Garnet Wolseley
of the British army, who wrote his impressions of what he saw
there, especially his impression of the simplicity and acces-
sibility of the commanding general.

In visiting the headquarters of the Confederate generals, particularly those of General Lee, any one accustomed to see European
armies in the field can not fail to be struck with the great absence
of all the pomp and circumstance of war in and around their encampments.

Lee's headquarters consisted of about seven or eight pole tents pitched, with their backs to a stake-fence, upon a piece of ground so rocky that it was unpleasant to ride over it, its only recommendation being a little stream of good water which flowed close by the General's tent. In front of the tents were some three or four army wagons, drawn up without any regularity, and a number of horses turned loose about the field. The servants—who were, of course, slaves—and the mounted soldiers called couriers, who always accompany each general of division in the field, were unprovided with tents and slept in or under the wagons. Wagons, tents and some of the horses were marked "U.S.," showing that part of that huge debt in the North has gone to furnishing even the Confederate generals with camp equipment.

No guard or sentries were to be seen in the vicinity, no crowd of aides-de-camp loitering about making themselves agreeable to visitors and endeavoring to save their generals from receiving those who had no particular business. A large farm-house stands close by, which in any other army would have been the general's residence *pro tem;* but, as no liberties are allowed to be taken with personal property in Lee's army, he is particular in setting a good example himself.* His staff are crowded together, two or three in a tent; none are allowed to carry more baggage than a small box each, and his own kit is but very little larger. Every one who approaches him does so with marked respect, although there is none of that bowing and flourishing of forage caps which occurs in the presence of European generals; and, while all honor him and place implicit faith in his courage and ability, those with whom he is most intimate feel for him the affection of sons to a father.

---

* Colonel Wolseley could not know it at the time, but there was an amusing story in connection with the location of the camp. General Long relates the circumstances: "The army had preceded the General and taken possession of every desirable camping-place. After a long and fatiguing search a farm-house was discovered, surrounded by a large shady yard. The occupants of the house with great satisfaction gave permission for the establishment of General Lee not only in the yard, but insisted on his occupying a part of the house. Everything being satisfactorily settled, the wagons were ordered up; but just as their unloading began the General rode up and flatly refused to occupy either yard or house. No one expected him to violate his custom by occupying the house, but it was thought he would not object to a temporary occupation of the yard. Being vexed at having to look for another place for headquarters, I ordered the wagons into a field almost entirely covered with massive stones. The boulders were so large and so thick that it was difficult to find space for the tents. When the tents were pitched, the General looked around with a smile of satisfaction, and said, 'This is better than the yard. We will not now disturb those good people.'"

Old General Scott was correct in saying that when Lee joined the Southern cause it was worth as much as the accession of 20,000 men to the "rebels." Since then every injury that it was possible to inflict the Northerners have heaped upon him. Notwithstanding all these personal losses, however, when speaking of the Yankees he neither evinced any bitterness of feeling nor gave utterance to a single violent expression, but alluded to many of his former friends and companions among them in the highest terms. He spoke as a man proud of the victories won by his country and confident of ultimate success under the blessing of the Almighty, whom he glorified for past successes, and whose aid he invoked for all future operations.

15

Lee's capacity for subordinating his private feelings and interests to the duties of his official position is impressively shown in a touching story told by Colonel Taylor:

Tidings reached General Lee, soon after his return to Virginia [from Maryland] of the serious illness of one of his daughters—the darling of the flock [Annie]. For several days apprehensions were entertained that the next intelligence would be of her death. One morning the mail was received, and the private letters were distributed as was the custom; but no one knew whether any home news had been received by the general. At the usual hour he summoned me to his presence to know if there were any matters of army routine upon which his judgment and action were desired. The papers containing a few such cases were presented to him; he reviewed and gave his orders in regard to them. I then left him, but for some cause returned in a few moments and, with my accustomed freedom, entered his tent without announcement or ceremony. I was startled and shocked to see him overcome with grief, an open letter in his hands. That letter contained the sad intelligence of his daughter's death. . . .

His army demanded his first thought and care; to his men, to their needs, he must first attend, and then he could surrender himself to his private, personal affairs. Who can tell with what anguish of soul he endeavored to control himself and maintain a calm exterior, and who can estimate the immense effort necessary to still the heart filled to overflowing with tenderest emotions, and to give attention to the important trusts committed to him before permitting the more selfish indulgence of private meditation, grief and prayer? "Duty first" was the rule of his life, and his every thought, word and action was made to square with duty's inexorable demands.

12

Fredericksburg and Chancellorsville

IT IS related that when General Lee went to Richmond late in October to confer with President Davis he was hardly recognized at the War Department, so white had his beard become—and surely his experiences of the past two months had been sufficient to add that touch of frost to his head. But now he must make plans for the future. The Federal Army was again on the south side of the Potomac, and would not remain forever inactive. He must be ready to move when they moved.

As Lee, through his scouts, alertly watched the enemy, President Lincoln, displeased with McClellan's failure to take aggressive steps against his opponent, removed him from the command of the Army of the Potomac and replaced him with General Ambrose E. Burnside. The news of McClellan's dismissal was received by Lee with mixed emotions. In later years he expressed the opinion that McClellan was the ablest of all the Northern generals who had opposed him. To his wife at this time he wrote jestingly, "I hate to see McClellan go. He and I had grown to understand each other so well." It was obvious, on the other hand, that Burnside had been placed in command of the Federal Army for no other reason than to get it into action, so Lee redoubled his vigilance to meet whatever action might be taken.

Burnside, within a few days of assuming command, submitted to Halleck a plan to advance on Richmond by way of Fredericksburg. It was said (after the plan failed) that Halleck and Lincoln had both doubted the wisdom of the movement and consented to it with reluctance. On the other hand, Burnside later claimed that the scheme had been forced on him by the Washington authorities. At any rate, it was agreed that the movement should be made. Burnside started his army by the left flank on the fifteenth of November; and Lee, quickly informed of the movement, divined the destination of the marching Federals and immediately started to move his own forces to Fredericksburg on the southern side of the Rappahannock, to oppose Burnside's crossing.

1

A good description of the lay of the land and the placement of the troops at Fredericksburg is given by one who played a prominent part in the subsequent battle there and the events leading up to it, General James Longstreet.

We made a forced march and arrived on the hills around Fredericksburg about 3 o'clock on the afternoon of the 21st. . . . Very soon after I reached Fredericksburg the remainder of my corps arrived from Culpeper Court House, and as soon as it was known that all the Army of the Potomac was in motion for the prospective scene of battle Jackson was drawn down from the Blue Ridge. In a very short time the Army of Northern Virginia was face to face with the Army of the Potomac. . . .

At a point just above the town, a range of hills begins, extending from the river out a short distance and bearing around the valley somewhat in the form of a crescent. On the opposite side are the noted Stafford Heights, then occupied by the Federals. At the foot of these hills flows the Rappahannock River. On the Confederate side nestled Fredericksburg, and around it stretched the fertile bottoms from which fine crops had been gathered and upon which the Federal troops were to mass and give battle to the Confederates. On the Confederate side nearest the river was Taylor's Hill, and south of it the now famous Marye's Hill; next, Telegraph Hill, the highest of the elevations on the Confederate side (later known as Lee's Hill, because during the battle General Lee was there most of the time), where I had my headquarters in the field; next was a declination through which Deep Run Creek passed on its way to the Rappahannock River; and next was the gentle elevation at

Hamilton's Crossing, not dignified with a name, upon which Stone-wall Jackson massed thirty thousand men.

It was upon these hills that the Confederates made their preparations to receive Burnside whenever he might choose to cross the Rappahannock. The Confederates were stationed as follows: On Taylor's Hill next the river and forming my left, R. H. Anderson's division; on Marye's Hill, Ransom's and McLaws's divisions; on Telegraph Hill, Pickett's division; to the right and about Deep Run Creek, Hood's division, the latter stretching across Deep Run Bottom.

On the hill occupied by Jackson's corps were the divisions of A. P. Hill, Early and Taliaferro, that of D. H. Hill being in reserve on the extreme right. To the Washington Artillery, on Marye's Hill, was assigned the service of advising the army at the earliest possible moment of the Federal advance. General Barksdale, with his Mississippi brigade, was on picket duty in front of Fredericksburg on the night of the advance.

The hills occupied by the Confederate forces, although over-crowned by the heights of Stafford, were so distant as to be outside the range of effective fire of the Federal guns and, with the lower receding grounds between them, formed a defensive series that may be likened to natural bastions. Taylor's Hill on our left was unassailable; Marye's Hill was more advanced toward the town, was of a gradual ascent and of less height than the others, and we considered it the point most assailable, and guarded it accordingly. The events that followed proved the correctness of our opinion on that point. Lee's Hill, near our center, with its rugged sides retired from Marye's and rising higher than its companions, was comparatively safe.

This was the situation of the 65,000 Confederates massed around Fredericksburg, and they had twenty-odd days in which to prepare for the approaching battle.

The Federals on Stafford Heights carefully matured their plans of advance and attack. General Hunt, chief of artillery, skillfully posted 147 guns to cover the bottoms upon which the infantry was to form for the attack, and at the same time play upon the Confederate batteries as circumstances would allow. Franklin and Hooker had joined Sumner, and Stafford Heights held the Federal

army, 116,000 strong, watching the plain where the bloody conflict was soon to be. In the meantime the Federals had been seen
along the banks of the river, looking for the most available points
for crossing. President Lincoln had been down with General Halleck, and it had been suggested by the latter to cross at Hoop-pole
Ferry, about 28 or 30 miles below Fredericksburg. We discovered
the movement, however, and prepared to meet it, and Burnside
abandoned the idea and turned his attention to Fredericksburg,
under the impression that many of our troops were down at Hoop-
pole, too far away to return in time for this battle.

The soldiers of both armies were in good fighting condition, and
there was every indication that we would have a desperate battle.
We were confident that Burnside could not dislodge us, and patiently awaited the attack.

2

Lee had determined his tactical course—to permit Burnside
to cross the Rappahannock unopposed, and then fight off any
attack he might make on the strong Confederate defensive position. There was hardly more than a token opposition by a
few sharpshooters when the Federals threw their pontoon
bridges across the river, crossed over to the south side and
massed in Fredericksburg and the fields about it. The battle of
Fredericksburg was opened on December 13 with an attack
on Jackson's end of Lee's defensive line, the Confederate right.
A participant in the repulse of the attack, J. H. Moore, tells of
that brisk engagement.

The morning of the 13th dawned with a dense fog enveloping
the plain and city of Fredericksburg, through which the brilliant
rays of the sun struggled about 10 in the morning. In front of the
right of the Confederate army was the vast force of Franklin,
marching and countermarching, hastily seeking the places assigned
for the coming conflict. Here was a vast plain, now peopled with
an army worthy of its grand dimensions. A slight but dazzling
snow beneath, and a brilliant sun above, intensified the leaping
reflections from thousands of gleaming bayonets. Officers on rest-

less horses rushed from point to point in gay uniforms. Field-artillery was whisked into position as so many fragile toys. Rank and file, foot and horse, small-arms and field-ordnance presented so magnificent a pageant as to call forth the unbounded admiration of their adversaries. In a word, this was the grandest martial scene of the war. The contrast between Stonewall Jackson's corps and Franklin's grand division was very marked, and so far as appearances went the former was hardly better than a caricature of the latter.

When all was in readiness, [the Federal] adjutants stepped to the front and, plainly in our view, read the orders of the day. This done, the fatal advance across the plain commenced. With gay pennants, State, regimental and brigade standards flying, this magnificent army advanced in three closely compacted lines of battle. At intervals in front, preceded by horse-artillery and flanked on either side by numerous field-pieces, hundreds of heavy field-pieces from the north bank of the Rappahannock belched forth their missiles of destruction and swept the plain in advance of Franklin's columns, while at the same moment his smaller field-pieces in front and on the flanks joined in to sweep the open space on all sides. This mighty cannonading was answered by the Confederate ordnance. Onward, steady and unwavering, these three lines advanced, preceded by a heavy skirmish line, till they neared the railroad, when Jackson's right and right center poured into these sturdy ranks a deadly volley from small-arms. Spaces, gaps and wide chasms instantly told the tale of a most fatal encounter. Volley after volley of small-arms continued the work of destruction, while Jackson's artillery posted on the Federal left and at right angles to their line of advance kept up a withering fire on the lessening ranks. The enemy advanced far in front of the River road and, crossing the railroad . . . charged the slopes upon which our troops were posted, but at length wavered, halted and suddenly retreated to the protection of the railroad embankments.

The struggle was kept up by sharpshooters for some time, when another general advance was made against a furious cannonade of small-arms and artillery. Again the scene of destruction was repeated; still the Federals crossed the railroad, when a gap in Jackson's line between Archer's and Thomas's brigades was discovered by some of the assailants. This interval was rushed for by a part of Franklin's troops as a haven of safety, while the rest of his command was repulsed in confusion.

The left of Archer's brigade . . . believing they were about to be surrounded, gave way. Their comrades on the right, unaware of the condition of affairs on the left and seeing the enemy routed in their front, were amazed at this confusion. Officers and men on the right were enraged at what seemed to be cowardice, and, rushing toward the broken lines, leveled their pistols . . . and fired into these fleeing comrades.

Presently the true condition of affairs appeared when the victorious brigades of Franklin emerged from the woods. Line and field officers rushed to and fro, wildly shouting, "Into line! Into line!" and, even in the face of a flanking foe, the gallant Colonel Turney, who temporarily commanded Archer's brigade, succeeded in re-forming his regiments at right angles to the former line of attack. This gave a brief check to the victors. Still the infantry and artillery fire scourged the line. The rout or capture of the Confederates seemed inevitable. Turney was struck by a minie-ball, which entered his mouth and came out at his neck, and his apparently lifeless body was hurriedly placed on a blanket, and four of his devoted followers attempted to carry him to the rear. They had not proceeded far when a shell burst among them, and they in turn lay helpless by the side of their bleeding commander. . . .

Up to the time of the break in our line no one in the ranks apprehended any danger. Those in front and near this scene of defeat and confusion made desperate efforts to rally the men and prevent a stampede, for we looked for nothing but defeat or capture. We were unaware of the fact that we had any reserves. Presently Early's division, in the very mood and spirit that had characterized Archer's brigade before the breaking of the lines, came at double-quick to our relief, jesting and yelling at us: "Here comes old Jubal! Let old Jubal straighten that fence! Jubal's boys are always getting Hill out of trouble!"

A desperate encounter followed. The Federals fought manfully, but the artillery on our right, together with the small-arms, literally mowed them down. Officers and men lost courage at the sight of their lessening ranks, and in the utmost confusion they again sought the shelter of the railroad. . . .

As the battle opened in the morning, the enemy was plainly in our view, and we could distinctly see their approach to the railroad in our front and to the left, where in every attempt to advance they halted. Now and then they would make an effort to advance from the railroad to our lines. We who were on the right had no trouble to repulse those in our front, and, in fact, we successfully met every assault made on our right, and that too with little or no loss. We regarded the efforts of the Federals, so far as the right was concerned, as futile in the extreme. In fact, their assaults on this part of the line appeared like the marching of men to certain defeat and slaughter. Our infantry fire, aided by fifteen pieces of artillery placed at our right, did terrible execution as the poor fellows emerged from a slight railroad cut in front of a part of our line.

On the morning of the 13th General Jackson rode down his lines dressed in a new suit, presented to him, as we understood, by General Stuart. Some of our men facetiously remarked that they preferred seeing him with his rusty old cap on, as they feared he wouldn't get down to work. He inspected all of his positions, riding alone. After halting near the extreme right, the artillery fire was begun, and here I had an excellent opportunity to see him under fire. I watched him closely and was unable to detect the slightest change in his demeanor. In a few minutes he rode off in the direction of Lee's headquarters. . . .

The next morning the scenes of carnage were heart-sickening. To intensify the horrible picture, the dead and the mortally wounded were in many instances burned in the sedge-grass, which was set on fire by bursting shells.

3

General Lee, from his position on Telegraph Hill, had witnessed the panoramalike spectacle of the attack and repulse of the Federals on Jackson's position, and it was on this occasion that he exclaimed: "It is well that war is so terrible! We should

grow too fond of it!" Burnside, undismayed by his thrust at
the Confederate right, made the tragic error of launching a
frontal attack on the strong left of the line held by Longstreet's
corps. The spearhead of the assault was directed at the well-
nigh impregnable position on Marye's Hill, and a thrilling account of the bloody battle on this front is available in the words
of Longstreet himself.

In front of Marye's Hill is a plateau, and immediately at the base
of the hill there is a sunken road known as the Telegraph Road.
On the side of the road next to the town was a stone-wall, shoulder-
high, against which the earth was banked, forming an almost un-
approachable defense. It was impossible for the troops occupying
it to expose more than a small portion of their bodies. Behind this
stone-wall I had placed about twenty-five hundred men, being all
of General T. R. R. Cobb's brigade, and a portion of the brigade
of General Kershaw, both of McLaws's division. It must now be
understood that the Federals, to reach what appeared to be my
weakest point, would have to pass directly over this wall held by
Cobb's infantry.

An idea of how well Marye's Hill was protected may be obtained
from the following incident: General E. P. Alexander, my engineer and superintendent of artillery, had been placing the guns,
and in going over the field with him before the battle I noticed an
idle cannon. I suggested that he place it so as to aid in covering the
plain in front of Marye's Hill. He answered: "General, we cover
that ground now so well that we will comb it as with a fine-tooth
comb. A chicken could not live on that field when we open on it."

A little before noon [on the 13th] I sent orders to all my batteries to open fire through the streets or at any points where the
troops were seen about the city, as a diversion in favor of Jackson.
This fire began at once to develop the work in hand for myself.
The Federal troops swarmed out of the city like bees out of a hive,
coming in double-quick march and filling the edge of the field in
front of Cobb. This was just where we had expected attack, and I
was prepared to meet it. As the troops massed before us, they were
very much annoyed by the fire of our batteries. The field was
literally packed with Federals from the vast number of troops that

had been massed in the town. From the moment of their appearance began the most fearful carnage. With our artillery from the front, right and left tearing through their ranks, the Federals pressed forward with almost invincible determination, maintaining their steady step and closing up their broken ranks. Thus resolutely they marched upon the stone fence behind which quietly waited the Confederate brigade of General Cobb. As they came within reach of this brigade, a storm of lead was poured into their advancing ranks and they were swept from the field like chaff before the wind. A cloud of smoke shut out the scene for a moment and, rising, revealed the shattered fragments recoiling from their gallant but hopeless charge. The artillery still plowed through their retreating ranks and searched the places of concealment into which the troops had plunged. A vast number went pell-mell into an old railroad cut to escape fire from the right and front. A battery on Lee's Hill saw this and turned its fire into the entire length of the cut, and the shells began to pour down upon the Federals with the most frightful destruction. They found their position of refuge more uncomfortable than the field of the assault.

Thus the right grand division of the Army of the Potomac found itself repulsed and shattered on its first attempt to drive us from Marye's Hill. Hardly was this attack off the field before we saw the determined Federals again filing out of Fredericksburg and preparing for another charge. The Confederates under Cobb reserved their fire and quietly awaited the approach of the enemy. The Federals came nearer than before, but were forced to retire before the well-directed guns of Cobb's brigade and the fire of the artillery on the heights. By that time the field in front of Cobb was thickly strewn with the dead and dying Federals, but again they formed with desperate courage and renewed the attack and again were driven off. At each attack the slaughter was so great that by the time the third attack was repulsed the ground was so thickly strewn with dead that the bodies seriously impeded the approach of the Federals.

General Lee, who was with me on Lee's Hill, became uneasy when he saw the attacks so promptly renewed and pushed forward with such persistence, and feared the Federals might break through our line. After the third charge, he said to me: "General, they are massing very heavily and will break your line, I am afraid." "General," I replied, "if you put every man now on the other side of the Potomac on that field to approach me over the same line, and give me plenty of ammunition, I will kill them all before they reach my line. Look to your right; you are in some danger there, but not on my line."

I think the fourth time the Federals charged, a gallant fellow came within one hundred feet of Cobb's position before he fell. Close behind him came some few scattering ones, but they were either killed or they fled from certain death. This charge was the only effort that looked like actual danger to Cobb, and after it was repulsed I felt no apprehension, assuring myself that there were enough of the dead Federals on the field to give me half the battle. The anxiety shown by General Lee, however, induced me to bring up two or three brigades, to be on hand, and General Kershaw, with the remainder of his brigade, was ordered down to the stone-wall—rather, however, to carry ammunition than as a reënforcement for Cobb. Kershaw dashed down the declivity and arrived just in time to succeed Cobb, who, at this juncture, fell from a wound in the thigh and died in a few minutes from loss of blood.

A fifth time the Federals formed and charged and were repulsed. A sixth time they charged and were driven back, when night came to end the dreadful carnage and the Federals withdrew, leaving the battle-field literally heaped with the bodies of their dead. Before the well-directed fire of Cobb's brigade, the Federals had fallen like the steady dripping of rain from the eaves of a house. Our musketry alone killed and wounded at least 5,000; and these, with the slaughter by the artillery, left more than 7,000 killed and wounded before the foot of Marye's Hill. The dead were piled sometimes three deep; and, when morning broke, the spectacle we saw upon the battle-field was one of the most distressing I ever witnessed. The charges had been desperate and bloody, but utterly hopeless. I thought, as I saw the Federals come again and again to their death, that they deserved sucess if courage and daring could entitle soldiers to a victory.

During the night a Federal strayed beyond his lines and was taken up by some of my troops. On searching him, we found on his person a memorandum of General Burnside's arrangements and an order for the renewal of the battle the next day. This information was sent to General Lee and immediately orders were given for a line of rifle-pits on the top of Marye's Hill for Ransom, who had been held somewhat in reserve, and for other guns to be placed on Taylor's Hill.

We were on our lines before daylight, anxious to receive General Burnside again. As the gray of the morning came without the battle, we became more anxious; yet, as the Federal forces retained position during the 14th and 15th, we were not without hope. There was some little skirmishing, but it did not amount to anything. But when the full light of the next morning revealed an abandoned field, General Lee turned to me, referring in his mind to the dispatch I had captured and which he had just re-read, and said, "General, I am losing confidence in your friend General Burnside." We then put it down as a *ruse de guerre*. Afterward, however, we learned that the order had been made in good faith but had been changed in consequence of the demoralized condition of the grand divisions in front of Marye's Hill. During the night of the 15th the Federal troops withdrew, and on the 16th our lines were re-established along the river. . . .

After the [Federals'] retreat, General Lee went to Richmond to suggest other operations, but was assured that the war was virtually over and that we need not harass our troops by marches and other hardships. Gold had advanced in New York to two hundred, and we were assured by those at the Confederate capital that in thirty or forty days we would be recognized and peace proclaimed. General Lee did not share in this belief.

4

Fredericksburg was, of course, a great victory for the Confederates; but, the first elation over, there were some who found fault with General Lee for not transforming the victory into an annihilation of Burnside's army. John Esten Cooke tells of the postbattle reaction.

General Lee has not escaped criticism. . . . The Southern people were naturally dissatisfied with the result—the safe retreat of the

Federal army—and asked why they had not been attacked and captured or destroyed. The London *Times,* at that period, and a military critic recently, in the same journal, declared that Lee had it in his power to crush General Burnside, "horse, foot and dragoons," and, from his failure to do so, argued his want of great generalship. It is proper to insert here General Lee's own explanation of his action:

"The attack on the 13th," he says, "had been so easily repulsed, and by so small a part of our army, that it was not supposed the enemy would limit his efforts to one attempt which, in view of the magnitude of his preparations and the extent of his force, seemed to be comparatively insignificant. Believing, therefore, that he would attack us, it was not deemed expedient to lose the advantages of our position and expose the troops to the fire of his inaccessible batteries beyond the river, by advancing against him. But we were necessarily ignorant of the extent to which he had suffered, and only became aware of it when, on the morning of the 16th, it was discovered that he had availed himself of the darkness of night and the prevalence of a violent storm of wind and rain, to recross the river."

This statement was no doubt framed by General Lee to meet the criticisms which the result of the battle occasioned. In conversing with General Stuart on the subject, he added that he felt too great responsibility for the preservation of his troops to unnecessarily hazard them. "No one knows," he said, "how *brittle* an army is."

The word may appear strange, applied to the Army of Northern Virginia which had certainly vindicated its claim, under many arduous trials, to the virtues of toughness and endurance. But Lee's meaning was plain, and his view seems to have been founded on good sense. The enemy had in all probably two hundred pieces of artillery, a large portion of which were posted on the high ground north of the river. Had Lee descended from his ridge and advanced into the plain to attack, this large number of guns would have greeted him with a rapid and destructive fire which must have inflicted upon him a loss nearly as heavy as he had inflicted upon General Burnside at Marye's Hill. From such a result he naturally shrunk. . . . The Federal troops, brave as they were, had been demoralized by such a fire; and Lee was unwilling to expose his own troops to similar slaughter.

5

A revealing and entertaining little episode is provided by the unofficial visit of a Confederate officer to the Federal head-quarters following the battle. Major W. Roy Mason, whose home in Fredericksburg was in the direct path of the action there, was sent by General Lee to meet a flag-of-truce boat on the southern side of the Rappahannock, and thereby hangs the tale.

After Burnside had withdrawn his forces across the Rappahan-nock, General Lee rode over to Marye's Heights where I then was and said to me: "Captain, those people (meaning the enemy) have sent over a flag of truce, asking permission to send a detachment to bury their dead. They have landed near your house, 'The Sentry Box.' Have you any objection to taking this reply down?" As he spoke, he handed me a sealed envelope directed to General Burn-side. I accordingly rode into the town and made my way down to the river-front of my residence, from which Burnside had only that morning removed his pontoons. There I found a Federal lieuten-ant-colonel with two soldiers in a boat, holding a flag of truce. I handed him the dispatch and at the same time asked where Burn-side was. He answered: "Just up the hill across the river, under an old persimmon tree, awaiting the dispatch." Telling him my name, I said: "Give my regards to General Burnside, and say to him that I thought he was too familiar with the surroundings of Fredericks-burg to butt his brains out deliberately against our stone-walls."

"Do you know General Burnside?" inquired the officer.

"Oh, yes," I replied, "he is an old acquaintance of mine."

"Then will you wait until I deliver your message and return? He may have something to say."

"I will wait then" was my answer.

In a very short time the flag of truce returned with a request from Burnside that I would come over in the boat to see him. I thoroughly appreciated the fact that I was running the risk of a court-martial from my own side in thus going into the enemy's lines without permission; but being that rather privileged person, a staff-officer, from whom no pass was required and of whom no questions were asked, I determined to accept this invitation and go over.

After passing the river and walking leisurely up the hill, the idle Federal soldiers, seeing a Confederate officer on their side and feeling curious about it, ran down in numbers toward the road. For the first time I was frightened by this result of my act, as I feared that our generals on the hills with their strong glasses, seeing the commotion, might inquire into it. As soon as I approached Burnside, who met me with the greatest cordiality, I expressed to him this fear. He at once sent out couriers to order the soldiers back to camp, and we then sat down on an old log and, being provided with crackers, cheese, sardines and a bottle of brandy (all luxuries to a Confederate), we discussed this lunch as well as the situation. General Burnside seemed terribly mortified and distressed at his failure, but said that he wanted me to tell his old army friends on the other side that he was not responsible for the attack on Fredericksburg in the manner in which it was made, as he was himself under orders, and was not much more than a figure-head, or words to that effect.

6

Following the battle there were several weeks of inaction, but late in January General Burnside made another attempt to attack Lee which was almost ludicrous in its ineptitude. Colonel Taylor tells about this "Mud March," as it was called in derision by the troops on both sides.

General Burnside's plan, as arranged after conference with General Halleck, was to cross the Rappahannock at the fords above the city of Fredericksburg and assail General Lee's army on that flank, hoping that by thus turning his left he would defeat General Lee in battle or compel him to evacuate the position held by his army at Fredericksburg.

On the 19th reports were made to headquarters of great activity on the part of the enemy and of a movement in force toward the upper fords; and on the 20th the larger part of Burnside's army was massed in the vicinity of Hartwood Church, and the troops heretofore stationed about Fairfax were advancing toward the Rappahannock. Orders were at once issued by General Lee for the strengthening and reinforcing of our positions at Banks's Ford and United States Ford, where it was evident the enemy would attempt to cross. Late in the evening it commenced to rain heavily, and continued with slight intermission for two days. This rain interfered very much with the Federal plans.

At the appointed hour on the 20th the Federal troops started for their proper positions, but the storm was so severe as to greatly retard their movements. It was almost impossible to move the pontoons and the artillery, and after struggling in the mud for two days, the attempt to cross the river was abandoned. General Burnside ascribes his failure to the elements and the unavoidable delay in getting his troops in position. He says in his report: "It was quite apparent during the forenoon of the 21st that the enemy had discovered our movement and had commenced their preparations to meet us. . . . On the 22nd I determined to abandon the attempt."

Thus ended what was thereafter known as the "Mud March" of General Burnside. The result was anything but inspiriting to the Federal troops. Open and undisguised sentiments of disgust were manifested by the leading officers of Burnside's army. . . . On January 25th, by order of the President, General Burnside was relieved of his command of the Army of the Potomac at his own request, and General Hooker was assigned to its command.

On January 27th another storm commenced, and continued until the morning of the 29th. The ground was now covered with snow. Under such conditions the roads were impracticable for active operations, and both armies settled down into winter quarters.

7

The winter was a hard one, and during these months the hardships of campaigning began to show their effects on Lee's health. In letters to his wife, however, he made light of his difficulties: "This morning the whole country is covered with a mantle of snow fully a foot deep. It was nearly up to my knees as I stepped out this morning, and our poor horses were enveloped. We have dug them out and opened our avenues a little, but it will be terrible and the roads impassable. No cars from Richmond. I fear our short rations for man and horse will have to be curtailed. Our enemies have their troubles too. They are very strong immediately in front, but have withdrawn their troops above and below us back toward Aquia Creek. I owe Mr. F. J. ["Fighting Joe"] Hooker no thanks for keeping me here. He ought to have made up his mind long ago what to do. (Later) The cars have arrived and brought me a young French officer, full of vivacity and ardent for service with me. I think the appearance of things will cool him. If they do not, the night will—for he brought no blankets."

But within the same month of February he was writing to his son Custis at Richmond in a strain of unwonted frankness and bitterness: "As far as I can judge at this distance, the proper authorities in Richmond take the necessities of the Army generally very easy. I hope there will be no cause to repent. But now every exertion should be made to put the Army everywhere on the strongest footing for vigorous work in the spring. Our salvation will depend on the next four months, and yet I can not ever get regular promotions made to fill vacancies in regiments while Congress seems to be laboring to pass laws to get easy places for some favorites or constituent, or get others out of active service. I shall feel very much obliged to them if they will pass a law relieving me from all duty and legislating some one in my place, better able to do it."

It was characteristic of Lee's devotion to duty that, despite the pressure of his military responsibilities, he found time in December to perform a troublesome and exacting task inforced on him by Mr. Custis's will. This will had specified that all the Custis slaves should be set free within a specified time, and as this time limit was now reached he took steps to have delivered to all the family servants their legal papers of manumission.

"They are entitled to their freedom and I wish to give it to them," he wrote. "I hope they will all do well and behave themselves."

Colonel Walter Taylor gives us a close-up picture of Lee in his winter quarters.

The headquarters camp of General Lee was never of such a character as to proclaim its importance. An unpretentious arrangement of five or six army tents, one or two wagons for transporting equipage and personal effects, with no display of bunting and no parade of sentinels or guards, only a few orderlies, was all there was of it. General Lee persistently refused to occupy a house and was content with an ordinary wall-tent but little, if any, larger than those about it. . . .

General Lee, as can well be understood, constantly had his rest disturbed by reason of the great responsibilities resting upon him. The many matters of great import pressing upon his mind caused him to lie awake for hours, and he more than once suggested to me not to arouse him before midnight, unless for a matter of importance admitting of no delay, as one hour of sleep before midnight was to him worth more than two hours after midnight. Of course, I refer here to despatches concerning some movement of the enemy, and not to the matters of detail coming from the different commands of our army. For these army communications he had so great a dislike that I endeavored to spare him as much as possible, and would only submit for his action such matters as were of a nature to demand the personal consideration and decision of the commander of the army.

On one occasion when an audience had not been asked of him for several days, it became necessary to have one. The few papers requiring his action were submitted. He was not in a very pleasant mood. Something irritated him, and he manifested his ill humor by a little nervous twist or jerk of the neck and head, peculiar to himself, accompanied by some harshness of manner. This was perceived by me, and I hastily concluded that my efforts to save him annoyance were not appreciated. In disposing of some case of a vexatious character, matters reached a climax. He became really worried and, forgetting what was due to my superior, I petulantly threw the paper down at my side and gave evident signs of anger. Then in a perfectly calm and measured tone of voice he said, "Colonel Taylor, when I lose my temper, don't you let it make you angry."

Was there ever a more gentle and considerate and yet so positive a reproof? General Lee was naturally of a positive temperament—firm, resolute, occasionally irascible, but always responsive to the sober second thought and ready to make the *amende honorable,* holding himself in check by the exercise of his will and conscience. He was not one of those invariably amiable men whose temper is never ruffled; but when we consider the immense burden which rested upon him, and the numberless causes for annoyance with which he had to contend, the occasional cropping out of temper which we who were constantly near him witnessed, only served to show how great was his habitual self-command; and it was frequently observed and commented upon that after any such trifling ebullition of temper he always manifested a marked degree of affability, as if desirous of obliterating all recollection of the unpleasant episode.

The idea prevails with some that General Lee possessed great austerity of manner, rendering him not easy of approach. Such was not the case. Although naturally a man of much dignity, in which he was never deficient when occasion called for the manifestation of that trait, his intercourse with those around him was marked by a suavity of manner that removed all restraint and invited closer fellowship. In our small circle of the personal staff, there was between General Lee and his military family a degree of *camaraderie* that was perfectly delightful. Our conversation, especially at table, was free from restraint, unreserved as between equals, and often of a bright and jocular vein. He was very fond of a joke, and not infrequently indulged in the pastime of teasing those about him in a mild way. While it would never occur to any one of us to be otherwise than perfectly deferential in our manner toward him, and respectful in our deportment toward each other in his presence, there was an utter absence of the rigid formality and the irksome ceremonial regarded by some as essential features of

the military etiquette appertaining to the station of the commander-in-chief of an army.

His simplicity of taste . . . was especially noticeable in the *mén-
age* at army headquarters. All the appointments were of the simplest kind. The table furniture was of tin, and while we never
really wanted for food, unless by reason of accidental separation
from our camp wagons, we only enjoyed what was allotted to the
army generally. Ours was the regular army ration, supplemented
by such additions from the country as could be procured by our
steward by the use of a little money. General Lee never availed
himself of the advantages of his position to obtain dainties for his
table or any personal comfort for himself. The use of spirituous
liquors, while not forbidden, was never habitual in our camp.
There was no general mess-supply and rarely, if ever, a private nip.
I used to think that General Lee would have been better off if he
had taken a little stimulant.

8

Lee did not spend the winter at Fredericksburg in inactivity.
A strong line of fortifications was constructed, stretching from
Banks's Ford to Port Royal; and Lee bombarded the war office
at Richmond with appeals for additional men and supplies.
"The enemy will make every effort to crush us between now
and June," he said, "and it will require all our strength to resist him." But nothing was done to strengthen Lee's army. On
the contrary, he was weakened by the dispatch of Longstreet
with two of his divisions to the south of Richmond to guard
against a possible attack from that quarter and to gather pro-
vender. Not despairing, Lee did his best to recruit and organize his force against the expected advance of the Federals with
the coming of spring. To add to his difficulties, however, he
was at this time stricken with a severe illness, affecting his
throat and heart, which incapacitated him for a while during
the days of early spring. As April advanced there were increasing signs of activity on Hooker's part, and Lee's scouts were
alerted all along the extended Confederate line. During the

latter days of April Stuart reported that the Federal cavalry was concentrating on the upper Rappahannock. Lee redoubled his final efforts to prepare for Hooker's thrust. Dr. James Power Smith tells how it came, on April 29.

At daybreak on the morning of the 29th of April, 1863, sleeping in our tents at corps headquarters, near Hamilton's Crossing, we were aroused by Major Samuel Hale, of Early's staff, with the stirring news that Federal troops were crossing the Rappahannock on pontoons under cover of a heavy fog. General Jackson . . . was at once informed of the news, and promptly issued orders to prepare for action. At his direction I rode a mile across the fields to army headquarters, and finding General Robert E. Lee still slumbering quietly . . . I entered the General's tent and awoke him. Turning his feet out of his cot, he sat upon its side as I gave him the tidings from the front. Expressing no surprise, he playfully said: "Well, I thought I heard firing, and was beginning to think it was time some of you young fellows were coming to tell me what it was all about. Tell your good general that I am sure he knows what to do. I will meet him at the front very soon."

It was Sedgwick who had crossed and, marching along the river front to impress us with his numbers, was now intrenching his line on the river road under cover of Federal batteries on the north bank. All day long we lay in the . . . lines . . . watching the operation of the enemy. Nor did we move through the next day. . . . During the forenoon of the 29th General Lee had been informed by General J. E. B. Stuart of the movement in force by General Hooker across the Rappahannock upon Chancellorsville; and during the night of Thursday, April 30th, General Jackson withdrew his corps, leaving Early and his division with Barksdale's brigade to hold the old lines from Hamilton's Crossing along the rear of Fredericksburg.

By the light of a brilliant moon, at midnight . . . the troops were moved . . . out of sight of the enemy, and about 11 A.M. of Friday, May 1st, they reached Anderson's position, confronting Hooker's advance from Chancellorsville . . . on the Plank Road. To meet the whole Army of the Potomac, General Lee had of all arms about 60,000 men.

9

Hooker was vastly pleased with himself for what he considered his master stroke of strategy in moving his army south of the river on Lee's flank, and in his exultation declared: "The rebel army is now the legitimate property of the Army of the Potomac. They may as well pack up their haversacks and make for Richmond, and I shall be after them!" He also issued an enthusiastic congratulatory order to his army which he termed "the finest army on the planet," telling them that the position they then occupied was so strong that "the enemy must either ingloriously fly or come out from behind his defences and give us battle on our own ground, where certain destruction awaits him." But affairs did not work out that way. Hooker had unwittingly placed his own army where, opposed by the combined genius of Lee and Jackson, he eventually found it necessary himself to fly ingloriously to avoid certain destruction. John Esten Cooke describes that tangled country, the Wilderness, where the two armies now confronted each other.

The "Wilderness," as the region around Chancellorsville is called . . . is a nearly unbroken expanse of dense thicket pierced only by narrow and winding roads, over which the traveler rides mile after mile without seeing a single human habitation. It would seem, indeed, that the whole barren and melancholy tract had been given up to the owl, the whippoorwill and the moccasin, its original tenants. The plaintive cries of the night-birds alone break the gloomy silence of the desolate region, and the shadowy thicket stretching in every direction produces a depressing effect upon the feelings.

Chancellorsville is in the center of this singular territory, on the main road, or rather roads, running from Orange Court-House to Fredericksburg, from which latter place it is distant about ten miles. In spite of its imposing name, Chancellorsville was simply a large country-house, originally inhabited by a private family but afterward used as a roadside inn. A little to the westward the "Old Turnpike" and Orange Plank-road unite as they approach the spot, where they again divide, to unite a second time a few miles

to the east where they form the main highway to Fredericksburg
From the north come in roads from United States and Ely's Fords,
Germanna Ford is northwest; from the south runs the "Brock
Road" in the direction of the Rapidan, passing a mile or two west
of the place.

The whole country, the roads, the chance houses, the silence,
the unending thicket, in this dreary wilderness, produce a sombre
effect. A writer familiar with it says: "There all is wild, desolate
and lugubrious. Thicket, undergrowth and jungle stretch for
miles, impenetrable and untouched. Narrow roads wind on forever between melancholy masses of stunted and gnarled oak. Little
sunlight shines there. The face of nature is dreary and sad. . . .
Into this jungle . . . General Hooker penetrated. It was the wolf
in his den, ready to tear any one who approached. A battle there
seemed impossible. Neither side could see its antagonist. Artillery
could not move; cavalry could not operate; the very infantry had
to flatten their bodies to glide between the stunted trees. That an
army of one hundred and twenty thousand men should have chosen
that spot to fight forty thousand, and not only chosen it but made
it a hundred times more impenetrable by felling trees, erecting
breastworks, disposing artillery *en masse* to sweep every road and
bridle-path which led to Chancellorsville—this fact seemed in-
credible."

It was no part of the original plan of the Federal commander to
permit himself to be cooped up in this difficult and embarrassing
region where it was impossible to manoeuver his large army. The
selection of the Wilderness around Chancellorsville as the ground
of battle was dictated by Lee.

10

It was painfully obvious to Lee that, outnumbered nearly
two to one, he had nothing to gain by a head-on collision with
the superior forces of his enemy. But here in this tangled country was an opportunity for the exercise of that tactical genius
with which he was so richly endowed; and so developed one of
the most brilliant and renowned maneuvers of military history—the hurling of Jackson's corps on Hooker's exposed

right flank, deep in the Wilderness. It was a daring maneuver, leaving Lee himself in Hooker's immediate front with less than 20,000 men to keep up a show of opposition while Jackson moved swiftly through the Wilderness by back roads until he arrived at his target, the Federals' exposed right wing. Dr. Smith has written a stirring account of the falling of the Confederate thunderbolt on General Howard's unsuspecting corps that mild May evening.

It must have been between 5 and 6 o'clock in the evening, Saturday, May 2nd, when these [Jackson's] dispositions were completed. Upon his stout-built, long-paced little sorrel, General Jackson sat, with visor low over his eyes and lips compressed, and with his watch in his hand. Upon his right sat General Robert E. Rodes, the very picture of a soldier and every inch all that he appeared. Upon the right of Rodes sat Major Blackford.

"Are you ready, General Rodes?" said Jackson.

"Yes sir!" said Rodes, impatient for the advance.

"You can go forward then," said Jackson.

A nod from Rodes was order enough for Blackford, and then suddenly the woods rang with the bugle call, and back came the responses from bugles on the right and left, and the long line of skirmishers, through the wild thicket of undergrowth, sprang eagerly to their work, followed promptly by the quick steps of the line of battle. For a moment all the troops seemed buried in the depths of the gloomy forest, and then suddenly the echoes waked and swept the country for miles, never failing until heard at the headquarters of Hooker at Chancellorsville—the wild "rebel yell" of the long Confederate lines.

Never was assault delivered with grander enthusiasm. Fresh from the long winter's waiting, and confident from the preparation of the spring, the troops were in fine condition and high spirits. The boys were all back from home or sick leave. "Old Jack" was there upon the road in their midst; there could be no mistake and no failure. . . .

Alas! for Howard and his unformed lines, and his brigades with guns stacked, and officers at dinner or asleep under the trees, and butchers deep in the blood of beeves! Scattered through field and forest, his men were preparing their evening meal. A little show of earth-work facing the south was quickly taken by us in reverse from the west. Flying battalions are not flying buttresses for an army's stability. Across Talley's fields the rout begins. Over at Hawkins's hill, on the north of the road, Carl Schurz makes a stand, soon to be driven into the same hopeless panic. By the quiet Wilderness Church in the vale, leaving wounded and dead everywhere, by Melzi Chancellor's, on into the deep thicket again, the Confederate lines pressed forward—now broken and all disaligned by the density of bush that tears the clothes away; now halting to load and deliver a volley upon some regiment or fragment of the enemy that will not move as fast as the others. Thus the attack upon Hooker's flank was a grand success, beyond the most sanguine expectation. . . .

I was ordered to remain at the point where the advance began, to be a center of communication between the general and the cavalry on the flanks, and to deliver orders to detachments of artillery still moving up from the rear. . . . About 8 P.M., in the twilight . . . I gathered my couriers about me and went forward to find General Jackson. The storm of battle had swept far on to the east, and become more and more faint to the ear, until silence came with night over the fields and woods. As I rode along that old turnpike, passing scattered fragments of Confederates looking for their regiments, parties of prisoners concentrating under guards, wounded men by the roadside and under the trees at Talley's and Chancellor's, I had reached an open field on the right, a mile west of Chancellorsville, when in the dusky twilight I saw horsemen near an old cabin in the field. Turning toward them, I found Rodes and his staff engaged in gathering the broken and scattered troops that had swept the two miles of battle-field.

"General Jackson is just ahead on the road, Captain," said Rodes. "Tell him I will be here in this cabin if I am wanted."

I had not gone a hundred yards before I heard firing, a shot or two, and then a company volley upon the right of the road, and another upon the left. A few moments farther on I met Captain Murray Taylor, an aide of A. P. Hill's, with tidings that Jackson and Hill were wounded, and some around them killed, by the fire of their own men. Spurring my horse into a sweeping gallop, I soon

passed the Confederate line of battle and, some three or four rods
on its front, found the general's horse beside a pine sapling on the
left, and a rod beyond a little party of men caring for a wounded officer. The story of the sad event is briefly told and, in essentials,
very much as it came to me from the lips of the wounded general
himself, and in everything confirmed and completed by those who
were eye-witnesses and near companions.

When Jackson had reached the point where his line now crossed
the turnpike, scarcely a mile west of Chancellorsville, and not half
a mile from a line of Federal troops, he had found his front line
unfit for the farther and vigorous advance he desired, by reason of
the irregular character of the fighting. . . . Division commanders
found it more and more difficult as the twilight deepened to hold
their broken brigades in hand. Regretting the necessity of relieving the troops in front, General Jackson had ordered A. P.
Hill's division, his third and reserve line, to be placed in front.
While this change was being effected, impatient and anxious, the
general rode forward on the turnpike, followed by two or three
of his staff and a number of couriers and signal sergeants. . . . Fired
at by one or two muskets [from the enemy], he turned and came
back toward his line, upon the side of the road to his left. As he
rode near to the Confederate troops, just placed in position and
ignorant that he was in the front, the left company began firing to
the front and two of his party fell from their saddles dead. . . .
Spurring his horse across the road to his right, he was met by a
second volley from the right company of Pender's North Carolina
brigade. Under this volley, when not two rods from the troops,
the general received three balls at the same instant. One penetrated the palm of his right hand, and was cut out that night from
the back of his hand. A second passed through the wrist of the
left arm and out through the left hand. A third ball passed through
the left arm halfway from shoulder to elbow. The large bone of
the upper arm was splintered to the elbow-joint, and the wound
bled freely. His horse turned quickly from the fire, through the
thick bushes, which swept the cap from the General's head and
scratched his forehead, leaving drops of blood to stain his face. . . .

Laid upon the ground, there came at once to his succor General
A. P. Hill and members of his staff. I reached his side a minute

after, to find General Hill holding the head and shoulders of the wounded chief. Cutting open the coat-sleeve from wrist to shoulder, I found the wound in the upper arm, and with my handkerchief I bound the arm above the wound to stem the flow of blood. Couriers were sent for Dr. Hunter McGuire, the surgeon of the corps and the general's trusted friend, and for an ambulance. Being outside of our lines, it was urgent that he should be moved at once. With difficulty litter-bearers were brought from the line near by, and the general was placed upon the litter and carefully raised to the shoulder, I myself bearing one corner. . . .

A dispatch was sent to the commanding general to announce formally his disability. There came back the following note:

"General: I have just received your note, informing me that you were wounded. I can not express my regret at the occurrence. Could I have directed events, I should have chosen, for the good of the country, to have been disabled in your stead. I congratulate you upon the victory, which is due to your skill and energy. Most truly yours, R. E. LEE, GENERAL.

11

The Confederate attack was renewed the next morning. Hooker's army, despite its superior numbers, was thrown off balance and bewildered by the crushing of its right wing, and was driven in confusion through the dark tangle of the Wilderness. As Jackson's corps, now commanded by Stuart, pressed on, Lee attacked from his side, and it soon became apparent that the battle of Chancellorsville was a great Confederate victory. Cooke, who was present and a participant, gives a moving account of the last stages of the battle, one of the high spots in the military career of Robert E. Lee.

The attack . . . compelled the front line of the Federal army to retire to the stronger ground in the rear. When this was reached, and the troops of Lee saw before them the last citadel, the steady advance became a rush. The divisions of Anderson and McLaws on the right made a determined charge upon the great force under Generals Hancock, Slocum and others in that quarter, and Stuart closed in on the Federal right, steadily extending his line to join on to Anderson.

The spectacle here was superb. As the troops rushed on, Stuart shouted, "Charge! and remember Jackson!" and this watchword seemed to drive the line forward. With Stuart leading them and singing in his joyous voice, "Old Joe Hooker, will you come out of the Wilderness!"—for courage, poetry and seeming frivolity were strangely mingled in this great soldier—the troops went headlong at the Federal works, and in a few moments the real struggle of the battle of Chancellorsville had begun.

From this instant, when the lines respectively commanded in person by Lee and by Stuart closed in with the enemy, there was little manoeuvering of any description. It was an open attempt of Lee by hard fighting to crush in the enemy's front and force them back upon the river. In this arduous struggle it is due to Stuart to say that his generalship largely decided the event, and the high commendation which he afterward received from General Lee justifies the statement. As his lines went to the attack, his quick military eye discerned an elevated point on his right, from which it appeared an artillery fire would filade the Federal line. About thirty pieces of cannon were at once hastened to this point, and a destructive fire opened on the lines of General Slocum, which threw his troops into great confusion. So serious was this fire that General Slocum sent word to General Hooker that his front was being swept away by it, to which the sullen response was "I cannot make soldiers or ammunition!"

General Hooker was indeed, it seems, at this moment in no mood to take a hopeful view of affairs. The heavy assault of Jackson appears to have as much demoralized the Federal commander as his troops. During the night he had erected a semi-circular line of works, in the form of a redan, in his rear toward the river, behind which new works he no doubt contemplated falling back. He now awaited the result of the Southern attack, leaning against a pillar of the porch at the Chancellorsville House, when a cannon-ball struck the pillar, throwing it down and so stunning the general as to prevent him from retaining the command, which was delegated to General Couch.

The fate of the day had now been decided. The right wing of

the Southern army, under Lee, had gradually extended its left to meet the extension of Stuart's right; and, this junction of the two wings having been effected, Lee took personal command of all and advanced his whole front in a decisive assault. Before this the Federal front gave way and the disordered troops were huddled back— now only a confused and disorganized mass—upon Chancellorsville. The Southern troops pursued with yells, leaping over the earthworks and driving all before them.

A scene of singular horror ensued. The Chancellorsville House, which had been set on fire by shell, was seen to spout flame from every window, and the adjoining woods had in like manner caught fire and were heard roaring over the dead and wounded of both sides alike. The thicket had become a scene of the cruellest of all agonies for the unfortunate unable to extricate themselves. The whole spectacle in the vicinity of the Chancellorsville House, now in Lee's possession, was frightful. Fire, smoke, blood, confused yells and dying groans mingled to form the dark picture.

Lee had ridden to the front of his line, following up the enemy, and as he passed before the troops they greeted him with one prolonged, unbroken cheer in which those wounded and lying upon the ground united. In that cheer spoke the fierce joy of men whom the hard combat had turned into blood-hounds, arousing all the ferocious instincts of the human soul. Lee sat on his horse, motionless, near the Chancellorsville House, his face and figure lit up by the glare of the burning woods, and gave his first attention, even at this exciting moment, to the unfortunates of both sides, wounded and in danger of being burned to death. While issuing his orders on this subject, a note was brought to him from Jackson, congratulating him upon his victory. After reading it with evidences of much emotion, he turned to the officer who brought it and said: "Say to General Jackson that the victory is his, and that the congratulation is due to him."

12

Meanwhile the skeleton force left at Fredericksburg had been having troubles of its own. Lieutenant William Miller Owen of the Washington Artillery, who was engaged in the action there, tells how roughly the Confederates were handled by General Sedgwick's superior force.

In the evening [of the 2nd of May] the enemy on the right began pushing in our skirmishers and advancing on the hills towards Hamilton's Crossing, where Early's division is posted. . . . It was now quite dark, and, to deceive the enemy, innumerable camp fires were lighted all along Lee's Hill, to make it appear that there was a heavy force bivouacking there—that we had been heavily reinforced. There can't be less than 20,000 men in front of us, perhaps more. A deserter came in and told us that it was the *corps d'armee* of Sedgwick. We are evidently playing a big game of bluff to keep these 20,000 men off of Lee at Chancellorsville.

. . . On the morning of May 3d Capt. Miller . . . of the Washington Artillery, was ordered to take position on Marye's Hill, on the plank-road. Col. Walton protested against this order, and told General Barksdale it was not right to send the guns to this exposed position when the supports were so meagre. . . . The general insisted, and the guns were sent. . . .* Early in the morning the enemy made an advance in very strong force against the hills, and were gallantly repulsed by the Mississippians and Miller's and Brown's guns on Marye's Hill. . . . At 9:30 A.M. a flag of truce came out of the town. . . . The enemy requested permission to take off their killed and wounded, but Col. Griffin very properly refused their untimely request; but it was noticed . . . that the bearers of the flag peered intently at the foot of the hill where our infantry were, and our men would lift their heads up, showing plainly how small their numbers were. This was just what the enemy wanted to discover, and, being satisfied, retired to their own lines. . . .

At about 10 o'clock, emboldened by the discovery of our weakness, made under a flag of truce, the enemy suddenly appeared to spring out of the ground, in line of battle, from behind the ridge near the town. At the same time thirty or forty guns opened upon

---

* About midnight I went to Gen. Barksdale's bivouac on Lee's Hill to learn the result of the consultation with Gen. Early. I found him wrapped in his war blanket, lying at the root of a tree. "Are you asleep, general?" "No, sir. Who could sleep with a million of armed Yankees all around him?" he answered, gruffly. He then informed me that it was determined by Gen. Early to hold Marye's Hill at all hazards; but that his brigade and a portion of the Washington Artillery had to do it.—*Gen. B. G. Humphreys, ex-Governor of Mississippi and Colonel Twenty-first Regiment.*

our positions from the Stafford Heights. It was a beautiful sight, but a terrible one for us. . . . Their efforts to stay the tide of the assaulting columns were unavailing against such great odds. . . . Looking towards Marye's Hill, I saw it was crowded with the enemy; they had evidently overrun our small force. . . . On the left Gen. Barksdale was rallying the remnants of the Eighteenth and Twenty-first Mississippi regiments. . . .

After the first surprise everything was rallied into shape again and we fell back in good order, and retired, firing, to the line of the mine road, where were concentrated Early's division . . . and the remnants of Barksdale's brigade. . . .

One of our boys, who had stood by his gun until all hope was gone, was passing through Gen. Pendleton's reserve artillery; he was as mad as he could be, and his hands and face covered with burnt powder. One of the reserves called out, "Hello, Washington Artillery! where are your guns?" He replied sharply, "Guns be damned! I reckon now the people of the Southern Confederacy are satisfied that Barksdale's brigade and the Washington Artillery can't whip the whole damned Yankee army. . . ." He had about told the story of the fight. Early had under his command about nine thousand men, but less than two thousand were engaged with Sedgwick's corps. . . .

After driving our troops from Marye's Hill Sedgwick took up his line of march along the plank-road towards Chancellorsville, to aid Gen. Hooker, whose army Gen. Lee was furiously attacking, and successfully. . . . At sunrise on the 4th of May, in obedience to the orders of Gen. Lee, Early moved forward, and again reoccupied Marye's Hill. . . . Leaving Barksdale behind the stone-wall to look out for any of the enemy who might still be in Fredericksburg, he thence followed Sedgwick with his division.

13

Lee was kept informed of the progressive steps in Early's debacle at Fredericksburg, and was painfully aware of the perilous position in which he was placed. Although Hooker was routed, Lee's rear was now threatened by the advance of Sedgwick's victorious corps. Robert Stiles gives an intimately interesting picture of the Confederate commander's poise and calm in this crisis.

General Lee, convinced that there was, for the present at least, no more dangerous fight in Hooker, had ridden through to General McLaws' position to talk with him about turning back to help Early take care of Sedgwick. He and McLaws were conferring, I think, at the moment on horseback. . . . I was walking down the front of the captured regiment [of hundred-day men from New Haven, Conn.], kept, however, at proper distance by the guard which had been placed over them. I had heard where the prisoners hailed from and was carefully scanning their faces, recognizing many of them. At last a little fellow who had been in my Sunday-school class in New Haven recognized me. How he happened to do this is a mystery, as there was not a trace of my former self visible, except my height and my muscular figure. I had lost my hat, my hair was close-shingled, skin tanned red-brown; I had on my only flannel shirt, pants, belt and shoes; shirt front wide open, sleeves rolled up, clothes and skin spattered black with powder water from the sponge—indeed I was, all in all, about as desperate-looking a ruffian as could well be found or imagined. But when this little chap, through all this disguise and transformation, recognized me and called out my name, there was a simultaneous shout of "Bob Stiles" from many throats. General Lee called me to him and asked whether I really knew "those people"—the peculiar phrase he employed habitually in speaking of the Northern people or the Federal soldiery—and upon my telling him that I did, he ordered the guard to pass me in the lines, telling me to find out what I could and let him know. He also offered to do anything in his power for any prisoner whose circumstances I might think required his intervention, and in this way I arranged a special exchange for a young man named Sheldon whom I had known at school in New Haven. . . .

Shortly after I left General McLaws, he and General Lee resumed their conference and, just as they did so, there occurred an incident which beautifully revealed the equipoise of General Lee's character and the charm of his manner.

If any of the minor characters mentioned in these reminiscences

has a distinct personality every way worthy of approval and remembrance, it was "Brother William," the consecrated, courageous
chaplain of the Seventeenth Mississippi, or rather of Barksdale's
brigade—the real hero of the great revival at Fredericksburg. He,
of course, had remained behind there, with his brigade, under the
general command of Early, to watch Sedgwick.

I was standing in the shade of a tree, near our guns, which had
been ordered to draw out on the road, head of column to the rear,
that is toward Fredericksburg—an order and movement which we
all well understood—when my attention was called to a horseman
coming at full speed from the direction in which we were heading,
and as he drew near I saw it was Brother William, and that he was
greatly excited. . . . He did not have a saddle, but was riding upon
a blanket or cloth of some kind, and his horse was reeking with
sweat and panting from exertion. When his eye fell upon General
Lee he made directly for him, and I followed as fast as I could. He
dashed to the very feet of the commanding general, indeed, almost
upon him, and gasping for breath, his eyes starting from their sock-
ets, began to tell of dire disaster at Fredericksburg—Sedgwick had
smashed Early and was rapidly coming on in our rear!

I have never seen anything more majestically calm than General
Lee was; I felt painfully the contrast between him and dear little
Brother William. Something very like a grave, sweet smile began
to express itself on the General's face, but he checked it, and raising his left hand gently, as if to protect himself, he interrupted the
excited speaker, checking and controlling him instantly, at the
same time saying very quietly:

"I thank you very much, but both you and your horse are fatigued and overheated. Take him to that shady tree yonder and
you and he blow and rest a little. I'm talking to General McLaws
just now. I'll call you as soon as we are through."

. . . Brother William was at once dominated and controlled—
but not quite satisfied. He began a mild protest: "But, General!"
but he did not persist in it—he simply could not. He had already
dismounted and he started back with me to the tree, leading his
horse.

Unfortunately I had none of General Lee's power over him and
he began to pour out to me his recital of disaster and prediction of

ruin. All was lost below, Sedgwick had stormed the heights and seized the town, the brigade had been cut off and, he feared, captured; Early had been beaten and pushed roughly aside, and at least 30,000 victorious troops were rapidly pressing on in our rear. Substantially, he alone was left to tell the tale, and had fortunately been able to secure this horse on which to come to tell it. If not already too late, it very soon would be, to do anything even to moderate the calamity.

In vain I suggested that General Lee could not be ignorant of all this; that his scouts had, doubtless, given him information; that General Early certainly would have found means to communicate with him; that Lee had beaten Hooker and his calm and self-reliant bearing clearly indicated that he felt himself to be master of the entire situation. But Brother William would not be comforted or reassured. General Lee had not been upon the spot and could not know; he had been there and did know. The very calmness of the general showed he did not appreciate the gravity of the situation. While we were thus debating the matter, General Lee finished with McLaws, who at once started his division on the back track to reinforce Early and help him take care of Sedgwick—and, true to his promise, Marse Robert now called for Brother William and, as he approached, greeted him with a smile, saying:

"Now, what were you telling us about Major Sedgwick?"

Brother William again told his tale of woe—this time with somewhat diminished intensity and less lurid coloring. When he had finished the general thanked him, saying again:

"I am very much obliged to you; the major is a nice gentleman; I don't think he would hurt us very badly, but we are going to see about him at once. I have just sent General McLaws to make a special call upon him."

I did not at the time quite appreciate the marked peculiarity of General Lee's allusion to Sedgwick; but, as I now understand, the latter had been a major in the old service of the regiment of which Lee was colonel, and they had been somewhat intimate friends.

14

McLaws and Early did take care of Sedgwick, and soon sent

him in rapid retreat to the nearest ford. Next day Hooker withdrew his whole army from the south side of the river; Lee had won one of his greatest and most brilliant victories. But the sweet taste of victory turned bitter in his mouth when news was brought to him that Stonewall Jackson had died. Lee's sense of loss at the death of Jackson, and the close relations— military and personal—which existed between the two great Confederate leaders, are effectively set forth by Edmund Lee Childe.

This illustrious lieutenant of Lee had become his right hand, and Lee felt his loss cruelly. Since the opening of hostilities no name had won so much public favour as that of Jackson. In the short space of two years the brilliant manner in which he executed the missions with which he was charged and the continued triumphs which he gained rendered his name, previously utterly unknown, famous. He came out of an early struggle, difficult and unequal, in the Valley of Virginia, a conqueror, although he had to do with forces very superior to his own. These victories, at a time so critical and on a frontier so important, contributed not a little to electrify the inhabitants of Richmond and, indeed, of all the Confederacy. He then took a very important part in the Seven Days' battle against McClellan in 1862 on the Chickahominy. Sent towards the north, he defeated Pope's van at Cedar Mountain, commanded Lee's left wing in the turning movement against Pope's flank, destroyed Manassas, maintained himself until the arrival of his chief, and largely contributed to the victory which followed. Hence he crossed into Maryland, marched on Harper's Ferry and mastered it; he was by Lee's side in the battle of Sharpsburg and there kept his ground without stumbling before the rude assaults of the enemy. If this contest remained indecisive instead of being a defeat for the South, the merit is chiefly due to Lee as general and Jackson as soldier. When the Confederates retired, Jackson remained in the Valley to embarrass McClellan. In this he perfectly succeeded, then suddenly reappeared in Fredericksburg, where he received and repulsed one of the two great Federal attacks. In the following spring was fought the sanguinary battle of Chancellorsville, the last battle of the heroic Jackson. With this glorious conflict finished the career of him who had become Lee's *alter ego.*

It is not difficult to estimate what the general-in-chief felt on losing a man who was at once the soldier on whom he most relied and the friend he most dearly cherished. The connection between Lee and Jackson had, from the first, been most cordial. Never had a shadow arisen to disturb the reciprocal feelings of affection and admiration which they had for one another. Never had they asked of each other what place they occupied in the public esteem, which of the two had the greatest share in the respect and love of their fellow-citizens. On the contrary, it was impossible to please Lee better than by setting forth the splendour of Jackson's services. He was, under all circumstances, the first to acknowledge publicly how much was owing to his illustrious lieutenant, to express in high terms all the admiration which he felt for his military talents, and to attribute to him as, in fact, he wrote after the battle of Chancellorsville, all the merit of the victory.

The spectacle of two soldiers loving and admiring each other, without any mental reservation, without a shadow ruffling their self-respect, is a beautiful one. As for Jackson, his love for his chief was more profound; it contained as much of veneration as of admiration. To give birth to such feelings in such a man, Lee must not only have been a military genius of the highest rank but also a man endued with great moral qualities and great piety. Jackson's opinion never varied, and his confidence and attachment remained unshaken to the end. He invariably defended his chief against criticism. Some one, one day, reproached Lee with being slow. Jackson, who was present, habitually very silent, this time could not restrain himself. "General Lee," said he, "is not slow. No one knows the weight upon his heart—his great responsibilities. He is commander-in-chief, and he knows that if an army is lost it can not be replaced. No! there may be some persons whose good opinion of me may make them attach some weight to my views, and if you ever hear that said of General Lee, I beg you will contradict it in my name. I have known General Lee for five-and-twenty years. He is cautious; he ought to be. But he is not slow. Lee is a phenomenon. He is the only man whom I would follow blindfolded!"

Such an encomium, from such a man, speaks for itself. Time only increased these sentiments with Jackson. He submitted his whole will to his chief. The least word of Lee was sacred to his lieutenant; all he did could not be otherwise than right. Only once was he of a different opinion—when, after his wound and victory at Chancellorsville, he received from Lee that little word of congratulation. "General Lee," said he, "is very kind; but he should give the glory to God!"

Lee returned this affection fully. He consulted Jackson always and regarded him as his bosom friend. Rarely was there a question between them as to the relations of superior to subordinate, except when in his quality of commander-in-chief Lee had to come to a decision. In details he depended entirely on Jackson, certain that he would always act for the best.

Lee's affection showed itself in a striking manner after Chancellorsville. Jackson, seriously wounded, was at an inn in the Wilderness. Lee, retained on the battlefield by the critical state of the situation, rendered still more so by Jackson's absence, could not steal away for a moment to press the invalid's hand. Not looking upon the wound as dangerous (and, indeed, it did not become so till the last moment), he unceasingly sent for news of him and forwarded these words of friendship: "Give him my affectionate regards," said he to one of his aides-de-camp. "Tell him to make haste and get well and come back to me as soon as he can. He has lost his left arm, but I have lost my right."

When, shortly after, the symptoms grew worse and it began to be whispered that the end would be fatal, Lee was deeply moved and exclaimed: "Surely General Jackson must recover! God will not take him from us, now that we need him so much. Surely he will be spared to us, in answer to the many prayers which are offered for him!" He became silent for a moment, an evident prey to violent and sorrowful emotion. Then, addressing an officer whom he was sending to the wounded general, he said: "When you return, I trust you will find him better. When a suitable occasion offers, give him my love and tell him that I wrestled in prayer for him last night as I never prayed, I believe, for myself."

The grief which Lee felt at Jackson's death was too profound for tears. God alone knows what that order of the day cost him, in which he imparted the tidings of this loss to the army!

"Headquarters Army of Northern Virginia
May 11, 1863

"General Order No. 61

With deep grief the Commanding General announces to the army the death of Lieutenant General T. J. Jackson, who expired on the 10th inst., at quarter past 3 P.M. The daring, skill and energy of this great and good soldier, by the decree of an All Wise Providence, are now lost to us. But while we mourn his death we feel that his spirit still lives and will inspire the whole army with his indomitable courage and unshaken confidence in God as our hope and strength. Let his name be a watchword to his corps, who have followed him to victory on so many fields. Let his officers and soldiers emulate his invincible determination to do everything in the defence of our beloved country.

R. E. LEE, GENERAL."

15

After he had got safely back across to the north side of the Rappahannock, General Hooker attempted to gloss over the magnitude of his defeat in adroitly worded reports and congratulatory orders to his troops. The Northern people were not deceived by this, however, as indicated by the report one of the war correspondents with the Army of the Potomac sent back to his paper.

We had men enough, well enough equipped and well enough posted to have devoured the ragged, imperfectly armed and equipped host of our enemies from off the face of the earth.

Their artillery horses are poor, starved frames of beasts, tied on to their carriages and caissons with odds and ends of rope and strips of raw hide. Their supply and ammunition trains look like a congregation of all the crippled California emigrant trains that ever escaped off the desert out of the clutches of the rampaging

Camanche Indians. The men are ill-dressed, ill-equipped and ill-provided—a set of ragamuffins that a man is ashamed to be seen among, even when he is a prisoner and can't help it.

And yet they have beaten us fairly, beaten us all to pieces, beaten us so easily that we are objects of contempt even to their commonest private soldiers, with no shirts to hang out of the holes in their pantaloons and with their cartridge-boxes tied round their waists with strands of rope.

16

The battle of Chancellorsville was followed by much discussion as to whether the brilliant flank movement so flawlessly executed by Jackson was conceived by him or by General Lee. Lee, with characteristic modesty, made no claims for himself, nor did he permit himself to become involved in the discussion until four years later when Dr. A. T. Bledsoe, editor of the *Southern Review,* wrote him a letter on the subject which demanded a reply. Lee, with his gift for tactful and restrained expression, answered in a way which could hardly be misunderstood but which cast no discredit on his great lieutenant.

In reply to your inquiry, I must acknowledge that I have not read the article on Chancellorsville in the last number of the *Southern Review,* nor have I read any of the books published on either side since the termination of hostilities. I have as yet felt no desire to revive my recollections of those events, and have been satisfied with the knowledge I possessed of what transpired. I have, however, learned from others that the various authors of the "Life of Jackson" award to him the credit of the success gained by the Army of Northern Virginia where he was present, and describe the movements of his corps or command as independent of the general plan of operations and undertaken at his own suggestion and upon his own responsibility.

I have the greatest reluctance to do anything that might be considered as detracting from his well-deserved fame, for I believe that no one was more convinced of his worth or appreciated him more highly than myself; yet your knowledge of military affairs, if you have none of the events themselves, will teach you that this could not have been so. Every movement of an army must be well considered and properly ordered, and every one who knows General Jackson must know that he was too good a soldier to violate this fundamental military principle.

In the operations round Chancellorsville I overtook General Jackson, who had been placed in command of the advance, as the skirmishers of the approaching armies met, advanced with the troops to the Federal line of defenses, and was on the field until their whole army recrossed the Rappahannock. There is no question as to who was responsible for the operations of the Confederates or to whom any failure would have been charged.

What I have said is for your own information.

17

The battle of Chancellorsville was a great victory for the Confederate arms; but it was not possible for Lee to rest on his well-earned laurels. There was work to be done, and plenty of it. One of his first steps was to bring his army to its fullest possible strength by calling Longstreet and his divisions back from the neighborhood of Suffolk. It was then necessary, because of the loss of Stonewall Jackson, to reorganize the army. In this reorganization three corps were set up, A. P. Hill and Richard S. Ewell being named to command two of them; Longstreet retained command of the First Corps. The question then presented itself: Should the Army of Northern Virginia assume the offensive or remain on the defensive? Various military moves were discussed, but the opinion prevailed in Richmond that if the smashing victory at Chancellorsville could be followed up by a similar success on a battlefield in the enemy's country it would not only bring European recognition, but would impel the people of the North to demand the ending of the war. Accordingly Lee began, early in June, to move by his left flank in the direction of Culpeper. The spirits of the commander and his army were high; but at the very inception of the campaign the weight of Lee's burden of anxiety was increased by a personal misfortune—the wounding and subsequent capture of his son, Rooney. Rooney's brother Robert has left an account of the episode, in which he played a part.

About June 5th most of the army was gathered around Culpeper. Its efficiency, confidence and morale were never better. On June 7th the entire cavalry corps was reviewed on the plain near Brandy Station in Culpeper by General Lee. We had been preparing ourselves for this event for some days, cleaning, mending and polishing, and I remember we were very proud of our appearance. In fact, it was a grand sight—about eight thousand well-mounted men riding by their beloved commander, first passing him in a walk and then in a trot. He writes to my mother next day —June 8, 1863:

". . . I reviewed the cavalry in this section yesterday. It was a splendid sight. The men and horses looked well. They have recuperated since last fall. Stuart was in all his glory. Your sons and nephews [two sons and three nephews] were well and flourishing. The country here looks very green and pretty, notwithstanding the ravages of war. What a beautiful world God . . . has given us! What a shame that men endowed with reason and knowledge of right should mar His gifts. . . ."

The next day, June 9th, a large force of the enemy's cavalry, supported by infantry, crossed the Rappahannock and attacked General Stuart. The conflict lasted until dark, when

"The enemy was compelled to recross the river, with heavy loss, leaving about five hundred prisoners, three pieces of artillery and several colours in our hands."

During the engagement, about 3 P.M., my brother, General W. H. F. Lee, my commanding officer, was severely wounded. In a letter dated the 11th of the month, my father writes to my mother:

". . . My supplications continue to ascend for you, my children and my country. When I last wrote I did not suppose that Fitzhugh would be so soon sent to the rear disabled, and I hope it will be for a short time. I saw him the night after the battle—indeed, met him on the field as they were bringing him from the front. He is young and healthy, and I trust will soon be up again. He seemed to be more concerned about his brave men and officers, who had fallen in the battle, than about himself. . . ."

It was decided, the next day, to send my brother to "Hickory Hill," the home of Mr. W. F. Wickham, in Hanover County, about twenty miles from Richmond, and I was put in charge of him to take him there and to be with him until his wound should heal. . . .

In a letter to my brother's wife, written on the 11th, his love and concern for both of them are plainly shown:

"I am so grieved, my dear daughter, to send Fitzhugh to you wounded. But I am so grateful that his wound is of a character to give us full hope of a speedy recovery. With his youth and strength to aid him, and your tender care to nurse him, I trust he will soon be well again. I know that you will unite with me in thanks to Almighty God, who has so often sheltered him in the hour of danger, for his recent deliverance. . . . As some good is always mixed with the evil in this world, you will now have him with you for a time, and I shall look to you to cure him soon and send him back to me. . . ."

My brother reached "Hickory Hill" quite comfortably, and his wound commenced to heal finely. His wife joined him, my mother and sisters came up from Richmond, and he had all the tender care he could wish. He occupied "the office" in the yard, while I slept in the room adjoining and became quite an expert nurse. About two weeks after our arrival, one lovely morning as we all came out from the breakfast table, stepping into the front porch with Mrs. Wickham, we were much surprised to hear two or three shots down in the direction of the outer gate, where there was a large grove of hickory trees. Mrs. Wickham said some one must be after her squirrels, as there were many in those woods, and she asked me to run down and stop whoever was shooting them.

I got my hat and at once started off to do her bidding. I had not gone over a hundred yards toward the grove when I saw, coming up at a gallop to the gate I was making for, five or six Federal cavalrymen. I knew what it meant at once, so I rushed back to the office and told my brother. He immediately understood the situation and directed me to get away—said I could do no good by staying, that the soldiers could not and would not hurt him, and there was nothing to be gained by my falling into their hands; but that, on the contrary, I might do a great deal of good by eluding them, making my way to "North Wales," a plantation across the Pamunkey River, and saving our horses.

So I ran out, got over the fence and behind a thick hedge, just as I heard the tramp and clank of quite a body of troopers riding up. Behind this hedge I crept along until I reached a body of woods, where I was perfectly safe. From a hill near by I ascertained that there was a large raiding party of Federal cavalry in the main road, and the heavy smoke ascending from the Court House, about three miles away, told me that they were burning the railroad buildings at that place. . . .

I saw my brother brought out from the office on a mattress and placed in the "Hickory Hill" carriage, to which was hitched Mr. Wickham's horses, and then saw him driven away, a soldier on the box and a mounted guard surrounding him. He was carried to the "White House" in this way, and then sent by water to Fortress Monroe. This party had been sent out especially to capture him, and he was held as a hostage (for the safety of some Federal officers we had captured) for nine long, weary months.

18

Lee's primary concern, of course, was with the military activities of the Army of Northern Virginia. He realized, however, that the ultimate objective of the army's activities was to win an honorable peace, and he did not wish to overlook any opportunity to bring about such a peace at the earliest possible time. His grasp of current political and diplomatic factors is reflected in a thoughtful letter he sent to President Davis on June 10.

I beg leave to bring to your attention a subject with reference to which I have thought that the course pursued by writers and speakers among us has had a tendency to interfere with our success. I refer to the manner in which the demonstration of a desire for peace at the North has been received in our country.

I think there can be no doubt that journalists and others at the South, to whom the Northern people naturally look for a reflection of our opinions, have met these indications in such wise as to weaken the hands of the advocates of a pacific policy on the part of the Federal Government, and give much encouragement to those who urge a continuation of the war. . . .

Conceding to our enemies the superiority claimed by them in numbers, resources and all the means and appliances for carrying on the war, we have no right to look for exemption from the military consequences of a vigorous use of these advantages, except by such deliverance as the mercy of Heaven may accord to the courage of our soldiers, the justice of our cause and the constancy and prayers of our people. . . . It is the part of wisdom to carefully measure and husband our strength and not to expect from it more than in the ordinary course of affairs it is capable of accomplishing. We should not, therefore, conceal from ourselves that our resources in men are constantly diminishing, and the disproportion in this respect between us and our enemies, if they continue united in their efforts to subjugate, is steadily augmenting. The decrease of the aggregate of this army as disclosed by the returns affords an illustration of this fact. Its effective strength varies from time to time, but the falling off in its aggregate shows that its ranks are growing weaker and that its losses are not supplied by recruits.

Under these circumstances we should neglect no honorable means of dividing and weakening our enemies, that they may feel some of the difficulties experienced by ourselves. It seems to me that the most effectual mode of accomplishing this object now within our reach is to give all the encouragement we can, consistently with the truth, to the rising peace party of the North.

Nor do I think we should, in this connection, make nice distinction between those who declare for peace unconditionally and those who advocate it as a means of restoring the Union, however much we may prefer the former. We should bear in mind that the friends of peace at the North must make concessions to the earnest desire that exists in the minds of their countrymen for a restoration of the Union, and that to hold out such a result as an inducement is essential to the success of their party. Should the belief that peace will bring back the Union become general, the war would no longer be supported; and that, after all, is what we are interested in bringing about.

When peace is proposed to us it will be time enough to discuss its terms, and it is not the part of prudence to spurn the proposition in advance merely because those who wish to make it believe, or affect to believe, that it will result in bringing us back to the Union. We entertain no such apprehension, nor doubt that the desire of our people for a distinct and independent national existence will prove as steadfast under the influence of peaceful measures as it has shown itself in the midst of war.

If the views I have indicated meet the approval of your Excellency, you will best know how to give effect to them. Should you deem them inexpedient or impracticable, I think you will nevertheless agree with me that we should at least carefully abstain from measures or expressions that tend to discourage any party whose purpose is peace. . . . I leave to your better judgment to determine the proper course to be pursued.

13

High Tide of the Confederacy

Aside from the diplomatic and political considerations which were of such interest to the Richmond authorities, Lee regarded the invasion of Pennsylvania as being sound strategy from a strictly military standpoint. He viewed it as promising the twofold beneficial result of enabling him to live off the enemy's supplies and provisions during the approaching summer, and at the same time forcing the Federal Army to withdraw from Virginia. Back of it all, he had the sound basic idea that his presence in the enemy's territory would force the Federals to withdraw troops from other points in the South, notably Vicksburg, thus relieving pressure at those points, and he also believed that his idea of strengthening the peace party in the North would be advanced by a successful invasion.

Lee's movements were hampered by the fact that after he left Winchester he was in ignorance of the whereabouts of the Federal Army. Unfortunately he had given Stuart generalized instructions which were capable of being misconstrued, and Stuart had gone off on a dramatic raid around the opposing army, getting himself entirely out of touch with Lee. The Army of Northern Virginia, therefore, moved on northward like a blind man groping in the dark. By June 28 Lee's forces were strung out over a wide territory in Pennsylvania. Ewell's corps, the first to cross the Potomac, had reached Carlisle, and was under orders to move on to Harrisburg. Early had already captured and occupied York. Lee himself was at Chambersburg with Longstreet and Hill, planning to move eastward with them, cross the Susquehanna and seize the railroad between Harrisburg and Philadelphia.

1

At Chambersburg Lee issued a general order to his troops, establishing a pattern for their conduct during their stay in the enemy's country.

General Orders No. 73

The commanding general has observed with marked satisfaction the conduct of the troops on the march, and confidently anticipates results commensurate with the high spirit they have manifested.

No troops could have displayed greater fortitude or better performed the arduous marches of the past ten days. Their conduct in other respects has, with few exceptions, been in keeping with their character as soldiers, and entitles them to approbation and praise.

There have, however, been instances of forgetfulness on the part of some that they have in keeping the yet unsullied reputation of the army, and that the duties exacted of us by civilization and Christianity are not less obligatory in the country of the enemy than in our own.

The commanding general considers that no greater disgrace could befall the army, and through it our whole people, than the perpetration of the barbarous outrages upon the unarmed and defenseless and the wanton destruction of private property that have marked the course of the enemy in our own country.

Such proceedings not only degrade the perpetrators and all connected with them, but are subversive of the discipline and efficiency of the army and destructive of the ends of our present movement. It must be remembered that we make war only upon armed men, and that we cannot take vengeance for the wrongs our people have suffered without lowering ourselves in the eyes of all whose abhorence has been excited by the atrocities of our enemies, and offending against Him to whom vengeance belongeth, without whose favor and support our efforts must all prove in vain. The commanding general therefore earnestly exhorts the troops to abstain with most scrupulous care from unnecessary or wanton injury to private property, and he enjoins upon all officers to arrest and bring to summary punishment all who shall in any way offend against the orders on this subject.

R. E. LEE
GENERAL

2

Lee's strict orders against foraging in Pennsylvania were sometimes honored in the letter of the law rather than the spirit. The irrepressible Texan, J. B. Polley, writes amusingly of his "purchase" of food, and also of his entertainment by a hospitable Pennsylvania family.

Just after crossing the boundary line into Pennsylvania, I went to a farmhouse in sight of the road and inquired if the owner had any bacon for sale. Answered in the affirmative, I asked the price and was told that it was fifteen cents a pound. Reflecting that in Virginia the price was two dollars a pound, and bacon almost impossible to buy at that, I determined to lay in a good supply. So, selecting from his well-filled smoke-house two sides which weighed exactly eighty pounds and were streaked with lean and fat in exactly the right proportion, I tied them together with a piece of old rope and, throwing them across the loins of my horse, handed the farmer a twenty-dollar Confederate bill.

"Oh!" said he, as he took it gingerly between thumb and fore-finger and eyed it as if suspicious it were unclean, "I can't pass this kind of money here in Pennsylvania."

"Yes, indeed, you can, my dear sir," said I, speaking with the fervor of absolute conviction. "Can't you see from the army passing by that we intend to take possession of this little neck of the woods? You will need our money to pay taxes and for many other purposes, and you had better begin to get hold of it."

"But I can't change this bill, for I haven't got any of the same kind," he whined.

"Oh! that's a small matter," said I; "just give me greenbacks—I ain't afraid of them."

"I'll see what I can do," he answered after a moment's hesitation, and walked into the house. In less than a minute I heard the shrill voice of an angry woman scolding vigorously and, guessing that the farmer was encountering opposition that might interfere with the trade, deemed it prudent to mount my steed and be prepared for emergencies. I had scarcely settled myself in the saddle when the farmer appeared and, extending the bill toward me, said, "Here, Mister, give me back that bacon and take your money—I can't make the change, for I ain't got eight dollars in the house."

Fully equal to the imperative demands of the occasion, and assuming the most lordly Southern air of which I was capable, I said, "Then just keep the change, sir," touched my weather-beaten hat with the politeness of a Chesterfield and, giving free rein to my horse, soon overtook a wagon and unloaded my prize into it. . . .

An old Dunkard gave us such an early breakfast next morning that when at noon we halted before a large and elegant mansion, surrounded by beautiful grounds, we were as hungry as bears. It fell to my lot to ask for entertainment and, dismounting, I rapped gently at the front door. A well-preserved lady of fifty opened the door and, her face as white as a sheet, looked silently at me. Raising my hat, I stated my errand. She looked at me from head to foot and glanced in the direction of my companions, then said in a tremulous voice, "You are Rebels, are you not?"

"That is what you call us, Madam, I suppose; but we call ourselves Confederates," I explained.

"Orders have been published," said she, "prohibiting citizens from giving any aid or comfort to the Confederates."

"I shall regret very much, Madam," I rejoined, "to have the orders obeyed in our particular case, for in that event we will have to ask elsewhere for food, and we are quite hungry."

"That alters the case," she replied quickly, smiling for the first time. "The Bible commands us to feed the hungry, and it is of higher authority than the orders of man. Ask your friends in. I will give you dinner." . . .

Within half an hour eight Confederates sat around a long table in a spacious dining room, eating huge slices of light bread, cold ham, corned beef and roast mutton, interspersed liberally with sweet pickles, jam, jelly and apple butter, drinking genuine coffee and the richest of milk and, between sups and bites, chatting as merrily with our hostess, her three handsome daughters, and an old gentleman whom the girls called "Uncle John," as if they were acquaintances of long and intimate standing. . . .

We sat there fully three hours; then Captain Mills suggested departure and, calling me to one side, quietly dropped a treasured five-dollar gold piece into my hand, saying in a low voice, "Here, Joe, pay for our dinner with this. They have been too kind to us to be offered Confederate money." Turning to the hostess I offered the coin and asked if it would satisfy her for her trouble.

"Yes, sir, it would were I willing to accept pay," said she, drawing back rather indignantly. "But I am not. We have heard horrible stories of the treatment we might expect from Confederates, but if all are gentlemen like yourselves, I will make them as welcome to my house and table as you have been." And when I said good-by, she clasped my hand warmly and said, "Good-by, my dear boy; and remember, if you get sick or wounded and will only let us know where you are, you shall be brought here and nursed until you are well again."

3

Colonel Taylor, in telling of Lee's preparations for the Pennsylvania invasion, shows how the Confederate commander attempted to foresee every contingency, again pointing out the advantages to be derived by arousing fears for the safety of Washington through the organization of an "effigy" army at Culpeper—a suggestion that was not acted on by the Richmond authorities.

General Lee commanded the army operating with him in the field, but not the disposition of all the troops available for the execution of his plans. While he was operating in the field the authorities at Richmond were nervous and apprehensive about the safety of that city. Far removed as he was at times, he was handicapped in his movements by the knowledge that his army was relied upon to defend the capital from any expedition the enemy might direct against it. . . . On the 23rd of June General Lee wrote to President Davis:

"At this distance I can see no benefit to be derived from maintaining a large force on the southern coast during the unhealthy months of summer and autumn, and I think that a part, at least, of the troops in North Carolina and of those under General Beauregard can be employed at this time to great advantage in Virginia. If an army could be organized under the command of General Beauregard and pushed forward to Culpeper Court House, threatening Washington from that direction, it would not only effect a diversion most favorable for this army, but would, I think, relieve us of any apprehension of an attack upon Richmond during our absence. . . . If success should attend the operations of this army—and what I now suggest would greatly increase the probability of that result—we might even hope to compel the recall of some of the enemy's troops from the West."

And again, under date of the 25th of June, to President Davis he wrote:

"You will see that the apprehension for the safety of Washington and their own territory has aroused the Federal government and people to great exertions, and it is incumbent upon us to call forth all our energies. In addition to the one hundred thousand troops called for by President Lincoln to defend the frontier of Pennsylvania, you will see that he is concentrating other organized forces in Maryland. . . . It is plain that if all the Federal army is concentrated upon this, it will result in our accomplishing nothing and being compelled to return to Virginia. If the plan that I suggested the other day of organizing an army, even in effigy, under General Beauregard at Culpeper Court House can be carried into effect, much relief will be afforded. . . . I have not sufficient troops to maintain my communications and therefore must abandon them. I think I can throw General Hooker's army across the Potomac and draw troops from the South, embarrassing their plan of campaign in a measure, if I can do nothing more and have to return."

4

Evidence of the South's blind confidence in General Lee's invincibility and of its unlimited belief in the credibility of Confederate news sources is provided by an enthusiastic editorial in the *Daily Citizen* of Vicksburg, Mississippi, on July 2—just two days before the surrender of that city and Lee's retreat from Pennsylvania.

Again we have reliable news from the gallant corps of General Lee in Virginia. Elated with success, encouraged by a series of brilliant victories, marching to and crossing the Rappahannock, defeating Hooker's right wing and thence through the Shenandoah Valley, driving Milroy from Winchester and capturing 6,000 of his men and a large amount of valuable stores of all descriptions, re-entering Maryland, holding Hagerstown, threatening Washington City, and within a few miles of Baltimore—onward and upward their war cry—our brave men under Lee are striking terror to the hearts of all Yankeedom. Like the Scottish chieftain's braves, Lee's men are springing up from moor and brake, crag and dale, with flashing steel and sturdy arm, ready to do or die in the great cause of national independence, right and honor.

To-day the mongrel administration of Lincoln, like Japhet, are in search of a father—for their old Abe has departed for parts unknown. Terror reigns in their halls. Lee is to the left of them, the right of them, in front of them, and all around them; and daily do we expect to hear of his being down on them. Never were the French in Algeria more put out by the mobile raids of Ab Del Kader than are the Federals of Maryland, Washington City, Pennsylvania and Ohio by the mercureal movements of Lee's cavalry. Like Paddy's flea are they to the Federals—now they have got them and now they haven't. The omnipresence of our troops and their throwing dust in the eyes, or rather on the heels, of the panic-stricken Federals in Maryland and Pennsylvania clearly prove that Lee just now is the right man in the right place.

To-day Maryland is ours; tomorrow Pennsylvania will be; and the next day Ohio—now midway like Mahommed's coffin—will fall.

Success and glory to our arms! God and right are with us.

5

As has been frequently pointed out, the battle of Gettysburg was an accidental battle. On June 28 Lee was at Chambersburg, expressing concern at his ignorance of the whereabouts of Hooker's army, but entertaining no idea that a collision with his adversary was imminent. Then on the twenty-ninth he received the surprising and disquieting news that the Federal army, now under General George G. Meade, who had succeeded Hooker, had crossed the Potomac several days previously and was moving northward. Lee still did not know where Meade's forces were at that time, but he was painfully aware of the fact that in the circumstances his own army was too widely scattered, and so he immediately issued orders for a concentration of his troops east of the Blue Ridge at Cashtown and Gettysburg. In accordance with these orders Ewell and Early moved in the direction of Gettysburg and Lee, accompanying Longstreet and Hill, crossed over South Mountain toward Cashtown.

Entirely unknown to Lee, the advance guard of the Federals, under General Buford, reached Gettysburg on the twenty-ninth. Hill, in the Confederate van, stumbled up on Buford's dismounted troopers in the outskirts of Gettysburg, a brisk skirmish resulting. Contact being thus unexpectedly established with the enemy, Lee found it necessary to make a quick, extemporized readjustment of his plans. General Maurice explains simply and clearly the military conditions which governed Lee's decision.

On July 1st, both armies were concentrating toward Gettysburg as rapidly as might be, for Hill and Buford were drawing their armies after them like magnets, and early that morning Hill began a cautious advance, cautious because he did not know what was in front of him. Buford, again handling his troopers skilfully, kept him off until Reynolds arrived with the First Corps of the Army of the Potomac. Some stiff fighting followed in which the gallant Reynolds was killed, but the arrival of Howard with the eleventh Federal Corps kept the Confederates at bay until Ewell began to come down on Gettysburg from the north, when the Federals were driven from the greater part of the town. Things were going badly with them, for the Confederates were in superior numbers, when

Hancock, sent forward by Meade to take command, put new life into the defence. Meade had given him discretion to stand at Gettysburg or fall back on Pipe's Creek, and Hancock, knowing that reënforcements were coming up fast, and realising the natural strength and importance of the ridge south of Gettysburg, elected to hold it.

So far the two commanders-in-chief had done little more than direct their troops toward a place of strategical importance. Neither had yet definitely decided on battle, and the course of events had been directed by their subordinates.

Lee reached the battlefield about 3 P.M., and soon learned that his men were engaged with two Federal corps, and that others were coming up. His troops had gained some preliminary success, but in view of his uncertainty as to the position of Meade's troops he decided not to press on immediately.

He had now to consider what he would do next. He had four alternatives open to him. He could fall back on the South Mountains and there await attack, he could await attack where he was, he could move round the Federal left and interpose between it and Washington, and lastly he could make a direct attack on the Federal army where it stood. The first two of these Lee has disposed of in his report: "It had not been intended," he says, "to deliver a general battle so far from our base unless attacked, but coming unexpectedly upon the whole Federal army, to withdraw through the mountains with our excessive trains would have been difficult, and dangerous. At the same time we were unable to await an attack, as the country was unfavourable for collecting supplies in the presence of the enemy, who could restrain our foraging parties by holding the mountain passes with local and other troops. A battle had therefore become in a measure unavoidable, and the success already gained gave hope of a favourable issue."

Lee had skinned the Cumberland Valley to feed his 73,000 men, and the greater part of its produce was either in his men's stomachs or in his wagons. When these were empty, he had no immediate means of refilling them. He could not, therefore, allow his adversary to take his own time in offering battle. The harassed Confederate Quartermaster General had said airily: "If Lee wants supplies, let him seek them in Pennsylvania," but quartermasters do

not always realise how much their proposals affect the strategy of
their generals. The poverty in resources of the Confederacy imposed strict limits upon Lee's choice of action.

During the night of the 1st-2nd of July, Longstreet, as averse as
ever to offensive tactics, urged a movement round the Federal left.
But Lee rejected it, and rightly. It was from the direction of
Washington that Meade was advancing, and Lee did not know
where were the Federal troops, who were marching up to Gettysburg Ridge. Jackson's turning movement at Chancellorsville had
been justified by exact knowledge of Hooker's position, but to
have made a turning movement on July 2nd, in the absence of
Stuart's cavalry and of all detailed information, would have been
wildly rash.

It remained then to attack the Federals where they stood. During the night Lee received information that only a part of Meade's
army was opposite him. He knew that the two Federal corps which
had opposed him had suffered severely, and he decided to attack
next morning as early as practicable. Obviously his greatest chance
of victory lay in attacking before all Meade's troops were up. Lee's
plan was to make his main attack against the Federal left with
Longstreet's corps, while Ewell kept their right occupied. This
was tactically the soundest plan, but it was a singular misfortune
for Lee that the disposition of his troops forced him to entrust it
to a lieutenant who was notoriously averse to initiating attack.

6

Probably no battle in the history of the world has attracted
the attention of so many historical writers as has the battle of
Gettysburg. Many volumes and innumerable magazine and
newspaper articles have been written about the details of its
tactics, the mistakes, the conflict of views, the lost opportunities, the heroism and the tragedy of that bloody field. For a
graphic, over-all, bird's-eye view of the engagement it is hard
to find anything better than the observations recorded by a British army officer, Lieutenant Colonel Arthur Fremantle of the
Coldstream Guards. Colonel Fremantle was on a tour of observation of the Confederate States, and had joined the Army

of Northern Virginia on its march into Pennsylvania. His day-by-day entries in his journal reflect vividly the impact of the battle—and of Lee and his army—on this observant British soldier.

30th June (Tuesday)—This morning, before marching from Chambersburg, General Longstreet introduced me to the Commander-in-Chief. General Lee is, almost without exception, the handsomest man of his age I ever saw. He is fifty-six years old, tall, broad-shouldered, very well made, well set up—a thorough soldier in appearance; and his manners are most courteous and full of dignity. He is a most perfect gentleman in every respect. I imagine no man has so few enemies or is so universally esteemed. Throughout the South, all agree in pronouncing him to be as near perfection as a man can be. . . . I never saw him carry arms, and the only marks of military rank are the three stars on his collar. He rides a handsome horse, which is extremely well groomed. He himself is very neat in his dress and person, and in the most arduous marches he always looks smart and clean. . . . The relations between him and Longstreet are quite touching—they are almost always together. Longstreet's corps complains of this sometimes, as they say that they seldom get a chance of detached service, which falls to the lot of Ewell. It is impossible to please Longstreet more than by praising Lee. I believe these two Generals to be as little ambitious and as thoroughly unselfish as any men in the world. . . . I had a long talk with many officers about the approaching battle, which evidently can not now be delayed long and will take place on this road instead of in the direction of Harrisburg as we had supposed. . . .

1st July (Wednesday)—We did not leave our camp till noon, as nearly all General Hill's corps had to pass our quarters on its march towards Gettysburg. . . . At 2 P.M. firing became distinctly audible in our front, but although it increased as we progressed, it did not seem to be very heavy. A spy who was with us insisted upon there being "a pretty tidy bunch of blue-bellies in or near Gettysburg," and he declared that he was in their society three days ago. . . .

At 3 P.M. we began to meet wounded men coming to the rear,

and the number of these soon increased most rapidly, some hobbling alone, others on stretchers carried by the ambulance corps, and others in the ambulance waggons; many of the latter were stripped nearly naked and displayed very bad wounds. This spectacle, so revolting to a person unaccustomed to such sights, produced no impression whatever upon the advancing troops, who certainly go under fire with the most perfect nonchalance: they show no enthusiasm or excitement, but the most complete indifference. This is the effect of two years' almost uninterrupted fighting. . . .

At 4:30 P.M. we came in sight of Gettysburg and joined General Lee and General Hill who were on the top of one of the ridges which form the peculiar feature of the country round Gettysburg. We could see the enemy retreating up one of the opposite ridges, pursued by the Confederates with loud yells. The position into which the enemy had been driven was evidently a strong one. His right appeared to rest on a cemetery on the top of a high ridge to the right of Gettysburg as we looked at it. . . .

I climbed up a tree in the most commanding place I could find, and could form a pretty good general idea of the enemy's position, although, the tops of the ridges being covered with pine woods, it was very difficult to see anything of the troops concealed in them. The firing ceased about dark, at which time I rode back with General Longstreet and his staff to his headquarters at Cashtown, a little village eight miles from Gettysburg. At that time troops were pouring along the road, and were being marched towards the position they are to occupy to-morrow. . . .

2nd July (Thursday)—We all got up at 3:30 A.M., and breakfasted a little before daylight. . . . I arrived at 5 A.M. at the same commanding position we were on yesterday, and I climbed up a tree in company with Captain Schreibert of the Prussian army. Just below us were seated Generals Lee, Hill, Longstreet and Hood in consultation—the two latter assisting their deliberations by the truly American custom of whittling. General Heth was also present: he was wounded in the head yesterday, and although not allowed to command his brigade, he insists upon coming to the field.

At 7 A.M I rode over part of the ground with General Longstreet, and saw him disposing McLaws's division for to-day's fight.

The enemy occupied a series of high ridges, the tops of which were covered with trees, but the intervening valleys between their ridges and ours were mostly open, and partly under cultivation. The cemetery was on their right, and their left appeared to rest upon a high rocky hill. The enemy's forces, which were now supposed to comprise nearly the whole Potomac army, were concentrated into a space apparently not more than a couple of miles in length. The Confederates enclosed them in a sort of semi-circle, and the extreme extent of our position must have been from five to six miles at least. Ewell was on our left, his headquarters in a church with a high cupola; Hill in the centre; and Longstreet on the right. Our ridges were also covered with pine woods at the tops and generally on the rear slopes. The artillery of both sides confronted each other at the edges of these belts of trees, the troops being completely hidden. The enemy were evidently intrenched, but the Southerns had not broken ground. A dead silence reigned till 4:45 P.M., and no one would have imagined that such masses of men and such a powerful artillery were about to commence the work of destruction at that hour. Only two divisions of Longstreet were present to-day—viz., McLaws's and Hood's—Pickett being still in the rear. . . .

At 2 P.M. General Longstreet advised me, if I wished to have a good view of the battle, to return to my tree of yesterday. I did so, and remained there with Lawley and Captain Schreibert during the rest of the afternoon. But until 4:45 P.M. all was profoundly still, and we began to doubt whether a fight was coming off to-day at all. At that time, however, Longstreet suddenly commenced a heavy cannonade on the right. Ewell immediately took it up on the left. The enemy replied with at least equal fury, and in a few moments the firing along the whole line was as heavy as it is possible to conceive. A dense smoke arose for six miles; there was little wind to drive it away, and the air seemed full of shells—each of which appeared to have a different style of going and to make a different noise from the others. . . .

So soon as the firing began, General Lee joined Hill just below our tree and he remained there nearly all the time, looking through his field-glass—sometimes talking to Hill and sometimes to Colonel Long of his staff. What I remarked especially was that during the whole time the firing continued he only sent one message and only received one report. It is evidently his system to arrange the plan thoroughly with the three corps commanders and then leave to them the duty of modifying and carrying it out to the best of their ability.

When the cannonade was at its height, a Confederate band of music, between the cemetery and ourselves, began to play polkas and waltzes, which sounded very curious, accompanied by the hissing and bursting of the shells.

At 5:45 all became comparatively quiet on our left and in the cemetery; but volleys of musketry on the right told us that Long-street's infantry were advancing, and the onward progress of the smoke showed that he was progressing favourably; but about 6:30 there seemed to be a check, and even a slight retrograde move-ment. Soon after 7 General Lee got a report by signal from Long-street to say "We are doing well." A little before dark the firing dropped off in every direction and soon ceased altogether. We then received intelligence that Longstreet had carried everything before him for some time, capturing several batteries and driving the enemy from his positions; but when Hill's Florida Brigade and some other troops gave way, he was forced to abandon a small portion of the ground he had won, together with the captured guns, except three. His troops, however, bivouacked during the night on ground occupied by the enemy this morning. . . .

3rd July (Friday)—At 6 A.M. I rode to the field with Colonel Manning, and went over that portion of the ground which, after a fierce contest, had been won from the enemy yesterday evening. . . . We joined Generals Lee and Longstreet's staff: they were re-connoitring and making preparations for renewing the attack. . . . The plan of yesterday's attack seems to have been very simple—first a heavy cannonade all along the line, followed by an advance of Longstreet's two divisions and part of Hill's corps. In conse-quence of the enemy's having been driven back some distance, Longstreet's corps (part of it) was in a much more forward situa-tion than yesterday. But the range of heights to be gained was still most formidable, and evidently strongly entrenched.

The distance between the Confederate guns and the Yankee posi-tion was at least a mile—quite open, gently undulating and exposed to artillery the whole distance. This was the ground which was to be crossed in to-day's attack. Pickett's division, which had just come up, was to bear the brunt in Longstreet's attack, together with Heth and Pettigrew in Hill's corps. At noon all Longstreet's dispositions were made; his troops for attack were deployed into line and lying down in the woods; his batteries were ready to open. The General then dismounted and went to sleep for a short time. The Austrian officer and I now rode off to get, if possible, into some commanding position from whence we could see the whole thing without being exposed to the tremendous fire which was about to commence. . . .

7

Colonel Fremantle was not able to find a satisfactory place from which to view the impending action, and so determined to return to Longstreet's position. While thus moving to and fro he missed the dramatic highlight of the whole battle— Pickett's historic charge. Fremantle mentions "Colonel Long of his staff" as one of those at General Lee's side during the action, and Colonel (later General) Long supplies a vivid description of that bloody debacle.

Pickett's division was fresh, having taken no part in the previous day's fight, and to these veterans was given the post of honor in the coming affray, which promised to be a desperate and terrible one.

About twelve o'clock the preparations for the attack were completed and the signal for battle was given, which was immediately followed by the concentrated fire of all the Confederate artillery on Cemetery Hill, which was promptly responded to by the powerful Federal batteries. Then ensued one of the most tremendous artillery engagements ever witnessed on an open field: the hills shook and quivered beneath the thunder of two hundred and twenty-five guns as if they were about to be torn and rent by some powerful convulsion. . . . For more than an hour this fierce artillery conflict continued, when the Federal guns began to slacken their fire under the heavy blows of the Confederate batteries, and ere long sank into silence—an example which was quickly followed by the Confederates.

A deathlike stillness then reigned over the field, and each army remained in breathless expectation of something yet to come still more dreadful. In a few moments the attacking column, consisting of Pickett's division, supported on the left by that of Heth commanded by Pettigrew, and on the right by Wilcox's brigade of Anderson's division, appeared from behind a ridge and, sweeping over its crest, descended into the depression that separated the two armies. The enemy for a moment seemed lost in admiration of this gallant array as it advanced with the steadiness and precision of a review. Their batteries then opened upon it a spasmodic fire, as if recovering from a stunning blow.

The force that moved to the attack numbered about 15,000 men. It had a terrible duty to perform. The distance which it was obliged to traverse was more than half a mile in width, and this an open plain in full front of the enemy, who thickly crowded the crest of the ridge, and within easy range of their artillery.

But the tempest of the fire which burst upon the devoted column quickly reduced its strength. The troops of Heth's division, decimated by the storm of deadly hail which tore through their ranks, faltered and fell back in disorder before the withering volleys of the Federal musketry. This compelled Pender's division, which had marched out to support the movement, to fall back, while Wilcox, on perceiving that the attack had grown hopeless, failed to advance, leaving Pickett's men to continue the charge alone. The other supports, Hood's and McLaws's divisions, which had been expected to advance in support of the charging column, did not move, and were too remote to offer any assistance. The consequence was that Pickett was left entirely unsupported.

Yet the gallant Virginians marched steadily forward, through the storm of shot and shell that burst upon their devoted ranks, with a gallantry that has never been surpassed. As they approached the ridge their lines were torn by incessant volleys of musketry as by a deadly hail. Yet with unfaltering courage the brave fellows broke into the double-quick and with an irresistible charge burst into the Federal lines and drove everything before them toward the crest of Cemetery Hill, leaping the breastworks and planting their standards on the captured guns with shouts of victory.

The success which General Lee had hoped and expected was gained, but it was a dearly-bought and short-lived one. His plan had gone astray through the failure of the supporting columns. Now was the time that they should have come to the aid of their victorious comrades; but, alas! Heth's division, which had behaved with the greatest gallantry two days before, had not been able to face the terrible fire of the Federal lines, while the other supports were too remote to afford timely relief. The victory which seemed within the grasp of the Confederate army was lost as soon as won. On every side the enemy closed in on Pickett's brigades, concentrating on them the fire of every gun in that part of their lines. It was impossible to long withstand this terrific fusillade. The band of heroes broke and fell back, leaving the greater part of their number dead or wounded upon the field or captive in the hands of their foes. . . .

Colonel Walter H. Taylor, adjutant general on the staff of General Lee, states as follows: ". . . The attack was not made as designed: Pickett's division, Heth's division and two brigades of Pender's division advanced. Hood and McLaws were not moved forward. There were nine divisions in the army; seven were quiet, while two assailed the fortified line of the enemy. Had Hood and McLaws followed or supported Pickett, and Pettigrew and Anderson been advanced, the design of the commanding general would have been carried out: the world would not be so at a loss to understand what was designed by throwing forward, unsupported, against the enemy's stronghold so small a portion of our army. . . . He felt strong enough to carry the enemy's lines, and I believe success would have crowned his plan had it been faithfully carried out."

The author can add his testimony to that of Colonel Taylor. The original intention of General Lee was that Pickett's attack should be supported by the divisions of McLaws and Hood, and General Longstreet was so ordered . . . verbally by General Lee in the presence of Colonel Long and Major Venable of his staff and other officers of the army.

8

Colonel Fremantle arrived back at Longstreet's headquarters as the bleeding survivors of Pickett's shattered division were limping back through the woods. He provides an impressive picture of the behavior of Lee and Longstreet and the other Confederate leaders in the face of this staggering reverse.

When I got close up to General Longstreet, I saw one of his regiments advancing through the woods in good order; so, thinking I was just in time to see the attack, I remarked to the General that "I wouldn't have missed this for anything." Longstreet was seated at the top of a snake fence at the edge of the wood, and looked perfectly calm and unperturbed. He replied, laughing, "The devil you wouldn't! I would like to have missed it very much; we've attacked and been repulsed." . . . The General told me that Pickett's division had succeeded in carrying the enemy's position and capturing his guns, but after remaining there twenty minutes it had been forced to retire, on the retreat of Heth and Pettigrew on its left. No person could have been more calm or self-possessed than General Longstreet under these trying circumstances. . . . He asked for something to drink: I gave him some rum out of my silver flask, which I begged he would keep in remembrance of the occasion: he smiled and, to my great satisfaction, accepted the memorial. . . .

Soon afterwards I joined General Lee, who had in the meanwhile come to that part of the field on becoming aware of the disaster. If Longstreet's conduct was admirable, that of General Lee was perfectly sublime. He was engaged in rallying and encouraging the broken troops, and was riding along in front of the wood quite alone—the whole of his staff being engaged in a similar manner further to the rear. His face, which is always placid and cheerful, did not show signs of the slightest disappointment, care or annoyance; and he was addressing to every soldier he met a few words of encouragement, such as, "All this will come right in the end; we'll talk it over afterwards; but, in the meantime, all good men must rally. We want all good and true men just now," etc. He spoke to all the wounded men that passed him, and the slightly wounded he exhorted to "bind up their hurts and take a musket" in this emergency. Very few failed to answer his appeal, and I saw many badly wounded men take off their hats and cheer him. He said to me, "This has been a sad day for us, Colonel—a sad day; but we can't expect always to gain victories." He was also kind enough to advise me to get into some more sheltered position, as the shells were bursting round us with considerable frequency.

Notwithstanding the misfortune which had so suddenly befallen him, General Lee seemed to observe everything, however trivial. When a mounted officer began licking his horse for shying at the bursting of a shell, he called out, "Don't whip him, Captain; don't whip him. I've got just such another foolish horse myself, and whipping does no good." . . .

I saw General Willcox (an officer who wears a short round jacket and a battered straw hat) come up to him and explain, almost crying, the state of his brigade. General Lee immediately shook hands with him and said cheerfully, "Never mind, General, all this has been *my* fault—it is *I* that have lost this fight, and you must help me out of it the best way you can." In this manner I saw General Lee encourage and reanimate his somewhat dispirited troops and magnanimously take on his own shoulders the whole weight of the repulse. It was impossible to look at him or to listen to him without feeling the strongest admiration. . . .

Soon afterwards I rode to the extreme front, where there were four pieces of rifled cannon almost without any infantry support. To the non-withdrawal of these guns is to be attributed the otherwise surprising inactivity of the enemy. I was immediately surrounded by a sergeant and about half-a-dozen gunners, who seemed in excellent spirits and full of confidence, in spite of their exposed situation. The sergeant expressed his ardent hope that the Yankees might have spirit enough to advance and receive the dose he had in readiness for them. They spoke in admiration of the advance of Pickett's men and the manner in which Pickett himself had led it. When they observed General Lee they said, "We've not lost confidence in the old man: this day's work won't do him no harm. 'Uncle Robert' will get us into Washington yet, you bet!"

9

A close-up view of General Lee in the last minutes preceding the final charge on the Federal position is given by a member of one of the Tennessee regiments participating in the charge, W. H. Swallow.

The men who composed the assaulting column proper . . . were composed of troops from five states: Virginia, Tennessee, North Carolina, Alabama and Mississippi. Their strength was as follows: Pickett's division, 4,500; Heth's division, 5,000; while the two brigades of Scales and Lane of Pender's division, commanded by General Trimble, mustered about 2,500. The assaulting column therefore contained about 12,000 men. There were nine brigades engaged in the direct column of attack.

Immediately after the column was formed, Generals Lee, Longstreet and Pickett rode along the lines several times, reviewing the troops and inspecting the different assignments. They then rode aside and had an earnest and animated conversation together, after which all three again rode along the column and retired together. Their whole conduct showed in a manner not to be mistaken how extremely dangerous and full of doubt these officers regarded the proposed assault.

General Trimble, who commanded Pender's division and lost his leg in the assault, lay wounded with the writer at Gettysburg for several weeks after the battle. He told me that when General Lee was closing the inspection of the column in front of Scales' brigade, which had been fearfully cut up in the first day's conflict, and noticing many of Scales' men with their heads and hands bandaged, he said to General Trimble: "Many of these poor boys should go to the rear; they are not able for duty." Passing his eyes searchingly along the weakened ranks of Scales' brigade, he turned to General Trimble and touchingly added: "I miss in this brigade the faces of many dear friends."

As he rode away he looked mournfully at the column and muttered, more to himself than to General Trimble, "The attack must succeed."

10

General John B. Imboden of the Confederate cavalry, who was entrusted with the duty of guarding Lee's wagon train on the retreat from Gettysburg, has left a striking account of his last interview with Lee on the battlefield on the evening of July 3, and of the defeated commander's reaction to his tragic hour.

It was a warm summer's night; there were few camp-fires, and the weary soldiers were lying in groups on the luxuriant grass of the beautiful meadows, discussing the events of the day, speculating on the morrow, or watching that our horses did not straggle off while browsing. About 11 o'clock a horseman came to summon me to General Lee. I promptly mounted and . . . guided by the courier who brought the message, rode about two miles toward Gettysburg to where half a dozen small tents were pointed out, a little way from the roadside to our left, as General Lee's headquarters for the night. On inquiry I found that he was not there, but had gone to the headquarters of General A. P. Hill, about half a mile nearer to Gettysburg. When we reached the place indicated, a single flickering candle, visible from the road through the open front of a common wall-tent, exposed to view Generals Lee and Hill seated on camp stools with a map spread upon their knees. Dismounting, I approached on foot. After exchanging the ordinary salutations, General Lee directed me to go back to his headquarters and wait for him. I did so, but he did not make his appearance until about 1 o'clock, when he came riding alone, at a slow walk, and evidently wrapped in profound thought.

When he arrived there was not even a sentinel on duty at his tent, and no one of his staff was awake. The moon was high in the clear sky and the silent scene was unusually vivid. As he approached and saw us lying on the grass under a tree, he spoke, reined in his jaded horse, and essayed to dismount. The effort to do so betrayed so much physical exhaustion that I hurriedly rose and stepped forward to assist him, but before I reached his side he had succeeded in alighting, and threw his arm across the saddle to rest; and fixing his eyes upon the ground leaned in silence and almost motionless upon his equally weary horse—the two forming a striking and never-to-be-forgotten group. The moon shone full upon his massive features and revealed an expression of sadness that I had never before seen upon his face. Awed by his appearance, I waited for him to speak until the silence became embarrassing, when, to break it and change the silent current of his thoughts, I ventured to remark in a sympathetic tone and in allusion to his great fatigue:

"General, this has been a hard day on you."

He looked up and replied mournfully:

"Yes, it has been a sad, sad day for us," and immediately relapsed into his thoughtful mood and attitude.

Being unwilling again to intrude upon his reflections, I said no more. After perhaps a minute or two, he suddenly straightened up to his full height and, turning to me with more animation and excitement of manner than I had ever seen in him before, for he was a man of wonderful equanimity, he said in a voice tremulous with emotion:

"I never saw troops behave more magnificently than Pickett's division of Virginians did to-day in that grand charge upon the enemy. And if they had been supported as they were to have been— but, for some reason not yet explained to me, were not—we would have held the position and the day would have been ours." After a moment's pause he added in a loud voice, in a tone almost of agony: "Too bad! *Too bad!* OH! TOO BAD!" I shall never forget his language, his manner, and his appearance of mental suffering.

In a few moments all emotion was suppressed, and he spoke feelingly of several of his fallen and trusted officers. . . . He invited me into his tent, and as soon as we were seated he remarked:

"We must now return to Virginia. As many of our poor wounded as possible must be taken home. I have sent for you because your men and horses are fresh and in good condition, to guard and conduct our train back to Virginia. The duty will be arduous, responsible and dangerous, for I am afraid you will be harassed by the enemy's cavalry."

11

The situation, as viewed from a Confederate standpoint, is outlined by Colonel Taylor.

After the assault on the enemy's works on the 3rd of July, there was no serious fighting at Gettysburg. The 4th passed in comparative quiet. Neither army evinced any disposition to assail the other. Notwithstanding the brilliant achievements of Ewell and Hill on the first day, and the decided advantage gained by Longstreet on the second, the failure of the operations of the third day deprived us, in a measure, of the prestige of our previous successes, and gave a shadow of right to our adversary's claim of having gained a victory. Their exultation, however, should be tempered with moderation when it is considered that, after one day of absolute quiet, the Confederates withdrew from their front without serious molestation and, with bridges swept away and an impassable river in rear, stood in an attitude of defiance until their line of retreat could be rendered practicable, after which they safely crossed into Virginia. Then, again, so serious was the loss visited upon the Federals in the engagements of the first and second days, and so brilliant was the effort to capture their position on the third day, that they themselves were undecided as to whether they should stand or retreat. General Lee's army was in condition to have justified his moving by either flank to draw the enemy from his impregnable position, and so to have forced a battle on more even terms, with greater promise of success. The spirit of the army was superb; General Lee's confidence in his men was undiminished; and the lack of supplies and of ammunition alone constrained him to abandon the enemy's front and recross the Potomac.

12

A graphic account of the retreat from Gettysburg, as viewed through the eyes of a neutral foreign observer, is given by Fitzgerald Ross, an Austrian army officer who was visiting the Army of Northern Virginia as a military observer.

The road was crowded with waggons, as the whole train had but two roads to move on—the Fairfield and the Cashtown one. When Lee's army entered Maryland the waggon-train alone, without the artillery, was forty-two miles long, and it was now larger than ever, though most of the waggons and teams procured in Pennsylvania had been already sent to the rear.

Bream's tavern, house, stables, barn and every out-building

were full of wounded men, some of whom were being moved into the ambulances, and others more badly wounded were being removed to better accommodations left thereby vacant.

It was a grievous sight to see these fine young fellows, many of them probably crippled for life, and yet all were cheerful and smiling. Looks of deep sympathy greeted them on every side as they were borne past on stretchers. And sometimes the wounded men would address a few encouraging words to some friend who stood near, himself too sad to speak. Many were to be left behind, too severely wounded to bear removal; and it struck me very much that it should be they who would speak words of comfort to their more fortunate friends who had escaped the dangers of the battle. No one complained. All bore themselves in the same proud manly way. . . .

When it was dusk we went on a mile or two farther on the Fairfield road, and presently came upon a blazing fire around which were Generals Lee and Longstreet with all their staff. We were to remain here until the train had passed, when the main body of the army would be withdrawn from its position and join the retreat.

It soon grew pitch dark, and then the rain began again. Oh, how it did pour! I never saw anything like it. Now and then it would relax a little, and then again and again would rush down in torrents. . . . It was certainly a dismal night. The fire was kept up and protected from the rain by continually piling on fresh wood, and it was a roaring one, yet I wondered that it was not extinguished. It lighted up the scene with a strange glare.

Lee and Longstreet stood apart engaged in earnest conversation, and around the fire in various groups lay the officers of their staffs. Tired to death, many were sleeping in spite of the drenching rain. . . . Again and again during the night reports came in from Law, McLaws, Ewell, etc., stating that the enemy had retreated and that they had nothing but cavalry in front of them. General Lee said, a few days afterwards, that he had hesitated whether he should not countermand his own retreat, which he certainly would not have commenced if he had anticipated such dreadfully bad weather. But the waggon-trains were now well on their way to the rear, and their safety might have been compromised if the army had not followed them. By eight o'clock next morning the whole waggon-train had got past us and the troops began to move. It had ceased raining, but the road was a sea of slush and mud and we got along very slowly . . . and it was dark before we reached Hagerstown. . . .

Two days after our return to Hagerstown . . . I visited General Lee in the afternoon, and he spoke very openly on the subject of the late campaign.

Had he been aware that Meade had been able to concentrate his whole army—for which he deserved great credit—he certainly should not have attacked him: indeed, it had not been his interest nor his intention to bring on a great battle at all; but, led away, partly by the success of the first day, believing that Meade had only a portion of his army in front of him, and seeing the enthusiasm of his own troops, he had thought that a successful battle would cut the knot so easily and satisfactorily that he had determined to risk it. His want of knowledge of the enemy's movements he attributed to Stuart's having got too far away from him with his cavalry. . . .

General Lee, when he had commenced his forward movement, had gained several days' march upon General Hooker, who was at that time opposed to him; but at Chambersburg he had been obliged to halt with his main force for three days, as there had been some delay in forwarding his supply-trains. This gave Meade, who had now superseded Hooker, time to concentrate his forces in the right direction. Otherwise, and if Lee had been able to follow closely upon Ewell's corps, which had advanced as far as Carlisle, he would have crossed the mountainous region of Pennsylvania and got into the rich and fertile valley of the Susquehanna without any opposition.

Here his army would have found plentiful means of subsistence, Philadelphia would have been threatened and Washington, Baltimore and the Army of the Potomac would have been cut off from their supplies and from all communication with the north except by sea. The communications of General Lee could not have been seriously interfered with without the Federal army entirely uncovering Washington and Baltimore. He might have taken up a position where it would have been very difficult for Meade to attack him; and, without further fighting, by merely maintaining his army at or near Harrisburg or some other central point, incalculable results might have been secured. But it was not so ordained.

13

The retreat from Gettysburg was a serious affair, fraught with the gravest danger, but Robert Stiles with his light touch gives an excellent impression of the temper of the men in the Army of Northern Virginia as they trudged homeward along the Pennsylvania roads.

Much has been said, and justly, of the unshaken condition of the Army of Northern Virginia when it retired from the Federal front at Gettysburg; and yet it is equally true that army had been through a most trying experience, and as it was still in hostile territory and a swollen and at the time impassable river flowed between it and the friendly soil of Old Virginia, Lee had great cause for anxiety, and it behooved him to be thoroughly informed and certified as to the real condition and spirit of his troops. With this view he directed his generals, particularly his generals of division, to make prompt and thorough investigation in this regard, and to report results to him. McLaws, our division general, made a special tour around the camp fires of his men one evening while we were in line of battle at Hagerstown, Maryland, waiting for Meade to attack, or for the Potomac to fall, so that we might in safety cross it, and I was at special pains to follow, and to see and hear what I could.

McLaws was rather a peculiar personality. He certainly could not be called an intellectual man, nor was he a brilliant and aggressive soldier; but he was regarded as one of the most dogged defensive fighters in the army. His entire make-up, physical, mental and moral, was solid, even stolid. In figure he was short, stout, square-shouldered, deep-chested, strong-limbed; in complexion, dark and swarthy, with coal-black eyes and black, thick, close-curling hair and beard. Of his type he was a handsome man, but the type was that of the Roman centurion; say that centurion who stood at his post in Herculaneum until the lava ran over him.

He was a Georgian, and his division, consisting of two Georgia brigades, one from South Carolina and one from Mississippi, was as stalwart and reliable as any in the service. Nothing of course could repress our Mississippians, but the general effect and influence of the man upon his command was clearly manifest in the general tenor of the responses he elicited. His men were respectful, but not enthusiastic on this occasion. For the most part they kept right on with what they happened to be doing when the General arrived—cooking, cleaning their arms and accoutrements, or whatever else it might be. He was riding a small, white pony-built horse, and as he rode into the circle of flickering light of camp fire after camp fire to talk with the men, he made quite a marked and notable figure. The conversation ran somewhat in this line:

"Well, boys, how are you?"

"We are all right, General!"

"They say there are lots of those fellows over the way there."

"Well, they can stay there; we ain't offerin' to disturb 'em. We've had all the fighting we want just now; but if they ain't satisfied and want any more, all they've got to do is to come over and get their bellies full."

"Suppose they do come, sure enough, boys? What are you going to do with them?"

"Why, just make the ground blue with 'em, that's all; just manure this here man's land with 'em. We ain't asking anything of them, but if they want anything of us, why just let 'em come after it, and they can get all they want; but they'll wish they hadn't come."

"Well, now, I can rely upon that, can I?"

"You just bet your life you can, General. If we're asleep when they come, you just have us waked up, and we'll receive 'em in good style."

"Well, good-night, boys. I'm satisfied."

McLaws' "boys" had no occasion upon that field to vindicate their own account of themselves. The enemy did not attack, the river did fall, and we returned to our own side of the Potomac, but not until the 13th of July. The day we got there, or perhaps the day following, "Tuck," the redoubtable wagon driver of the old battery had a memorable experience which he never tired of telling.

Tuck was a unique character. Up to the date of his enlistment his horizon had perhaps been more contracted and his opportunities fewer and lower than those of any other man among us. Naturally he gravitated to the wagon, but the man made the position. He was so quiet and steady and perfect in the discharge of his humble duties, that I question whether there was another private soldier in the battery as useful, or one more universally liked and respected, and he was as loyal and devoted to the company and his comrades as they were to him. He had a fine pair of mules, and his affection for them amounted almost to a passion. Indeed, his entire outfit—mules, harness and wagon—was always in better condition than any other I ever saw in the army, and if there was forage or food, for man or beast, to be had anywhere, Tuck was sure to get at least our share for us.

It was the very day we reached the soil of old Virginia, Tuck . . . was dragging along with his wagon, through the mud and mist, considerably in rear of the battery, grieving that his two faithful mules had gone supperless to bed the last night and taken breakfastless to the road that morning, when, glancing to the left, his eye lit upon a luxuriant field of grass he was just passing, and there, right abreast of his wagon, was an enticing set of draw-bars. On the instant he turned out to the side of the road, unhitched his mules, and taking them by their long, strong halter reins . . . let down the bars and led them into the field, and was enjoying their breakfast as much perhaps as the mules were, when a fine-looking officer, with a rubber cape over his shoulders, rode up to the fence and said in a kindly, pleasant voice:

"My man, I like that. I am glad to see you taking such good care of your mules, and they like it too. What a fine breakfast they are making. They are fine mules, too."

"What, my mules? You bet they are fine! Marse Robert ain't got no better mules in his army than these two."

"What are their names?"

"This here gray one, he's named Dragon, and that 'ere black one, his name's Logan. Dragon, he's a leetle the best of the two, but either one of 'em's good enough."

"Yes, indeed, I can well believe that, and I am glad to see you taking such good care of this man's property, too; keeping your mules in hand with the lines. I wish all the drivers in the army were as careful of their teams and of other people's property as you are. Now this is all right, but I wouldn't stay here too long. There are some gentlemen in blue back here on the road a little way, and——"

"What's that? the damn Yankees coming? Come, Dragon, come, Logan, we must git out o' this!"

"O, I wouldn't be in quite such a hurry. There is no danger yet awhile. Let them finish their breakfast. I only meant——"

"No, sir; I ain't taking no chances. The infernal Yankees shan't never git my mules. Come on here, Dragon and Logan—" leading them toward the bars—"we must git out 'o this, and mighty quick, too."

As he got his pets out in the road and was hitching them up again, Colonel Taylor and Colonel Marshall and the rest of General Lee's staff rode up and reported to Tuck's friend and took orders from him, and Tuck waked up to the fact that he had been talking with Marse Robert himself for the last five minutes.

"Great Scott!" he said, in relating his adventure, "I felt that I had been more impudent than the devil himself, and I wanted to get out o' sight as fast as ever I could; but I didn't feel like letting no common man speak to me for two or three days after that."

14

Lee's own views regarding the Pennsylvania campaign and the battle of Gettysburg are effectively summed up by Dr. Freeman.

What was his [Lee's] judgment of the battle and of the campaign? Said he: ". . . the loss of our gallant officers and men . . . causes me to weep tears of blood and to wish that I never could hear the sound of a gun again." More than 23,000 Southerners had been killed, wounded and captured by the enemy from the beginning of the campaign at Brandy Station to the return to the lines on the Rapidan (June 9–August 4). Five guns had been lost, approximately fifty wagons and more than thirty flags. Lee believed, however, that the enemy had paid a price in proportion, and he was far from thinking that the invasion had been fruitless. Much of what he hoped to achieve had been accomplished—the enemy had been driven from the Shenandoah Valley, the hostile forces on the coasts of Virginia and the Carolinas had been reduced, the Federal plan of campaign for the summer had been broken up, and there was little prospect of a resumption of the offensive that year by the Union forces in Virginia. He was no more prepared to admit a crushing defeat than Meade was to claim one, and perhaps he shared the philosophical view later expressed by General Early that if the army had remained in Virginia it would have been forced to fight battles with losses as heavy as those at Gettysburg. As criticism spread, Lee was quick to absolve his men of all responsibility for failure to attain the full objective. . . . He felt that he himself had been at fault in expecting too much of the army. His confidence in it, he frankly confessed, had carried him too far— an opinion that was shared by some of the men in the ranks. Overlooking all the tactical errors and all the mistakes due to the state of mind of his subordinates, he went straight to the underlying cause of failure when he said it was due primarily to lack of coordination. . . .

When the war had ended, General Lee was still reticent in writing and speaking to strangers about Gettysburg or about any other of his battles, and never went further than to say to them that if the assault had been co-ordinated success could have been attained. . . . But it is certain that in the last years at Lexington, as Lee viewed the Gettysburg campaign in some perspective, he concluded that it was the absence of Jackson, not the presence of Ewell or of Longstreet, that made the Army of Northern Virginia a far less effective fighting machine at Gettysburg than at Chancellorsville. Not long before his death, in a long conversation with his cousin Cassius Lee of Alexandria, the General said that if Jackson had been at Gettysburg he would have held the heights that Ewell seized.* And one afternoon, when he was out riding with Professor White, he said quietly, "If I had had Stonewall Jackson with me, so far as man can see, I should have won the battle of

---

* The reference would seem to be to the attack of Early on the afternoon of July 2, but it is possible that Lee was misunderstood and that he had in mind the opportunity of seizing Cemetery Hill that was lost on the afternoon of July 1.

Gettysburg." That statement must stand. The darkest scene in the great drama of Gettysburg was enacted at Chancellorsville when Jackson fell.

15

There is no doubt that Lee felt keenly the unsuccessful outcome of his invasion of the North. Conscientiously, and with no false modesty, he felt that perhaps the Army of Northern Virginia might do better—or, at least, might rise in the public esteem—if led by another commander. He therefore took the step—unquestionably a painful step—of submitting his resignation to President Davis in a letter written on August 8.

Mr. President: Your letters of July 28th and August 2nd have been received, and I have waited for a leisure hour to reply, but I fear that will never come. I am extremely obliged to you for the attention given to the wants of this army and the efforts made to supply them. Our absentees are returning, and I hope the earnest and beautiful appeal made to the country in your proclamation may stir up the whole people and that they may see their duty and perform it. Nothing is wanted but that their fortitude should equal their bravery to insure the success of our cause. We must expect reverses, even defeats. They are sent to teach us wisdom and prudence, to call forth greater energies, and to prevent our falling into greater disasters. Our people have only to be true and united, to bear manfully the misfortunes incident to the war, and all will come right in the end.

I know how prone we are to censure and how ready to blame others for the non-fulfilment of our expectations. This is unbecoming in a generous people, and I grieve to see its expression. The general remedy for the want of success in a military commander is his removal. This is natural, and in many instances proper. For no matter what may be the ability of the officer, if he loses the confidence of his troops disaster must sooner or later ensue.

I have been prompted by these reflections more than once since my return from Pennsylvania to propose to your excellency the propriety of selecting another commander for this army. I have seen and heard of expressions of discontent in the public journals at the result of the expedition. I do not know how far this feeling extends in the army. My brother officers have been too kind to report it, and so far the troops have been too generous to exhibit it. It is fair, however, to suppose that it does exist, and success is so necessary to us that nothing should be risked to secure it.

I therefore, in all sincerity, request Your Excellency to take measures to supply my place. I do this with the more earnestness because no one is more aware than myself of my inability for the duties of my position. I cannot even accomplish what I myself desire. How can I fulfil the expectations of others? In addition, I sensibly feel the growing failure of my bodily strength. I have not yet recovered from the attack I experienced last spring. I am becoming more and more incapable of exertion, and am thus prevented from making the personal supervision of the operations in the field which I feel to be necessary. I am so dull that in making use of the eyes of others I am frequently misled.

Everything, therefore, points to the advantages to be derived from a new commander, and I the more anxiously urge the matter upon Your Excellency from the belief that a younger and abler man than myself can readily be obtained. I know that he will have as gallant and brave an army as ever existed to second his efforts, and it would be the happiest day of my life to see at its head a worthy leader, one that would accomplish more than I could perform and all that I have wished. I hope Your Excellency will attribute my request to the true reason, the desire to serve my country and do all in my power to insure the success of her righteous cause.

I have no complaints to make of any one but myself. I have received nothing but kindness from those above me, and the most considerate attention from my comrades and companions in arms. To Your Excellency I am especially indebted for uniform kindness and consideration. You have done everything in your power to aid me in the work committed to my charge, without omitting anything to promote the general welfare. I pray that your efforts may at length be crowned with success, and that you may live long to enjoy the thanks of a grateful people.

16

President Davis rejected Lee's proffered resignation in a cordial letter expressing the most unreserved confidence in Lee's superior ability. "To ask me to substitute you," he wrote, "by some one in my judgment more fit to command, or who would possess more of the confidence of the army, is to demand an impossibility." Davis's own views as to the battle of Gettysburg, as expressed by him some twenty years later, are interesting.

The wisdom of the [General Lee's] strategy was justified by the result. The battle of Gettysburg was unfortunate. Though the loss sustained by the enemy was greater than our own, theirs could be repaired, ours could not.

Had General Lee been able to compel the enemy to attack him in position, I think we should have had a complete victory, and the testimony of General Meade . . . [before the Committee on the Conduct of the War] shows that he was not at all inclined to make the experiment. If General Lee, by moving to the right, would only have led General Meade to fall back on his preferred position of Pipe Creek, his ability to wait and the impossibility under such circumstances for General Lee to supply his army for any length of time seem to me an answer to that point in the criticism to which our great Captain has been subjected. To compel Meade to retire would have availed but little to us, unless his army had first been routed. To beat that army was probably to secure our independence. The position of Gettysburg would have been worth nothing to us if our army had found it unoccupied. The fierce battle that Lee fought there must not be considered as for the position; to beat the great army of the North was the object, and that it was of possible attainment is to be inferred from the various successes of our arms. . . . It is not admitted that our army was defeated, and the enemy's claim to a victory is refuted by the fact that, when Lee halted on the banks of the Potomac, Meade, instead of attacking as a pursuing general would a defeated foe, halted also, and commenced intrenching.

The battle of Gettysburg has been the subject of an unusual amount of discussion, and the enemy has made it a matter of extraordinary exultation. As an affair of arms it was marked by mighty feats of valor to which both combatants may point with military pride. It was a graceful thing in President Lincoln if, as reported, when he was shown the steeps which the Northern men persistently held, he answered, "I am proud to be the countryman of the men who assailed those heights."

14

Interlude on the Rapidan

LEE, following his return from the invasion of Pennsylvania, camped on the Rapidan near Orange Court House, and Meade stopped in the vicinity of Culpeper. There the two armies remained, comparatively inactive for several weeks. In an effort to bolster the strength and morale of Braxton Bragg's Army of Tennessee, Lee detached Longstreet's corps and sent it on temporary loan to Bragg, a move which was directly contributory to Bragg's victory at Chickamauga. Meade's army was also reduced by the transfer of two corps to New York City, where there had been rioting in opposition to the conscription laws; and, with his opponent thus weakened, Lee felt that he was justified in again assuming the offensive. The next three months were occupied in an interesting campaign of maneuver, interspersed with occasional engagements of cavalry and infantry, but without any real battles of serious importance.

The last clash of the campaign came during the latter days of November along the banks of Mine Run, in the tangled Wilderness not far from Chancellorsville, but the fighting here was inconclusive. The year ended with Meade back at Culpeper and Lee on the Rapidan near Orange—about the same relative position of the two opposing armies as in the summer of 1862 before the battle of Second Manassas.

1

The actions of the Army of Northern Virginia and the Army of the Potomac during the latter months of 1863 consisted

341

principally of a vast amount of marching and maneuvering and
entrenching, with occasional clashes which were hardly more
than glorified skirmishes. Neither Lee nor Meade seemed
willing to bring on a general engagement unless assured of
fighting under conditions advantageous to himself and detri-
mental to his adversary. More than once Lee thought he had
maneuvered Meade into position where he could be attacked
successfully, but on each occasion the wily Meade declined the
battle and withdrew. Dr. White summarizes this inconclusive
Mine Run campaign.

On October 9 Lee advanced his army across the Rapidan to
seek battle with Meade. By concealed and circuitous routes he
passed around Meade's right flank and threatened his rear *via*
Madison Court-House. Meade had marched all the way from Gettysburg to find a battle with Lee, but during the night of October
10 he moved backward rapidly until the Rappahannock rolled between the two armies.

Lee then crossed the river at the Warrenton Springs and again
moved around Meade's right flank to Warrenton. A halt was made
to apportion food to the troops. The delay gave Meade the opportunity to hasten eastward along the railroad and thus to reach
Bristoe Station before Lee could cut off his retreat. Hill led Lee's
advance-guard. As Hill drew nigh to Bristoe Station, the Fifth
Federal Corps was just crossing Broad Run in front of the Confederates. Without a reconnaissance, Hill pushed parts of two divisions over the Run to attack the rear of the Fifth. Suddenly the
fire of Warren's (Second) corps was poured into Hill's flank from
behind the railroad embankment. Nearly fourteen hundred Confederates were disabled or captured. The tardiness of both Hill
and Ewell had permitted the escape of Meade, but the greater
tardiness of Ewell allowed Warren thus to assail Hill's flank. Lee
listened to the latter's words of excuse for the mortifying disaster,
and then with grave sadness replied: "Well, well, General, bury
these poor men and let us say no more about it." Even yet, however, Meade's situation was "singularly precarious," says one of
his own officers, for his waggon trains were massed in the fields
away from the roads. At length the Federal army was on the north-

ern side of Bull Run and fortified itself in Centreville. Lee then decided to withdraw, and assigned the following reasons:

"Nothing prevented my continuing in his front but the destitute condition of the men, thousands of whom are barefooted, a greater number partially shod, and nearly all without overcoats, blankets or warm clothing. I think the sublimest sight of the war was the cheerfulness and alacrity exhibited by this army in the pursuit of the enemy under all the trials and privations to which it was exposed."

While the Confederates were returning toward the Rapidan, Stuart gave Meade's cavalry a staggering blow as they advanced in pursuit. The horsemen wrought heroic deeds during the entire campaign, both in the pursuit and in the withdrawal. Lee moved the main body of his troops across the Rappahannock and left two of Early's brigades on the northern bank in the redoubts near the site of the former railroad bridge. A sudden onset of the advanced Federal brigades in the late evening of November 7 secured possession of the redoubts before aid could be sent to Early's troops. Sixteen hundred prisoners, eight colours and several guns became Federal spoil. Just before this disaster Lee wrote as follows to his wife:

"I moved yesterday into a nice pine thicket, and Perry is to-day engaged in constructing a chimney in front of my tent which will make it warm and comfortable. I have no idea when Fitzhugh (General W. H. F. Lee) will be exchanged. The Federal authorities still resist all exchanges, because they think it is to our interest to make them. Any desire expressed on our part for the exchange of any individual magnifies the difficulty, as they at once think some great benefit is to result to us from it. His detention is very grievous to me and, besides, I want his services. I am glad you have some socks for the army. Send them to me. They will come safely. Tell the girls to send all they can. I wish they could make some shoes too. We have thousands of barefooted men. There is no news. General Meade, I believe, is repairing the railroad, and I presume will come on again. If I could only get some shoes and clothes for the men I would save him the trouble."

After Lee returned to the southern bank of the Rapidan, Meade essayed a movement of the Napoleonic sort. At the dawn of No-

vember 26 he ordered the Fifth and First Corps to cross the Rapidan at Culpeper Mine ford; the Second Corps was expected to
cross at the Germanna ford, while the Third and Sixth were to
seek passage higher up the stream. This host in five bands was
expected to seize the Orange turnpike and the Plank Road, which
run parallel to the Rapidan, and to follow these highways up-
stream against Lee's right flank. The Rapidan banks were difficult; other causes assisted in delaying Meade an entire day. The
Third Corps moved too far to the right on the 27th, and ran
against Edward Johnson's division of Ewell's corps. Stuart's vigilance had brought Lee the news, and the swift marching of Hill
united his corps with Ewell in the intrenchments hastily constructed by the troops on the western border of Mine Run. This
forest stream seeks the Rapidan in a northward course and formed
the right flank of Lee's position. On its rugged banks Lee arrayed
his eager veterans.

The gallant Johnson held the Federal Third Corps engaged,
and thus the rest of the Federal army was delayed. When Meade
advanced on the morning of the 28th to run riot in Lee's camp,
he was confronted in the Wilderness with one hundred and fifty
guns behind heavy works. Meade paused to devise further strategic movements. Warren led the Federal Second Corps and a part
of the Sixth to turn Lee's right flank. Sedgwick found what seemed
to be a vulnerable point in the defences of Lee's left wing. Warren's force was increased to twenty-six thousand, and Meade gave
his two lieutenants the order to crush the Confederate flanks. The
signal guns sounded early on the morning of November 30. Sedgwick on the Federal right was ready to move. Warren on the left
was ready but unwilling to assault. During the night Lee's heroes
had thrown up heavy breastworks and adorned them with cannon
for the defence of their right flank. Naught but wounds and death
did the Federal officers anticipate in advancing upon the grim
Confederate heroes. With chagrin, Meade withdrew his troops to
the fields of Culpeper. Though greatly out-numbering them, he
dared not attack the defiant Confederate veterans of Gettysburg. . . .

On the sixth day of February [1864] Meade marched down to
Morton's Ford to test the mettle of Lee's half-fed veterans. With

eager impetuosity the latter fell upon the division of Hays and sent it back across the Rapidan with loss. In the opening days of the month of March Kilpatrick and Dahlgren were leading a troop of Federal horsemen across the Ely Ford and through Spotsylvania toward Richmond. Dahlgren had great expectation of burning and sacking the Confederate capital and of capturing all the executive officers of the Confederacy. Instead of this, he lost his own life, and the entire expedition was another Federal disaster.

2

Following the frustration of the Dahlgren raid, Secretary of War Seddon advised General Lee of the raid and sent him copies of the papers found on Colonel Dahlgren, which indicated that the purpose of the enterprise was the burning of Richmond and the murder of President Davis and other officials. He asked for Lee's opinion as to the advisability of retaliatory measures, suggesting the possibility of executing some of Dahlgren's men who had been captured. Lee's opinions as to retaliation were firm, but in replying to the secretary he diplomatically and tactfully discussed the matter from the standpoint of policy and expedience as well as abstract justice, not failing to point out the beam in the eye.

I concur with you in thinking that a formal publication of these papers should be made under official authority, that our people and the world may know the character of the war our enemies wage against us, and the unchristian and atrocious acts they plot and perpetrate.

But I cannot recommend the execution of the prisoners who have fallen into our hands. Assuming that the address and secret orders of Colonel Dahlgren correctly state his designs and intentions, they were not executed; and I believe, in a legal point of view, acts in addition to intentions are necessary to constitute a crime. These papers can only be considered as evidence of his intentions. It does not appear how far his men were cognizant of them or that his course was sanctioned by his Government. It is only known that his plans were frustrated by a merciful Providence, his forces scattered and himself killed. I do not think it is right, therefore, to visit upon the captives the guilt of his intentions.

I do not pretend to speak the sentiments of the Army, which you seem to desire. I presume that the blood boils with indignation in the veins of every officer and man as he reads the account of the barbarous and inhuman plot, and under the impulse of the moment many would counsel extreme measures. But I do not think that reason and reflection would justify such a course. I think it better to do right, even if we suffer in so doing, than to incur the reproach of our conscience and posterity. Nor do I think that under present circumstances policy dictates the execution of these men. It would produce retaliation. How many and better men have we in the enemy's hands than they have in ours! But this consideration should have no weight, provided the course was in itself right. Yet history records instances where such considerations have prevented the execution of marauders and devastators of provinces.

It may be pertinent to this object to refer to the conduct of some of our men in the Valley. I have heard that a party of Gilmer's battalion, after arresting the progress of a train of cars on the Baltimore and Ohio Railroad, took from the passengers their purses and watches. As far as I know, no military object was accomplished after gaining possession of the cars, and the act appears to have been one of plunder. Such conduct is unauthorized and discreditable. Should any of that battalion be captured, the enemy might claim to treat them as highway robbers. What would be our course? I have ordered an investigation of the matter and hope the report may be untrue.

3

Between the Mine Run skirmishing and the opening of the Wilderness campaign the following May the Army of Northern Virginia had a prolonged stay in their winter quarters on the banks of the Rapidan, and there the close relations and understanding between the commanding general and the men

in the ranks were further developed and intensified, as Mr.
Childe relates.

Lee's headquarters during the autumn and winter were established in a wood on the southern slope of a high hill, Clarke's
Mountain, some miles to the east of Orange Court House. Surrounded by his staff, he there led almost a family life. Those who
had intercourse with him at that time are loud in their praises of
his sweetness and the perfect equilibrium of his moral qualities.
The charm of his society was very great. Not a shade of preten-
sion, the most perfect sincerity, the simplicity of a child; the more
one saw of him the more one loved him for, contrary to what generally happens, Lees was greater when near than when at a distance.

During those long weeks of inaction on the Rapidan, his soldiers
learned to know him better. In the rough campaigns of the past
two years the old warrior had shared their fatigues, and never once
had he neglected to watch over them and assist their needs. He
had led them under fire, exposing himself with the most perfect
indifference; but as much as possible he spared his men's lives and
often, to the displeasure of the civil authorities, he had insisted
that above all things care should be taken of his veterans. These
facts gradually came to their knowledge and, from the division
general to the lowest drummer, Lee was adored. The whole army
felt that this man—so undemonstrative, so simply clad, sleeping
like the commonest soldier in his tent, having in the midst of the
wood a single blanket—was its guide, its protector, incessantly attentive to its welfare, jealous of its dearly purchased fame, and always ready, as its commander and friend, to defend it.

This winter there arose among the Confederate soldiers a movement which often occurs in the United States, especially in the
parts most recently colonized and at certain times of the year. We
speak of a certain fermentation, a certain religious excitement.
The trials which the Southern populations had undergone, more
especially the events experienced by the Army of Northern Virginia, its present forced inaction, all contributed to reawaken those
religious ideas, always powerful with men of the old English or
Scotch race. Continually one came across the affecting spectacle
of old grey-bearded soldiers, devoutly kneeling in a circle, address-

ing their humble prayers to Him who had hitherto so visibly protected them. A commander-in-chief educated in a European school
would only have compassionately smiled at these sensational assemblies, or have paid them no attention, regarding them as beneath his notice. Lee, on the contrary, contemplated the religious
enthusiasm of his soldiers with a pleasure he did not conceal. He
went to see them, talking the matter over with the chaplains, and
lent the support of his authority to this good work, altogether joyful at witnessing the spread of religious sentiments in his army.
The most remarkable feature of this illustrious soldier, the one
most deeply rooted in him, the one which regulated all others, was
his love towards God. By the world this feeling was called love of
duty; but with Lee the word duty was only another name for the
divine will. To search out that will and execute it—such was, from
the first to the last moment of his life, the only aim of the great
Virginian. . . . The heart of this man of worth was profoundly
convinced of the existence of a Providence whose exalted wisdom
rules all things, and that he was resigned beforehand to its impenetrable decrees.

We are about to contemplate the spectacle of a courageous heart
meeting adversity and disaster with perfect calm and unflinching
resolution. Up to a certain point this impassivity could be attributed to the proud and valiant nature of the man. But a moment of trial approached in which it was no longer possible for
human nature, finding its only support here below, not to lose
courage entirely and give up the struggle. In this decisive moment Lee was still firm and would not succumb. Few persons
were in a position to explain whence came the absolute serenity of
his soul which, without illusion, could behold everything crum-
bling around him. Not only was it that the pride of the soldier did
not yield, but he was also sustained by a sentiment much stronger
than human courage: the consciousness of having done his duty,
the inward assurance that he was protected by God, whose sublime goodness best knows what is for our well-being.

The final struggle between the two armies still belonged to the
future. The veterans of the Army of Northern Virginia still
guarding the line of the Rapidan, their white-haired commander
from his tent in the woods attentively watched the movements of

the enemy. During these long winter months his official correspondence, as was usual, occupied him much, and the minute care which he gave to the welfare of his soldiers, as well as preparations for the spring campaign, absorbed the rest of his time. Often he visited the men in their tents. As soon as the general-in-chief appeared in the distance, clad in his grey uniform, covered with a felt hat of the same colour, and mounted on his dapple-grey courser, Traveller, his old warriors ran up to him on all sides, receiving him with all sorts of tokens of respect and affection. Sometimes his rides reached the borders of the Rapidan (the outposts), stopping sometimes with one officer, sometimes with another, conversing with all, gaining knowledge about everything and, in particular, never forgetting to exchange kind words with those who, like himself, were no longer young. His smile, full of good nature, was irresistible; and every old soldier, with his poor tattered uniform, felt how much the general-in-chief looked upon him as a friend and comrade.

4

During the summer of 1863, as the Army of Northern Virginia lay in its camps near Orange Court House, there were occasional interludes of pageantry in the way of reviews—always enjoyed by the whole army, officers and men alike. Robert E. Lee, Jr., tells of one of these reviews, that of A. P. Hill's corps.

The General was mounted on Traveller, looking very proud of his master, who had on sash and sword, which he very rarely wore, a pair of new cavalry gauntlets and, I think, a new hat. At any rate, he looked unusually fine, and sat his horse like a perfect picture of grace and power. The infantry was drawn up in columns by divisions, with their bright muskets all glittering in the sun, their battle-flags standing straight out before the breeze, and their bands playing, awaiting the inspection of the General, before they broke into column by companies and marched past him in review.

When all was ready, General Hill and staff rode up to General Lee, and the two generals, with their respective staffs, galloped around front and rear of each of the three divisions standing motionless on the plain. As the cavalcade reached the head of each division, its commanding officer joined in and followed as far as the next division, so that there was a continual infusion of fresh groups into the original one all along the lines. Traveller started with a long lope, and never changed his stride. His rider sat erect and calm, not noticing anything but the gray lines of men whom he knew so well. The pace was very fast, as there were nine good miles to go, and the escort began to become less and less, dropping out one by one from different causes as Traveller raced along without a check.

When the General drew up, after this nine-mile gallop, under the standard at the reviewing stand, flushed with the exercise as well as with pride in his brave men, he raised his hat and saluted. Then arose a shout of applause and admiration from the entire assemblage, the memory of which to this day moistens the eye of every old soldier. The corps was then passed in review at a quick-step, company front. It was a most imposing sight.

After it was all over, my father rode up to several carriages whose occupants he knew and gladdened them by a smile, a word or a shake of the hand.

5

Lee's genuine solicitude for the welfare of his troops, particularly in the matter of the soldiers' physical comfort and well-being, is emphasized by General Maurice.

During a recent visit to Winchester, in the Valley, a survivor of the Army of Northern Virginia told me a story which illustrates the extent to which this [the welfare of his troops] was in Lee's mind, and its effect upon the individual soldier. It happened that one day in the Valley Lee had gone into a house for a midday meal. He had just sat down at table with General Wade Hampton when a weary soldier in search of refreshment opened the door. The man's embarrassment, when he suddenly found himself in the presence of two generals, may be imagined, and that embarrassment was not diminished when a moment later he recognized the Commander of his army. Lee promptly rose and, saying to Hampton, "Come on, General, this man needs this food more than we do," made way for the private—who from that moment would have gone anywhere and done anything at a nod from his chief. We may believe that this story quickly made the round of the camps, and with others of a like kind created a spirit which no hardship or adversity could quell.

Marshall gives a more serious account of the effect upon his men of Lee's methods. "While the army was on the Rapidan, in the winter of 1863-4, it became necessary, as was often the case, to put the men upon very short rations. Their duty was hard, not only on the outposts during the winter, but in the construction of roads to facilitate communication between the different parts of the army. One day General Lee received a letter from a private soldier informing him of the work he had to do, and saying that his rations were hardly sufficient to enable him to undergo the fatigue. He said that if it was absolutely necessary to put him upon such short allowance he would make the best of it, but that he and his comrades wanted to know if General Lee was aware that his men were getting so little to eat; he was sure there must be some necessity for it. General Lee did not reply direct to the letter, but issued a general order* in which he informed the soldiers of his efforts on their behalf, and that he could not then relieve their privations, but assured them that he was making every exertion to procure sufficient supplies. After that there was not a murmur in the army, and the hungry men went cheerfully to their hard work."

---

* The order ran:
"General Order No. 7   Jan. 22, 1864

The commanding general considers it due to the army to state that the temporary reduction of rations has been caused by circumstances beyond the control of those charged with its support. Its welfare and comfort are the objects of his constant and earnest solicitude, and no effort has been spared to provide for its wants. It is hoped that the exertions now being made will render the necessity of short duration, but the history of the army has shown that the country can require no sacrifice too great for its patriotic devotion.

Soldiers! You tread with no unequal step the road by which your fathers marched through suffering, privations and blood, to independence. Continue to imitate in the future, as you have in the past, their valor in arms, their patient endurance of hardships, their high resolve to be free, which no trial could shake, no bribe seduce, no danger appal; and be assured that the just God who rewarded their efforts with success will in His own good time send down His blessing upon yours.

R. E. LEE
GENERAL"

6

Another side of Lee's character is revealed by Colonel
Charles S. Venable, one of his staff.

While he was accessible at all times, and rarely had even an orderly before his tent, General Lee had certain wishes which his
aides-de-camp knew well that they must conform to. They did not
allow any friend of soldiers condemned by court-martial (when
once the decree of the court had been confirmed by him) to reach
his tent for personal appeal, asking reprieve or remission of sentence. He said that with the great responsibilities resting on him
he could not bear the pain and distress of such applications, and to
grant them when the judge advocate-general had attested the fair-
ness and justice of the court's decision would be a serious injury to
the proper discipline of the army. Written complaints of officers as
to injustice done them in regard to promotion he would sometimes turn over to an aide-de-camp, with the old-fashioned phrase:
" 'Suage him, Colonel, 'suage him," meaning thereby that a kind
letter should be written in reply. But he disliked exceedingly that
such disappointed men should be allowed to reach his tent and
make complaints in person.

On one occasion in the winter an officer came with a grievance,
and would not be satisfied without an interview with the commanding general. He went to the general's tent and remained
some time. Immediately upon his departure General Lee came to
the adjutant's tent with flushed face, and said warmly, "Why did
you permit that man to come to my tent and make me show my
temper?" The views which prevail with many as to the gentle temper of the great soldier, derived from observing him in domestic
and social life, in fondling of children, or in kind expostulation
with erring youths, are not altogether correct. No man could see
the flush come over that grand forehead and the temple veins swell
on occasions of great trial of patience and doubt that Lee had the
high strong temper of a Washington, and habitually under the
same control.

Cruelty he hated. In the same early spring of 1864 I saw him
stop when in full gallop to the front (on report of a demonstration

of the enemy against his lines) to denounce scathingly and threaten with condign punishment a soldier who was brutally beating an artillery horse.

7

A sad blow to General Lee during this gloomy winter was the death of his daughter-in-law Charlotte, who was ill when her husband Rooney was wounded and captured and whose health steadily declined during his imprisonment. When it was apparent that she was dying, Rooney's brother Custis self-sacrificingly volunteered himself as a hostage for his brother, so Rooney could visit his wife before she died, but the request was denied. General Lee himself would not ask any special consideration for his son. In this connection Dr. Jones comments on the service of Lee's sons during the war, and of their father's attitude toward their service.

Absence of nepotism pre-eminently characterized General Lee in all of his recommendations of men for promotion. His son Robert served as a private in the ranks of the Rockbridge Artillery, sharing with his comrades of that corps all of their dangers, hardships, drudgery and privations, when a hint from his father would have secured him promotion to some place of honor. . . .

When General Echols was compelled by failing health to ask to be relieved from the command of southwest Virginia, he went to Richmond to confer with President Davis as to his successor. . . . Mr. Davis . . . said: "I know of no better man for that position than General Custis Lee. To show you my estimate of his ability, I will say that, when some time ago I thought of sending General Robert Lee to command the Western Army, I had determined that his son Custis should succeed him in command of the Army of Northern Virginia. Now I wish you to go up and see General Lee, tell him what I say, and ask him to order General Custis Lee to the command of your department. Tell him I will make his son major-general, lieutenant-general or, if need be, full general, so that he may rank any officer likely to be sent to that department."

General Echols promptly sought Lee's headquarters and delivered Mr. Davis's message. But to all of his arguments and entreaties the old chieftain had but one reply: "I am very much obliged to Mr. Davis for his high opinion of Custis Lee. I hope that, if he had the opportunity, he will prove himself in some measure worthy of that confidence. But he is an untried man in the field, and I cannot appoint him to that command. Very much against his wishes and my own, Mr. Davis has kept him on his personal staff and he has had no opportunity to prove his ability to handle an army in the field. Whatever may be the opinion of others, I can not pass by my tried officers and take for that important position a comparatively new man—especially when that man is my own son."

The records of the Confederate War Department would be searched in vain for any word of General Lee seeking place either for himself or son.

Rev. Dr. T. V. Moore . . . related the following in his memorial sermon:

"After the cartel for the exchange of prisoners during the war was suspended, one of his own sons was taken prisoner. A Federal officer of the same rank in Libby Prison sent for me, and wished me to write to General Lee, begging him to obtain the consent of the Confederate authorities to his release, provided he could, as he felt sure would be the case, induce the United States authorities to send General Lee's son through the lines to effect this special exchange.

"In a few days a reply was received in which, with the lofty spirit of a Roman Brutus, he respectfully but firmly declined *to ask any favor for his own son that could not be asked for the humblest soldier in the army. . . .*"

It will add greatly to the force of the above incident to recall the fact that the son . . . was closely confined in a casemate at Fortress Monroe and threatened with death by hanging in retaliation for alleged cruelty on the part of the Confederate authorities toward certain Federal prisoners.

Only those who knew how devoted to his children General Lee was can appreciate the noble self-denial which he exercised when, under these circumstances, the tenderest feelings of a loving father were sacrificed to his sense of duty to his country.

8

General Lee has sometimes been censured by the uninformed for his alleged concentration of his interest and activity on affairs in Virginia, to the exclusion of a broad-scale view of the whole Confederate front. It was proper, of course, that Lee should give first consideration to the Army of Northern Virginia, of which he was the commander, but that he was not unaware of or indifferent to the over-all military problems of the Confederacy is shown by his correspondence with Longstreet during this period.

Instead of impatiently urging Longstreet to return from Tennessee to Virginia, Lee counseled with his "old war horse" as to the best use that could be made of his corps. Far from overemphasizing the importance of the Virginia front, he wrote to Longstreet: "I am glad that you are casting about for some way to reach the enemy. If he could be defeated at some point before he is prepared to open his campaign, it would be attended by the greatest advantage. . . . If Grant could be driven back and Mississippi and Tennessee recovered, it would do more to relieve the country and inspirit our people than the mere capture of Washington."

And in February 1864 he wrote to President Davis: "The approach of spring causes me to consider with anxiety the probable action of the enemy and the possible operations of ours in the ensuing campaign. If we could take the initiative and fall upon them unexpectedly, we might derange their plans and embarrass them the whole summer. . . . If Longstreet could be strengthened or given greater mobility than he now possesses, he might penetrate into Kentucky, where he could support himself, cut Grant's communications so as to compel him at least to detach from Johnston's front, and enable him to take the offensive and regain the ground we have lost. I need not dwell upon the advantages of success in that quarter."

As late as March 8, 1864, Lee was writing to Longstreet urging that aggressive action be taken in Tennessee against Grant, then in command of the Federal forces around Chattanooga, his letter revealing a close study of and interest in the western theater of war: "If you and Johnston could unite and move into Middle Tennessee, where I am told provisions and forage can be had, it would cut the armies at Chattanooga and Knoxville in two and draw them from those points, where either portion could be struck at in succession as opportunity offered. This appears to me at this distance to be the most feasible plan. Can it be accomplished? By covering your front well with your cavalry, Johnston could move quietly and rapidly through Benton, across the Hiwassee, and then push forward in the direction of Kingston, while you, taking such a route as to be safe from a flank attack, would join him at or after his crossing the Tennessee River. The two commands upon reaching Sparta would be in a position to select their future course, would necessitate the evacuation of Chattanooga and Knoxville and by rapidity and skill unite on either army. I am not sufficiently acquainted with the country to do more than indicate the general plan. . . . A victory gained there will open the country to you to the Ohio. Study the subject, communicate with Johnston and endeavor to accomplish it or something better."

But Johnston, true to his nature, was determined to continue on the defensive, and rejected as impractical all offensive plans; Longstreet himself seemed none too confident of his own capacities after his unsuccessful campaign into East Tennessee; so eventually, as spring advanced, Longstreet's corps was ordered back to Virginia to join Lee and prepare to resist the great Federal offensive known to be impending.

A glimpse of Lee in his winter quarters near Orange is given by John Esten Cooke.

General Lee's headquarters remained throughout the autumn and winter of 1863 in a wood on the southern slope of the spur called Clarke's Mountain, a few miles east of Orange Court-House.

Here his tents had been pitched in a cleared space amid pines and cedars; and the ingenuity of the "couriers," as messengers and orderlies were called in the Southern army, had fashioned alleys and walks leading to the various tents, the tent of the commanding general occupying the centre. . . .

With the gentlemen of his staff General Lee lived on terms of

the most kindly regard. He was a strict disciplinarian and ab-
horred the theory that a commissioned officer, from considerations
of rank, should hold himself above the private soldiers; but there
was certainly no fault of this description to be found at army headquarters, and the general and his staff worked together in harmon-
ious coöperation. The respect felt for him by gentlemen who saw
him at all hours and under none of the guise of ceremony was
probably greater than that experienced by the community who
looked upon him from a distance. That distant perspective, hiding
little weaknesses and revealing only the great proportions of a human being, is said to be essential generally to the heroic sublime.
No man, it has been said, can be great to those always near him;
but in the case of General Lee this was far from being a fact. He
seemed greater and nobler day by day as he was better and more
intimately known. . . . To know him better was to love and admire
him more and more. The fact is easily explained. There was in
this human being's character naught that was insincere, assumed
or pretentious. It was a great and massive soul—as gentle too and
tender as a woman's or a child's—that lay beneath the reserved exterior and made the soldier more beloved as its qualities were better known. Other men reveal their weaknesses on nearer acquaintance—Lee only revealed his greatness, and he was more and more
loved and admired. . . .

In this autumn and winter of 1863 his army, lying around him
along the Rapidan, began to form that more intimate acquaintance
which uniformly resulted in profound admiration for the man. In
the great campaigns of the two past years the gray soldier had
shared their hardships and never relaxed his fatherly care for all
their wants; he had led them in battle, exposing his own person
with entire indifference; had never exposed *them* when it was possible to avoid it; and on every occasion had demanded, often with
disagreeable persistence, from the civil authorities that the wants of
his veterans should be supplied if all else was neglected. These
facts were now known to the troops and made Lee immensely popular. From the highest officers to the humblest private soldiers he
was universally respected and beloved. The whole army seemed to
feel that in the plainly-clad soldier, sleeping like themselves under
canvas in the woods of Orange, they had a guiding and protecting

head, ever studious of their well-being, jealous of their hard-earned fame, and ready both as friend and commander to represent them and claim their due. . . .

What the writer here tries to draw he looked upon with his own eyes—the figure of a great, calm soldier, with kindly sweetness and dignity, but, above all, a charming sincerity and simplicity in every movement, accent and expression. Entirely free from the trappings of high command, and with nothing to distinguish him from any other soldier save the well-worn stars on the collar of his uniform-coat, the commander-in-chief was recognizable at the very first glance, and no less the simple and kindly gentleman.

His old soldiers remember him as he appeared on many battle-fields, and will describe his martial seat in the saddle as he advanced with the advancing lines. But they will speak of him with even greater pleasure as he appeared in the winters of 1862 and 1863 on the Rappahannock and the Rapidan—a gray and simple soldier, riding among them and smiling kindly as his eyes fell upon the tattered uniforms and familiar faces.

9

General Lee's temperate and abstemious habits in connection with the use of alcoholic beverages were generally well known. That this knowledge had not penetrated to all the recesses of the Confederacy, including the remote nooks and crannies of the Valley of Virginia, contributed to the comfort and pleasure of one of General Rosser's scouts, Colonel Harry Gilmor, on a cold New Year's night in 1864. Colonel Gilmor, who did not share General Lee's aversion to the imbibing of spirituous liquors, tells with delight of how he profited by a Virginia housewife's ignorance of Lee's views on the subject.

Rosser and Fitz Lee left the Valley and marched toward the North Mountain on the 31st of December, 1863, intending to cross by a very bad, steep road at Orkney Springs. The day was terrible in the extreme, a heavy snow-storm prevailing, and intensely cold. The column continued on, but some officers of Fitz Lee's and Rosser's staff, with myself, took shelter at the Springs, intending to remain until the storm should abate.

Mr. Bradford, the proprietor, received us with his usual kindness and soon had our horses put up and a large fire built in a separate well-furnished cottage. Peach brandy and honey, the old Virginia drink, passed around briskly, and when summoned to supper we were happy as lords. The supper was excellent, for our host is celebrated for good living, and with appetites whetted by the keen air, to say nothing of the peach and honey, great piles of buckwheat cakes vanished as fast as snow would on the griddle that baked them.

After supper we took a look at the weather and decided unanimously that it was not judicious to attempt crossing the mountain in such a storm, and accordingly repaired to the snug little cabin, in which we found a roaring fire We determined to escort the old year out and welcome the new one in in regular old Virginia style; so we made a large tin bucketful of egg-nog and another of milk punch, and went in for making a night of it. . . . We made the night a very convivial one and, after an early breakfast, commenced the ascent of the mountain; but before reaching the top we encountered all the ordnance wagons and artillery stuck fast and unable to proceed, for from the top down on the western slope the road was one solid sheet of ice. One poor fellow had tried it, and he went over the side of a steep cliff, wagon, mules, and all.

With the greatest difficulty our party reached the valley below, called "the Cove," and, passing through a rugged gap in the Cove Mountain, stopped at a distillery kept by an old man named Basore. Rosser had been there before us, and had ordered him to sell no liquor, which obliged us to resort to strategy.

I had on a new uniform, a wide-brimmed slouched hat with a long plume, gold band and crossed sabres in front. The old man was sent out to the mill, and James Bailey with great pomposity introduced me to the madam as "General Lee," gravely informing her that I was almost perished with cold and would like to have something to drink, provided it was very good. The simple-hearted old lady was highly delighted to think she had General Lee in her house, while the children—and there seemed to be a score of them—crept under the bed to hide.

Very soon I received a wink and an invitation into an adjoining room where, after shutting the door, the old lady opened an old rusty hair trunk and took from a lot of finery, perhaps a hundred years old, a large square bottle full of a golden liquor. When she removed the stopper the room was filled with the delicious peach perfume; and, having set it down beside a glass of clear honey, she told me that her mother had given it to her when she married John Basore thirty-three years ago, and the cork had never been drawn and would not be for any one but General Lee.

I felt ashamed of myself for practicing such a deception and for a while hesitated; but a second glance at the golden liquid, with another sniff of the perfume, put all my scruples to flight. At the same time I must confess I looked very sheepish; but I have no doubt the old lady thought me an uncommon modest man.

I do not remember that I have ever before or since tasted anything that could compare with that brandy, and I begged the old lady to let me call in "my staff" and give them a taste. She would almost have given her life for General Lee, and of course my staff were called in; and it is needless to say that when we left the old lady had nothing but the bottle to awaken the memory of her "dear dead and gone mother." Not a drop of the peach was left as a souvenir of her wedding-day. We had some silver and gold to leave as recompense. She and all the children, and John Basore himself, came into the porch to see General Lee off!

15

It Took All Summer

In the spring of 1864 the military situation was decidedly favorable to the North. The whole Mississippi River was now open to the Federal gunboats, cutting the Confederacy in half. Bragg's Army of Tennessee had been defeated at Missionary Ridge and the Confederates had been driven out of nearly all of Tennessee. Lee and his Army of Northern Virginia, however, despite the unsuccessful outcome of their invasion of Pennsylvania, still maintained their position between Richmond and Washington, and three years of fighting in this territory had not produced the slightest crack in the defense of the Confederate capital. The commander of the Army of the Potomac had been changed six times, but all the Northern generals had found it impossible to break Lee's lines.

But down in Tennessee there had emerged a Federal general who had been having a remarkable run of good fortune. There was nothing showy or flashy about him; but, somehow or other, he was producing victories, and victories were what the Federals sorely needed in Virginia. So, somewhat in desperation, Stanton in March 1864 ordered Ulysses S. Grant to Washington, where he was advanced to the rank of lieutenant general, the only officer of that rank then in the Federal Army. He was placed in supreme command of all the Federal forces, with the duty of keeping them in co-operation, but he was most especially entrusted with the task of doing something to the Army of the Potomac that would get it out of its discouraging habit of being outwitted and outfought by the Army of Northern Virginia. Grant immediately went to Culpeper and personally assumed charge of the operations in Virginia, although Meade remained nominally in command of the Army of the Potomac.

On Clark's Mountain Lee and his generals watched, through their field glasses, the Federal preparations for the coming campaign. Lee had done everything he could to recruit and strengthen his army, but the man power of the Confederacy was waning and there was not much he could do except watch the enemy and wait for them to make the first move. Longstreet and his corps had returned from Tennessee, although Pickett's division was still in the Petersburg field. But with his utmost effort Lee's total force was but little more than 60,000 men. Grant had more than 125,000 men under arms, aside from nearly 15,000 cavalry. Furthermore, in the ensuing campaign Grant enjoyed the great advantage over Lee of having supreme command of all the Federal armies, with power to order up reinforcements when and as needed and ability to direct the movements of other armies so as to contribute to the support of his plans. Lee, on the other hand, was still merely the commander of the Army of Northern Virginia, with no authority whatever over any other Confederate troops. He could not demand or order reinforcements; he could only request such help—and his requests were generally fruitless.

1

An intimate view of Lee's vigilance and alertness—and his recognition of the inadequacy of his own force—is shown in a letter to his son, then on President Davis's staff at Richmond, written less than a week before Grant crossed the Rapidan with the Army of the Potomac and precipitated the long series of battles beginning with the engagement in the Wilderness.

Camp   30 Apl '64

My dear Custis:

Nothing of much interest has occurred during the past week. The reports of scouts all indicate large preparations on the part of the enemy and a state of readiness for action. The 9th Corps is reported to be encamped (or rather was on the 27th) on the O & A RR between Fairfax CH and Alexandria. This is corroborative of information sent the President yesterday, but there may be some mistake as to the fact or number of corps. All their troops north of Rappahannock have been moved South, their guards called in, etc. The garrisons, provost guards, etc., in Northern cities have been brought forward and replaced by state troops. A battalion of heavy artillery is said to have recently arrived in Culpeper, numbering 3,000. I presume these are the men stated in their papers to have been drawn from the forts in N. Y. Harbour.

I wish we could make corresponding preparations. If I could get back Pickett, Hoke and R. Johnston I would feel strong enough to operate. I have been endeavouring for the last eight or ten days to move Imboden against the B. & O. RR in its unprotected state, but have not been able. I presume he has his difficulties as well as myself. I am afraid it is too late now. I can not yet get the troops together for want of forage and am hoping for grass. Endeavour to get accurate information from Peninsula, James river, etc. My scouts have not returned from Annapolis and may get back too late.

Very affectionately your father,

R. E. LEE

Gen. G. W. Custis Lee

2

Lee was well aware that elaborate plans were being laid to overwhelm him. His preparations to meet the impending move of the Federals are outlined by Dr. Freeman.

Lee's balancing of the ponderables on the military scales was accurate. He could not realize, and few even in Washington could see, that an imponderable was tipping the beam. That imponderable was the influence of President Lincoln. The Richmond government had discounted his every moderate utterance and had capitalized his emancipation proclamation in order to stiffen Southern resistance. The Confederate people had mocked him, had despised him, and had hated him. Lee himself, though he had avoided unworthy personal animosities and doubtless had included Mr. Lincoln in his prayers for all his enemies, had made the most of the President's military blunders and fears. References to Lincoln in Lee's correspondence and conversation were rare. He was much more interested in the Federal field-commanders than in the commander-in-chief. After the late winter of 1863-64, had Lee known all the facts, he would have given as much care to the study of the mind of the Federal President as to the analysis of the strategical methods of his immediate adversaries. For that remarkable man, who had never wavered in his purpose to preserve the Union, had now mustered all his resources of patience and of determination. Those who had sought cunningly to lead him, slowly found that he was leading them. His unconquerable spirit, in some mysterious manner, was being infused into the North as spring approached. . . .

Lee studied with the utmost care the reports that came from his spies during this period of waiting, and on April 16 he was satisfied that three attacks were in the making—a main assault across the Rapidan, a diversion in the Valley of Virginia, and an attack on the flank or rear of the Army of Northern Virginia, probably directed against Drewry's Bluff on James River, so as to expose the water-line of Richmond.

How could this greatest offensive of the war be met? Lee believed that much might still be accomplished by aggressive Confederate action in the West, but from the beginning of the discussion of the next move in Tennessee, he had argued that the alternative to this was an advance in Virginia against Meade. "We are not in a condition," he told the President, "and never have been, in my opinion, to invade the enemy's country with a prospect of permanent benefit. But we can alarm and embarrass him to some extent, and thus prevent his undertaking anything of magnitude against us."

His judgment now told him that the prudent course was to bring Beauregard's army to defend Richmond and to hasten the movement of Longstreet's corps, which was moving very slowly from Bristol. This done, he desired to "move right against the enemy on the Rappahannock," as he phrased it to the President. He went on: "Should God give us a crowning victory there, all their plans would be dissipated, and their troops now collecting on the waters of the Chesapeake would be recalled to the defense of Washington."

Regretfully he had to add: "But to make this move I must have provisions and forage. I am not yet able to call to me the cavalry or artillery. If I am obliged to retire from this line, either by a flank movement of the enemy or the want of supplies, great injury will befall us. I have ventured to throw out these suggestions to Your Excellency in order that in surveying the whole field of operations you may consider all the circumstances bearing on the question. Should you determine it is better to divide this army and fall back toward Richmond I am ready to do so. I, however, see no better plan for the defense of Richmond than that I have proposed."

His confidence in his veterans was not at all shaken by the strength of the Army of the Potomac or by the prestige of General Grant. If the flanking movement against Richmond could be successfully met, he said quietly, "I have no uneasiness as to the result of the campaign in Virginia."

The offensive if practicable, the defensive if inevitable—between these courses the government had to decide, and decide not only according to its judgment of the strategic situation but also according to its ability to supply the army. Johnston was still unprepared to take the offensive in the West; the danger to Richmond from the East was increasing, while the threat against Charleston was neither more nor less formidable than before; the commissary could do little for the soldiers and the quartermaster general even less for the horses. Thus circumstanced, the embarrassed administration had to compromise. Longstreet's slow movement from Bristol to Charlottesville was continued to Gordonsville, so that he would be available as a reserve in case of an attack on Richmond from the east. Beauregard was hurried northward with part of his troops, and was put in charge of all the forces between the James and the Cape Fear Rivers. . . .

On the morning of May 2, he [Lee] climbed once again—and for the last time—to the observation post on Clark's Mountain, and after studying with his glasses the location of the corps spread out beneath him, and the rolling fields of Culpeper, he told his companions that the enemy's crossing would be at Ely's or at Germanna —the fords that led into the Wilderness where the ghost of "Stonewall" Jackson walked. The landscape below him was much as it had been when he had first ascended Clark's Mountain in August, 1862, but the military outlook was far different. Then there had been reserves of men and of food behind him; now there were neither. His it had been in '62 to plan how he would fall upon the foe; now he must exert himself to checkmate the enemy's advance. Yet he knew he could count on the valor of those who, since that August day, had fought the bloodiest battles that ever drenched America. The morale of the army, which had been high throughout the winter, was now at its finest fighting pitch. "Never," wrote Colonel Taylor, "was [the army] in better trim than now. There is no overweening confidence, but a calm, firm and positive determination to be victorious, with God's help."

The spirit of the army was the spirit of its leader. He was as surely the captain of his soul that day on Clark's Mountain as ever he had been in his life. "You must sometimes cast your thoughts on the Army of Northern Virginia," he told one of his young cousins, "and never forget it in your prayers. It is preparing for a great struggle, but I pray and trust that the great God, mighty to deliver, will spread over it His almighty arms and drive its enemies before it." And to his son he wrote: "Our country demands all our strength, all our energies. To resist the powerful combination now forming against us will require every man at his place. If victorious, we have everything to hope for in the future. If defeated, nothing will be left for us to live for. . . . My whole trust is in God, and I am ready for whatever He may ordain."

In that spirit he came down from the mountain.

3

On the fourth of May the Army of the Potomac, under the command of General Meade—and under the watchful eye of General Grant—moved out of its camps north of the Rapidan and without opposition crossed the river at Germanna and Ely's ford. General Long tells of subsequent developments.

This easy passage of the Rapidan does not seem to have been anticipated by General Grant. In his report he says: "This I regarded as a great success, and it removed from my mind the most serious apprehension I had entertained, that of crossing the river in the face of an active, large, well-appointed and ably-commanded army."

Lee had made no movement to dispute the passage of the stream. He could, had he chosen, have rendered its passage extremely difficult. But, perceiving that Grant was making the mistake that had proved so disastrous to Hooker, by plunging with his army into that dense and sombre thicket well named "The Wilderness," he took care to do nothing to obstruct so desirable a result.

On reaching the southern side of the stream, Grant established himself at the intersection of the Germanna and old plank roads and at Chancellorsville. This position embraced the upper part of what is known as the Wilderness of Spottsylvania. Lee simultaneously ordered the concentration of his forces at Mine Run, a position about four miles north-west of that occupied by Grant. The corps of Ewell and Hill and the artillery of Long and Walker gained their positions on Mine Run during the evening and night of the 4th; Longstreet's corps, which since its arrival from Tennessee had been posted at Gordonsville, distant twenty miles from the point of concentration, was necessarily delayed in reaching the scene of the coming struggle.

There seemed no good reason to believe that General Lee would risk the hazard of a fight in open field, and expose his small force to the danger of being overwhelmed by Grant's enormous army. That he would offer battle somewhere on the road to Richmond was unquestionable, but Grant naturally expected his adversary to select some point strong alike by nature and art, and which must be forced by sheer strength ere the march to Richmond could be resumed. He did not dream that Lee would himself make the attack and force a battle with no other intrenchments than the unyielding ranks of his veteran troops.

Yet Lee had already tried the woods in the Wilderness as a battlefield, and knew its advantages. Its intricacies, which were familiar to him and his generals, were unknown ground to Grant. In them he had already vanquished a large army with half its force. The natural hope of success in baffling his new opponent which this gave him he did not fail to avail himself of, and Grant found himself on his southward march unexpectedly arrested by the presence of the Confederate army in the wilds in which, just a year before, Hooker's confident army had been hurled back in defeat.

The writer spent the night of the 4th at Lee's headquarters, and breakfasted with him the next morning. The general displayed the cheerfulness which he usually exhibited at meals, and indulged in a few pleasant jests at the expense of his staff officers, as was his custom on such occasions. In the course of the conversation that attended the meal he expressed himself surprised that his new adversary had placed himself in the same predicament as "Fighting Joe" had done the previous spring. He hoped the result would be even more disastrous to Grant than that which Hooker had experienced. He was, indeed, in the best of spirits, and expressed much confidence in the result—a confidence which was well founded, for there was much reason to believe that his antagonist would be at his mercy while entangled in these pathless and entangled thickets, in whose intricacies disparity of numbers lost much of its importance.

4

The first clash between the opposing armies came in the afternoon of May 5. On the morning of that day the Confederates had advanced in two columns—Ewell by way of the Orange-Fredericksburg turnpike and A. P. Hill on the Plank Road. Ewell encountered the enemy outposts after advancing about three miles, and his divisions immediately deployed. Late in the afternoon the Federal right and the Confederate left made contact, and there was a short and bloody fight in the tangled underbrush which was brought to a close by darkness. On the right, Hill on the Plank Road met the Federals under Hancock head on, and they fought inconclusively until nightfall. Grant by this time realized that Lee was not inclined to let him advance without a contest, and put his whole army in line of battle in preparation for the next day. Ewell and Hill had connected their corps in a continuous line, and Lee sent word to Longstreet to hasten his advance. John Esten Cooke, who was there, tells of the fighting on the next day.

The morning of the 6th of May came and, with the first light of dawn, the adversaries as by a common understanding advanced at the same moment to attack each other.

The battle which followed is well-nigh indescribable, and may be said, in general terms, to have been naught but the blind and desperate clutch of two great bodies of men who could scarcely see each other when they were but a few feet apart, and who fired at random, rather by sound than sight. A Southern writer, describing the country and the strange combat, says:

"The country was sombre—a land of thicket, undergrowth, jungle, ooze, where men could not see each other twenty yards off, and assaults had to be made by the compass. The fights there were not even as easy as night attacks in open country, for at night you can travel by the stars. Death came unseen; regiments stumbled on each other and sent swift destruction into each other's ranks, guided by the crackling of the bushes. It was not war—military manoeuvring: science had as little to do with it as sight. Two wild animals were hunting each other: when they heard each other's steps they sprung and grappled. The conqueror advanced, or went elsewhere. The dead were lost from all eyes in the thicket. The curious spectacle was here presented of officers advancing to the charge in the jungle, *compass in hand,* attacking not by sight but by the bearing of the needle. . . . Here in blind wrestle as at midnight did two hundred thousand men in blue and gray clutch each other—bloodiest and wierdest of encounters. War had had nothing like it." . . .

The commanders of both armies labored under great embarrassments. General Grant's was the singular character of the country, with which he was wholly unacquainted; and General Lee's the delay in the arrival of Longstreet. Owing to the distance of the camps of the last-named officer, he had not at dawn reached the field of battle. As his presence was indispensable to a general assault, this delay in his appearance threatened to result in unfortunate consequences, as it was nearly certain that General Grant would make an early and resolute attack. Under these circumstances, Lee resolved to commence the action and did so, counting doubtless on his ability, with the thirty thousand men at his command, to at least maintain his ground. His plan seems to have been to make a heavy demonstration against the Federal right and, when Longstreet arrived, throw the weight of his whole centre and right against the Federal left, with the view of seizing the Brock Road, running southward, and forcing back the enemy's left wing into the thickets around Chancellorsville.

This brilliant conception which, if carried out, would have arrested General Grant in the beginning of his campaign, was very near meeting with success. The attack on the Federal right, under General Sedgwick, commenced at dawn and the fighting on both sides was obstinate. It continued with indecisive results throughout the morning, gradually involving the Federal centre; but, nearly at the moment when it began, a still more obstinate conflict was inaugurated between General Hancock, holding the Federal left, and Hill who opposed him on the Plank-Road. The battle raged in this quarter with great fury for some time; but. attacked in front and flank at once by his able opponent, Hill was forced back steadily a considerable distance from the ground which had witnessed the commencement of the action. At this point, however, he was fortunately met by Longstreet. That commander rapidly brought his troops into line, met the advancing enemy, attacked them with great fury and, after a bloody contest in which General Wadsworth was killed, drove them back to their original position on the Brock Road.

It now seemed nearly certain that Lee's plan of seizing upon this important highway would succeed. General Hancock had been forced back with heavy loss, Longstreet was pressing on and, as he afterward said, he "thought he had another Bull Run on them," when a singular casualty defeated all. General Longstreet, who had ridden in front of his advancing line, turned to ride back, when he was mistaken by his own men for a Federal cavalryman, fired upon, and disabled by a musket-ball. This threw all into disorder, and the advance was discontinued.

General Lee, as soon as he was apprised of the accident, hastened to take personal command of the corps and, as soon as order was restored, directed the line to press forward. The most bloody and determined struggle of the day ensued . . . and, as at Chancellorsville, a new horror was added to the horror of battle. A fire broke out in the thicket, and soon wrapped the adversaries in flame and smoke. They fought on, however, amid the crackling flames. Lee continued to press forward, the Federal breastworks along a portion of their front were carried, and a part of General Hancock's line was driven from the field. The struggle had, however, been decisive of no important results and, from the lateness of the hour when it terminated, it could not be followed up.

On the left Lee had also met with marked but equally indecisive success. General Gordon had attacked the Federal right, driven the force at that point in disorder from their works, and but for darkness this success might have been followed up and turned into a complete defeat of that wing of the enemy. It was only discovered on the next morning what important successes Gordon had effected with a single brigade; and there is reason to believe that with a larger force this able soldier might have achieved results of a decisive character.

5

One of the outstandingly dramatic incidents of the war took place during the battle of the Wilderness when Wilcox's attack on the Federals was met with such a savage defense that his forces were temporarily demoralized and forced back, and Gregg's Texas brigade was ordered to their support. Colonel Charles S. Venable of Lee's staff gives an eyewitness account of the episode.

The Texans cheered lustily as their line of battle, coming up in splendid style, passed by Wilcox's disordered columns and swept across our artillery pit and its adjacent breastworks. Much moved by the greeting of these brave men and their magnificent behavior, General Lee spurred his horse through an opening in the trenches and followed close on their line as it moved rapidly forward. The men did not perceive that he was going with them until they had advanced some distance in the charge; when they did, there came from the entire line, as it rushed on, the cry, "Go back, General Lee! Go back!" Some historians like to put this in less homely words ("Lee, to the rear!"), but the brave Texans did not pick their phrases. "We won't go unless you go back!" A sergeant seized his bridle rein. The gallant General Gregg, turning his horse towards General Lee, remonstrated with him. Just then I called General

Lee's attention to General Longstreet, whom he had been seeking, and who sat on his horse on a knoll to the right of the Texans, directing the attack of his divisions. General Lee yielded with evident reluctance to the entreaties of his men, and rode up to Longstreet's position. With the first opportunity I informed General Longstreet of what had just happened and he, with affectionate bluntness, urged General Lee to go further back.

6

Colonel William C. Oates of the Fifteenth Alabama Regiment was in the van of Longstreet's forces as they made their belated but timely entry into the Wilderness battle. He has recorded his impression of his first sight of General Lee, as Longstreet's men deployed into action.

To reach our position we had to pass within a few feet of General Lee. He sat his fine gray horse, "Traveller," with the cape of his black cloak around his shoulders, his face flushed and full of animation. The balls were flying around him from two directions. His eyes were on the fight then going on south of the Plank Road between Kershaw's division and the flanking column of the enemy. He had just returned from attempting to lead the Texas Brigade in a second charge, when those gallant men and their officers refused to let him do so. . . . A group of General Lee's staff were on their horses just in rear of him. He turned in his saddle and called to his chief of staff in a most vigorous tone, while pointing with his finger across the road, and said: "Send an active young offcer down there." I thought him at that moment the grandest specimen of manhood I ever beheld. He looked as though he ought to have been, and was, the monarch of the world. He glanced his eye down on the "ragged rebels" as they filed around him in quick time to their place in line, and inquired, "What troops are these?" And was answered by some private in the Fifteenth, "Law's Alabama brigade." He exclaimed in a strong voice, "God bless the Alabamians!" The men cheered and went into line with a whoop. The advance began.

7

So began the long and bloody duel between Grant and Lee that ended at Appomattox—Grant with his hammer, Lee with his rapier, to borrow John Esten Cooke's simile. Grant was unquestionably surprised and stunned by the unexpected and savage resistance he encountered in the Wilderness. One of his aides has written that on the evening of May 6, when he learned the full details of how roughly his great army had been handled, "he went into his tent and, throwing himself face downward on his cot, gave way to the greatest emotion." And another observer said: "I never saw a man so agitated in my life." Lee, too, was none too happy over the day's work. True, he had checked Grant, but he had suffered a heavy loss of his irreplaceable man power—and he had lost the services of his "old war horse," Longstreet. Neither army was active on the seventh, each content to lick its wounds and watch the other. Lee realized that Grant was no Hooker or Burnside or Pope. He did not expect the Federals to retreat to the north side of the river. With his extraordinary genius for reading his opponent's mind, he concluded that Grant's next move would be in the direction of Hanover, by way of Spotsylvania Court House, and he began to make his plans accordingly. Robert S. Henry tells about it.

Lee knew . . . that Grant, determined and tenacious, had the whole of the immense resources of the United States and the entire confidence of the government at his command; and that this time there was to be no letting up, no giving up, no going back. The conditions of the problem pointed to Spottsylvania Court House, behind and beyond Lee's right flank on the way to Richmond. And there, even before General Grant had issued the order for his secret movement, Lee was fixing his attention.

On the night of May seventh Grant began the first of the series of "sidling" movements by the left flank, which were to take him from the Rapidan to the James, across that river, clear around to the south of Petersburg and on to Appomattox Court House— eleven months later. On the morning of May eighth when the

Union advance reached the cleared field north of the quaint little white columned court-house of Spottsylvania, on the road from Fredericksburg to Richmond, there was Longstreet's corps, now commanded by R. H. Anderson, deployed and waiting for them.

During that day both armies were pushing troops to Spottsylvania, crowding them forward on roads roughly parallel, with the Confederates having somewhat the longer route, but making the better speed, probably because they had less to carry.

Spottsylvania was the beginning of "trench warfare" in the modern sense, twelve days of it, from May eighth to twenty-first; nearly two weeks with all the familiar sound of a 1916 communique. There was a day of marching in; three days of maneuvering and entrenching, without decisive results; a day of general assault all along the line. Hancock's Second Corps, concentrating most heavily on the salient north of the court-house, held by Johnson's division of Ewell's corps—the Bloody Angle, it was to be called— carried it and captured its defenders, only to be stopped by a desperate counter-attack by others of Ewell's men under Rodes. A week longer they fought about the lines of Spottsylvania, the Confederates holding the new and shorter line across the base of the Bloody Angle, and all the rest of their original position; the Union armies maneuvering and thrusting here and there, and waiting for reinforcements on their way from Washington. Nearly three thousand Union soldiers were killed, nearly fifteen thousand wounded, more than two thousand captured in the fighting. The wounded lay outside the Confederate lines, untended, while General Grant, as at Vicksburg, would not ask truce to care for them and to bury the dead, and no man could go into the no-man's land between the lines and live. . . .

Lee's losses at Spottsylvania were scarcely more than a third those of the Union army—but a man lost to Lee was irreplaceable, while Grant could draw to himself men from all the world. The pounding policy of attrition was beginning to work. . . .

While the infantry of the armies was at stalemate in the trenches about Spottsylvania, the cavalry was whirling down toward Richmond. . . . On the night of May eighth, as the battle lines were forming about Spottsylvania, Grant started Sheridan on his first raid to Richmond. . . . Its main purpose was to suck Stuart's cavalry away from Grant's flanks, where they were embarrassingly observant of his movements and projects, a purpose in which it succeeded beyond all hope. . . . During the night while Sheridan was busy destroying railroad tracks and trains at Beaver Dam Station, Stuart collected what cavalry he could and passed beyond him, to attack at dawn of the tenth in his front. . . . The next day, skirmishing about Yellow Tavern, six miles north of Richmond, General Stuart received a pistol ball in his abdomen, and was carried to Richmond to die. . . .

While Lee was checking Grant in the Wilderness and holding him at Spottsylvania, Beauregard, in command south of Richmond, succeeded in neutralizing Butler's army of the James—corked him in a bottle, to use General Grant's simile. . . .

Lee was still at Spottsylvania. Grant, having thoroughly tested the possibility of going through or over him, found it not to be done; again sidled to the left, on the night of May twentieth, and started for a crossing on the North Anna River, to Lee's right and rear.

Within a few hours of Grant's start Lee was on his way too—leaving the blasted lines of Spottsylvania, where great trees had been brought down by the constant chipping of bullets, and where the Confederate ordnance detachments had gathered up more than one hundred and twenty thousand pounds of precious Northern lead, to be recast and fired back at the Union troops before the war was to end.

By night of May twenty-second Lee's whole army was below the North Anna, with its center holding the south bank of the river between Jericho Mills Ford and the Chesterfield Bridge, where the Telegraph Road direct from Fredericksburg to Richmond crosses, and with flanks drawn back in entrenched lines running to Little River in the rear.

Grant's men appeared on the north bank of the river the next morning, to begin an immediate crossing, without real opposition. That day and the next, the twenty-fourth, Grant threw his corps across the stream, to left and right of the narrow center front held by Lee—to discover, when it was too late, that he had split his army on the head of the spear held toward him by Lee; that the Army of Northern Virginia was in an impregnable position between the

Union wings, which could reach each other only by a long detour and two crossings of the North Anna; that, in short, he was in a badly disjointed and exposed position.

8

Lee's freedom from bitterness, as well as something of his sense of humor, is revealed in a little interlude of byplay at this time.

The day after the great battle of Spottsylvania Court House, General Lee was standing near his lines conversing with two of his officers, one of whom was known to be not only a hard fighter and a hard swearer, but a cordial hater of the Yankees. After a silence of some moments, the latter officer, looking at the enemy with a dark scowl on his face, exclaimed most emphatically, "I wish they were all dead!"

General Lee, with the grace and manner peculiar to himself, replied, "How can you say so, General? Now I wish they were all at home, attending to their own business, leaving us to do the same."

Lee then moved off; and the first speaker, waiting until he was out of earshot, turned to his companions and in the most earnest tones said, "I would not say so before General Lee, but I wish they were all dead *and in hell!*"

When this "amendment" to the wish was afterwards repeated to General Lee, in spite of his goodness he could not refrain from laughing heartily at the speech, which was so characteristic of one of his favorite officers.

9

During the fighting at Spotsylvania there were further examples of Lee's almost reckless exposure of himself to danger, and of his men's unwillingness to allow him to do so. Dr. Jones tells of these, and of other evidences of the reverential attitude of the men in the ranks toward their commander.

On the 10th of May the Confederate lines were broken near Spottsylvania Court House. The Federal troops poured into the opening, and a terrible disaster seemed imminent. As Early's old division, now commanded by General John B. Gordon, was being rapidly formed to recapture the works, General Lee rode to the front and took his position just in advance of the colors of the Forty-ninth Virginia Regiment. He uttered not a word—he was not the man for theatrical display—but as he quietly took off his hat and sat his war-horse, the very personification of the genius of battle, it was evident to all that he meant to lead the charge, and a murmur of disapprobation ran down the line. Just then the gallant Gordon spurred to his side, seized the reins of his horse, and exclaimed with deep anxiety: "General Lee, this is no place for you! Do go to the rear. These are Virginians and Georgians, sir, men who have never failed, and they will not fail now—will you, boys? Is it necessary for General Lee to lead this charge?"

Loud cries of "No! no! General Lee to the rear! General Lee to the rear! We will drive them back if General Lee will only go to the rear," burst forth from the ranks. While two soldiers led General Lee's horse to the rear, Gordon put himself in front of his division, and his clear voice rang out above the roar of battle, "Forward! Charge! And remember your promise to General Lee." These brave fellows swept grandly forward, stemmed the tide, drove back five times their own numbers, reëstablished the Confederate line and converted a threatened disaster into a brilliant victory.

A similar scene was enacted on the memorable 12th of May, when Hancock had broken the Confederate lines, just in front of the "bloody angle," where General Lee was only prevented from leading Harris's Mississippi Brigade into the thickest of that terrible fight by the positive refusal of the men to go forward unless their beloved chieftain would go to the rear. . . .

These incidents will go on the page of history as among the grandest battle-scenes of the war. At this time there was the deepest anxiety all through the army and throughout the country lest General Lee should be killed in battle, and President Davis wrote him a touching letter begging that he would not needlessly expose his person. . . .

One day he met, coming to the rear, a gallant Georgian whose right arm was very badly shattered. "I grieve for you, my poor fellow," said the tender-hearted chief. "Can I do anything for you?" "Yes, sir!" replied the boy with a proud smile. "You can shake hands with me, General—if you will consent to take my left hand." General Lee cordially grasped the hand of the ragged hero, spoke a few kind words which he could never forget, and sent him on his way rejoicing that he had the privilege of suffering under such a leader.

One night some soldiers were overheard discussing the tenets of atheism around their camp-fire, when a rough, honest fellow cut short the discussion by saying: "Well, boys, the rest of us may have developed from monkeys; but I tell you none less than a God could have made such a man as Marse Robert!"

10

With Grant's army split in half across the North Anna, Lee was finally in position to strike his adversary a serious blow. But at this critical time the Confederate commander was laid low by debilitating disease and almost completely incapacitated. Dr. Freeman tells about Lee's illness and its effect on his operations.

Thus favorably situated, Lee was sanguine. His communications were shorter, and his strength was raised, at last, some 8,500 by the arrival of all of Pickett's division, Hoke's old brigade, and Breckinridge's command. The opportunity for which he had been waiting might come the very next day. But before it developed, Lee was attacked by a violent intestinal complaint, brought on, no doubt, by bad food and long hours. He was loath, as always, to yield to sickness, and on the 24th he tried to transact army business as usual. . . .

Lee was worse on the 25th and confined to his tent, but he insisted on receiving reports and he carried on his official correspondence, in which there was not even a hint that he was sick. Some of his staff were disposed to think that he should not have vexed himself with duty when he was almost incapacitated. But what could he do? Beauregard's hands were full at Bermuda Hundred, and to whom else could he turn over the command? To Ewell, senior corps chief, who was himself scarcely able to keep the field? To Hill, who had just failed on the left? To Anderson, who had been in corps command scarcely more than a fortnight? As long as he was able to direct operations, Lee had no alternative. He must endure the pain and the debilitating symptoms. In his dispatches he was able to keep his measured tone. Writing to the President of the heavy reinforcement of Grant, he again urged joint operations by his army and Beauregard's, and at whatever point most advantageous to Beauregard. His phrases were as considerate and as self-controlled as if he had been at his best. In his tent it was different. As he felt opportunity slipping away, his grip on himself weakened, and he had a violent scene with Colonel Venable, who argued some point with him. When Venable emerged from the General's tent he was, Major McClellan remembered, "in a state of flurry and excitement, full to bursting, and he blurted out, 'I have just told the old man that he is not fit to command this army, and that he had better send for Beauregard.' " Lee could not, would not give up, but he broke out vehemently: "We must strike them a blow—we must never let them pass us again—we must strike them a blow." To Doctor Gwathmey he said of Grant, "If I can get one more pull at him, I will defeat him."

11

But Lee was not to be able to take advantage of the disadvantageous tactical position into which he had lured his adversary. While he lay prostrate in his tent, Grant quickly discovered the dangerous nature of his position and on the night of May 26 withdrew to the north side of the North Anna and once more started moving his forces in another effort to get around Lee's right flank. Colonel Taylor traces the campaign's developments at this stage.

We were in constant contact with the enemy, and every day brought its episodes of excitement and struggling at different points of our line. It looks as if these evidences of a defiant and aggressive spirit furnished material for serious reflection to General Grant. He evidently began to waver in his persistency and to look for some other way to get to Richmond.

On May 25th he informed the authorities at Washington that General Lee was evidently making a determined stand between the North Anna and South Anna, and that it would take him two days in which to get in position for a general attack upon Lee's army. On the 26th, after stating the position of the several corps of the army and of those of General Lee, he wrote that to make a direct attack by either wing of his army would cause a slaughter of his men that even success would not justify—coming from General Grant, that meant a frightful amount of killing; that any attempt to turn Lee's right between the two Annas would be impossible of execution on account of the swamp upon which his right rested; and that it would be inexpedient to attempt to turn his left; General Lee's knowledge and experience as an engineer served him well in the matter of laying out his lines of defense—so he had determined to make another movement to his left and to cross the Pamunkey River near Hanover town. In the same despatch, however, General Grant informs General Halleck that "Lee's army is really whipped." It must have afforded General Halleck infinite satisfaction to know that; it was the main thing they were striving for.

General Grant then took a position on the south side of the Pamunkey River. General Lee moved on parallel lines, his army still confronting the enemy and his headquarters established at Atlee's Station.

When near Hanover Court House, General Lee was reinforced by General Breckinridge's command from southwestern Virginia and by Pickett's division of the First Corps; and at Cold Harbor he was further strengthened by the arrival of Hoke's division from North Carolina. The aggregate strength of these reinforcements was between fourteen and fifteen thousand.

12

Despite his illness and his inability to mount his horse, Lee did not entirely lose contact with the action in the field at this time. A cannoneer in the horse artillery tells of witnessing the

commander's unconventional visit to the front lines on the
North Anna at a critical time.

On top of one of the hills we had our pieces in position close
to the river and not far from the ford. . . . The enemy in our front
advanced to within about a mile and a quarter of our position and
established a battle line along the edge of a woods, with their cavalry in front of the infantry line. . . . We ceased firing in order to
save our ammunition for close work in case the enemy would have
attempted to force the river. . . .

A spirit of disquieting uneasiness and subdued excitement
seemed to prevail among officers and men as they gazed at the glittering line of the foe that was menacing us and ready to rush across
the plain in our front at any moment and attempt to crush and
wipe us out. . . . Then I heard the beating drums sounding the
alarming thrill of the long roll in General A. P. Hill's camp, about
a mile away in the direction of Hanover Junction, which meant
"to the rescue" of the cavalry and horse artillery.

After we had endured the nerve-trying suspense for an hour or
so, and every man was standing at his post ready for the fray . . .
some one remarked: "Yonder comes a carriage across the field." As
it was an unusual occurrence to see a carriage drive on a field that
was stripped ready for fight, I looked to the rear and saw a carriage
with a single horseman riding behind it, coming right toward our
position where we had our guns in battery. The carriage drove up
close to our guns and stopped. When the door opened, who should
step out but our beloved and confidence-inspiring General Robert
E. Lee, and the first glimpse of the grand old chieftain instilled new
life and vigor into the whole command and dispersed the gloomy
mist which was gathering around the star of Hope and lifted a
burden of anxiety that had settled along our line; I felt like a new
man all over.

General Lee came right to where my gun was in position and
leaned against a large pine tree not more than ten feet from my
piece; he then, without the least sign of agitation, slowly drew his
field glass from the case and carefully scanned the enemy's battle
line; he commenced the scrutinizing gaze at the right of their line
on that part which was farthest up the river. After he swept from

end to end with his glass he turned around and remarked to the horseman that accompanied him, "Orderly, go back and tell General A. P. Hill to leave his men in camp; this is nothing but a feint, the enemy is preparing to cross below." Then he put his glass back in the case, got in his carriage and went back toward Hanover Junction.

A single glance from the old warrior's eye, like a flash of genius, instantly penetrated and fathomed the depths of the enemy's design, for in less than ten minutes after he left his carriage he was back in it again and on his way to some other point lower down the river. As the day rolled by the developments of the enemy's manipulations and maneuverings proved the infallibility of General Lee's judgment and quick perception, for the enemy is now this evening crossing the North Anna below, just as he predicted, and the demonstration at the ford where we were was nothing but an extensive and well-planned feint.

13

The campaign was rapidly approaching its bloody climax. The Northern hammer blows had been skillfully parried by the Southern rapier. But Grant was still to make one final effort to overwhelm Lee by storming his lines—an effort which resulted in one of the most sanguinary brief engagements in all history. Colonel Taylor tells of the action at this time.

General Grant's next move was toward Cold Harbor. On June 1st General Fitzhugh Lee, whose cavalry on our extreme right occupied Old Cold Harbor, was compelled to retire by the advance of the enemy's infantry in force on that point. It being evident to General Lee that the enemy was moving in that direction, he immediately ordered an extension of his own lines. . . . The two armies were now on historic ground, and the Confederates took inspiration from the thought of the victory that here crowned their efforts two years before in the Seven Days' battles around Richmond.

On the afternoon of the 1st the enemy attacked in heavy force. Our positions had been hastily taken, and there was an interval between Hoke and Anderson. The enemy succeeded in penetrating this interval, but General Hoke was reinforced and quickly recovered the lost ground in his front. General Kershaw on Anderson's right advanced and recovered part of the lost ground, and assumed a new line connecting with Hoke. In the afternoon of the 2nd, by direction of General Lee, General Early moved with a portion of his corps to endeavor to get upon the enemy's right flank. Early's troops advanced with spirit, driving the enemy from his intrenchments and following him some distance before darkness put an end to the fight. . . .

General Grant now determined to make one supreme effort to crush the army opposed to him. Orders were given for the whole line to attack. General Lee was to be made to feel the tremendous power of the formidable Army of the Potomac, marshaled in compact form, two and three lines deep, and numbering fully one hundred and twenty thousand men. At an early hour of June 3rd the battle was opened by a vicious assault upon our right and right center. The attack upon the portion of the right occupied by Hoke's command was readily repulsed with great slaughter; that upon Breckinridge's front was, at first, more successful; but Finegan's Florida brigade and the Maryland Line were thrown in the breach and speedily drove the enemy back, recapturing the works and restoring our line.

Later the enemy massed in large force in Kershaw's front on Anderson's right and attempted to seize the salient constituting the weak spot in this part of the line, but their every assault was repulsed with terrible slaughter. Time and again the order was given to advance; new troops were moved to the front, and division after division was hurled against the works held by Kershaw and Hoke, where the cool veterans of Lee, with steady nerve and accurate aim, sent death and destruction to the advancing hosts of the enemy.

Similar results attended the assaults upon General Early on the left, who maintained his position of the previous evening. The din and confusion of the battle, that had been incessant and terrific, suddenly ceased on the Federal side. There was a pause along the whole line. We did not understand it then, but later learned that it was the silent verdict of the men that the task was hopeless. "The order was issued through the officers to their subordinate commanders, and from them descended through the wonted channels, to advance; but no man stirred, and the immobile lines pronounced a verdict—silent yet emphatic—against further slaughter."

Night found the lines of General Lee intact. The loss of the enemy was frightful to contemplate; the ground in our front was covered with their dead and wounded. The Confederate guns controlled the situation, and it took General Grant two days to make up his mind to ask a truce that he might bury his dead and care for his wounded.

And thus the campaign to capture the city of Richmond—from the Wilderness to James River—ended, with Victory perched upon the banner of General Lee.

General Grant now put his army in motion to cross to the south side of James River.... His dash to capture Petersburg on the 15th of June was unsuccessful, owing to some delay in the movement of his own troops, but more especially to the heroic defense of the city put up by Generals Beauregard and Wise with the comparatively small force at their command, consisting in great part of Home Guards.... On June 16th the advance of General Lee's army entered the lines around the city, and the siege of Petersburg began.

14

General Maurice has comprehensively summed up the campaign ending at Cold Harbor.

Once the vastly superior resources of the North were applied systematically and resolutely to the prosecution of the war, the end was certain. The fact that, though opposed by system and resolution, Lee accomplished what he did in the summer of 1864 is an index of the quality of his generalship. He began the campaign by forcing upon his opponent battle on ground of his own choice, ground which by its nature neutralised the superior numbers of the Army of the Potomac, and was peculiarly favourable to the Army of Northern Virginia. He continued the campaign foreseeing every movement which his enemy made, opposing every manoeuvre by timely counter-manoeuvre. He showed that as a tactician he was, in his employment of entrenchments, years ahead of his time, and as a strategist he never allowed himself to be surprised by an able enemy who throughout held and used the initiative.

If the campaign of 1862, from Richmond to the Potomac, is a model of what an army inferior in numbers may achieve in offence, the campaign from the Wilderness to Cold Harbour is equally a model of defensive strategy and tactics. Some commanders have excelled in the one method, some in the other; few in both, and amongst those few must be remembered Robert E. Lee.

16

Besieged

FROM Spotsylvania Grant had sent his famous
message to Washington: "I propose to fight it out on this line
if it takes all summer." But within less than a month, with the
summer hardly begun, he realized that it would not be possible
for him to fight it out on the line of direct approach to Richmond, and accordingly he decided on the move that had been
proposed by McClellan two years before and rejected. He
moved his entire army to the south side of the James River and
settled down to the reduction of Richmond through the siege
of Petersburg.

The capture of Petersburg had been one of the features of
Grant's over-all strategy as planned at the beginning of the
campaign, the task of taking the city being entrusted to General Ben Butler and his army of 30,000 men. But Butler's attacks had been skillfully fought off by Beauregard who was in
command at Petersburg with a makeshift army composed of a
few veteran troops, some militia and a Petersburg home guard
of boys and old men. Grant, after crossing the James, consoli-
dated Butler's army with Meade's, under his own immediate
supervision; and Lee moved into Petersburg to defend it
against the movement on Richmond from that direction.

Grant's move to the south of the James marked an entire
change in his plan of operations. Up until now he had been
actively on the aggressive, hammering away at Lee's army, trying to wear it away by killing and capturing as many as possible. But a month of this was enough to convince him that it
was not getting the desired results, so he settled down to the
patient siege of Petersburg, the key to the back door of Richmond. As a diversion Grant had sent General Hunter on a raid

up the Shenandoah Valley, and Lee had been compelled to weaken his force by detaching Early and his command to go to the Valley to meet Hunter.

So the campaign—and the war—entered its final phase.

1

Dr. Freeman expertly summarizes the situation confronting General Lee as he prepared for this final phase of the great struggle.

When General Lee went to church in Petersburg on June 19, 1864, the day after he reached the city, the military problem in the solution of which he sought divine guidance was as grave as any he had ever faced. The front of battle was now twenty-six miles in length—from the cavalry outposts at White Oak Swamp, to Chaffin's Bluff, thence on the south side of the James from Drewry's Bluff past Bermuda Hundred Neck to the Appomattox, and over that stream southward and westward in front of Petersburg, to a point beyond the Jerusalem plank road. The whole of this line had at all times to be held. Lee was required, in the second place, to prevent the enemy from seizing ground that would force the Confederate army back into the Richmond defense; thirdly, he had to cover the capital against surprise attack at any point not protected by his lines; and fourthly, he had to keep open the railroads, on which he was dependent for supplies.

In performing this task, for what assistance could he hope? Early might be able to change the gloomy outlook. Lee was satisfied that officer could drive back Hunter, and, indeed, on the second day at Petersburg, he received news that Hunter had retired from in front of Lynchburg. Perhaps, as Lee had planned ere he detached him, Early could advance down the Shenandoah Valley, spread terror in the North and thereby force General Grant either to detach a large part of his army for the defense of Washington, or else to attack Lee in the hope of compelling him to recall Early. Again, by some miracle, a great victory might be won in the far South that would release troops from that section to reinforce the Army of Northern

Virginia; but a miracle it would have to be, because Johnston had fallen back from Dalton to Kennesaw Mountain and was as hard beset by Sherman's hammering tactics as Lee had been by Grant's.

For the rest, Lee had to rely on his own army and Beauregard's, plus such conscripts as might be brought in and such convalescents as might return. Valiant as his army was, the limits to its possible accomplishments were manifest.. Although there was abundant reason for believing that the Federals were dispirited after the severe repulses they had sustained, Lee's own force had been so reduced by casualties and detachments that he had small chance of undertaking a sustained offensive unless Grant should be guilty of some serious blunder and present an opening. "General Grant," he told the President, "will concentrate all the troops here he can raise, from every section of the United States. . . . I hope Your Excellency will put no reliance in what I can do individually, for I believe that will be very little. The enemy has a strong position, and is able to deal us more injury than from any other point he has ever taken. Still we must try and defeat him. I fear he will not attack us but advance by regular approaches. He is so situated that I cannot attack him." Lee believed, however, that he could defend Richmond from a direct assault delivered on the northside, provided he could keep the Richmond-Petersburg Railroad in running order for the transfer of troops in an emergency.

The one advantage of the Confederate commander was this: Grant had approached Petersburg from the east. His lines ran north and south and had not yet been extended to the southwest or to the west. Lee's own lines, on the Confederate left, paralleled Grant's, but as Lee had to protect Petersburg fully, he drew his lines north and south and then to the west. On the sector east of Petersburg, little distance separated the trench systems that sweating thousands were now throwing up under the June sun; but from the point where Lee's line curved to the westward, while Grant's continued southward, the space between the two fronts widened gradually until it became as much as two miles. The extreme Confederate right, which was lightly held, quite overlapped the Federal front there. This situation gave Lee a certain freedom of manoeuvre on his right. He availed himself of this very promptly and employed his right division as a general reserve to strengthen the sector to the east, as occasion required, or to be moved across the James and aid Custis Lee in defending Richmond.

The question of subsistence was more serious than the prospect of being pinned to the Richmond-Petersburg defenses. Lee was almost entirely dependent on the railways to feed his army. These roads were four in number. Close to the Richmond defenses lay the long-contested Virginia Central. Directly south from Petersburg ran the Petersburg and Weldon Railroad, which was a link in the main coastal route leading to Wilmington and Charleston and thence to Atlanta. Southwestward from Richmond was the track of the Richmond and Danville. This was connected at Danville with the new Piedmont Railroad, leading to Greensboro, N. C. General Lee, it will be recalled, had been very anxious to have the Piedmont completed, in anticipation of a possible loss of the Petersburg and Weldon. Now that the Piedmont was at last open, though wretchedly constructed, it gave Richmond a second, if a slow and devious, connection with the rich corn belt of northwestern Georgia. Besides these lines, Lee had to defend the Southside Railroad, which led by way of Lynchburg to Bristol, on the Virginia-Tennessee border. This railroad was of no mean importance because it crossed at Burkeville the track of the Richmond and Danville. Supplies coming by way of Greensboro and Danville and intended for the army could be transferred to the Southside road at Burkeville and could be sent immediately to Petersburg. . . .

Surveying these lines of communication, Lee was satisfied that it would be almost impossible to hold permanently the Petersburg and Weldon, the northern end of which was less than three miles from the left flank of the Federals. His aim was to keep the enemy from that railway, if possible, until the harvest in Virginia, or as long as he could do so without heavy loss. Meantime, he urged that the Southside, the Richmond and Danville, and the Piedmont be supplied with ample rolling stock and defended by the second-line reserves, so that these lines could supply the army when the Petersburg and Weldon fell into the enemy's hands. "If this cannot be done," he told the Secretary of War, in as plain words as he had ever employed, "I see no way of averting the terrible disaster that will ensue."

2

Throughout the month of June Grant maintained a continuous series of energetic thrusts at the defenses of Petersburg, attempting to find a weak place in the Confederate armor, but by the first of July the Federal engineers had advised him of their conclusion that Lee's works were impregnable to direct assault. In this impasse, the Federals conceived the idea of breaching the works by digging a tunnel to a point under the Confederate lines and there exploding a blast which would supposedly wreck the defenses. The tunnel was constructed, with great ingenuity and skill on the part of the men who built it, and the mine was exploded on the morning of July 30. Dr. McCabe tells of the explosion.

The fort was literally blown in the air, and a breach was made in the Southern line thirty or forty yards wide. The fort was held by Pegram's battery of four guns and three regiments of South Carolina infantry. The explosion overturned the guns, and killed and wounded several of the artillerists and many of the infantry; the site of the fort was converted into a huge crater one hundred and fifty feet long, sixty-five feet wide, and from twenty-five to thirty feet deep; and the troops in the immediate vicinity were considerably demoralized by the sudden and appalling explosion.

The smoke had not floated away before every gun along the Federal line was opened in a furious cannonade, and at the same time Ledlie's division of Burnside's corps emerged from the Federal works, dashed across the intervening space, and entered the crater. Had they advanced beyond this they might have carried the line, for the Confederates had not yet recovered from their surprise. To the astonishment of every one, however, they huddled into the crater and sought shelter there and behind the breastworks. The divisions of Potter and Wilcox of the 9th Corps were also advanced, but they too crowded into the crater.

Taking advantage of this delay, the Confederates rapidly regained their self possession, and with admirable discipline formed to the right and left of the gap.

3

A news story in the *Petersburg Express* of August 1, 1864, gives an interesting contemporaneous account of the Confederates' defense against this dramatic effort to wreck their defenses.

As soon as the nature of the disaster was known, General Hill dispatched a courier to General Mahone's headquarters and that vigilant officer moved off immediately.

Arriving upon the ground, General Mahone found twelve of the enemy's flags waving upon the ramparts of that portion of our line carried by the explosion, and the whole vicinity swarming with white and black Yankee troops.

Getting his troops into position, General Mahone ordered his brigade to re-take a portion of his works, and ordered Wright's brigade to come up in such position as would insure the re-capture of the remaining portion. Under the command of Colonel Weisiger, acting brigadier, Mahone's brigade formed into line and were about to move up when the enemy sallied out and made a charge. The Confederates reserved their fire until they could "see the whites of the enemy's eyes," when they poured into them such a storm of bullets that the enemy recoiled and fell back in confusion. A charge was now ordered, and Weisiger's men dashed forward with a yell, driving the enemy up to and over the breastworks. On the works our men halted and delivered a plunging fire which proved so destructive that the enemy were never again rallied on this portion of the line, but left our men in undisturbed possession.

In the meantime Wright's brigade, commanded by Colonel Hall, instead of coming directly up, by some means deployed and came around and thus failed to re-take that portion of the line assigned to them.

At a later hour Wilcox's old brigade, now ably commanded by the young and intrepid Saunders, came gallantly up to their work and by a charge drove the enemy from the remaining portion of the works and thus enabled us to re-establish our lines, precisely as they were before the explosion.

The enemy, finding escape impossible, rushed for safety into the immense hole or chasm made by their explosion, and around the edge of this great basin our men closed in and fought hand-to-hand. This was done chiefly by Mahone's old brigade and Saunders' Alabamians. Here the slaughter was terrific, and here too many a gallant Confederate fell to rise no more. As an evidence of the desperate nature of the contest around and in this chasm, we would state that General Saunders' men, after removing a large number of wounded, buried in the hole on Saturday night fifty-five Yankee Negro troops and 178 of the whites.

The enemy opened a severe fire on the city with his siege guns simultaneously with the explosion, and for two hours his shells fairly rained upon our streets. Thanks to a kind Providence, but one accident occurred and that was the loss of a finger by the chief engineer of our fire department, Mr. Robert Green. It was cut off by the fragment of a shell. The few houses burned were old and of but little value.

4

The mine assault constituted Grant's final effort to carry Petersburg by direct attack, but he was by no means inactive during the succeeding months of the summer, autumn and winter. Steadily he attempted to extend his left around Petersburg to cut it off from the south, and without cessation continued his bombardment of the city and its defenses with his artillery, meanwhile attempting a succession of attacks against spots in the works around Petersburg and Richmond supposed to be vulnerable. It taxed Lee's limited resources to parry these unremitting assaults by a superior enemy, but by constant vigilance he was able always to meet each attack with sufficient force to repel it. The two armies had now settled down to a system of trench warfare, which was disagreeable and uncomfortable—but was a means of security to the individual soldiers. J. B. Polley, the observant member of the Texas Brigade, gives us a picture of the Confederate trench system as developed here.

Imagine a ditch eight feet wide and three or four deep, the dirt from which is thrown on the side next to the enemy and forms an embankment just high enough for a man to stand erect and look over. This embankment is the breastworks which protects us from the shots of the Yankees. The ditch extends for miles to the right and left—or, at any rate, as far as there is a necessity for protection. Leading back from the main ditch at acute or obtuse angles, according to the nature of the ground and situation of the enemy's works, and with the dirt likewise thrown on the side next to the enemy, are smaller ditches, called traverses, in which the soldiers sleep and do their cooking, washing, starching and ironing.

Here at Petersburg we found the lines of defense already prepared for occupancy, but until we reached these about Richmond we had to do our own digging; sometimes, too, in an emergency so great that resort was had to bayonets and tin cups in the absence of spades, shovels and picks.

Often there was neither time nor inclination to construct traverses, and then men who objected to sleeping in the main trench dug square, shallow holes in the ground just back of the main line.

5

In such trenches as these the Army of Northern Virginia lived for nearly a year. Among the soldiers in Lee's army in the trenches was Sidney Lanier, the great Southern poet. He has recorded a glimpse of the human side of Robert E. Lee in one of the general's rare interludes of repose.

The last time I saw him with mortal eyes—for with spiritual eyes many, many times have I contemplated him since—the scene was so beautiful, the surroundings were so rare, nay, time and circumstance did so fitly frame him as it were, that I think the picture should not be lost. There was nothing melodramatic in the circumstances, nothing startling, nothing sensational—which was all the more particularly in accord with his character, for this was one of those grand but modest, sweet souls that love simplicity and shrink from all that is loud and vulgar.

It was at fateful Petersburg on a glorious Sunday morning whilst the armies of Grant and Butler were investing our last stronghold there. It had been announced to those who happened to be stationed in the neighborhood of General Lee's headquarters that religious services would be conducted on that morning by Major General Pendleton of the artillery. At the appointed time I strolled over to Dunn's Hill where General Lee's tent was pitched and found General Pendleton ensconced under a magnificent tree, and a small party of soldiers with a few ladies from the dwellings near by, collected about him. In a few moments General Lee appeared with his camp chair and sat down. The services began. That terrible battery, Number Five, was firing very slowly, each report of the great gun making the otherwise profound silence still more profound. Even Hoke's line was quiet. I sat down on the grass and gazed, with such reverence as I had never given to mortal man before, upon the grand face of General Lee.

He had been greatly fatigued by loss of sleep. As the services progressed and the immortal words of the Christian doctrine came to our hearts and comforted us, sweet influences born of the liberal sunlight that lay warm upon the grass, of the waving leaves and trembling flowers, seemed to steal over the General's soul. Presently his eyelids closed and he fell gently asleep. Not a muscle of him stirred, not a nerve of his grand countenance twitched, there was no drooping of the head nor bowing of the figure. . . . As he slumbered so, sitting erect with his arms folded upon his chest in an attitude of majestic repose such as I never saw assumed by mortal man before; as the lazy cannon of the enemy anon hurled a screaming shell to within a few hundred yards of where we sat; as finally a bird flew into the tree overhead and piped small blissful notes in unearthly contrast with the roar of the war engines; it seemed to me as if the present earth floated off through the sunlight and the antique earth returned out of the past and some majestic god sat on a hill sculptured in stone presiding over a terrible yet sublime contest of human passions.

6

The two-year period of war had left its mark on General Lee. As he shouldered the task of defending Petersburg and Richmond from the overwhelming force arrayed against it, his form and visage showed the effects of the hard campaigns through which he had passed since he came to Richmond in 1861 to tender his sword to Virginia. John Esten Cooke, who was in frequent contact with him during that time, was impressed with the great changes that took place in his appearance and in his demeanor as the war progressed.

Any thing aiming to be a truthful picture of General Lee must present him under his different phases at different periods of the war. His personal appearance, and apparently his character, underwent a considerable change during the long struggle.

When I had the pleasure of seeing him for the first time, in the spring of 1861, soon after the resignation of his commission in the United States Army, and his arrival in Richmond to take command of the Virginia forces, he was in the ripe vigor of middle age, and his manner had in it a perceptible infusion of the unbending and formal air of the professional militaire. It was neither stiff nor cold—his innate simplicity and courtesy were too great for that; but it was formal and reserved. The face was not that of the popular pictures. He was close shaven, with the exception of a heavy, dark mustache covering the whole upper lip; and his figure was more rounded in outline and fuller than in the latter months of the war, when his proportions became somewhat gaunt and angular. He had the same erectness of carriage, but less suavity than afterward. This resulted, no doubt, from the mental trouble under which he is said to have labored at that time.

He is known now to have felt very painful emotion at abandoning, through stress of circumstances, the old flag to which he was deeply attached, and at seeing the South about to embark in a struggle which his military foresight told him would be long and bloody. These circumstances, no doubt, combined to make him melancholy and reserved, traits which I particularly noticed. He had sent for me to express his wishes in reference to a matter connected with the resignation of an officer of the United States Army, and his observations on the business were brief and to the point. His voice was ceremonious and extremely grave; no superfluous words were employed; and, having stated what he desired, he terminated the interview by a courteous but formal inclination of the head, which intimated plainly that his time was valuable.

If, in this reference to an interview of no importance whatever in itself, I have been able to convey an idea of the general's personal bearing at that time, the reader will understand how great the contrast was between the personality of the soldier in 1861 and in 1864-'65. During this latter period he wore a thick, gray beard, which covered nearly his entire cheeks, and resembled an old man. He was still erect and vigorous, but his frame had grown harder and less youthful in outline. The formal bearing had entirely disappeared, and given place to a grave sweetness of manner not unlike that which a father adopts toward his children. His mood seemed almost invariably sweet and patient. He was easily approached, was very kind and courteous, especially to the private soldiers, and produced upon you the impression of a sympathizing friend. This resulted, no doubt, from the peculiar position which he occupied as the war went on. It was impossible for him not to feel that he had thoroughly won the affection of the Southern people, and that they regarded him as their great bulwark, almost as their father. It was, indeed, with the air of a father looking upon his children that he regarded his "old soldiers," associated now with his own life in so many scenes of triumph and defeat, and joy and suffering.

The alteration here indicated in General Lee's appearance and demeanor may be said to have taken place as early as the winter of 1862, when the campaigns of the Chickahominy, the second Manassas, and Sharpsburg, had put him in thorough rapport with the troops. His grave patience and invariable amenity of manner were greatest in the last months of 1864 and the spring of 1865, but his personality had already assumed its second phase at this time. Those who were thrown in contact with him personally during this the middle period of the war find it difficult to convey a full idea of the remarkable calmness of his bearing under all circumstances. This calmness seemed scarcely, under any contingencies, to undergo the least alteration, and was as perfect in his hours of defeat and disappointment as when his movements were fully successful. Having observed him with interest and attention during some of the most trying scenes of the war, I was particularly impressed by this trait, and it persistently recurs to memory as one of the most striking of his individuality.

7

Calm though he may have appeared at this time to those who saw him, the responsibilities resting on him, the sufferings of his men and his growing recognition of the almost hopeless nature of his task must have weighed heavily on Lee's soul. Dr. McCabe tells of some of the miseries of that nightmarish winter at Petersburg.

When active operations ceased before Petersburg, both armies went into winter quarters—the Federals surrounded by every comfort their Government could furnish them with, and the Confederates to brave out the long, cold season, and battle with hunger and privation with little to encourage them, and a Government too indifferent to care for their sufferings.

During the winter the citizens of Richmond and Petersburg prepared to give Lee's army a New Year's dinner. Contributions were liberally made, but, owing to the unfortunate manner in which the distribution of the provisions was conducted, the good intentions of the citizens were practically defeated. The army suffered very greatly for food during the winter. Matters had, indeed, reached such a condition that it was impossible . . . to avert the horrors of a famine, this . . . brought about by the gross mismanagement of the Confederate Commissariat. . . . On the 5th of December the Commissary-General stated that he had on hand nine days' rations for General Lee's army, and at this time General Lee informed the Government that his troops were deserting for want of food—the rations issued to them being hardly sufficient to sustain life—and urged prompt action. . . . The Government took no steps to remedy the evil, and on the 14th of December General Lee informed the President that his army was without meat. Fortunately several vessels loaded with supplies had just arrived at Wilmington, and provisions were hurried forward to Petersburg and Richmond. But for this, the army would have been forced to disband or starve. . . .

Confederate Treasury notes were worth less than two cents on the dollar. A loaf of bread was worth three dollars in Richmond and Petersburg, and a month's pay would scarcely purchase the most trifling article of clothing. Yet, with its money so greatly depreciated as to be almost worthless, the Government was greatly in debt to the army. Not a single man had been given his full pay, and thousands had not received a cent for two years. . . .

The Conscription [Act] had ceased to bring forth men. On the 31st of December General Lee declared that it was diminishing rather than increasing the strength of his army. The result [of the pernicious system of enforcing conscription] was that the people set themselves against it and frequently resisted the enrolling officers with arms. . . .

Extravagant as the assertion may seem, it is nevertheless true that no Government ever did so much as the Confederacy to force its army to desert, for no army was ever so badly treated. . . . Hundreds deserted to the enemy, and fully twice as many went home. . . . [The President] steadily opposed the enforcing of the law against deserters, and finally it came to be generally understood that no one need fear being shot for desertion, as a commutation of the sentence, if not a pardon, was sure to be granted by the Executive.

About the last of November General Longstreet . . . said: "Over one hundred of General Pickett's men are in the guard-house for desertion, and the cause of it may be attributed to the numerous reprieves, no one being executed for two months." General Lee endorsed on this paper: "Desertion is increasing in the army, notwithstanding all my efforts to stop it. I think a rigid execution of law is mercy in the end. The great want in our army is firm discipline. . . ." Mr. Davis returned it with the following endorsement: "When deserters are arrested they should be tried, and if the sentences are reviewed and remitted, that is not a proper subject for the criticism of a military commander. . . ."

In order to supply the deficiency in troops it was proposed to arm the slaves. A large number of them were employed in the army as laborers, engineer troops and teamsters, and had given great satisfaction by their efforts, and it was believed that they could be made to fill up the ranks. They had been found to be good soldiers in the Federal army, and it was believed that they would accomplish still more in the Confederate army. . . . General Lee favored the proposition, and did all in his power to induce the Government to adopt it. His views were stated in the following letter [to Hon. E. Barksdale, a member of the Confederate Congress]:

". . . I do not think that our white population can supply the necessities of a long war without overtaxing its capacity, and imposing great suffering upon our people; and I believe we should prepare resources for a protracted struggle—not merely for a battle or a campaign. . . . In my opinion the Negroes, under proper circumstances, will make efficient soldiers. . . . Under good officers and good instructions, I do not see why they should not become soldiers. . . . I think those who are employed should be freed. . . . I have no doubt that if Congress would authorize their reception into service, and empower the President to call upon individuals or States for such as they are willing to contribute, with the condition of emancipation to all enrolled, a sufficient number would be forthcoming to enable us to try the experiment. . . ."

The proposition to arm the slaves was made in November 1864. It was not passed until March 1865, and then the Bill studiously set aside the recommendation of General Lee. The reward of freedom was not held out to the slaves. . . . The law having passed in this form, it was not reasonable to expect to raise black troops. Still the effort was made, and it failed. . . .

In January, 1865, an effort was made to secure peace. An interview was held between President Lincoln, Secretary Seward and others, on the Federal side, and Vice-President Stephens, Senator Hunter and others on the Confederate side, on board a steamer in Hampton Roads, but nothing was accomplished.

Towards the last of February, General Longstreet was informed by General Ord of the Federal army, that General Grant was willing to meet General Lee for the purpose of settling the terms of an honorable peace, provided General Lee was authorized to act in the matter. President Davis at once conferred upon Lee full powers, and the Confederate commander notified General Grant that he was ready to open the negotiations. It proved, however, that General Ord had misinformed General Longstreet, having mistaken General Grant's meaning. . . .

This last effort for peace having failed, like the first, there was nothing left to the South but to fight the war out to its close.

8

An evidence of the soldier's implicit confidence in General Lee, and of Lee's pleasant manner with his men even in times of stress, is afforded by a quotation from the journal of Colonel Owen of the Washington Artillery.

March 10—Congress passed a bill yesterday in Richmond to enroll and arm the Negroes. Think it a bad move, and too late. Still, if Gen. Lee says it is all right, why, go ahead! . . .

March 22—Negro troops parade to-day in Richmond for the first time. The darkies are very jubilant, and think it great fun. The music attracts them like flies around a molasses barrel. We are really suffering now for food. Yesterday I had to order some ground corn and shucks to be taken from the horses to be distributed to the men. The distribution of rations is very irregular and unreliable.

While riding down the plank road this A.M. with Col. Lindsey Walker, the Chief of Artillery of Hill's corps, we overtook Gen. Lee, riding with an orderly, going down to see the cavalry below Hatcher's Run. "Good morning, gentlemen," said the General. "I hope you are both well this morning." We returned his kind salutation. We rode in silence for a moment. Col. Walker was expecting daily his commission as Brigadier-General, and he had told me *I* was gazetted for a Lieutenant-Colonel's berth; but we had not received official notification of our appointments. Presently the General seemed to arouse himself from a revery, and, turning to me, asked—addressing me as Colonel—: "Colonel, have you seen Rooney Lee lately?" I told him I had not. He then said, "I didn't know but you had, Colonel; he is a gay young fellow like yourself. I thought may be you had seen him last evening at that *ball you attended in the city.*" Then, turning to Walker, he said, "General, have you seen him in your rides?" "I have not," said Walker. The General soon took a country road leading off to the right, and Walker and I exchanged winks. The General simply desired to inform us that our commissions were all right. Another one of his pleasantries.

9

Within the trenches around Petersburg Lee was not satisfied to remain on the defensive. In a letter to President Davis he expressed confidence in his ability to maintain his lines against General Grant—with the ominous and all-important proviso, "I am less uneasy about holding our position than about our ability to procure supplies for the army." Casting about for some means of resuming the offensive, and of returning to the depleted Confederate ranks some of the thousands of prisoners accumulating in Northern prisons since the adoption of Grant's policy of no exchanges, Lee proposed to Davis a desperate and audacious project. The detail in which he presents the plan is evidence of the careful thought he had devoted to it.

Great benefit might be drawn from the release of our prisoners at Point Lookout if it can be accomplished. The number of men employed for this purpose would necessarily be small, as the whole would have to be transported secretly across the Potomac where it is very broad, the means of doing which must first be procured. I can devote to this purpose the whole of the Marylanders of this army, which would afford a sufficient number of men of excellent material and much experience, but I am at a loss where to find a proper leader. As he would command Maryland troops and operate upon the Maryland soil, it would be well that he should be a Marylander. Of those connected with this army, I consider Colonel Bradley Johnson the most suitable. He is bold and intelligent, ardent and true, and yet I am unable to say whether he possesses all the requisite qualities. Everything in an expedition of this kind would depend upon the leader. . . .

By taking a company of the Maryland artillery armed as infantry, the dismounted cavalry and their infantry organization, as many men would be supplied as transportation could be procured for. By throwing them suddenly on the beach with some concert of action among the prisoners, I think the guard might be overpowered, the prisoners liberated and organized, and marched immediately on the route to Washington.

The artillery company could operate the guns captured at the Point. The dismounted cavalry with the released prisoners of that arm could mount themselves on the march, and the infantry would form a respectable force. Such a body of men, under an able leader, though they might not be able without assistance to capture Washington, could march around it and cross the upper Potomac where fordable. . . . The subject is one worthy of consideration, and can only be matured by reflection. . . . The sooner it is put in execution the better, if it is deemed practicable.

10

An impressive picture of Lee at this time, as he watched his cause crumble, is given by John Esten Cooke.

He had established his headquarters a mile or two west of Petersburg on the Cox Road, nearly opposite his centre, and here he seemed to await whatever the future would bring with a tranquillity which was a source of surprise and admiration to all who were thrown in contact with him. Many persons will bear their testimony to this extraordinary composure. His countenance seldom, if ever, exhibited the least traces of anxiety, but was firm and hopeful and encouraged those around him in the belief that he was still confident of success. . . . From the first, he seems to have regarded his situation, unless his army were largely reënforced, as almost desperate. Those reënforcements did not come; and yet, as he saw his numbers day by day decreasing, and General Grant's increasing in a still larger ratio, he retained his courage, confronting the misfortunes closing in upon him with unmoved composure, and at no time seemed to lose his "heart of hope."

Of this phenomenon the explanation has been sought in the constitutional courage of the individual and that instinctive rebound against fate which takes place in great organizations. This explanation doubtless is not without a certain amount of truth; but an attentive consideration of the principles which guided this eminent soldier throughout his career will show that his equanimity at a moment so trying was due to another and more controlling sentiment. This sentiment was his devotion to Duty—"the sublimest word in our language." . . . Great and unmoved in the dark hour as in the bright, he seemed to have determined to perform his duty to the last and to shape his conduct, under whatever pressure of disaster, upon the two maxims: "Do your duty" and "Human virtue should be equal to human calamity."

There is little reason to doubt that General Lee saw this "calamity" coming, for the effort to reënforce his small army with fresh levies seemed hopeless. . . . While the Federal army was regularly and largely reënforced, so that its numbers at no time fell below one hundred and fifty thousand men, Lee's entire force at Petersburg at no time reached sixty thousand and in the spring of 1865, when he still continued to hold his long line of defences, numbered scarcely half of sixty thousand. . . . General Grant's immense hammer continued to beat upon his adversary, wearing away his strength day by day. No new troops arrived to take the place of those who had fallen; and General Lee saw drawing closer and closer the inevitable hour when, driven from his works or with the Federal army upon his communications, he must cut his way southward or surrender. . . .

From the autumn of 1864 to the end in the spring of 1865 he was felt by the country and the army to be the sole hope of the Confederacy. To him alone now all men looked as the *deus ex machinâ* to extricate them from the dangers surrounding them. . . . It is doubtful if in any other struggle of history the hopes of a people were more entirely wrapped up in a single individual. All criticisms of the eminent soldier had long since been silenced, and it may indeed be said that something like a superstitious confidence in his fortunes had become widely disseminated. It was the general sentiment, even when Lee himself saw the end surely approaching, that all was safe while he remained in command of the army. This hallucination must have greatly pained him, for no one saw more clearly or was less blinded by irrational confidence. Lee fully understood and represented to the civil authorities—with whom his relations were perfectly friendly and cordial—that if his lines were broken at any point the fate of the campaign was sealed.

Feeling this truth, of which his military sagacity left him in no doubt, he had to bear the further weight of that general confidence which he did not share.

He did not complain, however, or in any manner indicate the desperate straits to which he had come. He called for fresh troops to supply his losses; when they did not arrive he continued to oppose his powerful adversary with the remnant still at his command. These were now more like old comrades than mere private soldiers under his orders . . . and they were devoted to their commander. For this devotion they certainly had valid reason. Never had leader exhibited a more systematic, unfailing and almost tender care of his troops. Lee seemed to feel that these veterans in their ragged jackets, with their gaunt faces, were personal friends of his own, who were entitled to his most affectionate exertions for their welfare. His calls on the civil authorities in their behalf were unceasing. . . . The men understood this care for them, and returned the affectionate solicitude of their commander in full. He was now their ideal of a leader and all that he did was perfect in their eyes. All awe of him had long since left them—they understood what treasures of kindness and simplicity lay under the grave exterior. The tattered privates approached the commander-in-chief without embarrassment, and his reception of them was such as to make them love him more than ever. . . .

Personally, he looked much older than at the beginning of the war, but by no means less hardy or robust. On the contrary, the arduous campaigns through which he had passed seemed to have hardened him—developing to the highest degree the native strength of his physical organization. His cheeks were ruddy and his eye had that clear light which indicates the presence of the calm, self-poised will. But his hair had grown gray, like his beard and mustache, which were worn short and well-trimmed. . . . The movements of this soldierly figure were as firm, measured and imposing as ever. It was impossible to discern in General Lee any evidences of impaired strength or any trace of the wearing hardships through which he had passed. He seemed made of iron, and would remain in his saddle all day and then at his desk half the night without apparently feeling any fatigue. He was still almost an anchorite in his personal habits, and lived so poorly that it is said he was compelled to borrow a small piece of meat when unexpected visitors dined with him.

11

A personal recollection of a soldier in the Army of Northern Virginia, Lieutenant William A. Obenchain, shows Lee in a characteristic attitude of quiet and unobtrusive kindness.

In the fall of 1864 I was a first lieutenant of engineers, assigned to the staff of the chief engineer of the Army of Northern Virginia, Gen. Walter H. Stevens. Our quarters were near the Osborne turnpike, about four miles below Richmond.

I had just returned to camp from a long hard day's duty. The weather was drizzly and I was thoroughly chilled. There were only a few coals and smoldering chunks where the fire had been. The servants were all away and our camp seemed deserted.

Dismounting and hitching my horse, I gathered some wood and small sticks, raked the coals together and began to make a fire. While on my knees, vigorously blowing the coals to ignite the kindling, I heard some one ride up and dismount. I felt so forlorn and was so intent on my undertaking that I did not look up to see who it was. In a few moments he walked up to where I was and stopped at my side. Still I did not look up. Imagine my surprise when, in a gentle and sympathetic voice, which I recognized at once, came the words: "My boy, let me show you how to make that fire." It was Gen. Robert E. Lee.

I arose instantly, saluted and attempted an apology. Then, stooping down with me, Gen. Lee pulled the wood open at the top and told me to take the coals and kindling from off the ground underneath and lay them in the opening. "This is the way," he said, "the old servants showed me how to make a fire when I was a boy," and then he explained the philosophy of it. In a short time we had a roaring fire, which we enjoyed alone until the other officers returned to camp.

That young engineer cherishes to this day the fact that the commander of all the armies assisted him in making a fire. The desolation of the place was transformed by the genial presence of Gen. Lee.

12

Another intimate glimpse of General Lee in these trying times is provided by Mrs. Davis, the wife of the Confederate President.

Toward the end of the war my husband's health was very precarious, and he was too weak to ride to headquarters. General Lee came up from camp one day, evidently worn out and worried, to find Mr. Davis lying quite ill on a divan in a little morning room in which we received only our intimate friends. General Lee, with a bow and excuse for coming in on the white carpet with his splashed boots, sat down and plunged at once into army matters. The outlook was not encouraging, and the two friends talked in a circle until both were worn out. There was a little silver saucepan on the hearth, and the general stopped abruptly and said: "That is a pretty little thing; what do you use it for?" And then what a delight it gave me to heat steaming hot the *cafe au lait* it contained and hand it to him in a little Sevres cup. When I attempted to ring for a servant to bring luncheon he said: "This drink is exquisite, but I cannot eat; do not call a servant, it is very cosy just so." Then, looking at the cup, he remarked with a twinkle in his eye, "My cups in camp are thicker, but this is thinner than the coffee." Behind the playful speech I saw the intense realization he had of the coarse ways and uncomfortable concomitants of a camp, and that, after four years, he missed the refinements of life to which he had been accustomed as he did at first.

13

In January 1865 Lee had a visit from another world-famous Confederate officer, Admiral Raphael Semmes of the Confederate States Navy. Semmes had just returned to Richmond, by way of Mexico and Texas, following the sinking of the *Alabama,* and after a courtesy call to President Davis he went to visit Lee, whom he had not seen since the time they had served together in the Mexican War.

As soon as I could command a leisure moment, I paid General Lee a visit at his headquarters near Petersburg and spent a night with him. I had served with him in the Mexican war. We discussed together the critical state of the country and of his army (we were now near the end of January, 1865), and I thought the grand old chieftain and Christian gentleman seemed to foreshadow in his conversation—more by manner than by words—the approaching downfall of the cause for which we were both struggling.

I had come to him, I told him, to speak of what I had seen of the people and of the army in my transit across the country, and to say to him that unless prompt measures could be devised to put an end to the desertions that were going on among our troops, our cause must inevitably be lost.

He did not seem to be at all surprised at the revelations I made. He knew all about the country, civil and military, but seemed to feel himself powerless to prevent the downward tendency of things. And he was right. It was no longer in the power of any one man to save the country. The body politic was already dead. The people themselves had given up the contest; and, this being the case, no army could do more than retard the catastrophe for a few months. Besides, his army was itself melting away. That very night—as I learned the next morning at breakfast—160 men deserted in a body! It was useless to attempt to shoot deserters when demoralization had gone to this extent.

14

The fatuous attitude of the Confederate Congress was one of the wonders of the dying days of the Confederacy. With its nation crashing in ruins about it, with its principal army starving on its threshold, members of Congress orated and declaimed. A good example is provided by the speech of Senator W. S. Oldham of Texas on January 30, speaking in support of the declaration that the thought of peace was inadmissable unless "coupled with our independence."

Why should any man doubt our final success? Sum up the results of the last campaign and it will be found that the loss of the enemy was five to our one. We beat them in ten battles to where we lost one. One of their main armies was almost annihilated; that of the Potomac has suffered beyond that of almost any army in history, and is now occupying a position which it could have taken last spring without the loss of a man. While the loss of the third army has been twice or thrice as great as that opposed to it. Sherman's march from Atlanta was actually a retreat; he could neither stay there nor return by the way he came. He availed himself of the only road of escape, on which there was no army to oppose him and on which he could with impunity forage upon a country filled with supplies for the support of his army.

Upon a calm review it will be found that the results of the last campaign furnish nothing to inspire the enemy with hope or us with despondency. What though Sherman has been allowed to escape from Atlanta and Hood has been driven out of Tennessee; what though Savannah and Fort Fisher have been lost? All is not lost; honor is not lost; liberty and independence are not lost, while we have the spirit to defend them. Should the enemy capture all our seaport towns and drive us from Richmond, they would weaken themselves to the amount of force required to hold them, and strengthen us by enabling us to concentrate our whole force, now divided, to defend those places and make our blows more effective. They have not as yet touched the vital point of the Confederacy. It has no vital point, but is vital in every part and can but by annihilation die.

It has recently been my duty, as Senators know, to look into the military resources of our country, and I unhesitatingly declare that they are ample to enable us to maintain ourselves indefinitely against any force the enemy can bring against us. We have men, arms, ammunition and provisions, and the means necessary to keep up the supply. To-day our army is nearer an equality with the enemy, in point of numbers, than at any past period of the war. Our enemy can never conquer us. If we stand firm to our position, he must yield. Could we but look into his resources and test the spirit of his people, we would doubtless discover much to encourage us. The gigantic scale upon which he has prosecuted the war has no doubt greatly impaired his resources and shaken the confidence of his people in the successful accomplishment of the work of our subjugation. His financial system can not much longer sustain the immense superstructure erected upon it. The crash must come, under the influence of which (if not before), and the continued destruction inflicted upon his armies, the war spirit of his people must eventually quail and succumb.

15

The Confederate Congress, fond as it was of debating abstractions and indulging in spread-eagle oratory, did sometimes take a constructive step. One such step—which came about four years too late—is related by Dr. McCabe.

In this hour of darkness the country turned to General Lee, as its last hope. During the entire period between June 1862 and April 1865, he was the only public man whose wisdom was believed in throughout the country, and whose integrity was never impeached; and now men came to the conclusion that if the cause was not already lost, General Lee was the only person capable of saving it. For several years there had been a growing desire to see him at the head of all the armies of the South, for since the fall of Vicksburg, it had been the chief wish of the people to take the control of the armies away from the President, in whose military capacity they had no confidence. Now the demand was made too powerfully to be resisted. The Legislature of Virginia passed a resolution declaring that "the appointment of General Robert E. Lee to the command of all the armies of the Confederate States would promote their efficiency and operate powerfully to reanimate the spirits of the armies, as well as of the people of the several States, and to inspire increased confidence in the final success of our cause."

This resolution was communicated to the President, who replied: "The opinion expressed by the General Assembly in regard to General Robert E. Lee has my full concurrence. Virginia cannot have a higher regard for him or greater confidence in his character and ability, than is entertained by me. When General Lee took command of the Army of Northern Virginia, he was in command of all the armies of the Confederate States by my order of assignment. He continued in this general command, as well as in the immediate command of the Army of Northern Virginia, as long as I would resist his opinion that it was necessary for him to be relieved from one of these two duties. Ready as he has ever shown himself to be to perform any service that I desired him to render to his country, he left it to me to choose between his withdrawal from the command of the army in the field, and relieving him of the general command of all the armies of the Confederate States. It was only when satisfied of this necessity that I came to the conclusion to relieve him from the general command, believing that the safety of the Capital and the success of our cause depended, in a great measure, on then retaining him in the command in the field of the Army of Northern Virginia. On several subsequent occasions, the desire on my part to enlarge the sphere of General Lee's usefulness has led to renewed considerations of the subject, and he has always expressed his inability to assume command of other armies than those now confided to him, unless relieved of the immediate command in the field of that now opposed to General Grant."

President Davis was right. General Lee had always shunned prominence. With a soldier's modesty, he had never sought to thrust himself forward, and had been satisfied to do his duty in whatever position he was placed by the lawful authority of the country. . . .

The position, however, which General Lee held in the spring of 1862, was not what the people now designed for him. Then he was acting "under the direction of the President"; now it was proposed to place the office of Commander-in-Chief beyond the control of the President. The truth is, the people and Congress wished to make General Lee a military dictator, as the last hope of saving the cause, and it is not likely, when it is remembered how extremely jealous of his power was Mr. Davis, that such a step was viewed with any favor by the Executive, even though the choice of the nation fell upon one so universally beloved as General Lee. . . . However this may be, the Bill [creating the office of Commander-in-Chief] was passed, and approved by the Executive, and on the 5th day of February 1865, a general order from the Adjutant-General's office directed General Lee to enter upon his new duties.

General Lee had not sought the high rank now bestowed upon him, and it came to him so unmistakably the act of the nation, that he felt he had no right to refuse it, . . . [He] entered upon his new command on the 9th of February 1865, and issued the following general order to the armies of the Confederacy:

"In obedience to General Order No. 3, Adjutant and Inspector-General's Office, 6th February, 1865, I assume command of the military forces of the Confederate States. Deeply impressed with the difficulties and responsibility of the position, and humbly invoking the guidance of Almighty God, I rely for success upon the courage and fortitude of the army, sustained by the patriotism and firmness of the people, confident that their united efforts, under the blessing of Heaven, will secure peace and independence.

"The Headquarters of the Army, to which all special reports and communications will be addressed, will be, for the present, with the Army of Northern Virginia. . . ."

By the middle of March, General Lee's army numbered about thirty-three thousand men. The troops had been half starved during the winter, they were badly clothed and poorly provided against the weather. Yet they were cheerful and willing to stand by their commander to the last, and it was a common saying with them that, though their lot was a hard one, they could stand it "as long as General Lee. . . ." [The men] saw nothing before them but defeat and still more suffering. It was a great trial to which their firmness was thus subjected, and only their stern patriotism, and their love for General Lee kept them true to their duty, for hope had completely departed from them.

16

Conditions being what they were, it was perhaps inevitable that Grant's superior forces before Petersburg would eventually overwhelm any defense that Lee could devise. For nearly nine months Lee skillfully parried every thrust of his adversary; but, with the coming of spring, it was generally felt that Grant would make a supreme effort to break down the Confederate defense. Grant began his preparations for this final thrust during the latter days of March, his objective being Lee's extreme right flank. Lee, with his habitual prescience, sensed the point of attack. But the Confederate resources were so strained that the slightest accident, the smallest failure, could bring sudden disaster. Sure enough, a straw broke the Confederate camel's back—or rather, a shad bake, as Otto Eisenschiml and E. B. Long bring out in their account of the disaster at Five Forks.

The iron ring which Grant had forged around Richmond and Petersburg was drawing closer and now threatened to crush the two remaining railroads over which flowed the sustenance of the army and the civilian population. How to prevent this calamity in face of an overwhelming enemy superiority, numerical and material, was a problem to which the Confederate leaders had vainly tried to find a solution.

Lee's position had indeed become desperate. So far he had met each new enemy front with one of his own, but now his lines were stretched to the breaking point. In some spots the trenches were manned by scarcely more than pickets. Grant kept harassing the defenders by constant thrusts, lest Lee pull out his troops surreptitiously some night and join General Joseph E. Johnston, who commanded the only other Eastern Confederate army still in the field. Johnston was somewhere in North Carolina, and if the two leaders combined their forces the war would go on. So far Grant had not been able to force the issue for lack of sufficient cavalry, but Philip H. Sheridan had recently arrived from the Shenandoah Valley and filled this want. Something was bound to happen soon.

Lee saw the picture clearly. He reasoned correctly that the Union armies would push westward to break the vital Southside Railroad. If that went, Petersburg and Richmond would go too. There would be left then only the railroad to Danville, over which the government and the troops must be evacuated if they were to avoid capture or starvation. To avert this danger, Lee scraped together his last reserves. Rosser was ordered to report to General George Pickett, of Gettysburg fame, who was to ward off the expected blow. Together with six thousand men on foot and Fitzhugh Lee's cavalry, the total number of this detached force was swelled to ten thousand, about one-quarter of Lee's entire army.

The decision to deplete the trenches by so many men was a desperate gamble. It meant that the Confederates must leave their fortifications and fight in the open, where the losses on both sides would be more equal; but there was nothing else Lee could do. If Pickett could not halt the Federal advance, all was lost. The prayers of millions were with him.

Rosser immediately set his troops in motion. He had been instructed to join Pickett at Five Forks, an important crossroad a few miles north of Dinwiddie Court House, between that settlement and the Southside Railroad. Since the distance he had to traverse was short, he did not hurry. On the way he had to cross the Nottoway River, and it occurred to him that he might take a few hours off and go fishing. Should he be lucky, it would help conserve his meager supply of provisions; if not, he would at least spend a peaceful afternoon. Accordingly he borrowed a seine from a neighboring farmer and set out on his foraging expedition.

The success of his short excursion surpassed all his expectations. The shad he caught were more than could be consumed before they would spoil. He and his officers feasted for a day, and what was left of the fish Rosser loaded into an ambulance. Tomorrow was another day and would bring with it renewed appetites which had to be satisfied.

When Rosser reported to Pickett he was ordered to the rear. There, two miles north of Five Forks and behind a small stream called Hatcher's Run, he was to guard the train and act as a general reserve.

Lee's uncanny ability to read Grant's mind, so successfully displayed in the campaign of the Wilderness, again proved itself. As Lee had anticipated, Sheridan began his march toward Dinwiddie Court House, expecting to overlap and turn the Southern defense line at Petersburg. From Dinwiddie Court House Sheridan struck northward, to gain the Southside Railroad. Up to then he had advanced unhindered, but now he found Pickett across his path, offering not passive but active opposition. Lee, always anxious to keep the initiative, had directed Pickett to take the offensive so as to disrupt the Federal plan. On March 30 the two forces met and Sheridan was thrown back. The victors then lay down at Five Forks for a much-needed night's rest.

The next morning, March 31, General Lee in person watched the onset of his left wing and was satisfied with its early progress. He then left for his headquarters. The troops, however, could not retain their forward position. By sundown the left wing had been forced back again to the vicinity of its starting point. The right wing under Pickett and Fitzhugh Lee had fared no better. It had come to within a few hundred yards of Dinwiddie Court House, then also had been forced to withdraw in the face of vastly superior forces and the concentrated fire of repeating rifles. When Lee was advised of the day's events he expressed keen disappointment, something he rarely did, but ordered Pickett to "hold Five Forks at all hazards." The fate of Richmond depended on it, for the crossroads protected the White Oak Road and the Southside Railroad. The White Oak Road was the main artery between Five Forks and Petersburg; the Southside Railroad led to Danville, to General Johnston—and to food.

Rosser had not been engaged in the day's fighting. Mindful of his fish supply, he invited Pickett, upon the latter's return in the evening, to join him the next day in a shad bake at his camp. Fitzhugh Lee, second in command, was included in the invitation. Pickett's mouth watered, but he hesitated. His position at Five Forks offered no natural advantages, as it lay in a flat, heavily wooded country and had been strengthened only perfunctorily by hastily erected breastworks. Ordinarily the situation would have called for special precautions, but the comparative ease with which Pickett had repulsed Sheridan made him overconfident. In view of his success on the day before, he did not expect to be molested for some time. Perhaps he also did some wishful thinking. At any rate, the prospect of a shad bake was too tempting to be resisted. It would be a pleasant interlude in this eternal business of killing or being killed. . . .

It was about one o'clock in the afternoon when Pickett and Fitzhugh Lee left Five Forks for the shad bake. Just as they were about to start out, Brigadier General Thomas T. Munford, Fitzhugh Lee's chief lieutenant, was told of a stir among the pickets to the east . . . and so informed his commander. Fitzhugh, impatient to be off, took the matter lightly and ordered Munford to take proper measures if it meant anything more than a slight brush, which he thought unlikely. Together with Pickett he then rode to Rosser's headquarters where the promised meal awaited them.

Hardly had the two generals left when Munford discovered that what was happening to his left was more than a mere brush. His pickets were being driven in, and the White Oak Road was already swarming with Federal cavalry. Heavy groups of infantry were massing in its rear. This road had to be kept clear at all cost, or Pickett's ten thousand men would be cut off from the rest of Lee's army. The Southside Railroad, for the defense of which Lee had detached such a large body of valuable troops, would be periled.

The real cause of the disturbance had been successfully hidden from Munford's outposts. The entire Union 5th Corps, under General G. K. Warren, had arrived overnight and was stealthily executing a wide encircling movement, so wide that it was safe from enemy observation. Yet Munford began to suspect what was going on and knew that something had to be done. . . . Munford, however, did not dare run counter to Lee's explicit order that Five Forks had to be held at all hazards. Frantically he sent messengers in all directions, trying to locate his commanding officers, who had not advised him of their destination. One of the horsemen finally discovered the generals at Rosser's camp. The three officers were calmly munching shad and made light of Munford's fears. Everything was quiet; they had heard no firing; Munford was too excitable. They refused to interrupt their meal. . . .

Sheridan had conceived an excellent battle plan. Warren's infantry was to occupy White Oak Road quietly, far east of the crossroads and the enemy pickets. A sudden mass attack was then to be launched on the Confederate left flank and rear. Sheridan's dismounted cavalrymen meanwhile were to creep up in front and coordinate their assault with that of their comrades. . . .

At four o'clock every regiment was in position, and the assault hit Pickett's flank like an avalanche. . . . The gray line battled valiantly with the courage of desperation. But the weight of numbers told. . . . With its left flank crushed, the entire Confederate line became untenable and was rolled up like a scroll. Resistance ceased shortly; in less than an hour three to four thousand prisoners were marched off to Dinwiddie Court House. The number was to grow to five thousand before the day was over. The extreme right of the line still held; but it was only a question of minutes before it too dissolved.

The heavy firing . . . acted on the three picnicking generals at Rosser's camp like an electric shock. They suddenly realized how timely Munford's warning had been, and that by ignoring it they had blundered disastrously. The horror of their guilt must have struck them like a physical blow. Two miles away their troops had been surrounded, while they were feasting. Pickett was the first to recover. Throwing himself flat on his horse, he plunged across the bridge over Hatcher's Run and rode the long gantlet of a furious fusilade by Union troops, but none of the shots found its mark. The remnants of his broken forces rallied around him, and he led them in flight. Fitzhugh Lee and Rosser were completely cut off and only managed to mingle with the few fugitives who streamed confusedly across Hatcher's Run. On the banks of the little river Rosser's reserve cavalry stood guard, successfully disputing further pursuit.

Pickett's defeat was a disaster as unexpected as it was irreparable. In an hour's time Lee had lost his last reserves and his hope of keeping Grant out of Richmond. . . . Nor was the heartbreaking loss in men the worst consequence of Pickett's and young Lee's aberration. Still worse was their failure to notify their commander promptly of the catastrophe. By nightfall Lee had received only incomplete reports, one from a fugtive captain, the other from his nephew Fitzhugh. Both led him to believe that Pickett had suffered a slight setback. Pickett himself either could not or dared not communicate with Lee, who did not learn the full truth until the morning of April 2. Then it was brought home to him in a forceful manner.

He was sleeping at his headquarters, the Turnbull House on Edge Hill, about three miles out of Petersburg. General A. P. Hill had come over from his near-by headquarters and was resting on the floor. Longstreet, who had been recalled from the northern defenses, arrived about 4:00 A.M. It was still dark when Colonel Charles S. Venable of Lee's staff happened to stroll out through the gate. A rumbling of wagons driven at breakneck speed reached his ears. A few moments later, frantic teamsters rushed by, whipping up their horses and yelling that the Yankees were right behind them.

Venable immediately rushed into the house to warn Lee, then rode out with A. P. Hill to reconnoiter. Hill was never again seen alive. In the early dawn Venable became terror-stricken upon discovering that a few huts half a mile away were already in possession of Federal troops. They might have captured Lee and his staff had they been aware of their opportunity.

17

Lee knew all too well what it meant when he emerged from the Turnbull House and saw the tide of battle surging up to his very doorstep, but his equanimity did not fail him. One of his officers, John Esten Cooke, was by his side during this crisis, and has recorded the unflinching manner in which Lee met disaster face to face.

Standing on the lawn in front of his headquarters, General Lee now saw approaching rapidly a heavy column of Federal infantry, with the obvious design of charging a battery which had opened fire upon them from a hill to the right. ... He watched with attention, but with perfect composure, this determined advance of the enemy; and, although he must have realized that his army was on the verge of destruction, it was impossible to discern in his features any evidences of emotion. He was in full uniform, and had buckled on his dress-sword, which he seldom wore—having on this morning declared, it is said, that if he were compelled to surrender he would do so in full harness. Of his calmness at this trying moment the writer is able to bear his personal testimony. Chancing to hear a question addressed to a member of his staff, General Lee turned with great courtesy, raised his gray hat in response to the writer's salute, and gave him the desired information in a voice entirely measured and composed. It was impossible to regard a calmness so striking without strong sentiments of admiration, and Lee's appearance and bearing at this moment will always remain vividly impressed upon the writer's memory.

The Federal column was soon in dangerous proximity to the battery on the hill, and it was obliged to retire at a gallop to escape capture. An attempt was made to hold the ground near the head-quarters, but a close musketry-fire from the enemy rendered this also impossible—the artillery was withdrawn, and General Lee, mounting his iron-gray, slowly rode back, accompanied by a number of officers, toward his inner line. He still remained entirely composed and only said to one of his staff in his habitual tone: "This is a bad business, colonel."

"Well, colonel," he said afterward to another officer, "it has happened as I told them it would at Richmond. The line has been stretched until it has broken."

18

The breaking of Lee's line could have but one result from the military standpoint—the evacuation of Petersburg and Richmond. Dr. McCabe tells of the departure of Lee and his army from the scene of their last stand.

. . . The day closed with the Confederates in possession of Petersburg. But it was far from General Lee's intention to attempt to hold the city longer. Such a course would involve the capture or destruction of his army, and all that remained to him now was to abandon both Richmond and Petersburg, and endeavor to join Johnston near Danville. It was no longer possible to retreat by the south bank of the Appomattox, for all the roads were in possession of the enemy, and now the march must be made by the longer route north of the river. . . .

Having decided to abandon the cities he had so long defended, General Lee at eleven o'clock, on the morning of the 2nd of April, telegraphed to the Government that it was his intention to retire from Richmond and Petersburg that night at eight o'clock, and advised the authorities to have everything in readiness to leave the city that night, unless they heard from him to the contrary in the meantime. His efforts now were all directed to the task of holding his line until nightfall, in order that he might move off with his army under the cover of darkness. During the day the tobacco and cotton stored in Petersburg were destroyed, the huge warehouses containing them being given to the flames. Everything was gotten in readiness for the retreat, and the army only awaited the coming of night to begin its last and most memorable march. . . .

Sunday, the 2nd of April wore anxiously away . . . and when night came the army breathed freer. The sky was lit up with the glare of the burning warehouses, and the heavy reports of cannon shook the city to its foundations. At midnight the army commenced to withdraw from the trenches, and move rapidly and silently through the streets, towards the river. By three o'clock the army was safely on the Chesterfield side, and the bridge was fired. Instantly the magazine of Cummin's battery of siege guns exploded with a deafening roar, followed in a few moments by the magazine at Fort Clifton, on the north side of the river. Then, all along the whole line, from Petersburg to Richmond, heavy explosions followed in quick succession, shaking the ground as with an earthquake. Still the Federal army lay quietly within its own lines, never venturing to move forward to ascertain the cause of these suspicious sights and sounds.

After leaving Petersburg, the army marched northward to Chesterfield Court House, nearly midway between Petersburg and Richmond. There it was joined by the divisions of General Mahone, and the rest of the troops that had held the line south of the James, fronting Bermuda Hundreds; and a little later Ewell arrived with the troops from the lines of Richmond. The army was once more united, but it numbered now less than twenty-five thousand men. The march was resumed from Chesterfield Court House, westward, and by daylight on the morning of the 3d of April, the city of Petersburg was sixteen miles behind.

19

An impressive account of the evacuation of the Confederate capital has been written by Captain Clement Sulivane, C.S.A., who was the last uniformed Confederate to leave the surrendered city.

About 11:30 A.M. on Sunday, April 2nd, a strange agitation was perceptible on the streets of Richmond, and within half an hour it was known on all sides that Lee's lines had been broken below Petersburg, that he was in full retreat on Danville, that the troops covering the city at Chaffin's and Drewry's Bluffs were on the point of being withdrawn, and that the city was forthwith to be abandoned. A singular security had been felt by the citizens of Richmond, so the news fell like a bomb-shell in a peaceful camp, and dismay reigned supreme.

All that Sabbath day the trains came and went; wagons, vehicles and horsemen rumbled and dashed to and fro; and, in the evening, ominous groups of ruffians—more or less in liquor—began to make their appearance on the principal thoroughfares of the city. As night came on, pillage and rioting and robbing took place. The police and a few soldiers were at hand and, after the arrest of a few ring-leaders and the more riotous of their followers, a fair degree of order was restored. But Richmond saw few sleeping eyes during the pandemonium of that night.

The division of General G. W. C. Lee, of Ewell's corps, at that time rested in the trenches eight miles below Richmond, with its right on the James River, covering Chaffin's Bluff. I was at the time its assistant adjutant general, and was in the city on some detached duty connected with the "Local Brigade" belonging to the division—a force composed of the soldiers of the army detailed on account of their mechanical skill to work in the arsenals, etc., and of clerks and other employes of the War, Treasury, Quartermaster and other departments.

Upon receipt of the news from Petersburg I reported to General Ewell (then in Richmond) for instructions, and was ordered to assemble and command the Local Brigade, cause it to be well supplied with ammunition and provisions, and await further orders. All that day and night I was engaged in this duty, but with small result, as the battalions melted away as fast as they were formed, mainly under orders from the heads of departments who needed all their employes in the transportation and guarding of the archives, etc., but partly, no doubt, from desertions. When morning dawned, fewer than 200 men remained, under command of Captain Edward Mayo.

Shortly before day General Ewell rode to my headquarters and informed me that General G. W. C. Lee was then crossing the pontoon at Drewry's; that he would destroy it and press on to join the main army; that all the bridges over the river had been destroyed except Mayo's, between Richmond and Manchester; and that the wagon bridge over the canal in front of Mayo's had already been burned by Union emissaries. My command was to hasten to Mayo's bridge and protect it and the one remaining foot-bridge over the canal leading to it, until General Gary of South Carolina should arrive.

I hurried to my command and fifteen minutes later occupied Mayo's bridge, at the foot of 14th street, and made military dispositions to protect it to the last extremity. This done, I had nothing to do but listen for sounds and gaze on the terrible splendor of the scene. And such a scene probably the world has never witnessed. Either incendiaries or (more probably) fragments of bombs from the arsenals, had fired various buildings, and the two cities, Richmond and Manchester, were like a blaze of day amid the surrounding darkness. Three high arched bridges were in flames; beneath them the waters sparkled and dashed and rushed on by the burning city. Every now and then, as a magazine exploded, a column of white smoke rose up as high as the eye could reach, instantaneously followed by a deafening sound. The earth seemed to rock and tremble as with the shock of an earthquake, and immediately afterward hundreds of shells would explode in air and send their iron spray down far below the bridge. As the immense magazines of cartridges ignited, the rattle as of thousands of musketry would follow, and then all was still for the moment except the dull roar and crackle of the fast-spreading fires. At dawn we heard terrific explosions about "The Rockets," from the unfinished iron-clads down the river.

By daylight on the 3rd a mob of men, women and children, to the number of several thousands, had gathered at the corner of 14th and Cary streets and other outlets in front of the bridge, attracted by the vast commissary depot at that point; for it must be remembered that in 1865 Richmond was a half-starved city, and the Confederate government had that morning removed its guards and abandoned the removal of the provisions, which was impossible for the want of transportation. The depot doors were forced open and a demoniacal struggle for the countless barrels of hams, bacon, whisky, flour, sugar, coffee, etc., raged about the buildings among the hungry mob. The gutters ran whisky, and it was lapped as it flowed down the streets, while all fought for a share of the plunder. The flames came nearer and nearer, and at last caught in the commissariat itself.

At daylight the approach of the Union forces could be plainly discerned. After a little came the clatter of horses' hoofs galloping up Main street. My infantry guard stood to arms, the picket across the canal was withdrawn, and the engineer officer lighted a torch of fat pine. By direction of the Engineer Department barrels of tar, surrounded by pine knots, had been placed at intervals on the bridge, with kerosene at hand, and a lieutenant of engineers had reported for the duty of firing them at my order. The noisy train proved to be Gary's ambulances, sent forward preparatory to his final rush for the bridge. The muleteers galloped their animals about half-way down, when they were stopped by the dense mass of human beings. Rapidly communicating to Captain Mayo my instructions from General Ewell, I ordered that officer to stand firm at his post until Gary got up. I rode forward into the mob and cleared a lane. The ambulances were galloped down to the bridge, I retired to my post, and the mob closed in after me and resumed its wild struggle for plunder.

A few minutes later a long line of cavalry in gray turned into 14th street and, sword in hand, galloped straight down to the river. Gary had come. The mob scattered right and left before the armed horsemen, who reined up at the canal. Presently a single company of cavalry appeared in sight, and rode at headlong speed to the bridge. "My rear-guard," explained Gary. Touching his hat to me, he called out, "All over! Good-bye! Blow her to h——ll!" and trotted over the bridge. That was the last I ever saw of General Gary of South Carolina.

In less than sixty seconds Captain Mayo was in column of march, and as he reached the little island about half-way across the bridge, the single piece of artillery loaded with grape-shot that had occupied that spot arrived on the Manchester side of the river. The engineer officer, Dr. Lyons, and I walked leisurely to the island, setting fire to the provided combustible material as we passed along, and leaving the north section of Mayo's bridge wrapped in flame and smoke. At the island we stopped to take a view of the situation north of the river, and saw a line of blue-coated horsemen galloping in furious haste up Main street. Across 14th street they stopped, and then dashed down 14th street to the flaming bridge. They fired a few random shots at us three on the island, and we retreated to Manchester. I ordered my command forward, the lieutenant of engineers saluted and went about his business, and myself and my companion sat on our horses for nearly half an hour watching the occupation of Richmond. We saw another string of horsemen in blue pass up Main street, then we saw a dense column of infantry march by, seemingly without end; we heard the very welkin ring with cheers as the United States forces reached Capitol Square, and then we turned and slowly rode on our way.

20

The degree to which the hopes of the Confederacy had become bound up with Lee, and the confidence in him on the part of the people, even his former detractors, had a classic example in E. A. Pollard, the fiery editor of the *Richmond Examiner* who in 1861 had spoken of Lee's "absurd misconception of mountain warfare." Now his views had changed. Incensed by the *New York Herald's* declaration that the taking of Richmond was "one of the grandest triumphs that had crowned human efforts for centuries," Pollard fulminated.

Such stuff was characteristic of Northern newspapers. But looking to facts, we shall find a more precise language in which to describe the achievement of Gen. Ulysses S. Grant in the fall of Richmond.

It was simply the consummation of the disgrace of this commander—that he should have taken eleven months to capture a position at no time held by more than one third of his forces, having lost in the enterprise in killed and wounded more than double the numbers actually in arms against him! This sentence may grate on Northern pride; but it is founded upon plain, unyielding figures; it is the inexorable statement of the law of proportions; it can be no more contested than a mathematical demonstration. As long as the intelligent of this world are persuaded of the opinion that a great General is he who accomplishes his purpose with small, but admirably drilled armies; who defeats large armies with small ones; who accomplishes great military results by strategy, more than by fighting; who makes of war an intellectual exercise rather than a match of brute force, that title will be given to Robert E. Lee above all men in America, and the Confederate commander will be declared to have been much greater in defeat than Grant in his boasted victory.

17

Retreat to Surrender

I<small>N</small> N<small>OVEMBER</small> Lee had written to President Davis, emphasizing the numerical superiority of Grant's army, saying: "Unless we can obtain a reasonable approximation to his force, I fear a great calamity will befall us." The attainment of any such equality of force, however, had been impossible; and now, as he led his tired, hungry, ragged men out of the works protecting Richmond and Petersburg he saw looming ominously ahead of him that calamity he had predicted. In his dispatches and in his discussions with his officers he spoke hopefully of plans to unite with the forces under his old friend, Joe Johnston, in North Carolina; but, deep in his heart, he must have known that any such plans were hopeless. A well-fed, elated army of superior strength opposed his hungry, discouraged force of far fewer numbers. No amount of military skill in leadership could make up for the disparity in strength of the opposing forces.

So the Army of Northern Virginia set out on its *Via Dolorosa*, that last week which was a tortured nightmare. Days and nights were a dizzying muddle of marching and fighting, with never enough food and never enough sleep. As they stumbled along to the concluding scene of their tragic four years under arms, their senses told them that the end was near and was inevitable, although their hearts insisted on rousing the thought that had always been sufficient to inspire them to one more effort: "Marse Robert will get us out of this." But Marse Robert too had reached the end of his tether. Appomattox was just ahead.

1

A record of that last, sad march of the Army of Northern Virginia has been left by John Esten Cooke.

On the morning of the 3rd of April General Lee, after allowing his column a brief period of rest, continued his march up the north bank of the Appomattox.

The aspect of affairs at this time was threatening, and there seemed little ground to hope that the small force would be able to make good its retreat to North Carolina. General Grant had a short and direct route to the Danville Railroad—a considerable portion of his army was already as far west as Dinwiddie Court House—and it was obvious that he had only to use ordinary diligence to completely cut General Lee off in the vicinity of Burkesville Junction. . . . He could move over the chord, while Lee was compelled to follow the arc of the circle. Unless good fortune assisted Lee and ill fortune impeded his opponent, the event seemed certain—and it will be seen that these conditions were completely reversed.

Under the circumstances here stated it appeared reasonable to expect in Lee and his army some depression of spirits. The fact was strikingly the reverse. The army was in excellent spirits, probably from the highly agreeable contrast of the budding April woods with the squalid trenches, and the long unfelt joy of an unfettered march through the fields of spring. General Lee shared this hopeful feeling in a very remarkable degree. His expression was animated and buoyant, his seat in the saddle erect and commanding, and he seemed to look forward to assured success in the critical movement which he had undertaken.

"I have got my army safe out of its breastworks," he said on the morning of this day, "and in order to follow me the enemy must abandon his lines and can derive no further benefit from his railroads or James River."

The design of the Confederate commander . . . depended for success upon an important condition. This was a supply of food for his army. The troops during the whole winter had lived from day to day on quarter-rations, doled out to them with a sparing hand; and, in moving now from Petersburg, Lee saw that he must look to supplies somewhere upon his line of retreat. These he had

directed to be brought from the South and deposited at Amelia
Court House; and the expectation of finding at that point full subsistence for his men had doubtless a great effect in buoying up his
spirits. An evil chance, however, reversed all the hopes based on
this anticipation. From fault or misapprehension, the train loaded
with supplies proceeded to Richmond without depositing the rations at Amelia Court House; there was no time to obtain other
subsistence and when, after unforseen delay in consequence of high
water in the Appomattox, Lee, at the head of his half-starved soldiers reached Amelia Court House, it was only to find that there
was nothing there for the support of his army, and to realize that a
successful retreat under the circumstances was wellnigh hopeless.

Those who accompanied the Southern army on this arduous
march will recall the dismayed expression of the emaciated faces
at this unlooked-for calamity; and no face wore a heavier shadow
than that of General Lee. The failure of the supply of rations completely paralyzed him. He had intended, and was confident of his
ability, to cut his way through the enemy; but an army can not
march and fight without food. It was now necessary to halt and send
out foraging parties into the impoverished region around. Meanwhile General Grant with his great force was rapidly moving to
bar his adversary's further advance; the want of a few thousand
pounds of bread and meat had virtually terminated the war.

An anxious and haggard expression came to General Lee's face
when he was informed of this great misfortune; and, at once abandoning his design of cutting his way through to North Carolina, he
turned westward and shaped his march toward Lynchburg . . . on
the night of the 5th of April.

2

Honorable Francis Lawley, correspondent for the *London
Times,* who accompanied the Army of Northern Virginia on its
retreat from Petersburg, tells poignantly of the heartbreaking
hardships of this last forced march of the Army of Northern
Virginia.

The country through which we were passing was a tract of straggling woods and pine barrens with occasional little patches of

clearings. The foraging parties had to go so far afield in quest of food that they were taken prisoners by wholesale. In the face of such suffering as they left behind, it cannot be wondered at if some of the poor fellows courted capture.

Those foragers who returned to Lee brought little or nothing with them. The sufferings of the men from the pangs of hunger have not been approached in the military annals of the last fifty years. But the sufferings of the mules and horses must have been even keener; for the men assuaged their craving by plucking the buds and twigs of trees just shooting in the early spring, whereas the grass had not yet started from its winter sleep and food for the unhappy guadrupeds there was none. As early as the morning of the 4th, Lee sent off half his artillery toward the railroad to relieve the famished horses. This artillery making slow progress, thanks to the exhaustion of the horses, was captured by the Federals on the 8th, but not until General Lindsay Walker had buried many of his guns, which were of course subsequently exhumed (70 of them at one haul) by their captors.

It is easy to see that the locomotion of an army in such a plight must have been slow and slower. The retreat was conducted in the following fashion: About midnight the Confederates slipped out of their hasty works, which they had thrown up and held during the previous day, and fell back until ten or eleven o'clock the next morning. Then they halted, and immediately threw up earthworks for their protection during the day. It was not long before the wolves were again at their heels, and from their earthworks the Confederates exchanged a heavy fire with their pursuers throughout the day. Delayed by the necessity of guarding a train from thirty-five to forty miles in length, enfeebled by hunger and sleeplessness, the retreating army was able to make only ten miles each night. This delay enabled the active Sheridan to get ahead with his cavalry and destroy the depot of provisions along the railroad between Burkeville and Danville.

Upon the 5th, many of the mules and horses ceased to struggle. It became necessary to burn hundreds of wagons. At intervals the enemy's cavalry dashed in and struck the interminable train here or there, capturing and burning dozens upon dozens of wagons. Toward evening of the 5th, and all day long upon the 6th, hundreds of men dropped from exhaustion and thousands let fall their muskets from inability to carry them further.

The scenes of the 5th, 6th, 7th and 8th were of a nature which can be apprehended in its vivid reality only by men who are thoroughly familiar with the harrowing details of war. Behind and on either flank an ubiquitous and increasingly adventurous enemy —every mud-hole and every rise in the road choked with blazing wagons, the air filled with the deafening reports of ammunition exploding and shells bursting when touched by the flames, dense columns of smoke ascending to heaven from the burning and exploding vehicles—exhausted men, worn-out mules and horses lying down side by side—gaunt famine glaring hopelessly from sunken lack-lustre eyes—dead horses, dead mules, dead men everywhere— death many times welcomed as God's blessing in disguise—who can wonder if many hearts, tried in the fiery furnace of four years' unparalleled suffering and never hitherto found wanting, should have quailed in presence of starvation, fatigue, sleeplessness, misery, unintermitted for five or six days and culminating in hopelessness.

3

That retreat was an ordeal that tried men's souls—and women's souls, too, as Robert Stiles shows in his relation of an affecting and dramatic scene in which he played a part.

We halted at daylight at a country cross-road in Chesterfield to allow other bodies of troops to pass, the bulk of my men lying down and falling asleep in a grove; but seeing others about a well in the yard of a farm house over the way, I deemed it best to go there and see that nothing was unnecessarily disturbed.

Sitting on the porch were an old couple . . . and a young woman dressed in black, apparently their daughter, and, as I soon learned, a soldier's widow. My coat was badly torn and the young woman kindly offering to mend it, I thanked her and, taking it off, handed it to her. While we were chatting . . . the door of the house opened and another young woman appeared. She was almost beautiful, was plainly but neatly dressed. . . . She had evidently been weeping and her face was deadly pale. Turning to the old woman . . .

she said . . . "Mother, tell him if he passes here he is no husband of mine," and turned again to leave the porch. I rose, and placing myself directly in front of her, extended my arm to prevent her escape. She drew back with surprise and indignation.

"What do you mean, sir?" she cried.

"I mean, madam," I replied, "that you are sending your husband word to desert, and that I cannot permit you to do this in the presence of my men."

"Indeed! and who asked your permission, sir? And pray, sir, is he your husband or mine?"

"He is your husband, madam, but these are my soldiers. They and I belong to the same army with your husband, and I cannot suffer you, or anyone, unchallenged, to send such a demoralizing message in their hearing."

"Army! do you call this mob of retreating cowards an army? Soldiers! if you are soldiers, why don't you stand and fight the savage wolves that are coming upon us defenseless women and children?"

"We don't stand and fight, madam, because we are soldiers, and have to obey orders. . . ."

"Quite a fine speech, sir . . . but this thing is over and has been for some time. The Government has now actually run off, bag and baggage . . . and there is no longer any Government or any country for my husband to owe allegiance to. He does owe allegiance to me and to his starving children. . . ."

. The woman was quick as a flash and cold as steel. She was getting the better of me. She saw it, I felt it, and, worst of all, the men saw it and felt it too . . . and were evidently leaning strongly to the woman's side. This would never do.

I tried every avenue of approach to that woman's heart. It was congealed by suffering, or else it was encased in adamant. She had parried every thrust. . . . I was desperate, and with the nonchalance of pure desperation, I asked the soldier-question:

"What command does your husband belong to?"

She started a little, and there was a trace of color in her face as she replied with a tone of pride in her voice:

"He belongs to the Stonewall Brigade, sir. . . ."

"When did he join it?"

A little deeper flush, a little stronger emphasis of pride.

"He joined it in the spring of '61, sir. . . ."

Turning to the men, [I] said, "Men, if her husband joined the Stonewall Brigade in '61, and has been in the army ever since, I reckon he's a good soldier."

I turned to look at her. It was all over. Her wifehood had conquered. She . . . answered instantly, with head raised high, face flushing, eyes flashing:

"General Lee hasn't a better in his army!"

As she uttered these words she put her hand in her bosom, and drawing out a folded paper, extended it toward me, saying:

"If you doubt it, look at that. . . ."

It had been much thumbed and was much worn. It was hardly legible, but I made it out. Again I turned to the men.

"Take off your hats, boys, I want you to hear this with uncovered heads"—and then I read an endorsement on application for furlough, in which General Lee himself had signed a recommendation of this woman's husband for a furlough of special length on account of extraordinary gallantry in battle.

During the reading of this paper the woman was transfigured, glorified . . . sweetly radiant. Her bosom rose and fell with deep, quiet sighs; her eyes rained gentle, happy tears.

The men felt it all. . . . They were all gazing upon her. . . . I turned once more to the soldier's wife.

"This little paper is your most precious treasure, isn't it?"

"It is. . . ."

"And yet . . . you would disgrace this hero-husband of yours, stain all his noble reputation, and turn this priceless paper to bitterness; for the rear-guard would hunt him from his own cottage, in half an hour, a deserter and a coward."

Not a sound could be heard save her hurried breathing. The rest of us held even our breath.

Suddenly, with a gasp . . . she snatched the paper from my hand . . . and, turning once more to her mother, said:

"Mother, tell him not to come."

I stepped aside at once. She left the porch, glided down the path to the gate, crossed the road . . . climbed the hill . . . as she disappeared in the weedy pathway I caught up my hat and said:

"Now, men, give her three cheers."

Such cheers! Oh, God! shall I ever again hear a cheer which bears a man's whole soul in it?

4

Events of fateful import crowded rapidly into the next few days. Again we turn to John Esten Cooke for a view of Lee's fortitude in the face of impending disaster.

Under the pressure of circumstances so adverse that they seemed calculated to break down the most stubborn resolution, General Lee did not falter; and throughout the disheartening scenes of the retreat, from the moment when he left Amelia Court House to the hour when his little column was drawing near Appomattox, still continued to believe that the situation was not desperate and that he would be able to force his way through to Lynchburg.

On the evening of the 6th, when the army was near Farmville, a sudden attack was made by the Federal cavalry on the trains of the army moving on a parallel road, and the small force of infantry guarding them was broken and scattered. This occurrence took place while General Lee was confronting a body of Federal infantry near Sailor's Creek; and, taking a small brigade, he immediately repaired to the scene of danger. The spectacle which followed was a very striking and imposing one, and is thus described by one who witnessed it: "The scene was one of gloomy picturesqueness and tragic interest. On a plateau raised above the forest from which they had emerged, were the disorganized troops of Ewell and Anderson, gathered in groups, un-officered and uttering tumultuous exclamations of rage and defiance. Rising above the weary groups which had thrown themselves upon the ground were the grim barrels of cannon, in battery ready to fire as soon as the enemy appeared. In front of all was the still line of battle, just placed by Lee, and waiting calmly. General Lee had rushed his infantry over just at sunset, leading it in person, his face animated and his eye brilliant with the soldier's spirit of fight, but his bearing unflurried as before. An artist desiring to paint his picture ought to have seen the old cavalier at this moment, sweeping on upon his large iron-gray whose mane and tail floated in the wind, carrying his field-glass half-raised in his right hand, with head erect, gestures animated and in the whole face and form the expression of the hunter close upon his game. The line once interposed, he rode in the twilight among the disordered groups of men, and the sight of him aroused a tumult. Fierce cries resounded on all sides and, with hands clinched violently and raised aloft, the men called on him to lead them against the enemy. 'It's General Lee!' 'Uncle Robert!' 'Where's the man who won't follow Uncle Robert?' I heard on all sides—the swarthy faces full of dirt and courage, lit up every instant by the glare of the burning wagons. Altogether the scene was indescribable."

On the 7th the army pressed on beyond Farmville, still harassed as it advanced by the Federal infantry and cavalry; but in some of these encounters the pursuing force met with what was probably a very unexpected discomfiture. General Fitz Lee, bringing up the rear of the army with his force of about fifteen hundred cavalry on broken-down horses, succeeded not only in repulsing the attacks of the large and excellently mounted force under General Sheridan, but ... when General Gregg attacked with about six thousand horse, he was met, defeated and captured by General Fitz Lee, to the great satisfaction of General Lee, who said to his son, General W. H. F. Lee: "Keep your command together and in good spirits, general. Don't let them think of surrender. I will get you out of this."

On the 8th and 9th, however, this hope seemed unwarranted by the circumstances, and the commander-in-chief appeared to be almost the only human being who remained sanguine of the result. The hardships of the retreat, arising chiefly from want of food, began to seriously impair the resolution of the troops, and the scenes through which they advanced were not calculated to raise their spirits. .... It cannot, however, be said with truth that any considerable portion of the Southern forces were greatly demoralized, to use the military phrase, as the fighting of the last two days ... will show. The men were almost entirely without food, and were glad to find a little corn to eat; but those who were not physically unable longer to carry their muskets—and the number of these was large— still marched and fought with soldierly cheerfulness and resolution.

General Lee's spirits do not seem at any time to have flagged, and up to a late period of the retreat he had not seriously contemplated surrender. The necessity for this painful course came home to his corps commanders first and they requested General Pendleton, the efficient chief of artillery of the army, to inform General Lee that in their opinion further struggle was hopeless. General Pendleton informed General Lee of this opinion of his officers, and it seemed to communicate something like a shock to him.

"Surrender!" he exclaimed with a flash of the eye. "I have too many good fighting men for that!"

5

Upon General Grant's arrival at Farmville on April 7 he sent to General Lee his first official note suggesting the surrender of the Army of Northern Virginia. A bit of comic relief in the midst of the tragedy of defeat is provided by Captain H. H. Perry's account of his receipt of this note.

About five o'clock P.M., a flag of truce appeared in front of General Sorrell's brigade, of which I was the adjutant general. A courier was sent to division headquarters to announce it. Colonel Tayloe had been assigned temporarily to the command of General Sorrell's brigade, General Sorrell having been almost mortally wounded near Petersburg. In a short while General Tayloe was ordered to send a staff officer to answer the flag of truce.

I was assigned to this duty at the Confederate front lines. As the top of the earthworks was reached, a number of Federal sharpshooters fired at me and two balls passed through the uniform coat I wore and one ball wounded in the hand a Confederate soldier who had risen up with others from behind the works out of curiosity to see what was going to take place. That ended the truce business for that afternoon.

About nine o'clock at night, as soon as the moon was about to rise, Captain English (in charge of the line in front of our brigade) reported that a flag of truce was again offered on the Federal lines on our front. It was reported again at our division headquarters and I was again sent out to answer it as before. I put on an army revolver, put aside my sword, and advanced about fifty yards from our pickets, halted and called for the flag. There was a response to my call, and I advanced some distance and met a very handsomely dressed Federal officer. We stepped in front of each other, about seven or eight feet apart. I soon recognized the fact that my worn Confederate uniform and slouch hat, even in the dim light, would not compare favorably with his magnificence; but as I am six feet high I drew myself up as proudly as I could and put on the appearance as well as possible of being perfectly satisfied with my personal exterior. The officer spoke first, introducing himself as General Seth Williams of General Grant's staff. . . .

After I had introduced myself, he felt in his side pockets for documents, as I thought, but the "document" was a nice-looking silver flask, as well as I could distinguish. He remarked that he hoped I would not think it was an unsoldierly courtesy if he offered me some very fine brandy. I will own up now that I wanted that drink awfully. Worn down, hungry and dispirited, it would have been a gracious godsend if some old Confederate and I could have emptied that flask between us in that dreadful hour of misfortune. But I raised myself about an inch higher, if possible, bowed and refused politely, trying to produce the ridiculous appearance of having feasted on champagne and pound-cake not ten minutes before, and I had not the slightest use for as plebeian a drink as "fine brandy."

He was a true gentleman, begged pardon, and placed the flask in his pocket again without touching the contents in my presence. If he had taken a drink and my Confederate olfactories had obtained a whiff of the odor of it, it is possible that I should have "caved." The truth is, I had not eaten two ounces in two days, and I had my coat-tail then full of corn, waiting to parch it as soon as an opportunity might present itself. (I did not leave it behind me because I had nobody I could trust with it.) As an excuse which I felt I ought to make for refusing his proffered courtesy, I rather haughtily said that I had been sent forward only to receive any communication that was offered, and could not properly accept or offer any courtesies. In fact, if I had offered what I could, it would have taken my corn.

He then handed me a letter, which he said was from General

Grant to General Lee, and asked that General Lee should get it immediately if possible. I made no reply except to ask him if that was all we had to transact. He said that was all. We bowed very profoundly to each other and turned away.

In twenty minutes after I got back in our lines a Confederate courier riding a swift horse had placed in General Lee's hands the letter which was handed to me, the first demand for surrender of his devoted army.

6

The letter forwarded to General Lee by Captain Perry was the first in the historic series of notes exchanged by Grant and Lee, leading up to the final scene at Appomattox. In this letter, written by Grant at 5 P.M., April 7, addressed to "General R. E. Lee, Commanding C.S.A.," he said: "The results of the last week must convince you of the hopelessness of further resistance on the part of the Army of Northern Virginia in this struggle. I feel that it is so, and regard it as my duty to shift from myself the responsibility of any further effusion of blood by asking of you the surrender of that portion of the Confederate States army known as the Army of Northern Virginia."

Within an hour Lee replied: "General: I have received your note of this date. Though not entertaining the opinion you express of the hopelessness of further resistance on the part of the Army of Northern Virginia, I reciprocate your desire to avoid useless effusion of blood, and therefore, before considering your proposition, ask the terms you will offer on condition of its surrender."

On the morning of the 8th Grant wrote Lee: "Your note of last evening received. In reply would say that there is but one condition I would insist upon—namely, that the men and officers surrendered shall be disqualified for taking up arms against the Government of the United States until properly exchanged. I will meet you at any point agreeable to you, for the purpose of arranging definitely the terms upon which the surrender of the Army of Northern Virginia will be received."

This put the decision squarely up to Lee; but in making so

momentous a decision he wished the counsel of his generals. Accordingly he called them together for their last council of war.

There were present Generals Lee, Longstreet, Gordon and Fitz-hugh Lee. The commander-in-chief indicated to them their position and acquainted them with his correspondence with Grant. After a short conversation it was resolved that next morning the entire army should advance: if only the cavalry of Sheridan was before it, it should sweep it out of its way and pursue the march to Lynchburg; if, on the contrary, imposing masses of hostile infantry should be encountered beyond the Court House, what was impossible must not be attempted; a flag of truce should go forward to ask General Grant to concede an interview, in order to agree upon the conditions on which the Southern army should lay down its arms.

Much against his will, General Lee was compelled to approve these arrangements. Shortly afterward the generals separated, each divisionary saluting the commander-in-chief, who, on his side, returned their salutes with grave courtesy; then all went back to their posts.

At three in the morning Lee sent to ask Gordon, who commanded the vanguard, what probability there was of an attack succeeding. "Tell General Lee," replied Gordon, "that my old corps is reduced to a frazzle, and unless I am supported by Longstreet heavily I do not think we can do anything more." When this report was made to Lee, for the first time some words of discouragement escaped from his lips. After a moment's silence he said: "There is nothing left but to go to General Grant; and I would rather die a thousand deaths." His staff was around him. One of his officers made this observation: "What will history say of our surrendering, if there is any possibility of escape? Posterity will not understand it." "Yes, yes," replied Lee, "they will not understand our situation; but that is not the question. The question is, whether it is right; and if it is right, I take the responsibility."

An expression of quiet confidence, of serenity almost joyful, had appeared in his face instead of profound sadness. The thought of having to capitulate was to him bitterer than death. At the moment of quitting his tent, the acclamations of the soldiers were heard: "There is Uncle Robert!" Turning to one of his officers, he said to him, in a tone at once firm and sweet: "How easily I could get rid of all this and be at rest! I have only to ride along the lines and all will be over!" Then, after a moment's silence, he added with a deep sigh: "But it is our duty to live. What will become of the women and children of the South, if we are not here to protect them?"

At length the time had come when it would be decided whether retreat was still possible. To General Gordon, who had nobly distinguished himself in the later military operations, fell the command of the attacking column. The Confederate army consisted of only 8,000 men armed with rifles. Gordon's 2,000 men formed the van. The remains of various corps under Longstreet were in the rear. Between the two was placed all that was left of the army trains, together with several thousands of stragglers without arms, hardly able to drag themselves along, so much had cold and hunger played havoc with them. The cavalry, 2,000 sabres, mounted on gaunt, lean horses, were in no condition to render any service. Such was the army preparing to pierce the lines of Sheridan.

Marching beyond Appomattox Court House, Gordon briskly attacked the enemy, supported by Fitz Lee's cavalry and Colonel Carter's artillery. The dash of his soldiers was such that he drove all the Federal troops before him over a space of about a mile and a half. But then he found in his front a compact mass of infantry, estimated, on the authority of the Federal officers themselves, at 80,000 men. Having behind him only 5,000 bayonets, there was no possibility of advancing. Already the Federal mass was moving to rush on him, when the arrival of a flag of truce spared a carnage rendered useless. General Lee, appreciating the absolutely desperate condition in which he was, had despatched this flag of truce to Grant, asking him to treat.

7

How one of Lee's officers received his first intimation of the impending surrender is told by Colonel Owen of the Washington Artillery.

April 9—At 9 o'clock this morning the battalion was moved out into the road to resume the march. Just as we emerged, Gen. Lee was riding by, going towards the rear, accompanied by Cols. Marshall and Taylor of his staff. As I saluted him he reined up his horse and said, "Good-morning, Colonel! How are your horses this morning? Do you think you can keep up with the infantry today?" I replied I thought I could, that they had had a pretty good feed of shucks and appeared to be in tolerable condition. "But, General," I added, "I have no orders." He replied, "You will find Gen. Longstreet on the hill yonder; he will give you orders." And, touching his hat in acknowledgment of my salute, he continued his ride. I noted particularly his dress. He was in full uniform, with a handsome embroidered belt and dress sword, tall hat and buff gauntlets. His horse, "Old Traveller," was finely groomed, and his equipment, bridle, bit, etc., were polished until they shone like silver. All this seemed peculiar. I had never seen him before in full rig, and began to think something strange was to happen. He always wore during the campaigns a gray sack coat with side pockets, quite like the costume of a business man in cities; and after the Second Manassas I had never seen him carry a sword. . . . I moved the battalion forward towards the hill, where I was to find Gen. Longstreet. . . .

I espied Generals Longstreet and Alexander, chief of artillery, sitting on a log. Alexander got up and came towards me. I said to him, "General Lee instructed me to stop here for orders. What do you want me to do?" He replied, "Turn into that field on the right and park your guns." Then he added, in a low tone, "We are going to surrender to-day!" We had been thinking it might come to that, sooner or later; but when the shock came it was terrible. . . . I could not keep back the tears that came to my eyes.

8

It is fortunate that there is available an eyewitness account of the surrender by one of the participants, Colonel Marshall of Lee's staff, who accompanied his chief on this last sad errand. Marshall tells of how he and Lee, resting under a roadside apple tree, awaited the receipt of a reply to Lee's last note to

Grant. At length Colonel Babcock of Grant's staff was seen approaching with the fateful message.

General Lee got up and talked with Babcock a little while, and at last he called me and told me to get ready to go with him. I was in a very dilapidated state and I had to make some preparation before I could go. My friend, Colonel Henry Young, of Charleston, who was Judge Advocate General of the army, had a dress sword which he let me have. I had a very shabby sword that General Stuart had given me. . . . I didn't care to wear that plain thing, so I borrowed Young's sword, which was very handsome. He also had a pair of gauntlets, a thing I didn't possess, and I put them on. He also lent me a clean shirt collar. . . . Then I mounted my horse and we started off—General Lee, Colonel Babcock, Colonel Babcock's orderly, one of our orderlies and myself.

We struck up the hill towards Appomattox Court House. There was a man named McLean who used to live on the first battle field of Manassas, at a house about a mile from Manassas Junction. He didn't like the war, and having seen the first battle of Manassas, he thought he would get away where there wouldn't be any more fighting, so he moved down to Appomattox Court House. General Lee told me to go forward and find a house where he could meet General Grant, and of all people, whom should I meet but McLean. I rode up to him and said, "Can you show me a house where General Lee and General Grant can meet together?" He took me into a house that was all dilapidated and that had no furniture in it. I told him it wouldn't do. Then he said, "Maybe my house will do!" He lived in a very comfortable house, and I told him I thought that would suit. I had taken the orderly along with me, and I sent him back to bring General Lee and Babcock, who were coming on behind. I went into the house and sat down, and after a while General Lee and Babcock came in. Colonel Babcock told his orderly that he was to meet General Grant, who was coming on the road, and turn him in when he came along. So General Lee, Babcock and myself sat down in McLean's parlour and talked in the most friendly and affable way.

In about half an hour we heard horses, and the first thing I knew General Grant walked into the room. There were with him General Sheridan, General Ord, Colonel Badeau, General Porter, Colonel Parker and quite a number of other officers whose names I do not recall.

General Lee was standing at the end of the room opposite the door when General Grant walked in. General Grant had on a sack coat, a loose fatigue coat, but he had no side arms. He looked as though he had had a pretty hard time. He had been riding and his clothes were somewhat dusty and a little soiled. He walked up to General Lee and Lee recognized him at once. He had known him in the Mexican war. General Grant greeted him in a most cordial manner, and talked about the weather and other things in a very friendly way. Then General Grant brought up his officers and introduced them to General Lee.

I remembered that General Lee asked for General Lawrence Williams, of the Army of the Potomac. That very morning General Williams had sent word by somebody to General Lee that Custis Lee, who had been captured at Sailor Creek and was reported killed, was not hurt; and General Lee asked General Grant where General Williams was, and if he could not send for him to come and see him. General Grant sent somebody out for General Williams, and when he came, General Lee thanked him for having sent him word about the safety of his son.

After a very free talk, General Lee said to General Grant: "General, I have come to meet you in accordance with my letter to you this morning, to treat about the surrender of my army, and I think the best way would be for you to put your terms in writing." General Grant said: "Yes; I believe it will." So a Colonel Parker, General Grant's Aide-de-Camp, brought a little table over from a corner of the room, and General Grant wrote the terms and conditions of surrender on what we call field note paper, that is, a paper that makes a copy at the same time as the note is written. After he had written it, he took it over to General Lee.

General Lee was sitting at the side of the room; he rose and went to meet General Grant to take that paper and read it over. When he came to the part in which only public property was to be surrendered, and the officers were to retain their side arms and personal baggage, General Lee said: "That will have a very happy effect."

General Lee then said to General Grant: "General, our cavalrymen furnish their own horses; they are not Government horses. Some of them may be, but of course you will find them out—any property that is public property, you will ascertain that, but it is nearly all private property, and these men will want to plough ground and plant corn."

General Grant answered that as the terms were written, only the officers were permitted to take their private property, but almost immediately he added that he supposed that most of the men in the ranks were small farmers, and that the United States did not want their horses. He would give orders to allow every man who claimed to own a horse or mule to take the animal home.

General Lee having again said that this would have an excellent effect, once more looked over the letter, and being satisfied with it, told me to write a reply. General Grant told Colonel Parker to copy his letter, which was written in pencil, and put it in ink. Colonel Parker took the table and carried it back to a corner of the room, leaving General Grant and General Lee facing each other and talking together. There was no ink in McLean's inkstand, except some thick stuff that was very much like pitch, but I had a screw boxwood inkstand that I always carried with me in a little satchel that I had at my side, and I gave that to Colonel Parker, and he copied General Grant's letter with the aid of my inkstand and my pen.

There was another table right against the wall, and a sofa next to it. I was sitting on the arm of the sofa near the table, and General Sheridan was on the sofa next to me. While Colonel Parker was copying the letter, General Sheridan said to me, "This is very pretty country."

I said, "General, I haven't seen it by daylight. All my observations have been made by night and I haven't seen the country at all myself."

He laughed at my remark, and while we were talking I heard General Grant say this: "Sheridan, how many rations have you?" General Sheridan said: "How many do you want?" and General Grant said, "General Lee has about a thousand or fifteen hundred of our people prisoners, and they are faring the same as his men, but he tells me his haven't anything. Can you send them some rations?"

"Yes," he answered. They had gotten some of our rations, having captured a train.

General Grant said: "How many can you send?" and he replied, "Twenty-five thousand rations."

General Grant asked if that would be enough, and General Lee replied "Plenty; plenty; an abundance"; and General Grant said to Sheridan "Order your commissary to send to the Confederate Commissary twenty-five thousand rations for our men and his men."

After a while Colonel Parker got through with his copy of General Grant's letter and I sat down to write a reply. I began it in the usual way: "I have the honor to acknowledge the receipt of your letter of such a date," and then went on to say the terms were satisfactory. I took the letter over to General Lee, and he read it and said: "Don't say, 'I have the honor to acknowledge the receipt of your letter of such a date'; he is here; just say, 'I accept these terms.'" Then I wrote:

HEADQUARTERS OF THE ARMY OF NORTHERN VIRGINIA
April 9, 1865

I received your letter of this date containing the terms of the surrender of the Army of Northern Virginia proposed by you. As they are substantially the same as those expressed in your letter of the 8th instant, they are accepted. I will proceed to designate the proper officers to carry the stipulations into effect.

Then General Grant signed his letter, and I turned over my letter to General Lee and he signed it. Parker handed me General Grant's letter, and I handed him General Lee's reply, and the surrender was accomplished. There was no theatrical display about it. It was in itself perhaps the greatest tragedy that ever occurred in the history of the world, but it was the simplest, plainest and most thoroughly devoid of any attempt at effect, that you can imagine.

The story of General Grant returning General Lee's sword to him is absurd, because General Grant proposed in his letter that the officers of the Confederate Army should retain their side-arms. Why, in the name of common sense, anybody should imagine that General Lee, after receiving a letter which said that he should retain his side-arms, yet should offer to surrender his sword to General Grant, is hard to understand. The only thing of the kind that occurred in the whole course of the transaction—which occupied perhaps an hour—was this: General Lee was in full uniform. He had on the handsomest uniform I ever saw him wear; and he had on a sword with a gold, a very handsome gold and leather, scabbard that had been presented to him by English ladies. General Grant excused himself to General Lee towards the close of the conversation between them for not having his side arms with him; he told him that when he got his letter he was about four miles from his wagon in which his arms and uniform were, and he said that he had thought that General Lee would rather receive him as he was, than be detained while he sent back to get his sword and uniform. General Lee told him he was very much obliged to him and was very glad indeed that he hadn't done it.*

9

An account of the surrender proceedings, reflecting the Federal officers' respect for General Lee and their consideration of his feelings, is given by one of Grant's staff, General Horace Porter.

While the letters were being copied, General Grant introduced the general officers who had entered, and each member of the staff, to General Lee. The General shook hands with General Seth Williams, who had been his adjutant when Lee was superintendent at

---

* This little conversation is of peculiar interest because Lee first met Grant when he was a captain on General Scott's staff in the Mexican War, and Grant was a lieutenant of infantry. General Scott had issued an order that officers coming to headquarters were to do so in full dress. Grant had been making a reconnaissance and came to headquarters to report the result in his field dress, plentifully covered with the dust of Mexico, evidently thinking in 1847, as he did in 1865, that time was of more importance than appearance. Lee had to tell Grant to go back to his tent and return in full dress. One wonders whether, when apologizing to Lee a second time for his informal costume, Grant remembered what had happened eighteen years before.

West Point some years before the war, and gave his hand to some of the other officers who had extended theirs, but to most of those who were introduced he merely bowed in a dignified and formal manner. . . . Lee did not utter a word while the introductions were going on, except to Seth Williams, with whom he talked quite cordially. Williams at one time referred in rather jocose manner to a circumstance which occurred during their former service together, as if he wanted to say something in a good-natured way to break up the frigidity of the conversation, but Lee was in no mood for pleasantries, and he did not unbend or even relax the fixed sternness of his features. His only response to the allusion was a slight inclination of the head. . . .

After a little general conversation had been indulged in by those present, the two letters were signed and delivered and the parties prepared to separate. . . . At a little before 4 o'clock General Lee shook hands with General Grant, bowed to the other officers . . . and passed out to the porch. Lee signaled to his orderly to bring up his horse, and while the animal was being bridled the general stood on the lowest step and gazed sadly in the direction of the valley beyond where his army lay—now an army of prisoners. He smote his hands together a number of times in an absent sort of a way; seemed not to see the group of Union officers in the yard who rose respectfully at his approach, and appeared unconscious of everything about him. All appreciated the sadness that overwhelmed him, and he had the personal sympathy of every one who beheld him at this supreme moment of trial.

The approach of his horse seemed to recall him from his reverie, and he at once mounted. General Grant now stepped down from the porch and, moving toward him, saluted him by raising his hat. He was followed in this act of courtesy by all our officers present. Lee raised his hat respectfully, and rode off to break the sad news to the brave fellows whom he had so long commanded.

10

To Lee the saddest act in the tragedy of Appomattox was yet to come. Colonel Owen tells, simply but effectively, of Lee's affecting reception when he rode back into his own lines.

This terminated the interview [with Grant], and General Lee mounted his horse and rode back to his quarters, which were three-quarters of a mile north-east of the Court-House.

As soon as he was seen riding towards his army, whole lines of men rushed down to the roadside, and crowded around him to shake his hand; all tried to show him the veneration and esteem in which they held him. Filled with emotion he essayed to speak, but could only say, "Men, we have fought through the war together. I have done the best I could for you. My heart is too full to say more."

We all knew the pathos of those simple words, of that slight tremble in his voice, and it was no shame on our manhood that "something upon the soldier's cheek washed off the stains of powder," that our tears answered to those in the eyes of our grand old chieftain, and that we could only grasp the hand of "Uncle Robert," and pray, *"God help you, General!"*

As he rode on to his tent, and disappeared from our view, "the Army of Northern Virginia" passed away, leaving upon the page of history a record of valor and devotion never excelled; "its battle-flags were furled forever, never lowered in defeat, but in accordance with the orders of its beloved commander, who was himself yielding obedience to the dictates of a pure and lofty sense of duty to his men."

11

One of the most famous documents of the war was General Lee's "General Order No. 9," his celebrated farewell address to his troops. Colonel Marshall, who drafted this document, tells of the circumstances surrounding its preparation.

On the night of April 9th after our return from McLean's house General Lee sat with several of us at a fire in front of his tent, and after some conversation about the army and the events of the day in which his feelings towards his men were strongly expressed, he told me to prepare an order to the troops.

The next day it was raining and many persons were coming and going, so that I was unable to write without interruption until about 10 o'clock, when General Lee finding that the order had not been prepared, directed me to get into his ambulance, which stood near his tent, and placed an orderly to prevent anyone from approaching us. I made a draft in pencil and took it to General Lee who struck out a paragraph, which he said would tend to keep alive the feeling existing between the North and the South, and made one or two other changes. I then returned to the ambulance, recopied the order and gave it to a clerk in the office of the Adjutant General to write in ink.

After the first draft of the order had been made and signed by General Lee, other copies were made for transmission to the corps commanders and the staff of the army. All these copies were signed by the General and a good many persons sent other copies which they had made or procured and obtained his signature. In this way many of the orders had the General's name signed as if they were originals.

The full text of the order follows:

General Order No. 9

Headquarters Army of Northern Virginia, 10th April 1865

After four years of arduous service marked by unsurpassed courage and fortitude the Army of Northern Virginia has been compelled to yield to overwhelming numbers and resources.

I need not tell the survivors of so many hard fought battles, who have remained steadfast to the last, that I have consented to this result from no distrust of them. But feeling that valor and devotion could accomplish nothing that could compensate for the loss that would have accompanied the continuance of the contest, I determined to avoid the useless sacrifice of those whose past services have endeared them to their country.

By the terms of the agreement Officers and men can return to their homes and remain there until exchanged. You will take with you the satisfaction that proceeds from the consciousness of duty faithfully performed and I earnestly pray that a merciful God will extend to you his blessing and protection.

With an unceasing admiration of your constancy and devotion to your country and a grateful remembrance of your kind and generous consideration of myself, I bid you all an affectionate farewell.

R. E. Lee
General

12

There is no better account of the last dying days of the Army or Northern Virginia than that written by Robert E. Lee himself in his final report addressed to "His Excellency, Jefferson Davis" from Appomattox Court House on April 12.

Mr. President: It is with pain that I announce to your excellency the surrender of the Army of Northern Virginia.

The operations which preceded this result will be reported in full. I will therefore only now state that, upon arriving at Amelia Court-House on the morning of the 4th with the advance of the army on the retreat from the lines in front of Richmond and Petersburg and not finding the supplies ordered to be placed there, nearly twenty-four hours were lost in endeavoring to collect in the country subsistence for men and horses. This delay was fatal, and could not be retrieved.

The troops, wearied by continued fighting and marching for several days and nights, obtained neither rest nor refreshment, and on moving on the 5th on the Richmond and Danville Railroad I found at Jetersville the enemy's cavalry, and learned the approach of his infantry and the general advance of his army toward Burkeville. This deprived us of the use of the railroad, and rendered it impracticable to procure from Danville the supplies ordered to meet us at points of our march. Nothing could be obtained from the adjacent country. Our route to the Roanoke [river] was therefore changed and the march directed upon Farmville, where supplies were ordered from Lynchburg. The change of route threw the troops over the roads pursued by the artillery and wagon-trains west of the railroad, which impeded our advance and embarrassed our movements.

On the morning of the 6th General Longstreet's corps reached

Rice's Station on the Lynchburg Railroad. It was followed by the commands of Generals R. H. Anderson, Ewell and Gordon, with orders to close upon it as fast as the progress of the trains would permit, or as they could be directed, on roads farther west. General Anderson, commanding Pickett's and B. R. Johnson's divisions, became disconnected with Mahone's division forming the rear of Longstreet. The enemy's cavalry penetrated the line of march through the interval thus left and attacked the wagon train moving toward Farmville. This caused serious delay in the march of the centre and rear of the column, and enabled the enemy to mass upon their flank. After successive attacks, Anderson's and Ewell's corps were captured or driven from their position. The latter general, with both of his division commanders, Kershaw and Custis Lee, and his brigadiers, were taken prisoners. Gordon, who all the morning, aided by General W. H. F. Lee's cavalry, had checked the advance of the enemy on the road from Amelia Springs and protected the trains, became exposed to his combined assaults, which he bravely resisted and twice repulsed; but, the cavalry having been withdrawn to another part of the line of march, and the enemy massing heavily on his front and both flanks, he renewed the attack about 6 P.M. and drove him from the field in much confusion.

The army continued its march during the night, and every effort was made to reorganize the divisions which had been shattered by the day's operations; but, the men being depressed by fatigue and hunger, many threw away their arms, while others followed the wagon-trains and embarrassed their progress. On the morning of the 7th rations were issued to the troops as they passed Farmville but, the safety of the trains requiring their removal upon the approach of the enemy, all could not be supplied. The army, reduced to two corps under Longstreet and Gordon, moved steadily on the road to Appomattox Court-house, thence its march was ordered by Campbell Court-house through Pittsylvania toward Danville. The roads were wretched and the progress slow. By great efforts the head of the column reached Appomattox Court-house on the evening of the 8th, and the troops were halted for rest.

The march was ordered to be resumed at 1 A.M. on the 9th. Fitz Lee with the cavalry, supported by Gordon, was ordered to drive the enemy from his front, wheel to the left and cover the passage of the trains, while Longstreet, who from Rice's Station had formed the rear-guard, should close up and hold the position. Two battalions of artillery and the ammunition wagons were directed to accompany the army, the rest of the artillery and wagons to move toward Lynchburg. In the early part of the night the enemy attacked Walker's artillery train near Appomattox Station on the Lynchburg Railroad and were repelled. Shortly afterward their cavalry dashed toward the Court-house, till halted by our line.

During the night there were indications of a large force massing on our left and front. Fitz Lee was directed to ascertain its strength and to suspend his advance till daylight if necessary. About 5 A.M. on the 9th, with Gordon on his left, he moved forward and opened the way. A heavy force of the enemy was discovered opposite Gordon's right which, moving in the direction of Appomattox Court-house, drove back the left of the cavalry and threatened to cut off Gordon from Longstreet, his cavalry at the same time threatening to envelop his left flank. Gordon withdrew across the Appomattox River, and the cavalry advanced on the Lynchburg road and became separated from the army.

Learning the condition of affairs on the lines where I had gone under expectation of meeting General Grant, to learn definitely the terms he proposed in a communication received from him on the 8th in the event of the surrender of the army, I requested a suspension of hostilities until these terms could be arranged. In the interview which occurred with General Grant in compliance with my request, terms having been agreed on, I surrendered the Army of Northern Virginia which was on the field, with its arms, artillery and wagon trains, the officers and men to be paroled, retaining their side-arms and private effects. I deemed this course the best under all the circumstances by which we were surrounded.

On the morning of the 9th, according to the reports of the ordnance officers, there were 7,892 organized infantry with arms, with an average of 75 rounds of ammunition per man. The artillery, though reduced to 63 pieces with 93 rounds of ammunition, was sufficient. These comprised all the supplies of ordnance that could be relied on in the state of Virginia. I have no accurate report of the cavalry, but believe it did not exceed 2,100 effective men. The enemy was more than five times our numbers.

If we could have forced our way one day longer, it would have been at a great sacrifice of life, and at its end I did not see how a surrender could have been avoided. We had no subsistence for man or horse and it could not be gathered in the country. The supplies ordered to Pamplin's Station from Lynchburg could not reach us and the men, deprived of food and sleep for many days, were worn out and exhausted.

13

A penetrating analysis of the far-reaching psychological effects of Lee's attitude at this critical time has been made by Charles Francis Adams.

. . . On Sunday, the 9th of April, Lee found his further progress blocked. That morning General Alexander again met Lee. Both realized the situation fully. Moreover, as chief of artillery, Alexander was well aware that the limber-chests were running low; his arm of the service was in no condition to go into another engagement. Yet the idea of an abandonment of the cause had never occurred to him as among the probabilities. All night he had lain awake, thinking as to what was next to be done. Finally he had come to the conclusion that there was but one course to pursue. The Confederate army, while nominally capitulating, must in reality disperse, and those composing it should be instructed, whether individually or as part of detachments, to get each man to his own State in the most direct way and shortest possible time, and report to the governor thereof, with a view to a further and continuous resistance.

. . . General Alexander told me that, as he passed his batteries on his way to headquarters, the men called out to him, in cheery tones, that there were still some rounds remaining in the caissons, and that they were ready to renew the fight. He found Lee seated on the trunk of a fallen tree before a dying camp-fire. He was dressed in uniform, and invited Alexander to take a seat beside him. He then asked his opinion of the situation, and of the proper course to be pursued.

Full of the idea which dominated his mind, Alexander proceeded at once to propound his plan, for it seemed to him the only plan worthy of consideration. As he went on, General Lee, looking steadily into the fire with an abstracted air, listened patiently. Alexander said his full say. A brief pause ensued, which Lee finally broke in somewhat these words: "No! General Alexander, that will not do. . . . We have fought this fight as long as, and as well as, we know how. We have been defeated. For us, as a Christian people, there is now but one course to pursue. We must accept the situation. These men must go home and plant a crop, and we must proceed to build up our country on a new basis. We cannot have recourse to the methods you suggest."

I remember being deeply impressed with Alexander's comment, as he repeated these words of Lee. They had evidently burned themselves into his memory. He said: "I had nothing to urge in reply. I felt that the man had soared way up above me; he dominated me completely. I rose from beside him, silently mounted my horse, rode back to my command and waited for the order to surrender."

Then and there Lee decided its course for the Confederacy. And I take it there is not one solitary man in the United States to-day, North or South, who does not feel that he decided right. . . . Lee's great military prestige and moral ascendency made it easy for some of the remaining Confederate commanders, like Johnston, to follow the precedent he set; while others of them, like Kirby Smith, found it imposed upon them. A firm direction had been given to the course of events; an intelligible policy was indicated. . . .

Recalling the circumstances of that time, it is fairly appalling to consider what in 1865 must have occurred had Robert E. Lee then been of the same turn of mind as was Jefferson Davis, or as implacable and unyielding in disposition as Krüger or Botha have more recently proved. The national government had in arms a million men, inured to the hardships and accustomed to the brutalities of war; Lincoln had been freshly assassinated; the temper of the North was thoroughly aroused, while its patience was exhausted. An irregular warfare would inevitably have resulted, a warfare without quarter. The Confederacy would have been reduced to a smouldering wilderness. . . . In such a death grapple the North, both in morale and in means, would have suffered only less than the South. From both sections that fate was averted. . . .

I doubt if one single man in the United States, North or South—whether he participated in the civil war or was born since that war ended—would fail to acknowledge an infinite debt of gratitude to the Confederate leader who on the 9th of April, 1865, decided, as he did decide, that the United States, whether Confederate or Union, was a Christian community, and that his duty was to accept the responsibility which the fate of war had imposed upon him—to decide in favor of a new national life, even if slowly and painfully to be built up by his own people under conditions arbitrarily and by force imposed on them.

18

Civilian and College President

WITH the surrender of the Army of Northern Virginia the war was over. Everybody knew it—but some were slow to admit it. Jefferson Davis, fleeing with his Cabinet, continued to keep alive the shadow of a Confederate civil government, issuing pronouncements proclaiming continued resistance and predicting the eventual success of the Southern cause. Joe Johnston had the remnants of an army in the field in North Carolina, but within a few days it surrendered to Sherman; and shortly thereafter Kirby Smith in the Trans-Mississippi Department also gave up the ghost. The Confederate States of America was now a thing of the past.

With a heavy heart, Robert E. Lee returned from Appomattox to Richmond—a paroled prisoner of war. He was now a civilian, after a lifetime spent as a soldier, a civilian without means of livelihood, without so much as a home to call his own. The future stretched bleakly before him. A weaker man would have found it easy to spend his remaining days in bitter repining. But weakness and bitterness were not among his characteristics. History abundantly provides examples of men who have achieved greatness through success; seldom has there been such a shining example of greatness attained in the face of disastrous defeat and failure.

The years after the war provide the crowning glory of Robert E. Lee's life. From him there was no complaint, no whining, no apology, no explanation, no sulking, no resentment. He had pursued the course directed by duty; he had failed; he was now ready to pick up the scattered threads of his life and adjust himself to the changed conditions, being of as much service as possible to his country and his people.

He repeatedly advised those who sought his counsel to submit to all authority and become patriotic, law-abiding citizens of the United States. The questions which had been in dispute, he told them, having been referred to the decision of war and "having been decided against us, it is the part of candor to recognize the fact and the part of wisdom to acquiesce in the result." He sternly rebuked a Virginia woman who was speaking bitterly of the North, telling her that she should bury her old animosities and train her sons "to be loyal Americans."

But, although he did with a fine sense of sportsmanship acquiesce in the result of the war, Lee never receded from the conviction that he was right in 1861 when he cast his lot with Virginia and the South. "I could have taken no other course save with dishonor," he later said, "and if it were to be all gone over again, I would act in precisely the same way." Again he said: "I fought against the people of the North because I believed that they were seeking to wrest from the South dearest rights, but I have never cherished towards them bitter or vindictive feelings, and have never seen the day that I did not pray for them."

Robert E. Lee, the soldier, was great; Robert E. Lee, the good citizen and good loser, was greater.

1

His army surrendered, paroled and dispersed, Lee's military responsibilities were at an end and he could now return home—or, at least, he could return to Richmond where his wife and daughters were now living. Like many another Confederate soldier, he had no home now.

Dr. Freeman provides a moving account of the defeated commander's return to Richmond from Appomattox.

Quietly and unceremoniously he left his last headquarters on the 12th and started home. With him rode Taylor, Marshall and Cooke, the last-named sick and in an ambulance lent by the Federals. They took with them their headquarters wagon and Gen-

eral Lee's old ambulance, which Britt drove. Colonel Venable
started with them but parted company very soon, as his route to
reach his family in Prince Edward County was different from
theirs. . . .

The worst of the strain was over now. Rest had begun to restore
the nerves of the men, who had scarcely relaxed from the time they
left Petersburg until they surrendered. They already had exhausted the fighting and its outcome as a theme of conversation,
and as they went homeward through the budding trees, away from
the sounds of rumbling wagon trains and marching columns, they
talked freely and of many things, but little of the war. When Lee
did speak of the struggle and its outcome, his thought, as always,
was of those around him rather than of himself. He urged the
young officers to go home, to take whatever work they could find,
and to accept the conditions necessary for their participation in the
government.

The road they were following led northeastward from Appomattox to Buckingham Courthouse and thence eastward to Cumberland Courthouse, where it struck the old stage road from Lynchburg to Richmond by way of Farmville. As evening drew on, General Lee passed through Buckingham Courthouse, where he was
identified and greeted. Two miles beyond the village he came, according to Lawley, to the bivouac of Longstreet, and there he decided to make his camp, in woods owned by Mrs. Martha Shep-
herd. . . .

In some way the news of Lee's coming spread ahead of him.
Women hastened to cook provisions and brought them out to the
road, where they waited for him. "These good people are kind, too
kind," he is reported to have said. "Their hearts are as full as
when we began our first campaigns in 1861. They do too much—
more than they are able to do—for us." His only concern over food
was about some oats he had procured for Traveller, and was afraid
some one else might take. As the day wore on, Traveller cast a
shoe and became lame. Lee soon stopped at Flanagan's Mill, Cumberland County, where he spent the night under the friendly roof
of Madison Flanagan. The mount was shod that night and was
ready for the road the next morning.

On the 14th Major Cooke, who was still sick, bade his chief farewell and turned off the road. Accompanied now only by Taylor and Marshall and the drivers, Lee continued on his way. Ere long he overtook one of his youthful veterans, limping barefooted along the same road. The boy had obtained a mule at Appomattox, along with his parole, but had lost the animal when it had bolted from him. "My boy," said Lee, "you are too badly off for the long journey ahead of you; you have no shoes. I am going to spend the night at the home of my brother, Charles Carter Lee, who lives a few miles ahead at Fine Creek Mills. I will find you a pair of shoes and you must stop there to get them."

At evening Lee reached his brother's farm in Powhatan County. He was made welcome, of course, but as the house was crowded he insisted on using his own tent. He was then invited to "spend the night," in familiar Virginia phrase, at the residence of John Gilliam, whose farm adjoined that of C. C. Lee. He asked, instead, that the available room be given a sick officer and his wife, who had driven up. Learning from his brother's family that the Gilliams were disappointed at his refusal and were very anxious that he at least eat a meal at their table, he sent word that if it were agreeable he would take breakfast with them. Then, having procured a pair of shoes for the soldier, to whom he had promised them, he went into camp, immediately in front of the Gilliam home. It was his final bivouac, the last night he ever slept under canvas.

The next morning he ate with the Gilliam family. It probably was at this time, and in answer to a question from Mr. Gilliam, that he said many people would wonder why he did not make his escape before the surrender, when that course was practicable. The reason, he explained, was that he was unwilling to separate his fate from that of the men who had fought under him so long. He was unrestrained in his conversation and made much of a little girl about ten, the daughter of the Gilliams, who was presented to him. He took her on his knee and caressed her. "Polly," he said, "come with me to Richmond and I will give you a beau."

The company was swelled that morning by the arrival of Rooney Lee and the General's nephew, John Lee. Riders and vehicles soon got under way—there were twenty horses altogether—and went down the River road, through Powhatan and Chesterfield Counties. As they neared the capital of the dying Confederacy, in the midst of a gloomy spring downpour, General Lee and two of his officers went ahead of the wagons and of the ambulances. Ere long they reached Manchester, which was then a separate municipality on the south bank of James River, opposite Richmond. While the rain was at its heaviest he passed in the town the home of a Baptist minister who chanced to see the General, and later wrote of the scene in these moving words: "His steed was bespattered with mud, and his head hung down as if worn by long travelling. The horseman himself sat his horse like a master; his face was ridged with self-respecting grief; his garments were worn in the service and stained with travel; his hat was slouched and spattered with mud and only another unknown horseman rode with him, as if for company and for love. Even in the fleeting moment of his passing by my gate, I was awed by his incomparable dignity. His majestic composure, his rectitude and his sorrow were so wrought and blended into his visage and so beautiful and impressive to my eyes that I fell into violent weeping. To me there was only one where this one was. . . ."

The streets through which General Lee rode in Manchester cut off his view of Richmond until he was close to the James River, which he had made renowned in military history. Then he could see how deep and how hideous were the scars on the face of the city. Both bridges were gone: a line of Federal pontoons afforded the only crossing. Nearly the whole waterfront had been consumed in the fire of April 2-3 that had followed the evacuation. Arsenal, factories, flouring mills, tobacco warehouses, stores, dwellings—all were destroyed. . . .

General Lee probably was forced to wait a while at the pontoon bridge, for his wagons and companions overtook him and followed him across the river and up the streets of Richmond. If there was a halt, General Lee did not prolong it an unnecessary minute, for he was anxious to avoid a demonstration of any sort. Rumor had spread on the 12th that he had arrived, but it had been ascertained then that the General Lee who had come to town was Custis, who had been carried as a prisoner of war from Sayler's Creek to City Point and had been allowed to visit his mother. Still, it had been the supposition of all loyal Confederates that Lee would return directly from Appomattox to his family in Richmond. A certain informal lookout for him had been kept. Now word spread quickly that he was riding uptown. As many as could reach Main Street before he passed, hurriedly turned out to see him.

What met their gaze was not a pageant to stir martial ardor. He had put aside his best uniform and had on one that had seen long service, but he still wore a sword, though apparently not the handsome weapon he had carried at Appomattox. His mount was Traveller. With him now rode five others, Taylor, Marshall and Rooney Lee among them. These officers also carried their side arms, but all their horses were gaunt and jaded. Behind them rattled the General's old ambulance and the wagons the Federals had permitted the officers to bring away from Appomattox for the transportation of their personal effects. In these vehicles, along with the possessions of the others, were General Lee's camp equipment and those of the headquarters records that had escaped destruction on the road to Appomattox. No attempt was made to dress up the vehicles for a formal showing. One of them, lacking a canvas, was covered with an old quilt. But those who looked at the sad little procession understood and choked and wept. Along a ride of less than a mile, from the pontoons to the residence at 707 East Franklin Street, the crowd grew thicker with each block. Cheers broke out, in which the Federals joined heartily. Hats went off, and uniform caps of blue along with them. General Lee acknowledged the greetings by uncovering repeatedly, but he was manifestly anxious to finish his journey as quickly as he could.

Arriving in front of the house, he turned his horse over to one of the men attending the wagons. The heart-broken civilians of Richmond, widows, old men, maidens, thronged him as the soldiers had at Appomattox. They wanted to speak to him and to shake his hand, and if that was impossible, at the least to touch his uniform. He grasped as many outstretched palms as he could. In a moment, with his emotions strained almost to tears, he made his way to the iron gate, and up the granite steps. Bowing again to the crowd, he entered the house and closed the door. The cheers of the crowd died out, and it began to scatter. His marching over and his battles done, Robert E. Lee unbelted his sword forever.

2

Robert E. Lee, Jr., was a member of the post-war household
at the Lee home on Franklin Street, and he tells of his father's
life there during the time immediately following his return.

As well as I can recall my father at this time, he appeared to be
very well physically, though he looked older, grayer, more quiet
and reserved. He seemed very tired, and was always glad to talk of
any other subject than that of the war or anything pertaining
thereto. We all tried to cheer and help him. And the people of
Richmond and of the entire South were as kind and considerate
as it was possible to be. Indeed, I think their great kindness tired
him. He appreciated it all, was courteous, grateful and polite, but
he had been under such a terrible strain for several years that he
needed the time and quiet to get back his strength of heart and
mind. All sorts and conditions of people came to see him: officers
and soldiers from both armies . . . ministers of the Gospel, mothers
and wives to ask about husbands and sons of whom they had heard
nothing. To keep him from being overtaxed by this incessant
stream of visitors, we formed a sort of guard of the young men in
the house, some of whom took it by turns to keep the door and, if
possible, turn strangers away. My father was gentle, kind and polite
to all, and never willingly, so far as I know, refused to see any one.

Dan Lee, late of the Confederate States Navy, my first cousin,
and myself one day had charge of the front door, when at it appeared a Federal soldier, accompanied by a darkey carrying a large
willow basket filled to the brim with provisions of every kind. The
man was Irish all over, and showed by his uniform and carriage that
he was a "regular" and not a volunteer. On our asking him what
he wanted, he replied that he wanted to see General Lee, that he
had heard down the street that General Lee and his family were
suffering for lack of something to eat, that he had been with "the
Colonel" when he commanded the Second Cavalry, and, as long as
he had a cent, his old colonel should not suffer. My father, who
had stepped into another room as he heard the bell ring, hearing
something of the conversation, came out into the hall. The old
Irishman, as soon as he saw him, drew himself up and saluted and

repeated to the General, with tears streaming down his cheeks, what he had just said to us. My father was very much touched, thanked him heartily for his kindness and generosity, but told him that he did not need the things he had brought and could not take them. This seemed to disappoint the old soldier greatly, and he pleaded so hard to be allowed to present the supplies to his old colonel, whom he believed to be in want of them, that at last my father said that he would accept the basket and send it to the hospital for the sick and wounded, who were really in great need. Though he was not satisfied, he submitted to this compromise, and then to our surprise and dismay, in bidding the General good-bye, threw his arms around him and was attempting to kiss him when Dan and I interfered. As he was leaving he said: "Good-bye, Colonel! God bless ye! If I could have got over in time I would have been with ye!"

A day or two after that, when Dan was doorkeeper, three Federal officers, a colonel, a major and a doctor, called and asked to see General Lee. They were shown into the parlour, presented their cards, and said they desired to pay their respects as officers of the United States Army. When Dan went out with the three cards, he was told by some one that my father was upstairs engaged with some other visitor, so he returned and told them this and they departed. When my father came down, was shown the cards and told of the three visitors, he was quite put out at Dan's not having brought him the cards at the time, and that afternoon mounted him on one of his horses and sent him over to Manchester, where they were camped, to look up the three officers and to tell them he would be glad to see them at any time they might be pleased to call. However, Dan failed to find them.

He had another visit at this time which affected him deeply. Two Confederate soldiers in very dilapidated clothing, worn and emaciated in body, came to see him. They said they had been selected from about sixty other fellows, too ragged to come themselves, to offer him a home in the mountains of Virginia. The home was a good house and farm, and nearby was a defile in some rugged hills, from which they could defy the whole Federal Army. They made this offer of a home and their protection because there was a report that he was about to be indicted for treason. The

General had to decline to go with them, but the tears came into his eyes at this hearty exhibition of loyalty.

3

During that summer of 1865 in Richmond the air was electric with tension as the citizens of the erstwhile capital of the Confederacy strove to adjust themselves to the new living conditions imposed on them by the army of occupation. Lee overlooked no opportunity to set an example to his fellow citizens in accommodating themselves to the new situation. One of the communicants of St. Paul's Church tells of an incident with explosive potentialities at services there one June morning, which was resolved by Lee's tact.

It was communion day, and when Dr. Minnegerode was ready to administer the holy communion, a negro in the church arose and advanced to the communion table. He was tall, well-dressed and black. This was a great surprise and shock to the communicants, and others present. Its effect was startling upon the communicants, and for several moments they retained their seats in solemn silence and did not move, being deeply chagrined at this attempt to inaugurate the "new regime" to offend and humiliate them during their most devoted church services. Dr. Minnegerode was evidently embarrassed.

General Robert E. Lee was present and, ignoring the actions and presence of the negro, arose in his usual dignified and self-possessed manner, walked up the aisle to the chancel rail, and reverently knelt down to partake of the communion, and not far from the negro. This lofty conception of duty by General Lee under such provoking and irritating circumstances had a magic effect upon the other communicants, including myself, who went forward to the communion table.

4

A feature of General Lee's great service to the South after the war, the importance of which has not always been properly appreciated, was the influence he exerted by his example of patient and patriotic adjustment to the outcome of the war. Many of the soldiers and citizens of the Southern Confederacy had become so devoted to the cause that it was exceedingly difficult for them to adjust themselves to defeat. Some of them, in their bitterness, openly declared an unwillingness to resume an allegiance which they had terminated in 1861, and there was a strong tendency to encourage the emigration of unreconstructed Southerners to Mexico and South America. Dr. Jones points out the good effects of the example Lee set by his quiet submission and his effort to help the Southern people to the best of his ability by staying with them and working with them.

The conduct of Lee's soldiers after the end of the war has excited the attention and elicited the admiration of the world. There was much in the state of things just after the surrender to excite the serious apprehension of thinking people that these disbanded soldiers would render the condition of the South far worse by entering upon a career of lawlessness. After long exposure to the demoralizing influence of the camp and a long cessation from any industrial pursuit, these young men returned to find their fondly cherished hopes blighted, their fortunes ruined, their fields laid waste and, in not a few instances, blackened ruins marking the spot of their once-happy homes. It would not have been surprising if they had yielded to despair and had sought redress by taking the law into their own hands.

I claim to have thoroughly known the veterans of Lee's army and to have had some peculiar opportunities of seeing them after the close of the war. In traveling very extensively through the South I made it a point always to inquire after them, and the invariable response was: "They have gone to work and are quiet, orderly members of society." Many of them who had been raised in luxury and ease took off their coats and went into the corn, tobacco and cotton fields of the South or entered upon other pursuits with a zeal and earnestness truly marvelous to those who did not know the stuff of which these heroic men were made. They accepted the situation and, amid provocations and insults not a few, have proved themselves loyal to their every pledge—law-abiding citizens of whom any community might be proud.

If asked the explanation of this, the simplest answer would be: "The soldiers have continued to follow their commander-in-chief." General Lee was most scrupulous in observing the terms of his parole. He refused to attend political gatherings, avoided discussing the war or its issues (except with intimate friends and in the freedom of private intercourse), and gave the young men of the South a striking example of quiet submission to the United States authorities.

He was accustomed to say: "I am now unfortunately so situated that I can do no good; and, as I am anxious to do as little harm as possible, I deem it wisest for me to remain silent." And yet, as has been intimated, the good order and law-abiding spirit of the soldiers and people of the South were due in no small measure to the quiet example and influence of this noble man.

In the uncertainty as to the future of the South just after the close of the war, many of our best men were seriously thinking of seeking homes in foreign lands. General Lee's influence more than anything else prevented this. . . .

The following letter to the great scientist [Matthew Fontaine Maury] whom the whole world honored, who was General Lee's intimate friend and in whose society in Lexington he seemed so much to delight, will be read with peculiar interest:

"Near Cartersville, Va., September 8, 1865

"My dear Captain: I have just received your letter of the 8th ult. We have certainly not found our form of government all that was anticipated by its original founders, but that may be partly our effect in expecting too much and partly in the absence of virtue in the people. As long as virtue was dominant in the republic so long was the happiness of the people secure. I can not, however, despair of it yet. I look forward to better days and trust that time and experience, the great teachers of men, under the guidance of an ever-merciful God, may save us from destruction and restore to us the bright hopes and prospects of the past.

"The thought of abandoning the country and all that must be

left in it is abhorrent to my feelings, and I prefer to struggle for its restoration and share its fate rather than to give up all as lost. I have a great admiration for Mexico. The salubrity of its climate, the fertility of its soil and the magnificence of its scenery possess for me great charms; but I still look with delight upon the mountains of my native state. To remove our people with their domestics to a portion of Mexico which would be favorable to them would be a work of much difficulty. Did they possess the means and could the system of apprenticeship you suggest be established, the United States Government I think would interpose obstacles; and under the circumstances there would be difficulty in persuading the freedmen to emigrate.

"Those citizens who can leave the country and others who may be compelled to do so will reap the fruits of your considerate labor; but I shall be very sorry if your presence be lost to Virginia. She has now need for all her sons and can ill afford to spare you. I am very much obliged to you for all you have done for us, and hope your labors in the future may be as efficacious as in the past and that your separation from us may not be permanent."

The following, to the gallant and distinguished soldier with whom General Lee always preserved the kindliest relations, will be appropriately introduced in this connection:

"Lexington, Va., October 3, 1865

"General G. T. Beauregard, New Orleans, La.

"My dear General: I have received your letter of the 1st ult. and am very sorry to learn that the papers of yourself and Johnston are lost, or at least beyond your reach, and I hope they may be recovered. Mine never can be, though some may be replaced. . . . I hope both you and Johnston will write the history of your campaigns. Every one should do all in his power to collect and disseminate the truth, in the hope that it may find a place in history and descend to posterity.

"I am glad to see no indication in your letter of an intention to leave the country. I think the South requires the aid of her sons now more than at any period of her history. As you ask my purpose, I will state that I have no thought of abandoning her unless compelled to do so.

"After the surrender of the Southern armies in April, the revolution in the opinions and feelings of the people seemed so complete and the return of the Southern States into the Union of all the states so inevitable, that it became in my opinion the duty of every citizen, the contest being virtually ended, to cease opposition and place himself in a position to serve the country. . . . I need not tell you that true patriotism sometimes requires of men to act exactly contrary at one period to that which it does at another, and the motive that impels them—the desire to do right—is precisely the same. The circumstances which govern their actions change and their conduct must conform to the new order of things. History is full of illustrations of this. Washington himself is an example: at one time he fought against the French, under Braddock in the service of the King of Great Britain; at another he fought with the French at Yorktown, under the orders of the Continental Congress of America, against the King. He has not been branded by the world with reproach for this, but his course has been applauded."

The following to one of his favorite officers [General J. A. Early, who had emigrated to Mexico] expresses his feelings very freely on various points of interest:

"Lexington, Va., March 15, 1866

"My dear General: I am very much obliged to you for the copies of my letters forwarded with yours of the 25th January. I hope you will be able to send me reports of the operations of your commands in the campaign from the Wilderness to Richmond, at Lynchburg, in the Valley, Maryland, etc. All statistics as regards numbers, destruction of private property by the Federal troops, etc., I should like to have, as I wish my memory strengthened on those points. It will be difficult to get the world to understand the odds against which we fought; and the destruction or loss of all returns of the army embarrasses me very much. . . .

"I have been much pained to see the attempts made to cast

odium upon Mr. Davis, but do not think they will be successful with the reflecting or reformed portion of the country. The accusations against myself I have not thought proper to notice, or even to correct misrepresentations of my words and acts. We shall have to be patient and suffer for a while at least; and all controversy, I think, will only serve to provoke angry and bitter feelings and postpone the period when reason and charity may resume their sway. At present the public mind is not prepared to receive the truth.

"The feelings which influenced you to leave the country were natural and I presume were uppermost in the breasts of many. It was a matter which each man had to decide for himself, as he could only know the reasons which governed him. I was particularly anxious on your account, as I had the same apprehensions to which you refer. I am truly glad that you are beyond the reach of annoyance, and hope you may be able to employ yourself profitably and usefully . . .

"I hope in time peace will be restored to the country and that the South may enjoy some measure of prosperity. I fear, however, much suffering is still in store for her and that her people must be prepared to exercise fortitude and forbearance."

5

A visit to some of his relatives in the country afforded General Lee a pleasant interlude of quiet relaxation in this painful period of adjustment, as told by his son.

My father was at this time anxious to secure for himself and family a house somewhere in the country. He had always had a desire to be the owner of a small farm, where he could end his days in peace and quiet. The life in Richmond was not suited to him. He wanted quiet and rest, but could not get it there, for people were too attentive to him. So in the first days of June he mounted old Traveller and, unattended, rode down to "Pampatike"—some twenty-five miles—to pay a visit of several days to his relations there. This is an old Carter property, belonging then and now to Colonel Thomas H. Carter, who, but lately returned from Appomattox Court House, was living there with his wife and children. [His] father was a first cousin of General Lee's. . . .

At the old-fashioned dinner hour of three o'clock my father, mounted on Traveller, unannounced, unexpected and alone, rode up to the door. The horse and rider were at once recognised by Colonel Carter, and he was gladly welcomed by his kinsfolk. I am sure the days passed here were the happiest he had spent for many years. He was very weary of town, of the incessant unrest incident to his position, of the crowds of persons of all sorts and conditions striving to see him; so one can imagine the joy of master and horse when, after a hot ride of over twenty-miles, they reached this quiet resting-place.

My father, Colonel Carter tells me, enjoyed every moment of his stay. There were three children in the house, the two youngest little girls of five and three years old. These were his special delight, and he followed them around, talking baby-talk to them and getting them to talk to him. Every morning before he was up they went into his room, at his special request, to pay him a visit. Another great pleasure was to watch Traveller enjoy himself. He had him turned out on the lawn, where the June grass was very fine, abundant and at its prime, and would allow no corn to be fed to him, saying he had had plenty of that during the last four years, and that the grass and the liberty were what he needed. He talked to Colonel Carter much about Mexico, its people and climate; also about the old families living in that neighbourhood and elsewhere in the State, with whom both Colonel Carter and himself were connected; but he said very little about the recent war, and only in answer to some direct question.

6

General Lee was eager to get away from Richmond and settle down to the simple life of a Virginia farmer. He wrote to General Long: "I am looking for some little, quiet home in the woods, where I can procure shelter and my daily bread, if permitted by the victor. I wish to get Mrs. Lee out of the city as soon as practical." Such a retreat was found in a small cottage on the estate of Mrs. Elizabeth Randolph Cocke in Cumberland County, called Derwent, and during the latter days of June the General, Mrs. Lee, Custis and the daughters went there and spent the remainder of the summer. And here he was when he received the summons that was to determine the course of his future life.

Lee had been besieged with financially attractive proposals since the surrender. He was offered $50,000 a year to go to New York to head a firm being organized to promote trade with the South. An insurance company offered him $25,000 a year to act as its president. Another company proposed to pay him $10,000 a year merely for the use of his name. But his sense of personal honor did not permit of his accepting any of these efforts to capitalize his fame. "My name is not for sale at any price," he said simply. Nor did he hesitate when an admiring British nobleman offered him an estate in England as a home, with an annual income of $15,000. He wrote a grateful letter of appreciation to his generous admirer, but concluded: "I must abide the fortunes and share the fate of my people."

As these offers continued to pour in, one of his daughters remarked: "They are offering my father everything except the only thing he will accept: a place to earn honest bread while engaged in some useful work." And out of this remark grew the opportunity for Robert E. Lee, paroled prisoner of war, to end his days earning honest bread by useful work. Professor Nelson tells how the office sought the man.

When the war closed Washington College was a wreck, but the board of trustees, animated by indomitable Scotch-Irish pluck, determined to resuscitate it. It was announced that the board would meet on the 4th day of August, 1865. The members of the faculty were present by invitation, as most interested spectators.

Several highly respectable gentlemen and scholars were placed in nomination for president of the college and their merits discussed. At length the board seeemed ready to take the vote. Just then Col. Bolivar Christian arose and said, in a somewhat hesitating manner, that he deemed it his duty to make a statement, before the vote was taken, which might have some influence on the election. He then said that a lady friend of his who was also a friend of Miss Mary Lee, daughter of General Robert E. Lee, recently told him that Miss Mary Lee had remarked to her that while the Southern people were willing and ready to give her father everything that he might need, no offer had ever been made him by which he could earn a living for himself and family.

A member asked Colonel Christian if he nominated General Lee. No, he replied, he would not do that, but he merely wanted the board to know what Miss Mary Lee had said. Then various members of the board said what a great thing it would be for the college if the services of General Lee could be secured, and wondered if there was any chance of doing so. At length, after repeated urging, Colonel Christian did make the nomination. All other names were immediately withdrawn and the roll was called, and General Lee was unanimously elected.

Then there was a pause, and silence prevailed for some moments. The board seemed oppressed with the gravity of the situation, and seemed to feel that they had acted rashly. How could they announce to the world that they had elected to the presidency of a broken-down college not only the greatest man in the South but in many respects the greatest man in the world? And yet it was only brave men who could seize an opportunity like this. "There is a tide in the affairs of men which, taken at the flood, leads on to fortune."

At length a member summoned courage to say that, having taken that step, they must go forward; and he moved that a committee of five members, with the rector, be appointed to draft a letter to General Lee apprising him of his election and urging his acceptance. Another member suggested that it would not avail to send a letter through the mail, but that it must be conveyed by a personal representative, and that there was no one so well qualified for that mission as the rector.

Judge Brockenbrough, the rector, was a large man of imposing appearance, of courtly manners, a good talker and an eloquent speaker. He had been federal judge of the western district of Virginia, and had for many years conducted a flourishing law school in Lexington. The judge arose at once and, thanking the member for his kind words, said that he could not go; and, glancing down at his well-worn clothes, said he could not make an appearance in

General Lee's presence dressed as he was, and that those were the best clothes he had, and that he had no money whatever to buy others.

Mr. Hugh Barclay, a member of the board, who also was a large man, replied that one of his sons who lived in the North had sent him a suit of broadcloth which he thought would fit Judge Brockenbrough pretty well, and that if he would wear this suit he would be welcome to it. The judge thanked him, but said there was still another difficulty. It would be quite a journey to . . . where General Lee was residing, and would necessitate some expense, and he had no money and the college had none. Colonel McLaughlin, another trustee, who was ever alive to the interests of the college, and who knew everything that occurred in town, said there was a lady living in Lexington who owned a farm in Buckingham county and who had recently secured the money for a crop of tobacco, and that the college could borrow some of it.

Judge Brockenbrough, thus equipped and supplied, went on his mission. When he returned he reported that General Lee was willing to take the matter under consideration. On the 24th of August General Lee wrote that he would accept the office of President of Washington College under certain conditions, one of which was that he could not undertake to give instruction to classes but could only undertake general supervision. The conditions imposed were readily accepted by the board and the announcement of General Lee's acceptance was made public.

Money was borrowed and every effort made to place the college in working order. On the 18th of September, 1865, General Lee rode into town on Traveller.

7

If the board of trustees were surprised at their own temerity in offering General Lee a position paying $1,500 a year, there were also others who felt no hesitation in predicting that General Lee would not accept the position offered him. As one said: "There was a general expectation that he would decline the position as not sufficiently lucrative, if his purpose was to repair the ruins of his private fortune resulting from the war;

as not lifting him conspicuously enough in the public gaze, if
he was ambitious of office or further distinction; or as involving
too great labor and anxiety, if he coveted repose after the terrible contest from which he had just emerged." Lee himself, in
his letter of conditional acceptance, pointed out to the board
that he had been excluded from the President's terms of am-
nesty and was "an object of censure to a portion of the country" and that "I have thought it probable that my occupation
of the position of president might draw upon the college a feeling of hostility . . . and I could not consent to be the cause of
animadversion upon the college." But this objection was
brushed aside by the board. Bishop Wilmer gives a clear view
of the motives which impelled General Lee to accept the presidency of the run-down little college in Lexington.

At the close of the war his great mind harbored no resentments;
he uttered no complaints. He accepted the consequences of the
war with a spirit of resignation which few can emulate but which
we all can revere. We thought now that the sun had gone down
in night, but we were in error. The change in the life of this unconquerable man was not one from labor to idle repose and inan-
ity. He sought activity and usefulness, and he did not seek in vain.

I was seated at the close of the day in my Virginia home, when I
beheld through the thickening shades of evening a horseman entering the yard, whom I soon recognized as General Lee. The next
morning he placed in my hands the correspondence with the authorities of Washington College at Lexington. He had been invited to become president of that institution. His mind was perplexed and craved sympathy.

I confess to a feeling of momentary chagrin at the proposed
change—shall I say revulsion?—in his history. The institution was
one of local interest, and comparatively unknown to our people. I
named others more conspicuous which would welcome him with
ardour as their presiding head. I soon discovered that his mind
towered above these earthly distinctions—that in his judgment the
cause gave dignity to the institution, and not the wealth of its en-
dowments or the renown of its scholars—that this door and not another was opened to him by Providence, and he only wished to be

assured of his competency to fulfill the trust, and thus to make his few remaining years a comfort and blessing to his suffering country.

I had spoken to his human feelings; he had now revealed himself to me as one whose life was hid with Christ in God. My speech was no longer restrained. I congratulated him that his heart had been inclined to this great cause, and that he was spared to give to the world this august testimony to the importance of Christian education. How he listened to my feeble words; how he beckoned me to his side as the fullness of my heart found utterance; how his whole countenance glowed with animation when I spoke of the Holy Ghost as the great Teacher, whose presence was required to make education a blessing, which otherwise might be the curse of mankind. How feelingly he responded, how eloquently as I never. heard him speak before, can never be effaced from my memory, and nothing more sacred mingles with my reminiscences of the dead.

8

General Lee was not joined in Lexington by his wife and family for several weeks. His son, Robert, tells of the re-establishment of the household there in December.

We . . . arrived at Lexington on the morning of December 2nd. My father, on Traveller, was there to meet us and, putting us all in a carriage, escorted us to our new home. . . . The house was in good order—thanks to the ladies of Lexington—but rather bare of furniture, except my mother's room. . . . A handsomely carved grand piano, presented by Stieff, the famous maker of Baltimore, stood alone in the parlour. The floors were covered with the carpets rescued from Arlington—much too large and folded under to suit the reduced size of the rooms. Some of the bedrooms were partially furnished, and the dining-room had enough in it to make us very comfortable. We were all very grateful and happy—glad to get home, the only one we had had for four long years.

My father appeared bright and even gay. . . . [He] was much interested in all the arrangements of the house, even to the least thing. He would laugh merrily over the difficulties that appalled the rest of us. Our servants were few and unskilled, but his patience and self-control never failed. The silver of the family had been sent to Lexington for safe-keeping early in the war. When General Hunter raided the Valley of Virginia and advanced upon Lexington, to remove temptation out of his way, this silver, in two large chests, had been intrusted to the care of the old and faithful sergeant at the Virginia Military Institute, and he had buried it in some safe place known only to himself. I was sent out with him to dig it up and bring it in. We found it safe and sound, but black with mould and damp, useless for the time being, so my father opened his camp-chest and we used his forks, spoons, plates, etc., while his camp-stools supplied the deficiency in seats. . . .

He at once set to work to improve all around him, laid out a vegetable garden, planted roses and shrubs, set out fruit and yard trees, made new walks and repaired the stables, so that in a short time we were quite comfortable and very happy. He at last had a home of his own, with his wife and daughters around him, and though it was not the little farm in the quiet country for which he had so longed, it was very near to it, and it gave rest to himself and those he loved most dearly.

9

Robert E. Lee's service to the Lexington school (now Washington and Lee University) is well told by a spokesman of the school itself.

General Lee was inducted into office as president of Washington College on October 2, 1865. Immediately he applied his tireless energies to this new work, and quickly reduced it to perfect method.

This was a task that would have discouraged men unaccustomed to the effect of discipline and system in a large way; for as an educational institution, Washington College was then little more than a name, less than an efficient academy; with few students, and buildings pillaged, defaced and falling into ruins; with a slender faculty, and little endowment.

But his presence gave it instant prestige and vivified it with life that flows as naturally from such a character as electric current traverses the wire. Soon Washington College took on the semblance of a great university, and began to be known as an institution of learning that was to be reckoned among the greater colleges.

It was most natural that his character should become a lodestone to draw the flower of Southern youth to this point and that they should become surcharged with the elevation of his ideals. He was the fellow of every student, yet set apart by the commanding dignity with which he surrounded his office. Always sympathetic, helpful, thoughtful of the interest and future of the individual; constantly aligning the student body with that standard of conduct always his own, be brought to the office of educator an influence for good that well earned for him the encomium: *"General Lee as college president has ennobled every college in the land."*

His work was carried on with wonderful energy; prompt at the morning hour, lasting well through the day; always available to his developing faculty for counsel and direction; ready to see every caller, and with his innate courtesy, to answer every letter; like a father to his students.

Students came from every part of the South, many of his soldiers whose scholastic training had been interrupted by the war, and sons of other immortal veterans who had stood the shock of battle in the great victories around Richmond; at Second Manassas, Sharpsburg, Fredericksburg, Chancellorsville; in the epic of Gettysburg, and the battles sequent to the Maryland-Pennsylvania campaign: Wilderness, Spottsylvania, Cold Harbor—and through the long-drawn exhaustion of the Confederate forces, down to the hour when 8,000 footsore, ragged and hunger-stricken heroes, peers of Caesar's Tenth Legion and Napoleon's Old Guard, surrendered to the enveloping forces of Grant and Sherman. Great sacrifices were necessary to send these boys to General Lee's tutelage, but the deprivations gave to the South many of its leaders of thought and action, and formed the cornerstone of a structure to which the world now owes much in literature, art, jurisprudence and commerce.

The veterans' confidence was surely placed. He was "Marse Robert," the resourceful, the circumspect, the wise, the kind, translated to college halls from fields that had long bound commander and men in one sympathetic body.

Because of General Lee's presence, money came readily; the grounds were enlarged; additional buildings were erected; the faculty was increased; apparatus and library were extended, and the new president's broad plans of development went forward with the alacrity of a military campaign.

General Lee was unsparing of himself. The correspondence of the college was from his own hand; he was constantly in his office and always to be seen by callers, faculty, parents and students alike. His time seemed as flexible as the demand made on it, however much it should be. No letter was unanswered; no effort of courtesy was too insignificant to have his own painstaking audit.

Students found inspiration and stimulant in the knowledge of the president's familiarity with their scholastic standing, outside deportment, home life and athletic attainments, and although a request to appear before him was not received with equanimity, nevertheless the student knew that justice always attended the reproof and admonition that came from the head of the institution, and he was prepared to accept the justice of the reproof, couched as it invariably was in terms of courtesy and gentleness, yet so direct that the effect was never lost.

Professor Joynes, of General Lee's faculty, has related that "his sense of personal duty was also expanded into a warm solicitude for all who were associated with him. To the faculty, he was an elder brother, beloved and revered, and full of tender sympathy. To the students, he was a father in carefulness, in encouragement, in reproof. Their welfare and their conduct and character as gentlemen were his chief concern; and this solicitude was not limited to their collegiate years, but followed them abroad in life. He thought it to be the office of the college not merely to educate the intellect, but to make Christian gentlemen. The moral and religious character of the students was more precious in his eyes even than their intellectual progress, and was made the special object of his personal solicitude. In the discipline of the college his moral influence was supreme. A disciplinarian—but no seeker after small offences, or stickler for formal regulations. Youthful indiscretion found in him the most lenient of judges; but falsehood and meanness he did not tolerate."

General Lee constantly sought to eradicate feelings of bitterness and rancor resulting from the war. He carefully abstained from expressions and acts that may have been misconstrued, and discouraged praise of himself in the public utterances of students and faculty, from an intense desire that the war and its results be left to the past, and that all should resolutely face a future that held promise of peace and material prosperity.

10

How the president of Washington College appeared to a shy young freshman from Tennessee is told by John B. Colyar.

The morning after we reached Lexington we repaired to the office of General Lee for the purpose of matriculation and receiving instructions as to the duties devolving upon us as students. I entered the office with reverential awe, expecting to see the great warrior whose fame then encircled the civilized globe as I had pictured him in my own imagination. General Lee was alone, looking over a paper. He arose as we entered and received us with a quiet, gentlemanly dignity that was so natural and easy and kind that the feeling of awe left me at the threshold of his door. General Lee had but one manner in his intercourse with men. It was the same to the peasant as to the prince, and the student was received with the easy courtliness that would have been bestowed on the greatest imperial dignitary of Europe.

When we had registered, my brother asked the General for a copy of his rules. General Lee said, "Young gentlemen, we have no printed rules. We have but one rule here and it is that every student must be a gentleman." I did not until after years fully realize the comprehensiveness of his remark and how completely it covered every essential rule that should govern the conduct and intercourse of men.

I was so disappointed at not seeing the warrior that my imagination had pictured that my mind was left in a confused state of inquiry as to whether he was the man whose fame had filled the

world. He was so gentle, kind, and almost motherly, in his bearing
that I thought there must be some mistake about it. At first glance
his countenance was stern, but the moment his eye met that of his
entering guest it beamed with a kindness that at once established
easy and friendly relations—but not familiar. The impression he
made on me was that he was never familiar with any man.

He seemed to avoid contact with men, and the impression he
then made on me, seeing him every day, and which has since clung
to me, strengthening the impression then made, was that he was
bowed down with a broken heart. I never saw a sadder expression
than General Lee carried during the entire time I was there. It
looked as if the sorrow of a whole nation had been collected in his
countenance, and as if he was bearing the grief of his whole people.
It never left his face, but was ever there to keep company with his
kindly smile.

11

Dr. Jones tells of Lee's moderation and the breadth of
his views at this time.

Soon after the grand jury found its indictment against General
Lee, at a time when President Andrew Johnson was showing a purpose to carry out his threat to "make treason odious by hanging the
chief of the Rebel leaders," and when ultra men at the North were
clamoring for vengeance for what they claimed as "the complicity
of the South" in the assassination of Mr. Lincoln, a party of friends
were spending an evening at his house in Richmond, and the conversation naturally turned on these matters. Rev. Dr. ——— led the
conversation in expressing in terms of decided bitterness the indignation of the South at the indictment of General Lee. The General pleasantly remarked, "Well, it matters little what they may do
to me. I am old and have but a short time to live anyhow," and
very soon turned the conversation into other channels. Presently
Dr. ——— got up to go, and General Lee followed him out to the
door and said, "Doctor, there is a good old book which I read, and
you preach from, which says, 'Love your enemies, bless them that
curse you, do good to them that hate you, and pray for them which

despitefully use you.' Do you think your remarks this evening were quite in the spirit of that teaching?" Dr. ——— made some apology for the bitterness which he felt and had expressed, and General Lee added with that peculiar sweetness of tone and manner that we remember so well, "I have fought against the people of the North because I believed they were seeking to wrest from the South dearest rights. But I have never cherished toward them bitter or vindictive feelings, and have never seen the day when I did not pray for them."

If the world's history affords a sublimer spectacle than that of this stern warrior teaching a minister of the Gospel of Peace the duty of love to enemies, the present writer has failed to note it. . . .

One day in the autumn of 1869 I saw General Lee standing at his gate talking to an humbly clad man, who turned off, evidently delighted with his interview, just as I came up. After exchanging salutations the General pleasantly said, pointing to the retreating form, "That is one of our old soldiers who is in necessitous circumstances." I took it for granted that it was some veteran Confederate, and asked to what command he belonged, when the General quietly and pleasantly added, *"He fought on the other side, but we must not remember that against him now."*

The man afterwards came to my house, and said to me in speaking of his interview with General Lee, "Sir, he is the noblest man that ever lived. He not only had a kind word for an old soldier who fought against him, but he gave me some money to help me on my way."

What a beautiful illustration of the teaching of the apostle, "If thine enemy hunger, feed him; if he thirst, give him drink."

Upon the occasion of the delivery of an address at Washington College by a certain distinguished orator, General Lee came to me and said, "I saw you taking notes during the address. It was in the main very fine; but if you propose publishing any report of it I would suggest that you leave out all of the bitter expressions against the North and the United States Government. They will do us no good under our present circumstances, and I think all such expressions undignified and unbecoming."

Soon after the passage of some of the . . . so-called "Reconstruction Acts" two of the professors of the College were conversing with him, when one of them expressed himself in very bitter terms concerning the dominant party and their treatment of the people of the South. General Lee quietly turned to his table and, picking up a manuscript (which afterwards proved to be his memoir of his father), read the following lines:

> "Learn from your Orient shell to love thy foe,
> And store with pearls the hand that brings thee woe:
> Free like yon rock, from base vindictive pride,
> Emblaze with gems the wrist that rends thy side:
> Mark where yon tree rewards the stony shower,
> With fruit nectareous, or the balmy flower;
> All nature cries aloud, shall man do less
> Than heal the smiter and the railer bless?

He then said that these lines were written "in Arabia and by a Mussulman, the poet of Shivaz, the immortal Hafiz," and quietly asked, "Ought not we who profess to be governed by the principles of Christianity to rise at least to the standard of this Mohammedan poet and learn to forgive our enemies?"

12

The far-reaching effects of Lee's attitude in defeat, of his teaching and example to the students under his guidance, of his paradoxical plucking of the flower of success from the thistle of failure, is beautifully expressed by Gamaliel Bradford.

In point of fact, he was creating, or re-creating, a great nation still. His patience, his courage, his attitude towards the past, his attitude towards the future, his perfect forgiveness, his large magnanimity, above all, his hope, were reflected in the eager hearts about him and from them spread wide over the bruised and beaten South, which stood so sorely in need of all these things.

I have already referred to the immense importance of his general influence in bringing about reconciliation and peace. It is almost impossible to overestimate this. We have the high Northern evidence of Grant: "All the people except a few political leaders in the South will accept whatever he does as right and will be guided to a great extent by his example." Perhaps nothing will better illustrate the passionate testimony of Southerners than a simple anecdote. A Confederate soldier told General Wise that he had taken the oath of allegiance to the United States. "You have disgraced the family," said Wise. "General Lee told me to do it." "Oh, that alters the case. Whatever General Lee says is all right, I don't care what it is." Does not the knowledge of these things double the pathos of that profoundly pathetic sentence in one of Lee's last letters? "Life is indeed gliding away and I have nothing of good to show for mine that is past. I pray I may be spared to accomplish something for the benefit of mankind and the honor of God." If he had accomplished nothing, what shall be said of some of us?

Yet, in spite of all this, it must be admitted that Lee's life will always be regarded as a record of failure. And it is precisely because he failed that I have been interested to make this study of him.

Success is the idol of the world, and the world's idols have been successful. Washington, Lincoln, Grant, were doubtless very great. But they were successful. Who shall say just how far that element of success enters into their greatness? Here was a man who remains great, although he failed. America in the twentieth century worships success, is too ready to test character by it, to be blind to those faults success hides, to those qualities that can do without it. Here was a man who failed grandly, a man who said that "human virtue should be equal to human calamity," and showed that it could be equal to it, and so, without pretense, without display, without self-consciousness, left an example that future Americans may study with profit as long as there is an America.

A young sophomore was once summoned to the president's office and gently admonished that only patience and industry would prevent the failure that would inevitably come to him through college and through life.

"But, General, you failed," remarked the sophomore, with the inconceivable ineptitude of sophomores.

"I hope that you may be more fortunate than I" was the tranquil answer.

Literature can add nothing to that.

19

Last Days

THERE is something pleasing and soothing about
the last years of Lee's life. Not only was he engaged in a work
which he knew to be of vast importance to the South and to
the whole country and therefore very agreeable to him, but he
had ample opportunities for those social contacts which he enjoyed so much. There were visits to the homes of his married
sons and to other relatives in Virginia; there were the regular
pilgrimages to the various Virginia springs in the season; there
were occasional business trips to the cities, although he found
no pleasure in these.

Throughout it all he shrank from the public eye, avoided
politics and political discussions, and endeavored to live the
simple life of a quiet, loyal American citizen. The serenity of
his life was not undisturbed, however. A vindictive Federal
grand jury returned an indictment against him for treason—an
act of vengeance which was promptly frustrated by General
Grant's prompt declaration that Lee, like every other Confederate soldier, was protected by his parole. Lee was summoned
for questioning before the Congressional Reconstruction Committee, and subjected to a long siege of quizzing; but his ques-
tioners were not able to disturb his equanimity or extract from
him any expression of disloyalty or discontent.

And so the sands of his life ran out in the quiet little Virginia
mountain town.

1

A revealing insight into Lee's character and his views on the
war and current subjects may be gleaned from an examination

of some of his postwar correspondence as published by Dr. Jones.

His uniform courtesy and kindness were sometimes abused by thoughtless visitors who obtruded upon him at unseasonable hours, and still more by letters which flooded his mails, and to which he was very careful to reply. While at Washington College he received bushels of letters from all sorts of people on all sorts of subjects, and would worry himself to reply to them, when most men would have passed them by in silence.

He one day showed me a letter from a distressed damsel in St. Louis, who said that her lover had been a soldier "either in Mr. Lee's or Mr. Johnston's army," that she had not heard from him since the close of the war, and that his family reported him dead, but she believed that this was only a trick on their part to prevent him from marrying her. She wrote to beg that "Mr. Lee" would write her if he knew anything of him, and if he did not, that he would write for her to "Mr. Johnston" to see if he could give her any information. General Lee made the most diligent inquiries after the man in question, saying that he "would be very glad to relieve the poor woman if he could," and after all of his inquiries proved futile, he wrote her a kind letter of sympathy.

He received many letters from Federal officers, newspaper men, etc., and the mingled courtesy, tact and quiet humor with which he would reply would form a most interesting chapter if it were proper to publish the letters in full. I cannot, however, refrain from giving the following verbatim copy of a reply to a distinguished Federal general, who wrote to propound to him certain questions which were plainly indicated in General Lee's answer:

"Lexington, Virginia, January 18, 1869

"Dear Sir:

A reply to your letter of the 4th inst. would require more time than I can devote to it, and lead to a discussion of military affairs from which, for reasons that will occur to you, I hope that you will excuse me.

"I will, therefore, only say that the failure of the Confederate army at Gettysburg was owing to a combination of circumstances, but for which success might have been reasonably expected.

"It is presumed that General Burnside had good reasons for his move from Warrenton to Fredericksburg; and as far as I am able to judge, the earlier arrival of his pontoons at Aquia Creek would not have materially changed the result. Their appearance would only have produced an earlier concentration of the Confederate army at Fredericksburg.

"As regards General McClellan, I have always entertained a high opinion of his capacity, and have no reason to think that he omitted to do anything that was in his power.

"It is difficult for me to say what success would have attended the execution of your plan of moving the Federal army to Aquia Creek after its attack on Fredericksburg, and of threatening Richmond from Fortress Monroe with the available troops in that quarter and then entering the Rappahannock with the main army.

"I do not think that the Confederate army would have retreated to Richmond until the movement developed the necessity.

"After the accomplishment of an event it is so easy, with the aid of our after knowledge, to correct errors that arose from previous want of information that it is difficult to determine the weight that should be given to conclusions thus reached. . . ."

Upon another occasion he received a letter from some Spirit Rappers asking his opinion on certain great military movements. He wrote in reply a most courteous letter in which he said that the question was one about which military critics would differ; that his own judgment about such matters was but poor at best, and that inasmuch as they had power to consult (through their mediums) Caesar, Alexander, Napoleon, Wellington and all of the other great captains who have ever lived he could not think of obtruding his opinion into such company. . . .

Not long after the close of the war General Lee received a letter from General David Hunter of the Federal army, in which he begged information upon two points:

1. His (Hunter's) campaign in the summer of 1864 was undertaken on information received at the War Department in Washington that General Lee was about to detach forty thousand picked

troops to send to General Johnston. Did not his (Hunter's) movements prevent this and relieve Sherman to that extent?

2. When he found it necessary to retreat from before Lynchburg, did he not adopt the most feasible line of retreat?

General Lee wrote a very courteous reply in which he said, "The information upon which your campaign was undertaken was erroneous. I had *no troops* to spare General Johnston, and no intention of sending him any—*certainly not forty thousand, as that would have taken about all I had.* As to the second point, I would say that I am not advised as to the motives which induced you to adopt the line of retreat which you took, and am not, perhaps, competent to judge of the question; *but I certainly expected you to retreat by way of the Shenandoah Valley,* and was gratified at the time that you preferred the route through the mountains to the Ohio—leaving the Valley open for General Early's advance into Maryland."

2

Lee is seldom thought of as having been a man of a particularly humorous turn of mind, but those who knew him well were impressed with this characteristic. John Esten Cooke speaks of it.

General Lee is well known to have been a very grand specimen of a man, but he was also a thoroughly genuine individual specimen of his race, with many peculiarities which were not known to strangers and, in fact, rarely if ever exhibited by him in general society. One of these traits was a marked tendency to take a humorous view of things and indulge a certain playfulness, apparently inconsistent with the serious and solid mould of his organization. Even during the war, when he bore upon his broad shoulders the heavy weight of the public care, and was fully conscious of the enormous responsibilities incident to his post of commander-in-chief, he frequently relaxed and gave way to positive mirth. The bow, unbent for an instant, flew back in the opposite direction, and he exhibited a marked appreciation of the ludicrous and a love for the humorous side of things.

It is said—I do not know with what truth—that even in that hour of utter depression, amounting nearly to despair, when he found no rations awaiting him at Amelia Court-House, he gave way to this latter sentiment. A distinguished Confederate general made his appearance before him, wrapped in an old tattered blanket, covered with mud, his face streaked with earth-slums, like that of an Indian painted for battle—and at this spectacle General Lee is said to have burst into sudden laughter.

He seemed to enjoy the society of Stuart, especially on account of the high animal spirits of that jovial cavalier, whose tendency to mirth was as great as his unfaltering courage and elan in the field, and evidently derived great pleasure from the songs and perform-ance of Stuart's banjo-player, Sweeney, who was more than once taken to army headquarters to rattle away on his instrument, and sing "The Old Gray Horse," or some other comic ditty of the camp. This appreciation of the humorous was genuine and spontaneous, and he seemed to have a taste for every species—for the broad and comic as for the quiet.

His own humor was almost always quiet, playful, and rather sug-gested than fully conveyed the inner spirit of mirth moving him. The adjective playful, indeed, perfectly describes his tones and expression of face at such moments. This playfulness of disposi-tion is particularly exhibited in the private letters to his family.

3

A letter written to his nephew Fitzhugh during the last few weeks of his life gives an illuminating example of his playful sense of humor and his affectionate interest in all the members of his family.

Lexington, Va. 19 Sept., 1870

My dear Nephew—

Your letter on the dog question has been unavoidably delayed. I thank you very sincerely for recollecting my wishes on the subject and your steps to comply with them.

First I must inform you that it is not my purpose to put my dog to towing canal boats or hauling dirt carts, but want him to play the part of a friend and protector. His *disposition* is therefore of vital importance—he ought not to be too old to contract a friendship for me—neither is his size so important to me as a perfect form. In the second place I am promised by our connection, Genl. Bier of Md., a St. Bernard and Newfoundland puppy which I have been expecting for some weeks. He can come from Goshen in the stage, but how can your mammoth dog be accommodated? His plan would be to go to Lynchburg on the cars Monday, Wednesday or Friday, and take the packet boat that night and reach here the following morning. The expressman must request the captain in my name to take charge of him.

Now having the whole ground before you, you have full authority to act as judge for me in the matter. I shall be very glad to get the dog and hope that he may reach me safely. Either draw upon me through Mr. Burke and the Bank of Lexington for the price of the dog and transportation or let me know the amount and I will remit it to you.

We have had a pleasant visit from Fitzhugh. He was called home the other day but left his wife and boy with us. Robert is also here. I wish you were with us, my dear Nephew, and could gratify us in the same way that F. has. You and Custis must set out and do something creditable for yourselves. Give my love to your mother. All would join me did they know I was writing. Remember me to the boys. I have been much interrupted by the students who are coming in fast, arranging their studies and boarding houses, etc.

4

During the calm years of his civilian life in Lexington the deeply spiritual side of Lee's nature was intensified and commented upon by all who came in contact with him. There was nothing ostentatious or obtrusive about his religion; it was a part of him and manifested itself in his daily life in a quiet but effective manner. Dr. Jones, who was perhaps more closely in touch with this side of Lee's character than any other person, writes feelingly of it.

In this age of hero-worship there is a tendency to exalt unduly the virtues of great men and to magnify the religious character of one professing to be a Christian. This is so well understood that there may be with those who never came in contact with this great man a lingering doubt as to the genuineness of his piety—a fear that, with him as with many others, his profession of religion was merely nominal. A few incidents, culled from the many that might be given, will serve to dissipate any such impression and to show beyond all cavil that with General Lee vital godliness was a precious reality. . . .

General Lee always took the deepest interest in the work of his chaplains and the spiritual welfare of his men. He was a frequent visitor at the chaplains' meetings and a deeply-interested observer of their proceedings, and the faithful chaplain who stuck to his post and did his duty could be always assured of a warm friend at headquarters.

While the Army of Northern Virginia confronted General Meade at Mine Run, near the end of November 1863, and a battle was momentarily expected, General Lee with a number of general and staff officers was riding down his line of battle when, just in the rear of General A. P. Hill's position, the cavalcade suddenly came upon a party of soldiers engaged in one of those prayer-meetings which they so often held on the eve of battle. An attack from the enemy seemed imminent; already the sharpshooting along the skirmish-line had begun; the artillery was belching forth its hoarse thunder and the mind and heart of the great chieftain were full of the expectant combat. Yet, as he saw those ragged veterans bowed in prayer, he instantly dismounted, uncovered his head and devoutly joined in the simple worship. The rest of the party at once followed his example, and those humble privates found themselves leading the devotions of their loved and honored chieftains.

It is related that as his army was crossing the James in 1864 and hurrying on to the defenses of Petersburg, General Lee turned aside from the road and, kneeling in the dust, devoutly joined a minister present in earnest prayer that God would give him wisdom and grace in the new stage of the campaign upon which he was then entering. . . .

General Lee's orders and reports always gratefully recognized "the Lord of hosts" as the "Giver of victory," and expressed a humble dependence upon and trust in Him.

He thus began his dispatch to the President the evening of his great victory [in 1862] at Cold Harbor and Gaines's Mill: "Profoundly grateful to almighty God for the signal victory granted to us, it is my pleasing task to announce to you the success achieved by this army to-day."

His beautiful general order of congratulation to the troops on their series of splendid victories during the Seven Days' battles opened with these memorable words: "The commanding general, profoundly grateful to the Giver of all victory for the signal success with which He has blessed our arms, tenders his warmest thanks and congratulations to the army by whose valor such splendid results have been achieved."

His dispatch announcing the great victory at Fredericksburg contains the brief but significant sentence: "Thanks be to God."

In his dispatch to President Davis after Chancellorsville he said: "We have again to thank Almighty God for a great victory." And in his general order to his troops he uses this significant language: ". . . While this glorious victory entitles you to the praise and gratitude of the nation, we are especially called upon to return our grateful thanks to the only Giver of victory for the signal deliverance He has wrought. It is therefore earnestly recommended that the troops unite on Sunday next in ascribing unto the Lord of hosts the glory due unto His name."

In his dispatch announcing the result of the first day's battle in the Wilderness he says: ". . . By the blessing of God we maintained our position against every effort until night, when the contest closed." . . .

He closes his dispatch concerning the first day at Spottsylvania by saying: "I am most thankful to the Giver of all victory that our loss is small"; and that concerning the action of June 3, 1864, with "Our loss to-day has been small and our success, under the blessing of God, all that we could expect."

In his order assuming the command of all the Confederate forces [in February 1865] he said: ". . . Deeply impressed with the difficulties and responsibility of the position and humbly invoking the guidance of Almighty God, I rely for success upon the courage and fortitude of the army, sustained by the patriotism and firmness of the people, confident that their united efforts, under the blessing of Heaven, will secure peace and independence."

We give the above only as specimens of his dispatches and general orders, which all recognized in the most emphatic manner his sense of dependence upon and trust in God.

With the close of the war and the afflictions which came upon his loved land, the piety of this great man seems to have mellowed and deepened, and we could fill pages concerning his life at Lexington and the bright evidence he gave of vital, active godliness. He was a most regular attendant upon all of the services of his own church, his seat in the college chapel was never vacant unless he was kept away by sickness, and if there was a union prayer meeting or a service of general interest in any of the churches of Lexington, General Lee was sure to be among the most devout attendants. . . . He always devoutly knelt during prayer, and his attitude during the entire service was that of an interested listener or a reverential participant. . . .

He had also a most intelligent appreciation of the adaptation of religious services to particular occasions and of the appropriateness of prayers to the time and place in which they were offered. He once said to one of the faculty: "I want you to go with me to call upon Mr. ———, the new minister who has just come to town. I want to pay my respects to him and to invite him to take his turn in the conduct of our chapel exercises and to do what he can for the spiritual interests of our young men. And do you think that it would be any harm for me to delicately hint to him that we should be glad if he would make his morning prayers a little short? You know our friend is accustomed to make his prayers too long. He prays for the Jews, the Turks, the heathen, the Chinese and everybody else, and makes his prayers run into the regular hour for our college recitations. Would it be wrong for me to suggest to the new minister that he confine his morning prayers to us poor sinners at the college, and pray for the Turks, the Jews, the Chinese and the other heathen some other time?" . . .

General Lee was a member of the Episcopal Church and was sincerely attached to the church of his choice; but his large heart took in Christians of every name; he treated ministers of all denominations with the most marked courtesy and respect; and it may be truly said of him that he had a heart and hand ready to every good work. When once asked his opinion of a certain theological question which was exciting considerable discussion, he replied: "Oh, I never trouble myself about such questions. My chief concern is to try to be a humble, earnest Christian myself."

An application of a Jewish soldier for permission to attend certain ceremonies of his synagogue in Richmond was indorsed by his captain: "Disapproved. If such applications were granted, the whole army would turn Jews or shaking Quakers." When the paper came to General Lee he indorsed on it: "Approved, and respectfully returned to Captain —— with the advice that he should always respect the religious views and feelings of others." . . .

If I have ever come in contact with a sincere, devout Christian, one . . . whose piety constantly exhibited itself in his daily life, that man was General R. E. Lee.

5

General Lee during the latter years of his life conceived the idea of writing a history of the Army of Northern Virginia, but he died without having made any progress in the project beyond gathering some papers and making some notes. He very seldom discussed his campaigns and battles and with even less frequency wrote of them. Particular interest therefore attaches to a letter he wrote in 1868 to a Virginia gentleman who had asked him about the Maryland and Pennsylvania campaigns and also about the battle of Fredericksburg.

If you will refer to my official report of March 6, 1863, which was published in Richmond in 1864, you will find the general reasons which governed my actions; but whether they will be satisfactory to others is problematical.

In relation to your first question, I will state that in crossing the Potomac I did not propose to invade the North, for I did not believe that the Army of Northern Virginia was strong enough for the purpose, nor was I in any degree influenced by popular expectation. My movement was simply intended to threaten Washington, call the Federal army north of that river, relieve our territory and enable us to subsist the army. I considered it useless to attack the fortifications around Alexandria and Washington, behind which the Federal army had taken refuge, and indeed I could not have maintained the army in Fairfax, so barren was it of subsistence and so devoid were we of transportation. After reaching Frederick City, finding that the enemy still retained his positions at Martinsburg and Harper's Ferry and that it became necessary to dislodge him in order to open our communication through the Valley for the purpose of obtaining from Richmond the ammunition, clothing, etc., of which we were in great need—after detaching the necessary troops for the purpose, I was left with but two divisions, Longstreet's and D. H. Hill's, to mask the operation. That was entirely too weak a force to march on Baltimore, which you say was expected, even if such a movement had been expedient.

As to the battle of Gettysburg, I must again refer you to my official accounts. Its loss was occasioned by a combination of circumstances. It was commenced in the absence of correct intelligence. It was continued in the effort to overcome the difficulties by which we were surrounded, and it would have been gained could one determined and united blow have been delivered by our whole line. As it was, victory trembled in the balance for three days, and the battle resulted in the infliction of as great an amount of injury as was received and in frustrating the Federal campaign for the season.

I think you will find the answer to your third question in my report of the battle of Fredericksburg. In taking up the position there, it was with the view of resisting General Burnside's advance after crossing the Rappahannock rather than of preventing its passage. The plain of Fredericksburg is completely commanded by the heights of Stafford, which prevented our occupying it in the first instance. Nearly the whole loss that our army sustained during the battle arose from the pursuit of the repulsed Federal columns into the plain. To have advanced the whole army into the plain for the purpose of attacking General Burnside would have been to have insured its destruction by the fire from the continued line of guns on the Stafford Hills. It was considered more wise to meet the Federal army beyond the reach of their batteries than under their muzzles, and even to invite repeated renewals of their attacks. When convinced of their inutility, it was easy for them under cover of a long, dark and tempestuous night to cross the narrow river by means of their numerous bridges before we could ascertain their purpose.

6

An interesting record of a chance postwar encounter with two of his celebrated former companions in arms has been left by Colonel Mosby.

I met General Lee a few times after the war, but the days of strife were never mentioned. I remember the last words he spoke to me, about two months before his death, at a reception that was given to him in Alexandria. When I bade him good-by he said: "Colonel, I hope we shall have no more wars."

In March, 1870, I was walking across the bridge connecting the Ballard and Exchange hotels in Richmond, and to my surprise I met General Lee and his daughter. The General was pale and haggard, and did not look like the Apollo I had known in the army. After a while I went to his room; our conversation was on current topics. I felt oppressed by the great memories that his presence revived, and while both of us were thinking about the war, neither of us referred to it.

After leaving the room, I met General Pickett, and told him that I had just been with Lee. He remarked that if I would go with him he would call and pay his respects to the general, but he did not want to be alone with him. So I went back with Pickett; the interview was cold and formal, and evidently embarrassing to both. It was their only meeting after the war.

In a few minutes I rose and left the room, together with General Pickett. He then spoke very bitterly of General Lee, calling him "that old man."

"He had my division massacred at Gettysburg," Pickett said.

"Well, it made you immortal," I replied.

I rather suspect that Pickett gave a wrong reason for his unfriendly feelings. In May, 1892, at the University of Virginia, I took breakfast with Professor Venable, who had been on Lee's staff. He told me that some days before the surrender at Appomattox, General Lee ordered Pickett under arrest—I suppose for the Five

Forks affair. I think the professor said that he carried the order. I remember very well his adding that, on the retreat, Pickett passed them, and that General Lee said, with deep feeling: "Is that man still with this army?"

7

The summer seasons spent with his wife and daughters at the resorts in the near-by mountains—his favorite being the White Sulphur Springs, where the family had a cottage—were a source of pleasure and relief from care to Lee in his last days. Here he was always a center of interest, and his kindly courtesies and thoughtfulness added to the pleasure of all those with whom he came in contact. It was while spending one summer at "The White" that Lee met and became friendly with the great Northern philanthropist, George Peabody; and Peabody's endowment of the great teachers' college at Nashville bearing his name grew out of Lee's suggestion in answer to Peabody's inquiry as to how he might best do something to benefit the South. A pleasing view of Lee in his social contacts at White Sulphur Springs has been left by a Maryland lady who was there at the time.

Thoughtful as General Lee was for the happiness of every one, he was doubly solicitous for the small contingent of Northerners. Those among them who had been officers in the Union Army apparently avoided social intercourse with him, perhaps from consideration for his probable shrinking from contact with his conquerors. He, on the contrary, was concerned only for their enjoyment and for the Southern reputation for hospitality, and was uneasy at their comparative isolation, which offended his sense of Southern cordiality. By quiet attention to the ladies of their parties he drew them into his own circle and thus strove to break down the intangible barriers of separation. Truth to tell, his task was not always easy.

One evening, before the dancing began, a group of recent arrivals sat somewhat apart, with the air of mere lookers-on. They were from a Northern state, and the name was one celebrated in

the annals of the war. General Lee inquired of his young following whether they had welcomed the strangers. No one had made
their acquaintance. The grave suggestions of the General met
evasive answers. The reminder that we were on our own soil and
owed a sacred duty of hospitality fell on reluctant ears. In truth,
the manner of the Northern group was not inviting of courtesy.

"I have tried in vain," said the General finally, "to find any lady
who has made acquaintance with the party and is able to present
me. I shall now introduce myself, and shall be glad to present any
of you who will accompany me."

"I will go, General Lee, under your orders," I said, and proudly
arose to accompany him.

"Not under my orders," he gently corrected, "but it will gratify
me deeply to have your assistance."

And so we crossed the great room, but under the brilliant crystal
chandelier he paused and spoke words which went to the soul of
his young hearer. He told of the grief with which he found a spirit
of unreasoning resentment and bitterness in the young people of
the South, of the sinfulness of hatred and social revenge, of the
duty of kindness, helpfulness and consideration of others.

In a rush of unwonted feeling, the impulsive question came:
"But, General Lee, did you never feel resentment towards the
North?" ("Yankees" one might not say in his presence.)

Standing in the radiance of the myriad lighted crystals, his face
took on a far-away, almost inspired look, as his hand involuntarily
sought his breast. He spoke in low, earnest tones: "I believe I may
say, looking into my own heart, and speaking as in the presence of
God, that I have never known one moment of bitterness or resentment." After a pause he added, "When you go home, I want you
to take a message to your young friends. Tell them from me that
it is unworthy of them as women, and especially as Christian
women, to cherish feelings of resentment against the North. Tell
them that it grieves me inexpressibly to know that such a state of
things exists, and that I implore them to do their part to heal our
country's wounds."

We crossed the room at last and joined the formidable group.
The old soldier courteously presented himself and his young companion and accepted the proffered seats. The invisible restraint

which had existed in social intercourse between the representatives of different sections still remained, but the example and influence of the illustrious leader modified its expression and led to exchange of courtesies.

8

During December 1867 General Lee visited Petersburg for the first time since the days of the wartime siege. His son Rooney, who, it will be remembered, was widowed during his imprisonment during the war, was ending his widowhood by marrying Miss Mary Tabb Bolling of Petersburg, and Lee went there to attend the wedding. A letter written to Rooney on his return to Lexington reveals his reaction.

My visit to Petersburg was extremely pleasant. Besides the pleasure of seeing my daughter and being with you, which was very great, I was gratified in seeing so many old friends. When our army was in front of Petersburg, I suffered so much in body and mind on account of the good towns-people, especially on that gloomy night when I was forced to abandon them, that I have always reverted to them in sadness and sorrow. My old feelings returned to me as I passed well-remembered spots and recalled the ravages of hostile shot and shell. But when I saw the cheerfulness with which the people were working to restore their fortunes, and witnessed the comforts with which they were surrounded, a cloud of sorrow which had been pressing upon me for years was lifted from my heart.

9

Lee rarely complained of his health, but the rigors of four years of campaigning had left him in a debilitated condition. During the winter of 1869-1870 he contracted a severe cold, which it seeemed impossible to shake off. In March 1870 his doctors prevailed on him to take a trip to southern Georgia and Florida, to see if he would not be benefited by the warmer climate. Accordingly, accompanied by his daughter Agnes, he set out on what proved to be a fruitless search for health.

The first stop on the southward journey was at Warrenton Springs in North Carolina where his daughter Annie had died during the war and where she was buried. From there they proceeded on to Savannah, traveling in one of the new sleeping-cars, "very handsome and comfortable." At every station where the train stopped the news of his passage had preceded him and there were bands of music playing martial airs and crowds of cheering people crying "Lee! Lee!" Little boys named for him by admiring parents were brought to the stations to see him and have their heads patted. Old ladies craned their necks to look in the windows and murmur: "He is mightily like his pictures." One-armed and one-legged soldiers were very much in evidence. Little girls with bouquets; veterans of the Confederate army, from privates to generals; admirers with baskets of fruit—all these met the train wherever it stopped. It was the first opportunity that the people of the South had had to see him since the war, and the passage of five years and the fact that he was a defeated general had not dimmed their enthusiasm for him. They cheered him whenever he appeared where they could see him; and they serenaded him when he tried to go to sleep at night.

"I do not think that traveling in this way procures me much quiet and repose," he wrote his wife. "I wish I were back home." But he went on with his trip—to Cumberland Island to visit the grave of his father, then on to Palatka in Florida. They returned to Savannah, thence to Charleston, Wilmington, Norfolk and Richmond; and before he returned to Lexington he visited Rooney at the White House and Rob at Romancoke, and also paid a visit to Shirley on the James, the girlhood home of his mother, and to the homes of other relatives.

The trip to the South was a diversion, but it did the General's health no good. In June he went to Baltimore to consult the doctors there, but without much benefit. The pains in his chest still continued and grew worse. Back to Lexington he went; and then on to the Hot Springs where he took the baths and drank the water, read with close interest the newspaper accounts of the Franco-

Prussian War in Europe, and wrote letters home telling the gossip of the Springs and giving emphatic orders about the proper care of Traveller. But his health did not improve; on the contrary, he felt that he was growing weaker.

Early in September he returned to Lexington to look after the details of the opening of the college term, and the stimulation afforded by his interest in the school's affairs seemed to be of greater benefit to his health than all his visits to doctors and health resorts. On the morning of September 28th he wrote a cheerful letter to a friend in Baltimore in which he remarked that his health was improving. "My pains are less and my strength greater," he wrote.

10

General Lee's belief in the improvement of his health was sadly illusory. The day he wrote that cheerful letter to his Baltimore friend was in fact his last day of active life. That evening he was stricken fatally. The doctors gave as the cause of his death: "Mental and physical fatigue, inducing venous congestion of the brain which, however, never proceeded as far as apoplexy or paralysis but gradually caused cerebral exhaustion and death." This mental and physical fatigue, mentioned by the doctors, had been apparent to all who knew him during the declining days. Four years of campaigning had transformed him from a vigorous, middle-aged man in 1861 into a tired old man in 1865. And to this physical exhaustion, with its attendant bodily ills, was added the burden of sorrow at the fate of his cause and his people, a burden that was never lifted from his heart.

A moving account of the last days of the Confederate leader is given by Colonel William Preston Johnston—son of Lee's friend and fellow soldier, Albert Sidney Johnston—who sat by the stricken chieftain's side during those last hours and watched the flame of his life flicker out as he, like Stonewall Jackson in his dying delirium, called for A. P. Hill, and then murmured "Strike the tent."

Wednesday, the 28th of September, 1870, found General Lee at the post of duty. In the morning he was fully occupied with the

correspondence and other tasks incident to his office of president of
Washington College, and he declined offers of assistance from
members of the faculty of whose services he sometimes availed
himself.

After dinner, at four o'clock, he attended a vestry meeting of
Grace Episcopal Church. The afternoon was chilly and wet, and a
steady rain had set in which did not cease until it resulted in a
great flood, the most memorable and destructive in this region for
a hundred years. The church was rather cold and damp, and General Lee during the meeting sat in a pew with his military cape
cast loosely about him. In a conversation that occupied the brief
space preceding the call to order he took part and told with marked
cheerfulness of manner and kindliness of tone some pleasant anecdotes of Bishop Meade and Chief Justice Marshall.

The meeting was protracted until after seven o'clock by a discussion touching the rebuilding of the church edifice and the increase
of the rector's salary. General Lee acted as chairman and, after
hearing all that was said, gave his own opinion, as was his wont,
briefly and without argument. He closed the meeting with a characteristic act. The amount required for the minister's salary still
lacked a sum much greater than General Lee's proportion of the
subscription in view of his frequent and generous contributions to
the church and other charities; but just before the adjournment,
when the treasurer announced the amount of the deficit still remaining, General Lee said in a low tone: "I will give that sum."
He seemed tired toward the close of the meeting and, as was afterward remarked, showed an unusual flush; but at the time no apprehension was felt.

General Lee returned to his house and, finding his family waiting tea for him, took his place at the table, standing to say grace.
The effort was vain; the lips could not utter the prayer of the
heart. Finding himself unable to speak, he took his seat quietly
and without agitation. His face seemed to some of the anxious
group about him to wear a look of sublime resignation and to
evince a full knowledge that the hour had come when all the cares
and anxieties of his crowded life were at an end. His physicians,
Drs. H. T. Barton and R. L. Madison, arrived promptly, applied
the usual remedies and placed him upon the couch from which he

was to rise no more. To him henceforth the things of this world were as nothing, and he bowed with resignation to the command of the Master he had followed so long with reverence.

The symptoms of his attack resembled concussion of the brain, without the attendant swoon. There was a marked debility, a slightly impaired consciousness and a tendency to doze, but no paralysis of motion or sensation and no evidence of softening or inflammation of the brain. His physicians treated the case as one of venous congestion, and with apparently favorable results. Yet, despite these auspicious auguries drawn from his physical symptoms, in view of the great mental strain he had undergone, the gravest fears were felt that the attack was mortal.

He took without objection the medicines and diet prescribed and was strong enough to turn in bed without aid and to sit up to take nourishment. During the earlier days of his illness, though inclined to doze, he was easily aroused, was quite conscious and observant, evidently understood whatever was said to him, and answered questions briefly but intelligently. He was, however, averse to much speaking, generally using monosyllables, as had always been his habit when sick. When first attacked, he said to those removing his clothes, pointing at the same time to his rheumatic shoulder, "You hurt my arm."

Although he seemed to be gradually improving until October 10th, he apparently knew from the first that the appointed hour had come when he must enter those dark gates that, closing, reopen no more to earth. In the words of his physician, "he neither expected nor desired to recover." When General Custis Lee made some allusion to his recovery, he shook his head and pointed upward. On the Monday morning before his death Dr. Madison, finding him looking better, tried to cheer him: "How do you feel to-day, general?" General Lee replied, slowly and distinctly: "I feel better." The doctor then said: "You must make haste and get well; Traveller has been standing so long in the stable that he needs exercise." The general made no reply, but slowly shook his head and closed his eyes. Several times during his illness he put aside his medicine, saying, "It is of no use," but yielded patiently to the wishes of his physicians or children, as if the slackened cords of being responded to the touch of duty or affection.

On October 10th, during the afternoon, his pulse became feeble and rapid and his breathing hurried, with other evidences of great exhaustion. About midnight he was seized with a shivering from extreme debility, and Dr. Barton felt obliged to announce the danger to the family. On October 11th he was evidently sinking; his respiration was hurried and his pulse feeble and rapid. Though less observant, he still recognized whoever approached him, but refused to take anything unless presented by his physicians. It now became certain that the case was hopeless. His decline was rapid, yet gentle; and soon after nine o'clock on the morning of October 12th he closed his eyes and his soul passed peacefully from earth.

General Lee's physicians attributed his death in great measure to moral causes. The strain of his campaigns, the bitterness of defeat aggravated by the bad faith and insolence of the victor, sympathy with the subsequent sufferings of the Southern people, and the effort at calmness under these accumulated sorrows, seemed the sufficient and real causes that led to his death. Yet to those who saw his composure under the greater and lesser trials of life and his justice and forbearance with the most unjust and uncharitable, it seemed scarcely credible that his serene soul was shaken by the evil that raged around him.

General Lee's closing hours were consonant with his noble and disciplined life. Never was more beautifully displayed how a long and severe education of mind and character enables the soul to pass with equal step through this supreme ordeal; never did the habits and qualities of a lifetime, solemnly gathered into a few last sad hours, more grandly maintain themselves amid the gloom and shadow of approaching death. The reticence, the self-contained composure, the obedience to proper authority, the magnanimity and the Christian meekness, that marked all his actions still preserved their sway in spite of the inroads of disease and the creeping lethargy that weighed down his faculties.

As the old hero lay in the darkened room or with the lamp and hearth-fire casting shadows upon his calm, noble front, all the massive grandeur of his form and face and brow remained; and death seemed to lose its terrors and to borrow grace and dignity in sublime keeping with the life that was ebbing away. The great mind sank to its last repose almost with the equal poise of health. The few broken utterances that evinced at times a wandering intellect were spoken under the influence of the remedies administered; but as long as consciousness lasted there was evidence that all the high, controlling influences of his whole life still ruled, and even when stupor was laying its cold hand on the intellectual perceptions, the moral nature with its complete orb of duties and affections still asserted itself. A Southern poet has celebrated in song those last significant words, "Strike the tent"; and a thousand voices were raised to give meaning to the uncertain sound when the dying man said with emphasis, "Tell Hill he *must* come up!" These sentences serve to show most touchingly through what fields the imagination was passing; but generally his words, though few, were coherent— but for the most part indeed his silence was unbroken.

This self-contained reticence had an awful grandeur, in solemn accord with a life that needed no defense. Deeds, which required no justification, must speak for him. His voiceless lips, like the shut gates of some majestic temple, were closed not for concealment but because that within was holy. Could the eye of the mourning watcher have pierced the gloom that gathered about the recesses of the great soul, it would have perceived a Presence there full of an ineffable glory. Leaning trustfully upon the all-sustaining Arm, the man whose stature, measured by mortal standards, seemed so great, passed from this world of shadows to the realities of the hereafter.

11

Dr. Freeman's masterly summary provides a fitting final characterization of Robert E. Lee—great man, great military leader and great American.

There he lies, now that they have shrouded him, with his massive features so white against the lining of the casket that he seems already a marble statue for the veneration of the South. . . . Tomorrow a slow-footed procession will form to carry his body to the chapel of the college, and the press of the country will be praising his feats as a soldier and his high intellect as a leader, or else, once more, will be branding him traitor. . . . Let us look at him for the last time and read from his countenance the pattern of his life.

Because he was calm when others were frenzied, loving when they hated, and silent when they spoke with bitter tongue, they shook their heads and said he was a superman or a mysterious man. Beneath that untroubled exterior, they said, deep storms must rage; his dignity, his reserve, and his few words concealed sombre thoughts, repressed ambitions, livid resentments. They were mistaken. Robert Lee was one of the small company of great men in whom there is no inconsistency to be explained, no enigma to be solved. What he seemed, he was—a wholly human gentleman, the essential elements of whose positive character were two and only two, simplicity and spirituality.

When the nascent science of genetics is developed, Lee will be cited in the case-books along with those who appear in Galton's *Hereditary Genius*. For his most conspicuous qualities, it may be repeated, were derived in almost determinable proportions from his parents and from his grandparents. From his Grandfather Lee came a sense of system, the power of critical analysis that kept him free of illusion, and, along with these, perhaps, his love of animals. His good looks were an endowment from his maternal grandmother, the "Lowland Beauty," at the sight of whom the grave eyes of George Washington are said to have lighted up. To his Grandfather Carter, Robert E. Lee owed much of the religion in his nature, something of his kindness, his love of family life and his devotion to his kin. "Light-Horse Harry" Lee passed on to his youngest son his fine physique, his aptitude for military affairs, his great intelligence, his daring, his sense of public duty, and the charm of manner that made him so readily a captain. The characteristics of his mother that reappear were her religion, her thrift, her self-control, her social sense and her patience in adversity. If it seem unscientific, at first glance, to speak with so much assurance of Lee's inherited characteristics, it may be said that the celebrity of his forebears and the diligence of the family genealogists make the facts more apparent than in most cases. Were as much known of other great American families as of the Lees, as much might be said of their descendants.

Fortunate in his ancestors, Lee was fortunate most of all in that he inherited nearly all their nobler qualities and none of their worse. Genetists will say, perhaps, that this is the explanation of genius—a chance combination of genes. Beyond the frontier that these pioneers have not yet crossed lies the fact that at least four generations of the ancestors of Lee, prior to that of his immediate grandparents, had all married well. Back to Richard the immigrant, whose wife's family name is unknown, there was not one instance in which a direct progenitor of Lee mated with a woman of blood and station below his own. His line was not crossed in a century and a half with one that was degenerating. If blood means anything, he was entitled to be what he fundamentally was, a gentleman. . . .

In his labor he was swift and diligent, prompt and accurate, always systematic and instinctively thrifty. His ambition was in his labor, whatever its nature. He did not covet praise. Blushing to receive it, he assumed that others would blush when he bestowed it, and he spared what he thought were their feelings, though no man was quicker to appreciate and, at the proper time, to acknowledge the achievement of others. Place and advancement never lured him, except as promotion held out the hope of larger opportunity and better provision for his family. Even then he was meticulous regarding the methods he would employ to further himself financially, and he would never capitalize his name or draw drafts on the good opinion of friends or public. Yet he had all his life the desire to excel at the task assigned him. That was the urge alike of conscience, of obligation, of his regard for detail, and of his devotion to thoroughness as the prime constituent of all labor. He never said so in plain words, but he desired everything that he did, whether it was to plan a battle or to greet a visitor, to be as nearly perfect as he could make it. No man was more critical of his own performance because none demanded more of himself. The engineer's impulse in him was most gratified if something was to be created or organized, but if it concerned another's happiness or had a place in the large design of worth-while things, he considered the smallest task proper to perform. Only the useless was irksome.

He endured interruption of his work without vexation. Rarely was he embarrassed in his dealings with men. He met every visitor, every fellow-worker, with a smile and a bow, no matter what the other's station in life. Always he seemed to keep others at a judicious distance and did not invite their confidence, but he sought as a gentleman to make every right-minded person comfortable in his presence. With a tact so delicate that others scarcely noticed it, when he was busy he kept conversation to the question at issue, and he sought to make his interviews brief; but even so, his consideration for the sensibilities of others cost him many a precious hour. Wrangles he avoided, and disagreeable persons he usually treated with a cold and freezing courtesy. Should his self-control be overcome by stupidity or ill-temper, his eyes would flash and his neck would redden. His rebuke would be swift and terse, and it might be two hours or more before he was completely master of himself. Whoever visited him meantime would perhaps find him irascible, though sure to make amends. Exacting of his subordinates, he still reconciled himself often to working with clumsy human tools. Resentments he never cherished. When he found men unworthy of his confidence, he made it his practice to see them as little as possible and to talk to them not at all. Silence was one of his strongest weapons. During the war he summarized his code when he wrote these words on a scrap of paper that nobody saw until after his death:

"The forbearing use of power does not only form a touchstone, but the manner in which an individual enjoys certain advantages over others is a test of a true gentleman.

"The power which the strong have over the weak, the employer over the employed, the educated over the unlettered, the experienced over the confiding, even the clever over the silly—the forbearing or inoffensive use of all this power or authority, or a total abstinence from it when the case admits it, will show the gentleman in a plain light. The gentleman does not needlessly and unnecessarily remind an offender of a wrong he may have committed against him. He can not only forgive, he can forget; and he strives for that nobleness of self and mildness of character which imparts sufficient strength to let the past be but the past. A true man of honor feels humbled himself when he cannot help humbling others." . . .

This was the pattern of his daily life. There is every reason to believe it was the mirror of his own soul. Those who look at him through the glamor of his victories or seek deep meaning in his silence will labor in vain to make him appear complicated. His language, his acts, and his personal life were simple for the inescapable reason that he was a simple gentleman.

Simple and spiritual—the two qualities which constitute the man cannot be separated. The strongest religious impulse in his life was that given him by his mother. After that, in youth, he probably came most under the indirect influence of Reverend William Meade, later bishop. . . . He was content until he was past forty-five to hold the code of a gentleman rather than to the formal creed of a church. The experiences of the Mexican War, the gentle piety of the Fitzhughs at Ravensworth, the example and death of Mrs. Custis, the simple faith of Mrs. Lee, and, more immediately, the purpose of his daughters to enter into the full fellowship of the church induced Lee in 1853 to renew his vows. After that time, first his sense of dependence on God for the uprearing of his boys during his long absences from home, and then the developing tragedy of the war, deepened every religious impulse in his soul. . . .

To understand the faith of Robert E. Lee is to fill out the picture of him as a gentleman of simple soul. For him, as for his grandfather, Charles Carter, religion blended with the code of *noblesse oblige* to which he had been reared. Together, these two forces resolved every problem of his life into right and wrong. The clear light of conscience and of social obligation left no zone of gray in his heart: everything was black or white. There cannot be said to have been a "secret" of his life, but this assuredly was the great transparent truth, and this it was, primarily, that gave to his career its consistency and decision. . . . There was but one question ever: What was his duty as a Christian and a gentleman? . . . He could not have conceived of a Christian who was not a gentleman. . . .

Humility was another major implication of his religion. . . . Born of this humility, this sense of unworthiness in the sight of God, was the submission to the Divine will that has so often been cited in these pages to explain his calmness in hours that would have wrecked the self-control of lesser men. . . . Nothing of his serenity during the war or of his silent labor in defeat can be understood unless one realizes that he submitted himself in all things faithfully to the will of a Divinity which, in his simple faith, was directing wisely the fate of nations and the daily life of His children. This, and not the mere physical courage that defies danger, sustained him in battle; and this, at least equally with his sense of duty done, made him accept the results of the war without even a single gesture of complaint.

Of humility and submission, was born a spirit of self-denial that prepared him for the hardships of the war and, still more, for the dark destitution that followed it. This self-denial was, in some sense, the spiritual counterpart of the social self-control his mother had inculcated in his boyhood days, and it grew in power throughout his life. . . . If one, only one, of all the myriad incidents of his stirring life had to be selected to typify his message, as a man, to the young Americans who stood in hushed awe that rainy October morning as their parents wept at the passing of the Southern Arthur, who would hesitate in selecting that incident? It occurred in Northern Virginia, probably on his last visit there. A young mother brought her baby to him to be blessed. He took the infant in his arms and looked at it and then at her and slowly said: "Teach him he must deny himself."

That is all. There is no mystery there in front of the windows that look to the sunrise.

20

Epilogue

1

IN ANNOUNCING Lee's death, the *New York Herald* said:

On a quiet autumn morning, in the land which he loved so well and, as he held, served so faithfully, the spirit of Robert Edward Lee left the clay which it had so much ennobled and traveled out of this world into the great and mysterious land. The expressions of regret which sprang from the few who surrounded the bedside of the dying soldier and Christian on yesterday will be swelled today into one mighty voice of sorrow, resounding throughout our country and extending over all parts of the world where his great genius and his many virtues are known. For not to the Southern people alone shall be limited the tribute of a tear over the dead Virginian. Here in the North, forgetting that the time was when the sword of Robert Edward Lee was drawn against us—forgetting and forgiving all the years of bloodshed and agony—we have long since ceased to look upon him as the Confederate leader, but have claimed him as one of ourselves; have cherished and felt proud of his military genius as belonging to us; have recounted and recorded his triumphs as our own; have extolled his virtue as reflecting upon us—for Robert Edward Lee was an American, and the great nation which gave him birth would be to-day unworthy of such a son if she regarded him lightly.

Never had mother a nobler son. In him the military genius of America was developed to a greater extent than ever before. In him all that was pure and lofty in mind and purpose found lodgment. Dignified without presumption, affable without familiarity, he united all those charms of manners which made him the idol of his friends and of his soldiers and won for him the respect and admiration of the world. Even as in the days of his triumph glory did not intoxicate, so, when the dark clouds swept over him, adversity did not depress. From the hour that he surrendered his sword at Appomattox to the fatal autumn morning, he passed among men, noble in his quiet, simple dignity, displaying neither bitterness nor regret over the irrevocable past. He conquered us in misfortune by the grand manner in which he sustained himself, even as he dazzled us by his genius when the tramp of his soldiers resounded through the valleys of Virginia.

And for such a man we are all tears and sorrow today. Standing beside his grave, men of the South and men of the North can mourn, with all the bitterness of four years of war erased by this common bereavement. May this unity of grief, this unselfish manifestation over the loss of the Bayard of America, in the season of dead leaves and withered branches which this death ushers in, bloom and blossom like the distant coming spring into the flowers of a heartier accord. . . .

It is doubtful if there are many men of the present generation who unite so many virtues and so few vices in each of themselves as did General Lee. He came nearer the ideal of a soldier and Christian general than any man we can think of, for he was a greater soldier than Havelock and equally as devout a Christian. In his death our country has lost a son of whom she might well be proud and for whose services she might have stood in need had he lived a few years longer, for we are certain that had occasion required it General Lee would have given to the United States the benefit of all his great talents.

2

That Lee's fame was not confined to his own homeland is evidenced by the following extract from a tribute to him that appeared in the October 14, 1870, issue of the *Halifax* (Nova Scotia) *Morning Chronicle*.

"Ah, Sir Lancelot," he said, "thou wert head of all Christian knights; and now, I dare say", said Sir Ector, "thou, Sir Lancelot, there thou liest, that thou wert never matched of earthly knights' hand; and thou wert the courtliest knight that ever bare shield; . . .

and thou wert the kindest man that ever strake with sword; and thou wert the goodliest person that ever came among press of knights; and thou wert the meekest man and the gentliest that ever ate in hall among ladies; and thou wert the sternest knight to thy mortal foe that ever put spear in rest."—*The Mort d'Arthur of Sir Thomas Malory.*

With reverence and regret we repeat to-day Sir Ector's words of sorrow for the great Sir Lancelot, and apply them to the man who died yesterday—the noblest knight of our generation. The hero of the Arthurian legends, as he lay dead in Joyous-Gard with the record of a life made splendid by great deeds, might have revived other than kindly or ennobling recollections in the mourner's mind; for the wronged king and the breaking up of the goodly fellowship of the Round Table could not be forgotten, but lay like shadows upon the dead knight. But in the life of Robert Edward Lee there was no reproach of man or woman; his deeds were dimmed by no wrong done or duty unfulfilled; there was no stain upon his honor and no unrighteous blood upon his hands. He was, indeed, a good knight, noble of heart and strong of purpose, and both a soldier and a gentleman. The age that knew him, if not the age of chivalry, will yet be remarkable for having produced in him a man as chivalric as any that lives in history. . . .

Only nine years ago he was a colonel of cavalry in the United States army; and yesterday he died the greatest soldier in the world. Four years' service in the field at the head of an army gained for him this reputation, and though he was worsted at the last, it was a reputation that he did not lose with his losses. It is strong praise to give to him, but none the less deserved; for even his former enemies must concede to him the first place in the civil war, and we know of no living European general who possesses to the same extent those attributes of a soldier which so distinguished the Confederate leader. . . .

In every particular he possessed the requisites of a true soldier. He was brave; his whole military record and his life-long scorn of danger alike bear testimony to his bravery. He was wise; his great successes against great odds and his almost constant anticipation of the enemy's movements were proofs of his wisdom. He was skillful; his forced marches and unexpected victories assert his skill. He was patient and unyielding; his weary struggle against

the mighty armies of the North and his stern defense of Richmond
will forever preserve the memory of his patience and resolution.
He was gentle and just; the soldiers who fought under him and
who came alive out of the great fight, remembering and cherishing
the memory of the man, can one and all testify to his gentleness
and his justice. Above all, he was faithful; when he gave up his
sword there was no man in his own ranks or in those of the enemy
that doubted his faith or believed that he had not done all that
mortal could do for the cause which he had made such a noble
struggle. . . .

When the last chance was gone and all hope was at an end, the
old hero bowed to a higher will than his own and accepted the fate
of the South with calm grandeur. . . .

We cannot express all the truth that could be told about Lee,
nor can we do justice to his worth and fame, but perhaps the few
words of Sir Ector are the best after all. He was a good knight, a
true gentleman. Knowing this, let us leave him with fame and
posterity; with the rest, the light, the Resurrection and the Life.

3

Of laudatory Southern oratory there was virtually no end.
Perhaps the most eloquent of all of these was embodied in a
eulogistic memorial address by Senator Ben Hill of Georgia.

When the future historian shall come to survey the character of
Lee, he will find it rising like a huge mountain above the undulating plain of humanity, and he must lift his eyes high toward heaven
to catch its summit. He possessed every virtue of other great commanders without their vices. He was a foe without hate; a friend
without treachery; a victor without oppression, and a victim without murmuring. He was a public officer without vices; a private
citizen without reproach; a Christian without hypocrisy and a man
without guile. He was a Caesar without his ambition; Frederick
without his tyranny; Napoleon without his selfishness, and Washington without his reward. He was obedient to authority as a
servant, and loyal in authority as a true king. He was gentle as a
woman in life; modest and pure as a virgin in thought; watchful as
a Roman vestal in duty; submissive to law as Socrates, and grand in
battle as Achilles!

4

On the seventh day of January in 1907 the Lee Memorial Chapel at Lexington was crowded with an audience gathered there to honor the one hundredth anniversary of the birth of Robert E. Lee. The speaker of the occasion was not some hero-worshiping Southerner or Confederate veteran. The man who addressed them was a New England Yankee, a former soldier in the Army of the Potomac—Charles Francis Adams. The address he made on that occasion still stands as the classic tribute to Lee and justification of his course of conduct; the tribute of a former enemy to a Man of Character. Forthrightly Adams faced the fact that, in a large section of the country, Lee had been and by some was still an object of censure and reproba-bation. Adams met this issue frankly and eloquently, and quite effectively demolished it.

. . . The charge still most commonly made against Lee in that section of the common country to which I belong is that, in plain language, he was false to his flag—educated at the national academy, an officer of the United States Army, he abjured his allegiance and bore arms against the government he was sworn to uphold. In other words he was a military traitor. I state the charge in the ters-est language possible; and the facts are as stated. Having done so, and admitting the facts, I add as the result of much patient study and most mature reflection, that under similar conditions I would myself have done exactly what Lee did. In fact, I do not see how I, placed as he was placed, could have done otherwise. . . .

I maintain that every man in the eleven states seceding from the Union had in 1861, whether he would or no, to decide for himself whether to adhere to his state or to the nation; and I finally assert that, whichever way he decided, if only he decided honestly, put-ting self-interest behind him, he decided right. Paradoxical as it sounds, I contend moreover that this was indisputably so. It was a question of sovereignty—state or national; and from a decision of that question there was in a seceded state escape for no man. . . . But this, it will be replied, though true of the ordinary man and citizen, should not have been true of the graduate of the military academy, the officer of the Army of the United States. Winfield

Scott and George H. Thomas did not so construe their allegiance; when the issue was presented, they remained true to their flag and to their oaths. Robert E. Lee, false to his oath and flag, was a renegade!

The answer is brief and to the point: the conditions in the several cases were not the same; neither Scott nor Thomas was Lee. It was our Boston Dr. Holmes who long ago declared that the child's education begins about two hundred and fifty years before it is born; and it is quite impossible to separate any man—least of all, perhaps, a full-blooded Virginian—from his pre-natal traditions and living environment. From them he drew his being; in them he exists. Robert E. Lee was the embodiment of those conditions, the creature of that environment—a Virginian of Virginians. . . . To ask Lee to raise his hand against Virginia was like asking Montrose or the MacCallum More to head a force designed for the subjection of the Highlands and the destruction of the clans.

Where such a stern election is forced upon a man as then confronted Lee, the single thing the fair-minded investigator has to take into account is the loyalty, the single-mindedness of the election. Was it devoid of selfishness; was it free from any baser and more sordid worldly motive—ambition, pride, jealousy, revenge or self-interest? To this question there can, in the case of Lee, be but one answer. When, after long and trying mental wrestling, he threw in his fate with Virginia, he knowingly sacrificed everything which man prizes most—his dearly beloved home, his means of support, his professional standing, his associates, a brilliant future assured to him. Born a slave-holder in a race of slave-holders, he was himself no defender, much less an advocate, of slavery; on the contrary, he did not hesitate to pronounce it in his place " a moral and political evil." Later, he manumitted his slaves. He did not believe in secession; as a right reserved under the Constitution, he pronounced it "idle talk"; but, as a Virginian, he also added, "if the Government is disrupted I shall return to my native state and share the miseries of my people, and save in defence will draw my sword on none." Next to his high sense of allegiance to Virginia was Lee's pride in his profession. He was a soldier; as such, rank and the possibility of high command and great achievement were very dear to him. His choice put rank and command behind him. He quietly and silently made the greatest sacrifice a soldier can be asked to make. With war plainly impending, the foremost place in the army of which he was an officer was now tendered him; his answer was to lay down the commission he already held. Virginia had been drawn into the struggle; and, though he recognized no necessity for the state of affairs, "in my own person," he wrote, "I had to meet the question whether I should take part against my native state. I have not been able to make up my mind to raise my hand against my relatives, my children, my home."

It may have been treason to take this position. The man who took it, uttering these words and sacrificing as he sacrificed, may have been technically a renegade to his flag—if you please, false to his allegiance; but he stands awaiting sentence at the bar of history in very respectable company. Associated with him are, for instance, William of Orange, known as The Silent; John Hampden, the original *Pater Patriae;* Oliver Cromwell, the Protector of the English Commonwealth; Sir Harry Vane, once a governor of Massachusetts; and George Washington, a Virginian of note. In the throng of other offenders I am also gratified to observe certain of · those from whom I not unproudly claim descent. They were, one and all, in the sense referred to, false to their oaths—forsworn.

As to Robert E. Lee, individually, I can only repeat what I have already said—if in all respects similarly circumstanced, I hope I should have been filial and unselfish enough to have done as Lee did.

Mr. Adams closed his address on that January day in 1907 with a quotation of the words of Carlyle: "Whom shall we consecrate and set apart as one of our sacred men? Sacred, that all men may see him, be reminded of him and, by new example added to old perpetual precept, be taught what is real worth in man? Whom do you wish to resemble? Him you set on a high column, that all men looking at it may be continually apprised of the duty you expect from them."

And, Dr. Freeman has commented, "His heart-stirred audience was looking, as he spoke, past him—to the monument of Lee."

References

CHAPTER I

1—Brooks, *Lee of Virginia*, xi
2—Lee, Henry, *Memoirs*, 11
3—Lee, H., *Observations*, 141
4—Lee, Henry, *Memoirs*, 512
5—*Ibid.*, 41
6—Boyd, *Light-Horse Harry Lee*, 285

CHAPTER II

1—Armes, *Stratford*, 328
2—Jones, *Reminiscences*, 18
3—Mason, *Popular Life*, 91
4—Freeman, *R. E. Lee*, I, 34
5—Brock, *General Robert Edward Lee*, 149

CHAPTER III

1—Lee, Fitzhugh, *General Lee*, 22
2—Horn, *Boys' Life*, 24
3—Long, *Memoirs*, 40
4—Jones, *Reminiscences*, 201
5—Long, *Memoirs*, 45
6—Horn, *Boys' Life*, 32

CHAPTER IV

1—Long, *Memoirs*, 50
2—Jones, *Life and Letters*, 45
3—Brock, *General Robert Edward Lee*, 133
4—Lee, Fitzhugh, *General Lee*, 38
5—Long, *Memoirs*, 54
6—Semmes, *Afloat and Ashore*, 378
7—Long, *Memoirs*, 59
8—Maurice, *Robert E. Lee, the Soldier*, 34

CHAPTER V

1—Lee, Capt. R. E., *Recollections*, 6
2—*Ibid.*, 8
3—Jones, *Life and Letters*, 65
4—*"To Markie,"* 48
5—Rhodes, *Lee, The West Pointer*, 28
6—Lee, Fitzhugh, *General Lee*, 56
7—Long, *Memoirs*, 78
8—Jones, *Life and Letters*, 82
9—Lee, Fitzhugh, *General Lee*, 65

CHAPTER VI

1—*Report on Harper's Ferry Invasion*, 40
2—Jones, *Life and Letters*, 113
3—*Ibid.*, 120
4—*"To Markie,"* 58
5—*Confederate Veteran*, XIII, 167
6—Freeman, *R. E. Lee*, I, 435

CHAPTER VII

1—Maurice, *Robert E. Lee, the Soldier*, 43
2—Freeman, *R. E. Lee*, I, 455
3—*Southern Bivouac*, 538
4—Stiles, *Four Years*, 48
5—Taylor, *General Lee*, 24
6—*Ibid.*, 27
7—McCabe, *Life and Campaigns*, 40
8—Watkins, *"Co. Aytch,"* 18
9—Lee, Fitzhugh, *General Lee*, 125
10—*Confederate Veteran*, VI, 292
11—Long, *Memoirs*, 136
12—Jones, *Reminiscences*, 358

CHAPTER VIII

1—*Battlefields of the South*, 163
2—Freeman, *R. E. Lee*, II, 1
3—Maurice, *Robert E. Lee, the Soldier*, 67
4—*Ibid.*, 83
5—Davis, *Rise and Fall*, II, 83
6—Johnston, *Narrative*, 111
7—Davis, *Rise and Fall*, II, 88
8—Johnston, *Narrative*, 126
9—Reagan, *Memoirs*, 137
10—*Southern Bivouac*, II (1887), 651
11—Reagan, *Memoirs*, 140
12—*Battlefields of the South*, 28
13—Lee, Capt. R. E., *Recollections*, 70

CHAPTER IX

1—Maurice, *An Aide-de-Camp*, 60
2—Maurice, *Robert E. Lee, the Soldier*, 103
3—Maurice, *An Aide-de-Camp*, 67
4—Lee, Fitzhugh, *General Lee*, 142
5—Cooke, *Life*, 65
6—von Borcke, *Memoirs*, 37
7—Childe, *Life and Campaigns*, 84
8—*Battles and Leaders*, II, 347
9—Freeman, *R. E. Lee*, II, 119
10—Jones, *Diary*, I, 136
11—McCabe, *Life and Campaigns*, 128
12—*Battles and Leaders*, II, 447
13—*Southern Bivouac*, II, 655
14—Cooke, *Stonewall Jackson*, 228
15—Cooke, *Life*, 83
16—Long, *Memoirs*, 174
17—Stiles, *Four Years*, 97
18—*Battlefields of the South*, II, 163
19—Taylor, *General Lee*, 83
20—Freeman, *R. E. Lee*, II, 241
21—Stiles, *Four Years*, 108
22—Pollard, *Southern History*, 342
23—*Battles and Leaders*, II, 277
24—Brock, *R. E. Lee*, 322
25—Lee, Capt. R. E., *Recollections*, 73

CHAPTER X

1—McCabe, *Life and Campaigns*, 185
2—*Ibid.*, 644
3—Taylor, *General Lee*, 87
4—Mosby, *Memoirs*, 129
5—Long, *Memoirs*, 186
6—Cooke, *Life*, 115
7—*Battles and Leaders*, II, 528
8—Dooley, *Confederate Soldier*, 8
9—Maurice, *Robert E. Lee, the Soldier*, 142
10—Lee, Capt. R. E., *Recollections*, 76
11—Taylor, *General Lee*, 115

CHAPTER XI

1—Cooke, *Stonewall Jackson*, 308
2—*Official Records*, 19, Part 2, 605
3—*Battles and Leaders*, II, 604
4—*War Talks in Kansas*, 250
5—*Allan in Southern Bivouac*, II, 303
6—Owen, *Washington Artillery*, 136
7—Henry, *Story of the Confederacy*, 187
8—Lee, Capt. R. E., *Recollections and Letters*, 77
9—*Confederate Military History*, III, 356
10—*Battles and Leaders*, II, 681
11—Cooke, *Robert E. Lee*, 150
12—*Official Records*, Vol. 19, Part 2, 644
13—Cooke, *Robert E. Lee*, 154
14—Wolseley, *Blackwood's Magazine*, 93, 567
15—Taylor, *Four Years with General Lee*, 76

CHAPTER XII

1—*Battles and Leaders*, III, 70
2—*Ibid.*, 139
3—*Ibid.*, 78
4—Cooke, *Robert E. Lee*, 191
5—*Battles and Leaders*, III, 100
6—Taylor, *General Lee*, 152
7—*Ibid.*, 155
8—*Battles and Leaders*, III, 203
9—Cooke, *Robert E. Lee*, 219
10—*Battles and Leaders*, III, 207
11—Cooke, *Robert E. Lee*, 243
12—Owen, *Washington Artillery*, 211
13—Stiles, *Four Years*, 174
14—Childe, *Life and Campaigns*, 216
15—Pollard, *Southern History*, I, 612
16—Jones, *Reminiscences*, 158
17—Lee, Capt. R. E., *Recollections and Letters*, 95
18—*Official Records*, Vol. 27, Part 3, 882

CHAPTER XIII

1—*Official Records*, 27, Part 3, 943
2—Polley, *A Soldier's Letters*, 121
3—Taylor, *General Lee*, 215
4—*The Daily Citizen*, Vicksburg, Miss., July 2, 1863
5—Maurice, *Robert E. Lee*, 205
6—Fremantle, *Three Months*, 253
7—Long, *Memoirs*, 288
8—Fremantle, *Three Months*, 272
9—*Southern Bivouac*, I, 565
10—*Battles and Leaders*, III, 420
11—Taylor, *General Lee*, 211
12—Ross, *A Visit*, 69
13—Stiles, *Four Years*, 222
14—Freeman, *R. E. Lee*, III, 153
15—*Official Records*, Vol. 51, Part 2, 752
16—Davis, *Rise and Fall*, II, 447

CHAPTER XIV

1—White, *Robert E. Lee*, 326
2—*Official Records*, 33, 1200
3—Childe, *Life and Campaigns*, 263
4—Lee, Capt. R. E., *Recollections and Letters*, 106
5—Maurice, *Aide-de-Camp*, xxiii
6—*Battles and Leaders*, IV, 240
7—Jones, *Life and Letters*, 446
8—Cooke, *Robert E. Lee*, 371
9—Gilmor, *Four Years in the Saddle*, 134

CHAPTER XV

CHAPTER XVI

CHAPTER XVII

CHAPTER XVIII

CHAPTER XIX

1—Jones, *Life and Letters,* 452
2—*Appleton's Journal,* January 9, 1875
3—Letter in Compiler's Personal Collection
4—Jones, *Reminiscences,* 415
5—*Ibid.,* 266
6—Mosby, *Memoirs,* 380
7—Bond, *Memories,* 30
8—Jones, *Reminiscences,* 406
9—Horn, *Boys' Life,* 320
10—Jones, *Reminiscences,* 447
11—Freeman, *R. E. Lee,* IV, 493

CHAPTER XX
EPILOGUE

1—*Herald,* New York, N. Y.
2—*Morning Chronicle,* **Halifax,** Nova Scotia
3—Hill, *Address to Southern Historical Society,* February 17, 1874
4—Adams, *Lee's Centennial,* 14

Acknowledgments

In MAKING acknowledgments for a volume of this nature, the most obvious and immediate expressions of appreciation are due the writers and publishers of the material used. Such credit is given in the reference notes, aside from the complete bibliography. In addition, special appreciation is extended to the following publishers, for their permission to use matter protected by copyright:

From *Lee's Centennial,* by Charles Francis Adams, copyright 1948 by Americana House, reprinted by permission of the publisher.

From *General Lee,* by Fitzhugh Lee, copyright 1894 by D. Appleton & Company, reprinted by permission of Appleton-Century-Crofts, Inc.

From *Lee of Virginia,* by William E. Brooks, copyright 1932 by the Bobbs-Merrill Co., reprinted by permission of the publisher.

From *The Story of the Confederacy,* by Robert S. Henry, copyright 1931 by the Bobbs-Merrill Co., reprinted by permission of the publisher and the author.

From *As Luck Would Have It,* by Otto Eisenschiml and E. B. Long, copyright 1948 by the Bobbs-Merrill Co., reprinted by permission of the publisher and the authors.

From *Letters and Recollections of Robert E. Lee,* by Captain Robert E. Lee, Jr., copyright 1904, 1924, by Doubleday, Page & Co., reprinted by permission of Doubleday & Company.

From *John Dooley, Confederate Soldier,* edited by Joseph T. Durkin, S.J., copyright 1945 by Georgetown University Press, reprinted by permission of the publisher.

From *The Boys' Life of Robert E. Lee,* by Stanley F. Horn, copyright 1935 by Harper & Brothers, reprinted by permission of the publisher.

From *Lee, The American,* by Gamaliel Bradford, copyright 1912 by Gamaliel Bradford, Jr., reprinted by permission of the Houghton-Mifflin Company.

From *Lee at Appomattox and Other Papers,* by Charles Francis Adams, published by Houghton-Mifflin Company.

From *"To Markie,"* edited by Avery O. Craven, copyright 1933 by Harvard University Press, reprinted by permission of Henry E. Huntington Library and Art Gallery and Avery Craven.

From *The Memoirs of Colonel John S. Mosby,* copyright by Little, Brown & Co., reprinted by permission of the publisher.

From *General Robert E. Lee After Appomattox,* by Franklin R.

Riley, copyright 1922 by The Macmillan Company, reprinted by permission of the publisher.

From *An Aide-de-Camp of Lee,* by Major General Sir Frederick Maurice, published by Little, Brown and Company, and from *Robert E. Lee, The Soldier,* by Major General Sir Frederick Maurice, published by the Houghton-Mifflin Company, reprinted by permission of Major General Maurice and of Constable & Company, Limited.

From *Robert E. Lee and the Southern Confederacy,* by Henry A. White, copyright 1897 by G. P. Putnam's Sons, Inc., reprinted by permission of the publisher.

From *Memories of General Robert E. Lee,* by Christiana Bond, copyright 1926 by the Norman, Remington Company, reprinted by permission of the Remington Book Stores, Baltimore, Md.

From *Stratford Hall, the Great House of the Lees,* by Ethel Armes, copyright 1936 by Garrett & Massie, reprinted by permission of The Robert E. Lee Memorial Foundation.

From *R. E. Lee,* by Douglas Southall Freeman, copyright 1934 by Charles Scribner's Sons, reprinted by permission of the publisher and of Dr. Freeman.

From *Light-Horse Harry Lee,* by Thomas Boyd, copyright 1931 by Charles Scribner's Sons, reprinted by permission of the publisher.

From *Robert E. Lee, The West Pointer,* by General Charles Dudley Rhodes, copyright 1932 by the West Virginia Division of the Robert E. Lee Memorial Foundation, reprinted by permission of Colonel George S. Wallace.

From *Robert E. Lee, Soldier, Patriot, Educator,* published 1921 by Washington and Lee University, reprinted by permission of the publisher.

From *Stratford on the Potomac,* by Ethel Armes, copyright 1928 by William Alexander, Jr., Chapter, U. D. C., reprinted by permission of the publisher.

Aside from these acknowledgments, the editor wishes to express his personal thanks to Earl S. Miers for first suggesting the idea of the *Lee Reader* and for his gracious permission to make use of the idea under the sponsorship of another publisher. Special personal thanks are also extended to Paul M. Angle, editor of the *Lincoln Reader,* which is the source of the idea of this book and a guidepost in technique.

Bibliography

ADAMS, CHARLES FRANCIS, *Lee at Appomattox*. Houghton-Mifflin Co., Boston, Mass., 1902.
——, *Lee's Centennial*, Americana House, Chicago, Ill., 1948.
ALEXANDER, E. P., *Military Memories of a Confederate*. Charles Scribner's Sons, New York, N. Y., 1907.
ARMES, ETHEL, *Stratford on the Potomac*. William Alexander Jr. Chapter, United Daughters of the Confederacy, Greenwich, Conn., 1928.
BERNARD, GEORGE S., *War Talks of Confederate Veterans*. Fenn & Owen, Petersburg, Va., 1892.
BOWEN, J. J., *The Strategy of Robert E. Lee*. Thomas Y. Crowell Co., New York, N. Y., 1914.
BOYD, T. A., *Light-Horse Harry Lee*. Charles Scribner's Sons, New York, N. Y., 1931.
BRADFORD, GAMALIEL, *Lee, the American*. Houghton-Mifflin Co., Boston, Mass., 1912.
BROCK, R. A. (editor), *General Robert Edward Lee: Soldier, Citizen and Christian Patriot*. B. F. Johnson Publishing Co., Richmond, Va., 1897.
BROOKS, WILLIAM E., *Lee of Virginia*. The Bobbs-Merrill Co., Indianapolis, Ind., 1932.
CHILDE, EDWARD LEE, *Life and Campaigns of General Lee*. Chatto & Windus, London, Eng., 1875.
COOKE, JOHN ESTEN, *A Life of General Robert E. Lee*. D. Appleton-Century Co., Inc., New York, N. Y., 1875.
——, *Stonewall Jackson: A Military Biography*. D. Appleton & Co., New York, N. Y., 1866.
CRAVEN, AVERY (editor), *"To Markie."* Harvard University Press, Cambridge, Mass., 1933.
DAVIS, JEFFERSON, *The Rise and Fall of the Confederate Government*. D. Appleton-Century Co., Inc., New York, N. Y., 1881.
DEERING, JOHN R., *Lee and His Cause*. The Neale Publishing Co., New York, N. Y., 1907.
DURKIN, JOSEPH T., S.J. (editor), *John Dooley, Confederate Soldier, His War Journal*. Georgetown University Press, 1945.
EISENSCHIML, OTTO and LONG, E. B., *As Luck Would Have It*. The Bobbs-Merrill Co., Indianapolis, Ind., 1948.
ELLIS, EDWARD D., *The Camp-fires of General Lee*. Henry Harrison & Co., Philadelphia, Pa., 1886.

English Combatant, An (T.E.C.), *Battlefields of the South,* Smith Elder & Co., London, Eng., 1863.

FREEMAN, DOUGLAS SOUTHALL (editor), *Lee's Confidential Dispatches to Davis.* G. P. Putnam's Sons, New York, N. Y., 1897.

———, *R. E. Lee.* Charles Scribner's Sons, New York, N. Y., 1934.

FREMANTLE, COL. A. J. L., *Three Months in the Southern States.* William Blackwood and Sons, Edinburgh and London, 1863.

GILMOR, HARRY, *Four Years in the Saddle.* Harper & Brothers, New York, N. Y., 1866.

GORDON, GEN. JOHN B., *Reminiscences of the Civil War.* Charles Scribner's Sons, New York, N. Y., 1904.

HORN, STANLEY F., *The Boys' Life of Robert E. Lee.* Harper & Brothers, New York, N. Y., 1935.

JOHNSTON, J. E., *Narrative of Military Operation.* D. Appleton-Century Co., Inc., New York, N. Y., 1874.

JONES, CHARLES C., JR., *Reminiscences of the Last Days, Death and Burial of General Henry Lee.* Joel Munsell, Albany, N. Y., 1870.

JONES, J. B., *A Rebel War Clerk's Diary.* J. B. Lippincott Co., Philadelphia, Pa., 1866.

JONES, REV. J. WILLIAM, *Life and Letters of Robert Edward Lee, Soldier and Man.* The Neale Publishing Co., New York, N. Y., 1906.

———, *Personal Reminiscences, Anecdotes and Letters of General Robert E. Lee.* D. Appleton-Century Co., Inc., New York, N. Y., 1875.

LEE, EDMUND JENNINGS, M.D., *Lee of Virginia.* Philadelphia, Pa., 1895.

LEE, FITZHUGH, *General Lee.* D. Appleton-Century Co., Inc., New York, N. Y., 1894.

LEE, H., *Observations of the Writings of Thomas Jefferson.* Charles de Behr, New York, N. Y., 1832.

LEE, HENRY (edited by Robert E. Lee), *Memoirs of the War in the Southern Department of the United States.* University Publishing Co., New York, N. Y., 1869.

LEE, CAPT. ROBERT E., JR., *Recollections and Letters of General Robert E. Lee.* Doubleday, Page & Co., Inc., New York, N. Y., 1924.

LONG, A. L., *Memoirs of Robert E. Lee.* J. M. Stoddart & Co., Philadelphia, Pa., 1886.

LONGSTREET, JAMES, *From Manassas to Appomattox.* J. B. Lippincott Co., Philadelphia, Pa., 1896.

McCABE, JAMES D., *Life and Campaigns of General Robert E. Lee.* National Publishing Co., Philadelphia, Pa., 1870.

McCLELLAN, G. B., *McClellan's Own Story.* Charles L. Webster & Co., New York, N. Y., 1887.

McKIM, RANDOLPH H., *The Soul of Lee.* Longmans, Green and Co., New York, N. Y., 1918.

MASON, EMILY V., *Popular Life of General Robert Edward Lee.* John Murphy & Co., Baltimore, Md., 1872.

MAURICE, MAJ.-GEN. SIR FREDERICK (editor), *An Aide-de-Camp of Lee.* Little, Brown & Co., Boston, Mass., 1927.

———, *Robert E. Lee, the Soldier.* Houghton-Mifflin, Boston, Mass., 1925.

MEAD, EDWARD C., *Genealogical History of the Lee Family.* University Publishing Co., New York, N. Y., 1871.

NEESE, GEORGE M., *Three Years in the Confederate Horse Artillery.* The Neale Publishing Co., New York and Washington, 1911.

OATES, WILLIAM C., *The War Between the Union and the Confederacy.* The Neale Publishing Co., New York and Washington, 1905.

OWEN, WILLIAM MILLER, *In Camp and Battle with the Washington Artillery.* Ticknor & Co., Boston, Mass., 1885.

PAGE, THOMAS NELSON, *Robert E. Lee, Man and Soldier.* Charles Scribner's Sons, New York, N. Y., 1911.

———, *Robert E. Lee, the Southerner.* Charles Scribner's Sons, New York, N. Y., 1909.

POLLARD, E. A., *Southern History of the War.* Charles B. Richardson, New York, N. Y., 1866.

———, *The Lost Cause.* E. B. Treat & Co., New York, N. Y., 1866.

POLLEY, J. B., *A Soldier's Letters to Charming Nellie.* Neale Publishing Co., New York, N. Y., 1908.

PRYOR, MRS. ROGER A., *Reminiscences of Peace and War.* The Macmillan Co., New York, N. Y., 1905.

REAGAN, JOHN H., *Memoirs.* The Neale Publishing Co., New York and Washington, 1906.

Report of Select Committee of the Senate on the Harper's Ferry Invasion, Washington, D. C., 1860.

RHODES, CHARLES DUDLEY, *Robert E. Lee—The West Pointer.* The West Virginia Division of the Robert E. Lee Memorial Foundation, 1932.

RILEY, FRANKLIN L., *General Robert E. Lee, After Appomattox.* The Macmillan Co., New York, N. Y., 1922.

Robert E. Lee—Soldier, Patriot, Educator. Published for the Lee Memorial Fund, Lexington, Va., 1921.

ROSS, FITZGERALD, *A Visit to the Cities and Camps of the Confederate States.* William Blackwood and Sons, Edinburgh and London, 1865.

RUSSELL, CHARLES WELLS (editor), *Memoirs of Colonel John S. Mosby, The.* Little, Brown & Company, Boston, Mass., 1917.

SEMMES, RAPHAEL, *Service Afloat and Ashore During the Mexican War.* William H. Moore & Co., Cincinnati, Ohio, 1851.

———, *Memoirs of Service Afloat During the War Between the States.* Kelly, Piet & Co., Baltimore, Md., 1869.

SORRELL, G. MOXLEY, *Recollections of a Confederate Staff Officer.* The Neale Publishing Co., New York, N. Y., 1905.

Southern Military History (12 volumes), Atlanta, Ga., 1899.

STILES, ROBERT, *Four Years under Marse Robert*. The Neale Publishing Co., New York, N. Y., 1903.

TAYLOR, WALTER H., *Four Years with General Lee*. D. Appleton-Century Co., Inc., New York, N. Y., 1878.

———, *General Lee, His Campaigns in Virginia*. Nusbaum Book & News Co., Norfolk, Va., 1906.

VON BORCKE, HEROS, *Memoirs of the Confederate War for Independence*. London, Eng., 1866.

War Talks in Kansas (Military Order of the Loyal Legion). Franklin Hudson Publishing Co., Kansas City, Mo., 1906.

WATKINS, SAM R., *"Co. Aytch," Maury Grays*. Cumberland Presbyterian Publishing House, Nashville, Tenn., 1882.

WHITE, HENRY ALEXANDER, *Robert E. Lee and the Southern Confederacy*. G. P. Putnam's Sons, New York, N. Y., 1897.

WILMER, RT. REV. JOSEPH P. B., *General Robert E. Lee*. Nashville, Tenn., 1872.

WISE, JOHN S., *The End of an Era*. Houghton-Mifflin Co., Boston, Mass., 1900.

WOLSELEY, GARNET, "A Month's Visit to the Confederate Headquarters" in Blackwood's *Edinburgh Magazine*, January 1863 (Vol. 93).

Battles and Leaders of the Civil War. D. Appleton-Century Co., Inc., New York, N. Y., 1884-1888.

The Confederate Veteran, Atlanta, Ga.

The Confederate Veteran, Nashville, Tenn.

The Southern Bivouac (New Series), Louisville, Ky., 1886-1887.

The War of the Rebellion—Official Records of the Union and Confederate Armies. Government Printing Office, Washington, 1900-1901.

INDEX

Index